Excavations in the Burghfield Area, Berkshire
Developments in the Bronze Age and Saxon Landscapes

by C.A. Butterworth and S.J. Lobb

Excavations in the Burghfield Area, Berkshire
Developments in the Bronze Age and Saxon Landscapes

by C.A. Butterworth and S.J. Lobb

with contributions by
Michael J. Allen, Lynne Bell, Margaret Brooks, W.J. Carruthers, J. Coy,
J.G. Evans, R. Gale, P.A. Harding, Janet Henderson, Jacqueline I. McKinley,
L.N. Mepham, H. Rees, J.C. Richards, M. Robinson, Belinda Thompson,
J. Watson and A. Woodward

illustrations by
S. Garrett, K. Holt, S.E. James, K. Nichols, M. Tremayne,
and J. Vallender

artefacts photographed by Elaine Wakefield

Wessex Archaeology Report No. 1

Wessex Archaeology
1992

Published 1992 by the Trust for Wessex Archaeology Ltd
Portway House, Old Sarum Park, Salisbury, England, SP4 6EB

British Library Cataloguing in Publication Data
A catalogue record for this book is available from the British Library

ISBN 1–874350–01–9
ISSN 0965–5778

Produced by Wessex Archaeology
Printed by Henry Ling (Dorset Press) Ltd, Dorchester

Series Editor: Julie Gardiner

The publishers wish to acknowledge with
gratitude a grant from English Heritage for
the cost of publishing this volume

Front cover: Field Farm, looking west, Bronze Age ring-ditches 417 and 418 emerging after topsoil stripping
Back cover: Field Farm, Grave 87, skeleton with head to south

Contents

List of Figures

List of Plates

List of Tables

Acknowledgements

The investigations described in this volume are the result of a great deal of work by many people, during both fieldwork and post-excavation analysis.

Financial and other support was provided by Amey Roadstone Corporation Ltd (Southern) and English Heritage (Field Farm); English Heritage (Shortheath Lane); Berkshire County Council, the Englefield Charitable Trust, English Heritage, Newbury District Council, Reading Borough Council and Tarmac Roadstone (Southern) Ltd (Anslow's Cottages); William Cumber and Son (Theale) Ltd (Theale Industrial Site).

The report is the first of two volumes on the work of the Kennet Valley Survey, a project managed for Wessex Archaeology by Sue Lobb. Excavation supervisors at Anslow's Cottages were Nick Digby, Dave Farwell and Martin Trott; Lorraine Mepham, helped by Julie Lancley, was in charge of the on-site finds work. Dave Hopkins supervised the 1985 watching brief at Field Farm; Ian Barnes was Project Officer and Steve Tatler Project Supervisor for the 1988 excavations at that site.

A considerable debt of gratitude is owed to the many people who made up the various excavation teams, in particular those who took part in the first season of work at Anslow's Cottages, where working and living conditions were not always as pleasant as could have been wished for. Members of the Berkshire Field Research Group also provided invaluable help on many occasions. We would also like to thank Ian Fenwick for his advice on the soils at Field Farm, Anslow's Cottages and Theale Industrial Site.

Conservation was undertaken by the Ancient Monuments Laboratory (English Heritage), Portsmouth City Museum and Art Gallery, Reading Museum and Art Gallery, and Wiltshire Library and Museum Service Conservation Laboratory (Salisbury).

Archaeological Information was provided by the Sites and Monuments Record which is maintained by Berkshire County Council and thanks are due to Paul Chadwick (then County Archaeologist) for his help and support.

With the permission of the landowners, all finds and records will be deposited in Reading Museum and Art Gallery. In this respect we are grateful to the following for their cooperation: Amey Roadstone Corporation Ltd (Field Farm), the Englefield Estate (Anslow's Cottages), Brigadier D.C. Barbour (Shortheath Lane), and William Cumber and Son (Theale) Ltd (Theale Industrial Site).

We are grateful to all the contributors and to the illustrators S. Garrett, K. Holt, S.E. James, K. Nichols and J. Vallender. The casket reconstructions (Fig. 21) are based on originals supplied by Jacqui Watson, and the basketry (Fig. 43) was drawn by M. Tremayne. The finds were photographed by Elaine Wakefield. We are particularly grateful to Professor John Coles for his comments and editorial advice. Text editing was by Julie Gardiner and Chris Butterworth.

Abstract

Four sites were excavated on the gravels of the River Kennet in Berkshire, under the aegis of the Kennet Valley Survey.

At Field Farm, Burghfield, intermittent watching briefs, fieldwalking and excavation over a period of five years recovered material ranging from Mesolithic flintwork to a Saxon inhumation cemetery. A Neolithic hearth was associated with Mortlake Ware pottery, preceding the construction of a series of early–middle Bronze Age ring-ditches associated with Deverel-Rimbury and Collared Urn cremation burials. During the Saxon period the main ring-ditch appears to have acted as the focus for an inhumation cemetery. Bone preservation was very poor but grave-goods suggest a date in the 7th century. The location of any settlement associated with this cemetery remains unknown.

Rescue excavation along a short length of water pipeline at Shortheath Lane, Abbotts Farm Sulhampstead, recovered a number of Deverel-Rimbury Bucket Urns and small amounts of cremated human bone.

Large-scale excavations in advance of gravel extraction at Anslow's Cottages, Burghfield produced remarkable evidence of river related activities from the Bronze Age to post-medieval periods. Much of the material evidence consists of worked timbers relating to a series of river and riverside structures, supported by excellent environmental sequences derived principally from pollen, molluscan and insect assemblages.

A track or hollow way led to an apparent landing stage at the edge of a former river channel, associated with substantial quantities of later Bronze Age pottery. Rather ephemeral evidence of Roman activity consisted of a number of stakes within the river channel associated with early Roman pottery. A series of wooden structures including stake- and post-settings were constructed and repeatedly reconstructed within and across the channel during the Saxon period, culminating in a substantial structure comprising posts and planks pegged into a reused horizontal beam (possibly a threshold beam) set across the channel. Upstream from this, the remains of a basketry fish or eel trap were recovered.

The environmental sequences combine to reveal a clear distinction between wet and dry areas of the site. A predominantly lime woodland was selectively felled in the later Neolithic/earlier Bronze Age from which time the waterside areas were used for both pasture and cultivation, with summer crops of hay indicated through most of the occupation periods. Oak woodland surrounded the site with some indication of gradually increasing acidity and, more locally, the development of alder carr in marshy areas. Richly diverse and important molluscan and insect assemblages were recovered.

Small-scale excavations at Theale Industrial Site produced limited evidence for another timber structure of Saxon date within a former channel of the Kennet.

In the final chapter of the volume, the four sites are discussed together in order to provide a clearer picture of the developing landscape within the Kennet Valley during the later Prehistoric and Saxon periods.

1 Introduction

1 Introduction

This report describes investigations at four sites in close proximity to each other at the eastern end of the Kennet Valley in Berkshire; Field Farm (SU 675 704) and Anslow's Cottages (centred on SU 693 710) lie within Burghfield parish, and Shortheath Lane (SU 643 676) and Theale Industrial Site (SU 650 710) lie within the neighbouring parishes of Sulhamstead and Theale respectively (Fig. 1). The sites are not only linked geographically but also chronologically as the evidence from the excavations indicates predominantly Bronze Age and Saxon periods of occupation. In addition, the excavations have provided environmental evidence spanning the Neolithic–Saxon periods.

The excavations were all carried out within the broad remit of the Kennet Valley Survey which aimed to review the state of knowledge of settlement patterns in the prehistoric, Roman, and medieval periods in the lower part of the valley and to assess the changes and developments in landuse and the landscape in general. A programme of fieldwalking was undertaken and is reported elsewhere (Lobb and Rose forthcoming); as part of this survey the Burghfield area was selected for particular attention in order to examine more closely the context of the known and investigated sites. While the results of the collection of surface artefacts have enabled general interpretations to be made relating to settlement patterns and landuse, the excavations have provided more detailed information to complement this general statement.

2 Archaeological Background

The landscape of the Burghfield area has been considerably altered by gravel extraction, which has continued apace during the post-war years. Most of the gravel reserves have now been depleted and those that remain are either built on or threatened by redevelopment or further extraction (Fig. 2). Although much of the area was destroyed without any archaeological observation at all, sporadic monitoring of the quarries resulted in many small investigations which have provided a surprising amount of information.

Until the 1970s the archaeological response to this destruction was very haphazard, consisting largely of reported chance finds and, occasionally, opportune observations of exposed sites and sections (Boon and Wymer 1958). Ring-ditches threatened by the construction of the M4 were fully excavated at Burghfield by R.A. Rutland of Reading Museum (Lobb 1983–5) and at Englefield by Wymer and Ashbee (Anon. 1964; Healy forthcoming). In the early 1970s with the establishment of the Berkshire Archaeological Unit, a review of the available air photographs of the area (Gates 1975) indicated widespread and dense archaeological activity particularly on the river gravels. More systematic monitoring and watching briefs were undertaken by the Unit which resulted in the excavation and recording of several ring-ditches (Bradley and Richards 1979–80) and the later Bronze Age sites at Knight's Farm and at Aldermaston Wharf, 8 km upstream (Bradley et al. 1980). Large-scale excavation in advance of gravel extraction of the cropmark complex at Pingewood revealed a Romano-British farming settlement as well as a small, open, later Bronze Age settlement (Johnston 1983–5); subsequent watching-brief work and excavation in the remaining area of the quarry, to the east of the excavated site, investigated further archaeological features which include a Bronze Age ring-ditch, additional Romano-British ditches and early medieval occupation features (Lobb and Mills forthcoming).

In the 1980s Berkshire County Council was developing policies towards archaeology which included the evaluation of proposed development or extraction sites, where the archaeological potential was known or suspected, in advance of the determination of planning applications. This policy has now been adopted, with modifications, in the Replacement Structure Plan for Berkshire (Royal County of Berkshire 1989) and was put into practice during the period of consultation of the Draft Plan. The initial investigations at Anslow's Cottages and the evaluation at Theale were instigated as a result of this policy. The excavations at Field Farm and Shortheath Lane were carried out within the scope and funding of the Kennet Valley Survey. Within the same planning framework several other evaluations, sometimes followed up by further excavation, have been carried out in the Burghfield area, most notably at Reading Business Park at Small Mead Farm, Moores Farm and Hartley Court Farm, where evidence for extensive late Bronze Age settlement has been identified (Dawson and Lobb 1986; J. Moore pers. comm.).

3 Location of the Sites

To the south-west of Reading, between Theale and the southern outskirts of the town, the River Kennet passes from west to east through a broad floodplain, up to 0.75 km across, before turning sharply northwards and eastwards through a narrower gorge, approximately 0.30 km wide, and finally running into the Thames (Fig. 1). To the north of the river the ground rises abruptly onto the Chalk, Eocene clays and Plateau Gravels. To the south the alluvial floodplain is bounded by a broad

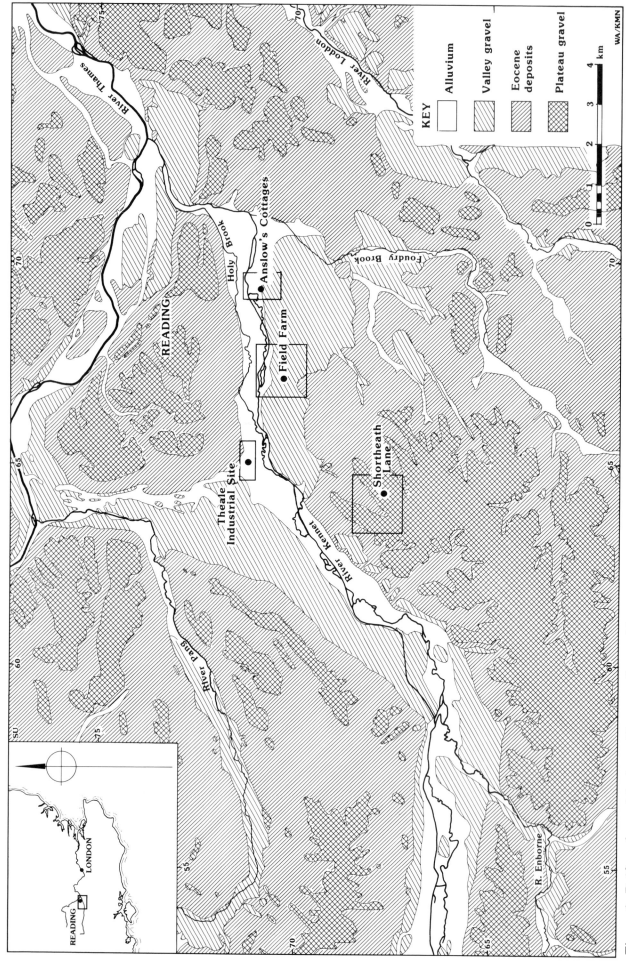

Figure 1 Drift geology of the lower Kennet valley and location of sites

3

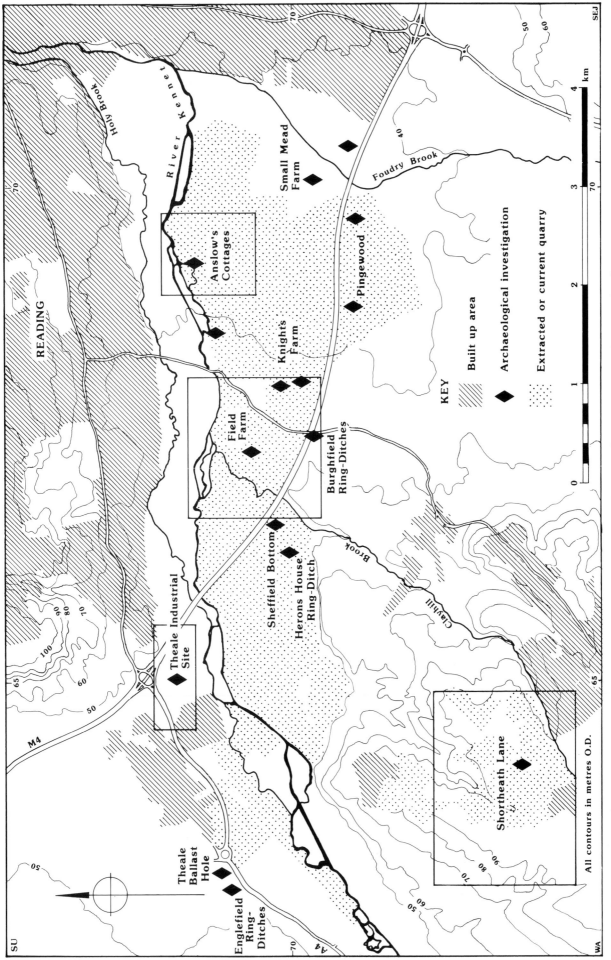

Figure 2 Map of the Burghfield area showing the sites discussed in this volume and previous investigations in the area

gravel terrace. The land rises gradually from the floodplain terrace onto the Plateau Gravel at Burghfield Common.

The gravel surface of the floodplain and floodplain terrace is traversed by a series of palaeo-channels, resulting from the braided river system of the Kennet. On the floodplain in the Burghfield area the gravel is overlain mainly by alluvial deposits of clays and calcareous silty clay loams often with thin layers of fine gravel or peaty material, 0.5 m and 0.2 m thick. The floodplain terrace is slightly higher than the floodplain itself although the junction between the two is not always clear on the ground. On the terrace the gravel is overlain by 0.5–0.2 m of brickearth which is covered by soils belonging to the Hurst series (Jarvis *et al.* 1979). The Plateau Gravels form a flat-topped ridge approximately 50 m above the level of the flood-plain, with a commanding view over the valley; the soils of this area are generally clayey and poorly drained. In recent years the floodplain has been used for watermeadow and pasture while the gravel terrace has supported both arable and pastoral farming; the Plateau Gravel terrace at Burghfield Common has been covered by woodland and scrub.

The site at Field Farm (Fig. 2) is located near the edge of the floodplain terrace between 50 m and 400 m south of the present course of the River Kennet at a height of 42 m OD. Shortheath Lane lies on a spur of the Plateau Gravel at a height of 94.5 m OD. overlooking the Kennet Valley to the north and north-west, and the broad river gravel terrace in the Burghfield area to the north-east; the site is located on a ridge between two small valleys. The Anslow's Cottages site, 2.5 km to the east of Field Farm, occupies a location at the junction of the alluvial floodplain and the gravel terrace, adjacent to the present course of the river; most of the site lies at about 39 m OD (heights range between 38.63 m and 39.65 m OD). Theale Industrial Site is situated on the alluvial floodplain some 160 m north of the river at its nearest point; the ground falls very slightly from west (44.86 m OD) to east (44.30 m OD) and is generally slightly lower than the riverbank (44.70 m OD in this area).

4 Dating

All radiocarbon dates referred to in the text are quoted as uncalibrated dates BP unless otherwise stated. Calibrated ranges for the dates recovered from the sites can be found in the relevant sections of each site report (Tables 1 and 14).

2 Excavations at Field Farm, Burghfield, Berkshire

1 Introduction

In 1982 planning permission was granted for gravel extraction from approximately 50 hectares of river gravels at Field Farm, Burghfield (Fig. 3). The area covered by the quarry included several features visible as cropmarks on aerial photographs taken in 1960 and 1961 by Cambridge University and by the Royal Commission on the Historical Monuments of England (RCHME) Air Photo Unit (Fig. 3). Several ring-ditches of differing size visible within the quarry site can be seen to be part of a group extending across the gravel terrace in this area. The area is fairly level (at about 42 m OD), although at least one former river channel was visible as a depression on the ground; two other river channels were visible on the aerial photographs and most of the area investigated occupied a prominent position between these channels (Fig. 3). In general, the gravel is overlain by a stony topsoil although peat appears to have developed in the north-west corner of the site adjacent to the river. To the north of the site the ground drops in level to the alluvial soils of the floodplain.

Most of the surrounding area has now been extracted and the investigations at Field Farm may be seen as complementary to the archaeological work previously carried out in this area. Gravel extraction began at the site in 1983, and archaeological investigations of varying quality and extent were carried out between 1984 and 1988 (Fig. 3); it is these investigations which are described in this report. The site was visited from time to time in 1983 and 1984 during topsoil stripping in the south-western corner of the site and a small number of features were observed and recorded. Also in 1983, the remaining part of the field was fieldwalked and surface finds collected. In 1985 excavations were carried out to investigate a large ring-ditch and the surviving half of a smaller one (both visible as cropmarks on aerial photographs). Watching briefs were subsequently carried out later in 1985, 1986 and 1987 during toposil stripping in and around the area of the excavation; a further small ring-ditch was partly examined. In 1988, in response to further expansion of the gravel workings, another small ring-ditch, as well as the two rectangular enclosures, were sampled by small scale excavation (Wessex Archaeology project no. W267). By 1990 only the extreme north-west corner of the quarry remained to be extracted.

Several phases of activity were recorded, dating principally to the late Neolithic and Bronze Age periods, but also including a mid-Saxon cemetery.

The prehistoric features have been described below by trench followed by a discussion of the Saxon cemetery.

2 Fieldwalking results

Surface finds were collected on a 25 m grid based on the National Grid; assuming transects of approximately 2 m width, this provides an 8% sample of the field surface (Richards 1985). An interpretation of the results is presented in Figure 4 and details can be found in archive.

A diffuse and low density scatter of largely undiagnostic worked flint was collected from the whole site. Two possible flint clusters were identified, at SU 674 706 (thirteen pieces) and SU 670 705 (seventeen pieces), not associated with any of the known archaeological features on the site. The second cluster is distinctive as the quantity and quality of the flakes contrast with the material from elsewhere; the concentration includes a crested flake which was probably removed from a multi-platform core during rejuvenation, a flake with a faceted butt from a core with opposed platforms and an undiagnostic scraper, and may represent a small cluster of Mesolithic date. Other finds of note include a fabricator (SF.75), made on a blade which has been retouched by bifacial flaking to a D–shaped cross section and a fragment of a reworked ground flint axe (SF.66).

The small amount of pottery recovered includes four sherds of later Bronze Age date, three of which may be Collared Urn (SU 67425 70550), four Romano-British sherds and four sherds of medieval date as well as a scatter of post-medieval material. Burnt flint concentrations were identified mainly along the northern edge of the field, corresponding to the edge of the gravel terrace and may be associated with the rectangular enclosures, and the possible Mesolithic flint scatters.

3 Dating Summary

The dating and phasing of the site is dependent on the artefactual evidence, supported in some cases by radiocarbon and archaeomagnetic dating (Table 1). On this basis the following broad phases of activity can be suggested:

1. Mesolithic: based on flint work only.
2. Neolithic: a hearth, dated by thermo-remanent magnetism to 3900–3000 Cal BC

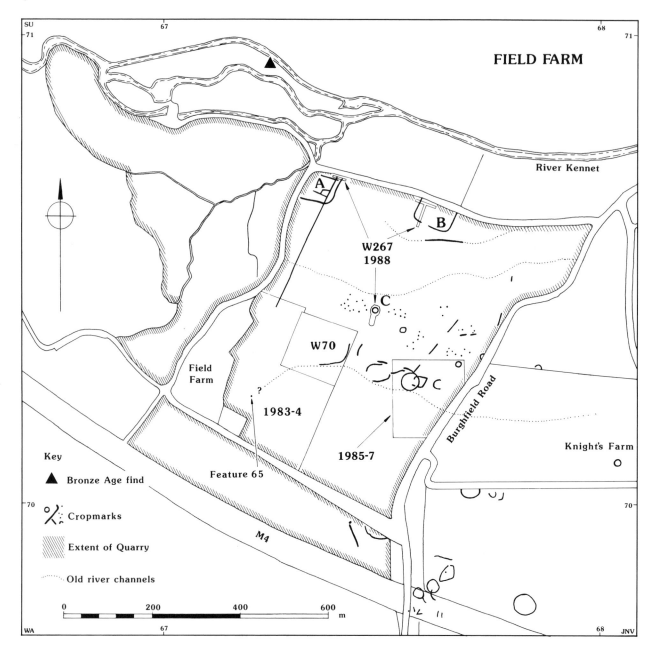

Figure 3   Field Farm: cropmarks and location of investigations

(AJC–63), with a Mortlake Ware bowl and associated features.

3.   Early Bronze Age: construction of ring-ditch 417 with associated central pit, dated by radiocarbon to 3650±80 BP (HAR–9139). After the initial silting of the ditch an episode of burning at its western side introduced a charcoal and ashy layer into the ditch which gave a radiocarbon date of 3569±70 BP (HAR–9142).

4.   Early/Middle Bronze Age: construction of ring-ditches 418, 604 and 032, with associated cremation burials. Secondary cremation burials in Collared Urns, Deverel-Rimbury Urns and unaccompanied,

around the edge of the suggested mound of ring-ditch 417, and between ring-ditches 417 and 418. A burnt post-hole (291) in the centre of ring-ditch 417 produced an archaeomagnetic date of 1859–1650 Cal BC (AJC–64). Charcoal from the fill of one of the Collared Urns within ring-ditch 417 produced a radiocarbon date of 2890±60 BP (HAR–9143).

5.   Late Bronze Age: a few pits and post-holes, widely distributed around the ring-ditches, appear to date to the late Bronze Age, although a few sherds of early Iron Age pottery indicate that the occupation might have been more prolonged.

6. Saxon: ring-ditch 417 appears to have acted as a focus for a Saxon inhumation cemetery. Many of the graves contained grave-goods which suggest a date in the 7th century AD.

4 Prehistoric Features

Watching brief 1983/84 (W70)

In 1983 and 1984 a minimal watching brief was carried out during site clearance in the area adjacent to the motorway and to the east of the farm buildings (Fig. 3); the site was visited only occasionally during the stripping of the soils overlying the gravels and only broad observations can be made. Some of the features visible on the aerial photographs in the southern field adjacent to the motorway were destroyed without any archaeological observation. Several linear and pit-like features were observed in the same field further east but remain undated. Further to the north, near the farm house, it appeared that archaeological features were of lower density than elsewhere on the site, with a large unoccupied area where the overburden was slightly deeper, possibly because of an old river channel.

Of particular note was the discovery of an apparently isolated pit (feature 65, Fig. 3) containing Neolithic flint and a single sherd of pottery. This feature had been partly removed by machine at the time of observation and was only 0.09 m deep. There appeared to be no other features in this area but it is possible that other shallow pits may have been entirely removed during machining.

A group of post-holes and pits was recorded towards the northern part of the watching brief area, all of which appear to be later Bronze Age in date, judging by the associated pottery. A plan of this area and other details of the watching brief observations are in archive; as only a small area was examined in detail it is not possible to indicate the extent of this activity.

1985 excavations

The 1985 excavations were carried out in response to the impending destruction of a large ring-ditch, 417, and the surviving half of a smaller one, 418 (Figs 3 and 5). Both ditches were clearly visible on aerial photographs, although in the case of the latter, the eastern half of the ditch had been destroyed by small-scale gravel extraction earlier this century. The main excavation of these features was carried out in July and August 1985 and was followed later in that year by a watching brief as overburden stripping continued in the surrounding area.

Ring-ditch 417 (Trenches A–M)
This ring-ditch was located on a low but prominent gravel bank adjacent to an old river channel (Fig. 3). A slight rise in the ground surface across the area of the ring-ditch was just perceptible, a levelled profile showing a maximum height of 0.40 m above the ground level of the surrounding area; very shallow depressions marking the ditch, 0.10 m deep

Table 1 Field Farm: summary of dating results

Radiocarbon

Ref.	Context	Material	Age BP	Calibrated date ranges 68%	95%
HAR–9139	fill of pit 297	charcoal	3650±80	2140–1922 BC	2280–1780 BC
HAR–9142	burnt layer in fill of ring-ditch 417	charcoal	3560±70	2010–1830 BC	2130–1710 BC
HAR–9143	fill of Collared Urn (Urn 1)	charcoal	2890±60	1190–1010 BC	1310–910 BC
HAR–9140	fill of Deverel-Rimbury Urn (Urn 625)	charcoal	3690±120	2270–1940 BC	2460–1740 BC

Calibrated using IML program, Stuiver and Reimer 1986

Archaeomagnetic

Ref	Context	Mean direction of thermoremanent magnetism Dec	Inc	alpha–95	Date of last heating @ 68% confidence
AJC–63	hearth 262	5.3°E	55.5°	5.5°	3900–3000 BC
AJC–64	?burnt post-hole 291	23.7°E	60.3°	4.3°	1850–1650 BC

References for calibration curves: Clark *et al.* 1988; Turner and Thompson 1982

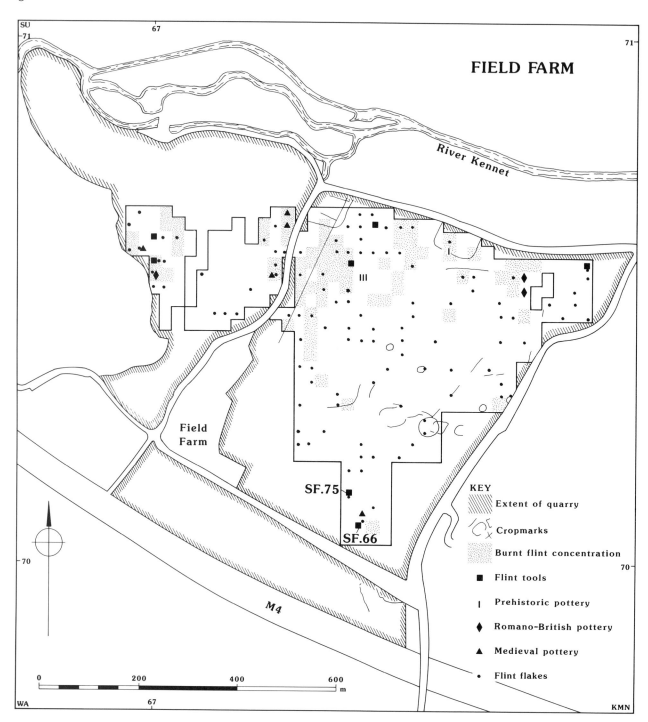

Figure 4   Field Farm: fieldwalking results

at most, were also recorded (Fig. 5). An initial survey with a fluxgate gradiometer failed to identify the ditch. The slightly higher area was taken as the focus for Trenches A–F, which were dug in a radial pattern around it; Trenches A and D were offset and extended inwards towards the centre of the ditch to give a complete cross-section. Additional areas (Trenches J and G) were opened to examine the central area. Trenches K, L and M were later excavated to allow further investigation of the Saxon cemetery (Fig. 5).

In all of the trenches except G, H and J, 0.25–0.45 m of topsoil and subsoil was removed by machine to expose the edges of the ditch. Once the arc of the ditch had been located and planned no further excavation was carried out in Trenches B, E and M; sections were excavated through the ditch in Trenches A, C, D and F, and all other features both within, across and beyond the ditch were dug by hand. Approximately 670 m^2 of the ditch and its interior were opened for examination, about 37% of the whole area of the ring-ditch.

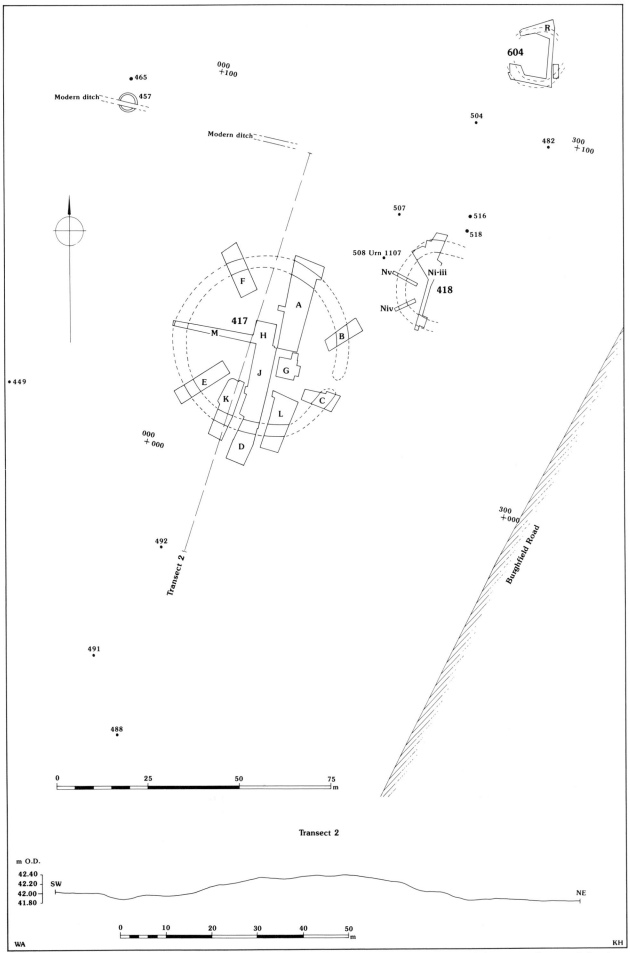

Figure 5   Field Farm: excavations 1985–6, location of trenches and additional features observed during the watching brief, and profile across ring-ditch 417 prior to excavation

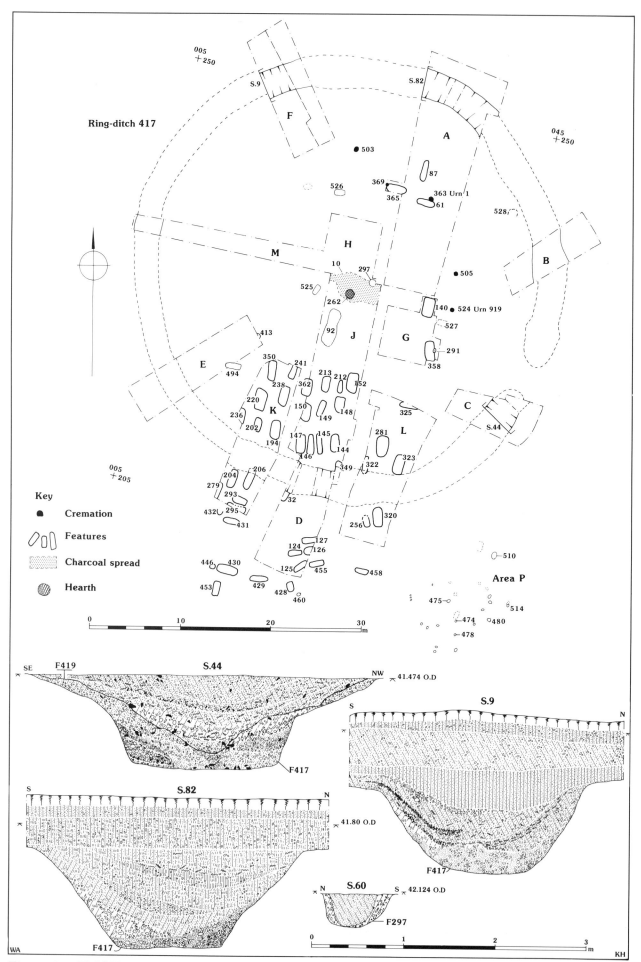

Figure 6   Field Farm: ring-ditch 417, feature plan and selected sections (for key see Figure 8)

A watching brief was carried out later in 1985 during the removal of overburden from the rest of the ring-ditch, when some additional features were planned; only a small number of these were examined.

The ditch

Although the aerial photographs suggested that the ditch formed an unbroken circle, observation during the watching brief in 1985 showed that there was a gap of a little over 3 m on the south-east side of the monument, between Trenches B and C (Fig. 6). Although Trench C had unknowingly been placed near the southern terminal, neither was fully examined. The ditch had an internal diameter of 41.50 m and an external diameter of 47.50 m.

Four sections through the ditch were excavated in Trenches A, C, D and F; sections from Trenches A, C and F are illustrated in Figure 6. The ditch was sealed by topsoil and a dark brown sandy clay loam subsoil which was deeper over the ditch; in Trenches D and L, the ditch and part of the interior were sealed by layers of gravelly silt loam, apparently the result of recent disturbance which had truncated the subsoil.

In all of the excavated sections the ditch was cut well down into the gravel, having a maximum depth of 1.10 m; average width of the top of the ditch was c.3 m, the sides usually falling quite steeply and symmetrically to a flat base, 1–1.20 m wide (Fig. 6, S9, S44 and S82). In Trench D the ditch had been truncated but survived to a depth of c.0.70 m. The ditch was widest in Trench C, in what later proved to be a position close to the terminal (Fig. 6), 3.80 m at the top and 1.60 m at the base, although the depth was consistent with those recorded in Trenches A and F.

Primary fills within the ditch were composed of clean, loose gravel, derived initially from the outer side of the ditch in most cases, but closely followed by similar clean gravel from the inner edge. Subsequent fills were predominantly sandy clays interspersed with lenses of gravel, the quantity of gravel decreasing through the upper part of the ditch.

In Trench F a dense lens of charcoal was recorded just above the primary fill (Fig. 6, S9); the underlying soil was slightly reddened, suggesting that burning might have occurred in situ. This horizon was not observed in any of the other ditch sections. A radiocarbon date was obtained for this charcoal layer of 3560±70 BP (HAR–9142).

In Trench C the upper fills of the ditch appeared to have been truncated by a later feature or recut, 419, with a shallow V–shaped profile, 0.82 m deep and slightly narrower (3.70 m) than the original ditch (Fig. 6, S44). This was filled with layers of gravelly silt loam containing large quantities of burnt flint and pottery, the latter indicating a late Bronze Age date.

Finds were scarce from all of the excavated ditch sections, with the exception of the later feature in Trench C, and were everywhere associated only with the upper fills.

The central area

A layer of yellowish brown sandy clay overlying the natural gravel was recorded only within the arc of the ditch (the highest part of the site); this soil was deeper nearer the ditch (up to 0.32 m deep c.6 m in from the ditch in Trench A), becoming shallower (0.16 m) nearer the centre. In Trenches D and L this layer was truncated by later disturbance. Its survival, especially in the centre of the circle where the topsoil was also shallowest, suggests that it may have been protected by a mound.

At the centre of the ring-ditch was a compact layer of mixed sandy loam, 10, which contained much charcoal together with some pottery and small quantities of knapped and burnt flint. This deposit, which covered an area of approximately $4m^2$ to a maximum depth of 0.14 m, overlay a layer of cleaner, although still charcoal-rich loam, 60; both layers sealed hearth 262. A substantial spread of charcoal surrounded and partly covered the hearth, an area of fire-reddened clay (burnt to a depth of 0.11 m) approximately 0.90 m in diameter. The upper layer of mixed sandy loam also sealed several stake-holes, 156–163, 215–218, 370, 534, which appeared to encircle a collapsed Mortlake Ware vessel (Fig. 7). Some difficulty was experienced in establishing which features were archaeological and which were the result of root action or animal disturbance. All were filled with very dark brown sandy loam often with much charcoal, probably from the overlying layer. The burnt clay of hearth 262 was sampled for archaeomagnetic dating and produced a date of 3900–3000 Cal BC (AJC–63). All of these features are thought to predate the construction of the ring-ditch, although they may not have been either contemporary or associated.

Cut through the lower charcoal-rich layer was a circular pit, 297, 0.37 m deep and 0.80 m in diameter (Fig. 6, S60; Fig. 7), which contained small quantities of early Bronze Age pottery, knapped and burnt flint, a little cremated bone and a few pieces of fired clay. Charcoal from the fill of this feature produced a radiocarbon date of 3650±80 BP (HAR–9139).

Other features were identified in this central area which may be of the same phase as pit 297 (Fig. 7). These include a second small pit, 167, two possible post-holes, 288 and 289, two stake-holes, 276 and 371, and a possible post-hole (not numbered) cut into the bottom of a shallow and amorphous hollow, 533.

A short distance away to the east in Trench G another small post-hole, 291, was recorded (Fig. 6) which contained much charcoal and burnt flint. The sandy clay through which it was cut showed clear signs of burning having taken place in situ. Archaeomagnetic analysis of this burnt clay produced a date of 1850–1650 Cal. BC (AJC–64). Also in the central area was a large pit, 92, which contained residual material from the earlier periods of activity but has been dated (by the pottery) to the later Bronze Age (Fig. 7). The original shape of this feature was unclear as it appeared to have been

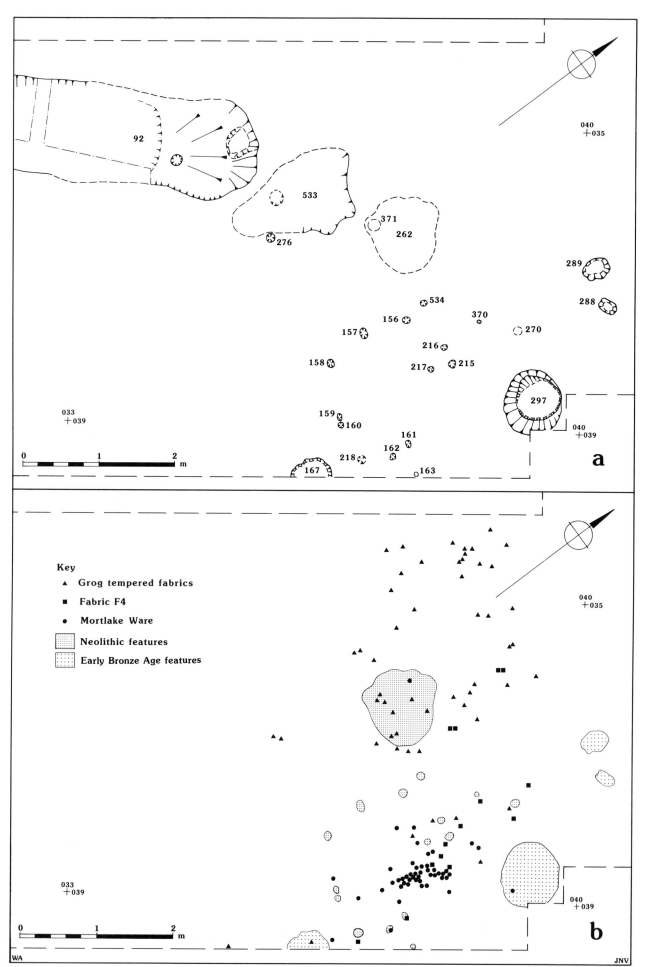

Figure 7   Field Farm: ring-ditch 417; a) detailed plan of features; b) distribution of Neolithic pottery

disturbed by animal burrowing and possibly by more recent features.

Cremations

Evidence of at least four, possibly five, cremations was found in the centre of ring-ditch 417, all 7.5–9.5 m from the inner edge of the ditch (Fig. 6). Two of them, 363 and 524, were contained within damaged but still partially complete Collared Urns (Urns 1 and 919 respectively); cremation 363 had been slightly damaged by the insertion of a Saxon grave (363) and both urns had been plough-damaged. The interiors of both were excavated in controlled conditions after their removal from the site in as complete a state as possible. Charcoal from the fill of Urn 1 produced a radiocarbon date of 2890±60 BP (HAR–9143). A third possible cremation, 369, had also been disturbed by a Saxon grave (365), the fill of which contained 22 fragments of Collared Urn.

The remaining urns were of Deverel-Rimbury character. Two survived in very fragmentary condition only. Cremation 505 had been severely damaged during topsoil stripping, if not by earlier ploughing, and showed only as a patch of burnt material within a ring of pottery so badly damaged and decayed that it was impossible to preserve. Of the possible fifth, 503, only the base of the vessel survived the passage of the scraper. Many of the Saxon graves contained fragments of cremated bone and prehistoric pottery and these may indicate that there were further cremations on the southern side of the ring-ditch.

Ring-ditch 418 (Trench N)

The smaller ring-ditch, 418, located c.15 m north-east of 417, was 18.5 m in internal diameter, 24.5 m external diameter. Only the western part of the ring-ditch could be investigated, the eastern half having already been destroyed by earlier gravel extraction.

This ditch was also located by excavating a number of radial trenches (Fig. 8). The first trench, Ni/iii, was machined across the projected diameter of the surviving ditch arc before being widened at its northern end to allow examination of part of the central area; the two opposed sections through the ditch were then excavated by hand. Two other small trenches, Niv and v, were machined across the line of the ditch to confirm its presence but were not further investigated (Fig. 8). An area of 92 m² was examined altogether, about 19% of the probable area of the whole ring-ditch, but c.40% of the part remaining.

The ditch

The ditch was cut into the gravel and sealed by up to 0.28 m of topsoil and probably by the intermittent underlying silty loam subsoil, although this was not always clear in the excavated sections. The profile was similar to that of 417, being fairly symmetrical, steep-sided and flat-bottomed, although in Trench Niii it had a less regular, more rounded profile, probably the result of being cut through less stable gravel in that area. In Trench Ni the ditch was stepped on the inner side, but it may have cut an earlier feature at that point (Fig. 8, S78).

Primary ditch fills were of mixed gravel, with noticeably larger stones lying toward the centre of the ditch in Trench Ni. Later fills were considerably more gravelly than those of the larger ditch, with few layers being completely stone-free; lenses of sandy silt and clay interspersed the gravel. Finds from the ditch sections were few and mostly from the upper levels, but included later Bronze Age material.

Internal features

It was not possible to examine the centre of the ring-ditch in detail in the limited time available. A sparse layer of sandy silt lay beneath subsoil and above gravel in the southern central area, similar to the deposit noted at the centre of ring-ditch 417, and perhaps indicative of an original mound. A charcoal-filled depression, 366, cut this layer (Fig. 8) but there were no associated finds. Also noted during the watching brief was a possible cremation, 520, apparently unaccompanied, surviving only as fragments of very friable bone in a shallow pit. Other possible features were seen during the watching brief but were not excavated.

Watching brief, 1985

From October to December 1985 a watching brief was carried out as the overburden was removed from the area around and to the west of ring-ditches 417 and 418. The aim of the watching brief was to record and investigate the extent and distribution of any additional features within or around the two ring-ditches, and any other features in the rest of the area being cleared. In practice, because of the large area involved and the speed at which the soil stripping was carried out only a small sample of features was recorded.

Area P, south-east of ring-ditch 417

A number of features were seen in this area, 11–17 m south of Trench C; the area between the recorded features and the ring-ditch was stripped without close scrutiny. At least 22 features, including possible pits and post-holes, were noted (Fig. 6) but there was only time to excavate six of them; many were seen to contain charcoal, pottery and burnt flint. All of the excavated features, 474, 475, 478, 480, 510, and 514, were larger than 0.30 m in diameter but none was more than 0.18 m deep; all were undoubtedly truncated during stripping. Pottery from the features was predominantly late Bronze Age in date.

Two features (other than Saxon graves) were excavated in the area just south of Trenches D and K, 446 and 460, but both were undated (Fig. 6).

North of ring-ditch 418

Several possible features were examined in this area (Fig. 5), four showing as areas of burning; the two smaller ones, 507 and 508, may have been

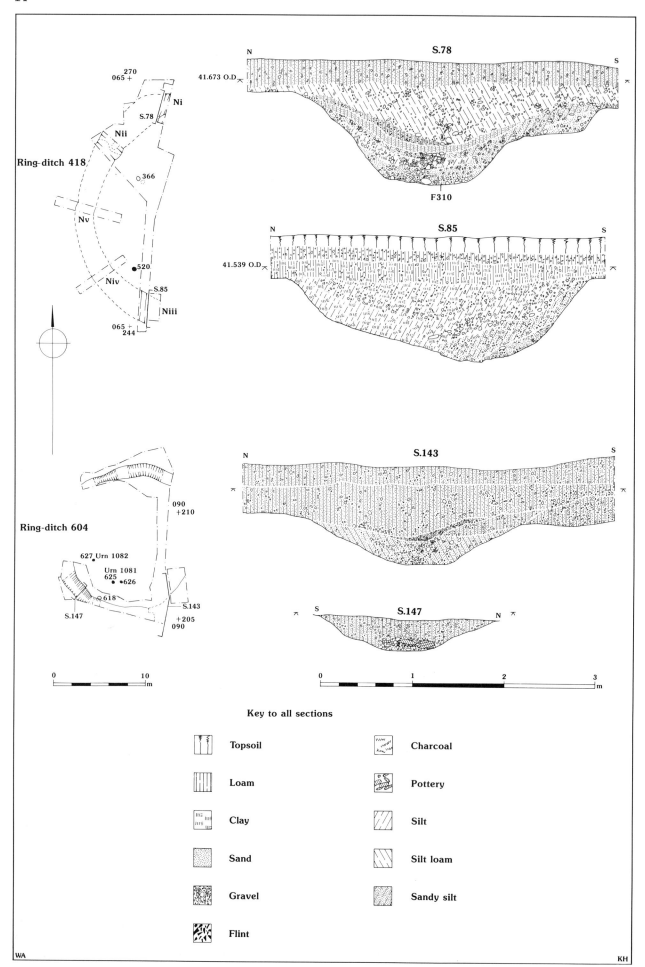

Key to all sections

	Topsoil		Charcoal
	Loam		Pottery
	Clay		Silt
	Sand		Silt loam
	Gravel		Sandy silt
	Flint		

Figure 8   Field Farm: ring-ditches 418 and 604, feature plans and selected sections

cremations although no bone was recovered from 507, and less than 5 g from 508. However, 508 was associated with a few sherds of Collared Urn. The two larger features, 516 and 518, lay within 2 m of each other and may originally have been joined. Features 504 and 482 were small pits thought to be of late Bronze Age date.

Other features
All other features investigated during the 1985 watching brief were widely dispersed. A fourth small ring-ditch, 457, was located c. 45 m north-west of ring-ditch 417 (Fig. 5). The feature, 4 m in diameter, was cut by a modern ditch, but had probably originally been a complete circle. The ditch was sectioned in three places, revealing a V–shaped profile. No evidence of internal or external banks could be seen. One sherd of early Bronze Age pottery was found in the ditch. A little over 3 m north of the ring-ditch was a shallow spread of black soil and charcoal, 465, 1.60 m x 0.80 m in area, which contained burnt flint but no artefacts.

Approximately 70 m west of ring-ditch 417 was a large circular pit, 449 (Fig. 5). Two quadrants were excavated from which 98 sherds of late Bronze Age and 21 sherds of Romano-British pottery were recovered. Three other features were recorded, widely dispersed, to the west and south of pit 449 (not on plan). These all produced pottery indicating a later Bronze Age date. The features investigated were undoubtedly only a small sample of the number of potential archaeological features of similar date, most of which could not be recorded with the time and manpower available.

1986 excavations

Ring-ditch 604
A small-scale excavation was carried out in October 1986 to locate and investigate a third ring-ditch, one of several of similar size in the northern central part of the site which showed as cropmarks on aerial photographs (Fig. 3).

The ring-ditch, located about 75 m to the north-east of 417 and 418, was 13.50 m in internal diameter, 16 m in external diameter. The interior of the ditch was not examined at that time, but cremations were recorded during the watching brief carried out in May 1987 (Fig. 8). An irregular trench forming three sides of a square, Trench R, was dug by machine to locate the ditch; three small sections were then excavated by hand through the remaining ditch fill.

The ditch
The ditch was sealed by up to 0.40 m of topsoil and subsoil and was cut into the gravel; it differed in profile from the two larger ditches, the sides sloping rather less steeply to a slightly rounded base and the angle between sides and base being less sharply defined (Fig. 8, S143). No evidence of an internal bank or mound was seen, but there was some suggestion of an external bank at the southern side

of the ditch where a marginally higher concentration of gravel occurred (the trenches were not cut cleanly enough to show this elsewhere).

There was no clear confirmation of an external bank from the ditch fills; in most sections the primary fill was gravel, slightly more of which could have derived from outside rather than inside the ditch. In one section the primary fill was relatively stone-free and lay beneath a much more gravelly deposit which contained a mass of broken pottery (Fig. 8, S147); 331 sherds were recovered, representing at least four Deverel-Rimbury Bucket Urns which were already broken before they were deposited in the ditch. Very few other finds were recovered.

Internal features
One small feature, 618, a possible post-hole, just cut the inner edge of the southern arc of the ditch; there were no associated finds. During the watching brief in 1987 two urns, 1081 and 1082 in features 625 and 627, both containing cremated bone, were found in the interior of the ditch. A third possible cremation, 626, apparently unaccompanied, was noted close to the other two but was not excavated; this feature showed only as a patch of dark soil and charcoal with small fragments of cremated bone.

Watching brief 1987

In the early summer of 1987 a further watching brief was carried out intermittently as overburden stripping extended into the north-east corner of the site. Some possible archaeological features were seen, but the gravel was spread and levelled after stripping so that they were almost entirely obscured. Three cremations in ring-ditch 604 were the only features excavated (see above).

1988 excavations (W267)
by J.C. Richards

Prior to the overburden removal in the north-western part of the field in 1988, investigation of some of the archaeological features in this area was undertaken. This enabled three specific cropmark features to be examined, initially by machine and, where appropriate, by manual excavation. The sites selected (Fig. 3) included:

A. A possible ditched enclosure in the north-west corner of the field.
B. A possible ditched enclosure near the northern boundary of the field and apparently continuing in the next field.
C. A ring-ditch located in the centre of the field within an area which the aerial photographs suggested also contained a number of pits.

The trenches were located as precisely as possible on the ground using information from available aerial photographs. The topsoil was

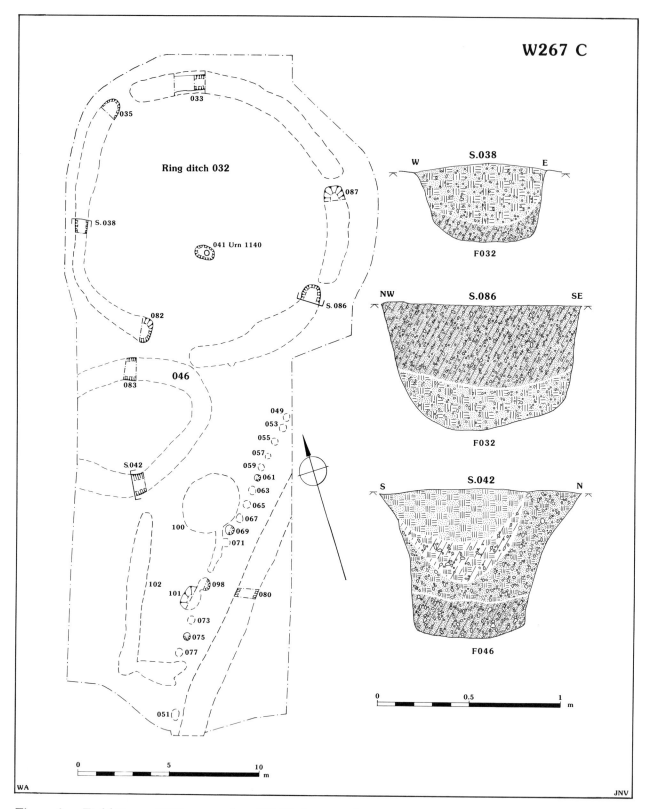

Figure 9   Field Farm: 1988 excavation (W267), feature plan and sections

removed by machine to expose a clean gravel surface. Where linear features were seen they were initially sectioned by machine in order rapidly to assess their depth, date and nature of filling. In the case of ring-ditch 032 (Trench C), trenches dug in order to locate the site were subsequently extended

in order to expose it entirely. A number of additional features were also recorded.

Enclosure A

The ditch which produced the cropmark was shown on excavation to be approximately 2.50 m wide and

0.80 m deep. Finds from its lower fill included fragments of brick suggesting a post-medieval or modern date.

Enclosure B

Sections excavated through the ditch in two places showed it to vary in size and complexity, but suggested that the enclosure might have been double-ditched. In the first section the two ditches were 3.25 m and 2 m wide and 0.48 m and 0.65 m deep respectively.

In contrast, the second section showed one ditch, nearly 9 m wide with a maximum depth of 1.4 m, and a second ditch 1.20 m wide and 0.35 m deep. No dating evidence was recovered from these sections but five sherds of pottery of later prehistoric date (probably late Iron Age) was recorded from unstratified contexts.

Ring-ditch 032 (Trench C)

This was shown on excavation to be irregular in shape, approximately 13 m in internal diameter, consisiting of four ditch segments separated by narrow causeways (Fig. 9). The ditch, where sectioned, varied considerably in both profile and depth, but was consistently less than 1m deep (Fig. 9, S038, S086).

To the south of the centre of the ring-ditch was a pit, 041, which contained an almost complete Barrel Urn inverted over a dense deposit of charcoal and 1.585 kg of cremated human bone (McKinley, this report). The urn was lifted complete with its contents, and the interior subsequently excavated and consolidated in the laboratory.

Other features

To the south of ring-ditch 032, a smaller, more irregular ring-ditch, 046, was located (Fig. 9); this was more oval in shape, approximately 5 m x 7 m (extrapolated). Two sections across the ditch indicated a steep sided profile with evidence for a recut, towards the outer edge, in the upper silts (Fig. 9, S042). No positive dating evidence was recovered from the ditch fill.

A ditch, 080, and a parallel row of small post-holes on the western side were recorded. Additional features were observed and planned although constraints of time meant that the majority of them could not be investigated. Pottery recovered from the top of feature 051 included eighteen sherds of coarse flint-tempered fabric, similar to Deverel-Rimbury Urns from the site. This feature was not excavated but it is possible that it may have been another cremation.

A complete sarsen saddle quern was found in the ploughsoil in this area, suggesting settlement activities.

Although only a small area was examined, it can be tentatively suggested that the ditch and fence may have separated a funerary area, represented by the ring-ditch with its cremation, from an area of more domestic activity.

5 The Anglo-Saxon Cemetery

Introduction

During excavation of ring-ditch 417 a group of Anglo-Saxon graves was discovered in Trench D; further graves were found in Trenches A,G,K and L, to north, west and east respectively of Trench D, and others were also identified during the 1985 watching brief, in Area P, the area south of the ring-ditch (Fig. 6). Altogether 50 graves were wholly or partly excavated. Four additional features, possibly graves were also noted (one was not excavated).

Thirty graves were recorded within ring-ditch 417. Twenty-five were concentrated in the central southern part of the interior (Plate 1), two were toward the centre, north-east of this group, and three were in the northern central area. A second large group of 20 graves lay outside the southern arc of the ditch. Four of these graves were partly cut into the filled ring-ditch and others may have been but remained unrecognised.

The excavated graves may indicate the external limits of the cemetery, although no evidence of boundaries was seen. A possible eastern edge is suggested by the line of graves 358, 325, 323, 320 and 458, perhaps with 61 and 140. Graves 494, 279, 432 and 453 could delineate the western edge of the cemetery. Although no such clear lines of graves mark the possible northern and southern cemetery limits, it would not be unreasonable to propose a line joining the southern ends of the suggested eastern and western boundaries south of graves 453 and 423 as a southern boundary. The northernmost limit may be represented only by a single grave, 87. No graves were seen beyond the area thus delineated during the excavation or watching brief, although it is possible that shallow graves may have been missed during machine stripping.

All of the graves in the centre of 417 lay directly beneath topsoil, most of those nearer to the ditch and outside it were also beneath an additional thin layer of subsoil, at depths of 0.25 m–0.30 m below the ground surface. In Trenches D and L the upper levels of the graves were truncated by later disturbance and were encountered at depths of as much as 0.80 m. At the centre of the ring-ditch they were cut only into the sandy silt above gravel; further out they were also cut through the gravel itself.

Grave depths varied between 0.05 m and 0.60 m, although the majority (32) were 0.16 m–0.35 m deep. Graves within the interior of the ring-ditch were cut at progressively higher levels the closer they were to the centre of the monument, with those cutting the filled ditch and outside it usually, but not always, the lowest-lying.

The dark brown, gravelly, silty loams filling most of the graves were not easy to distinguish from the soil filling the ditch, and graves could only be seen where they also cut the paler sandy silt beyond the ditch edges. Elsewhere, both within and without the

Plate 1   Field Farm: general view of the 1985 excavations looking north along Trenches K and D. The southern arc of ring-ditch 417 crosses the trenches in the foreground and beyond it are some of the Saxon graves

ditch, graves were more clearly recognisable and, once their appearance and likely density had been recognised, it was possible to look more closely at apparently 'empty' areas, but without addition to the total. Bone preservation was extremely poor, with only a single skeleton surviving in anything approaching a complete state (Plate 2). Grave-goods were present in 33 of the graves and it is these that indicate a late 6th–7th century date for the cemetery.

Grave Catalogue, by H. Rees and C.A. Butterworth

The orientation of the graves is given without reference to the position of the body; only in two instances, Graves 87 and 365, was the orientation of the body known from surviving bone, although it was sometimes indicated by the position of the grave-goods; this is stated where possible. Grave dimensions are given in the following order: length, width and depth (after the removal of topsoil). Not all graves were fully excavated; this is stated where relevant. The height above sea level of the base of each grave is given where known; it was not recorded for Graves 413–494 investigated during the watching brief. Where the base of a grave sloped markedly (by 0.05 m or more), values are given for both ends of the grave. Grave-fills are described and their context numbers given. Soilmarks within the graves are described where present.

Only graves which held grave-goods and Grave 87 are illustrated individually, with the exception of Grave 413, which was only observed in section.

The grave-goods are listed by their special find numbers, usually in numerical order; where a related group of items were found (such as the component parts of a shield) these are listed as a group. All grave-goods are of iron unless otherwise stated.

Preliminary identification of mineralised organic remains was carried out by Margaret Brooks of the Wiltshire Conservation Laboratory and further detailed examination and identification done by Jacqui Watson of the Ancient Monuments Laboratory; where identifications differ the initials of the relevant specialist are given after the identification.

Reconstruction of the casket from Grave 140 is by Jacqui Watson. The textiles were examined by Margaret Brooks. Identification of the human bone was carried out by Lynne Bell of University College, London.

Plate 2 Field Farm: Grave 87 showing the poor survival of the bone in the most complete skeleton excavated

Residual worked flint and pottery found within the grave-fills are noted where present and are discussed elsewhere in this volume.

Grave 32 (Fig. 12)
NE–SW; c.1.40 m, c.0.70 m, 0.35m; 41.07 m OD. Not fully excavated; cut through fill of ring-ditch 417. Filled with moderately gravelly dark brown sandy silt, 31.

Grave-goods:
SF.88   Tip of a **knife-blade**, perhaps of Böhner's type A (1958), preserving mineralised traces of its sheath, possibly leather.

Other finds:
One sherd of late Bronze Age pottery (unnumbered).

Grave 61 (Fig. 10)
WNW–ESE; c.2 m, c.0.65 m, 0.17 m; 41.73 m OD. Dark brown sandy silty loam with a little gravel, 53.

Grave-goods:
SF.237   These objects were found in close proximity. This, together with the fact that the shears were in closed position and both items preserve traces of mineralised leather, suggests that they may both have been part of a set, contained in a leather wrapping or bag.

Fragments of a **knife**, with probable straight cutting edge and curved back, mineralised leather on blade and mineralised horn handle.

Pair of **shears** with looped end and mineralised remains of leather on blades; length 145 mm.

Other finds:
Ninety-seven sherds of early/middle Bronze Age pottery; this grave cut a (damaged) Collared Urn *in situ* at the south side of the grave; two sherds of late Bronze Age pottery (SF.234–236, 238, 282, 283, 325, 326, 334–344, 398).

Grave 87 (Fig. 10; Plate 2)
NNE–SSW; 1.98 m, 0.65 m, 0.23 m; 41.50 m OD (north), 41.58 m OD (south). Dark brown silty loam, 86, over dark yellowish brown silty clay with a little gravel, 104.

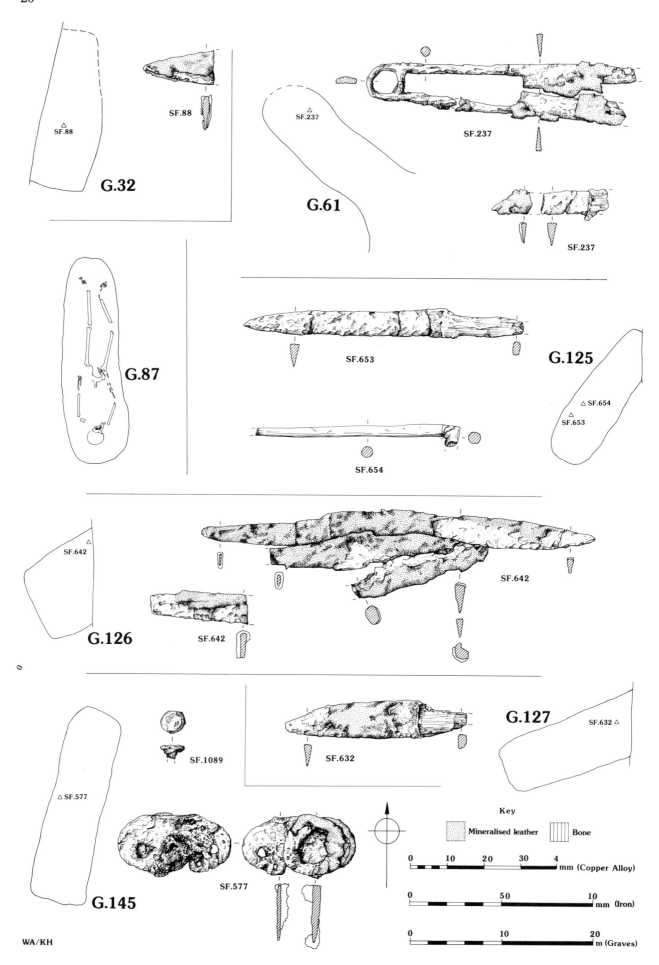

G.32

SF.88

SF.88

G.61

SF.237

SF.237

SF.237

G.87

SF.653

SF.654

G.125

SF.654

SF.653

G.126

SF.642

SF.642

SF.642

SF.642

G.127

SF.632

SF.1089

SF.632

G.145

SF.577

SF.577

Key

Mineralised leather   Bone

0   10   20   30   4
mm (Copper Alloy)

0   50   10
mm (Iron)

0   10   20
m (Graves)

WA/KH

Figure 10   Field Farm: Saxon grave plans and associated grave-goods

Bone:
Head at south: poor condition, sex not determined; 17–25 years; supine, skull turned to east, right arm across pelvis, right leg slightly flexed.

No grave-goods; no other finds.

Grave 124
ENE–WSW; 1.46 m, 0.48 m, 0.15 m; 41.16 m OD. Moderately gravelly dark brown silty clay, 109.

No grave-goods; no other finds.

Grave 125 (Fig. 10)
NE–SW: *c.*1.20 m, 0.46 m, 0.12 m; 41.20 m OD (north-east), 41.27 m OD (south-west). Not fully excavated but very little fill remaining. Moderately gravelly dark brown silty clay, 108.

Grave-goods:
SF.653   **Knife** of Böhner's type C, with mineralised organic material, possibly horn, on the tang; length 150 mm.

SF.654   Small **rod** of copper alloy, broken at one end and with right-angled hook at the other; length 55 mm. Mineralised fibres, probably of flax, are wound around the hook.

Grave 126 (Fig. 10)
ENE–WSW; +0.98 m; 0.80 m, 0.10 m; 41.17 m OD. Not fully excavated. Moderately gravelly dark brown silty clay, 110.

Grave-goods:
SF.642   These objects were found together and all show possible traces of mineralised leather; it is suggested that they were each part of a set, contained within a leather bag or case.

Long **knife** of Böhner's type A, with unidentifiable mineralised organic remains of the handle and possible traces of mineralised leather on the blade; length 217 mm.

Small **knife** of Böhner's type C, with unidentifiable mineralised organic remains of the handle and possible traces of mineralised leather on the blade; length 115 mm.

Sharpening steel with possible traces of mineralised leather; in two fragments, overall length *c.*123 mm.

Grave 127 (Fig. 10)
ENE–WSW; +1.60 m, 0.50 m, 0.20 m; 41.09 m OD. Not fully excavated. Moderately gravelly dark brown silty clay, 111.

Grave-goods:
SF.632   **Knife** of Böhner's type C with short broad blade. Possible traces of mineralised leather were found on the blade and evidence of a mineralised horn handle; length 98 mm.

Other finds:
Five sherds of late Bronze Age pottery (SF.615, 616, 621, 623, 631).

Grave 140 (Fig. 11; Plates 7 and 8)
NNE–SSW; 1.98 m, 1.20 m, 0.19 m; 41.91 m OD. Moderately gravelly dark yellowish brown–brown silty loam, 139/277, over brown sandy clay with a little gravel, 164.

Bone:
Cremated enamel fragments from four teeth; possible age 17–25 years.

Grave-goods:
These objects, which form the non-organic components of a casket, were found spread in the north western part of Grave 140, the handle, hasp and one of the corner fittings being in close association with each other. The functions of the pairs of incomplete and staple-like strips are not understood but they may have been purely decorative.

SF.855, 856, 875, 877   Four **corner-brackets**, each exhibiting mineralised maple wood (*Acer* sp.) along its internal surface and with wholly or partially remaining small nails with flat round heads *in situ*. Two, 875 and 877, also preserve external traces of textile in tabby weave.

SF.857, 858   Two **hinges** with leaf-shaped wings and rod-shaped centre, each with wholly or partially preserved small nails with flat round heads *in situ*. The internal surfaces of both objects exhibit traces of mineralised maple (*Acer* sp.) wood running across them.

SF.871, 872   Two incomplete **strips**, each with traces of mineralised maple (*Acer* sp.) wood on one surface; on 871 the grain runs across the strip, but on 872 it runs along it. (871 not illustrated).

SF.873   **Handle** with curving terminals attached to loop-headed **pins**. The latter have been manufactured differently, one being a split pin, the other butt-joined or thinned down onto itself. Mineralised maple (*Acer* sp.) wood is visible on the terminals and on the pins.

SF.873   **Hasp** with hinge loop and slot accommodating a fastening loop secured by means of a small wooden peg (the hinge and fastening loops have both broken

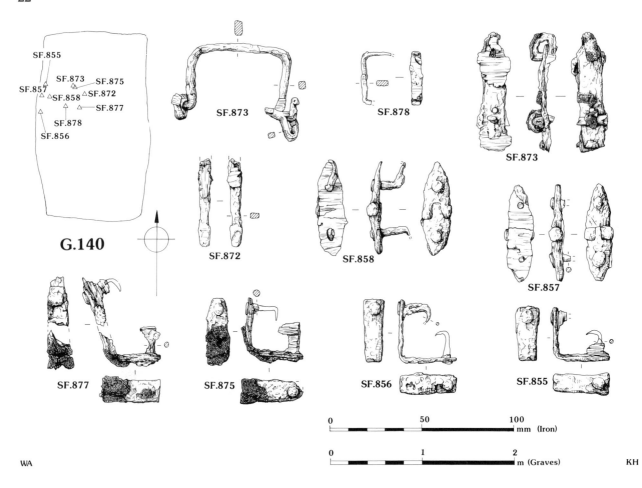

G.140

Figure 11   Field Farm: Saxon Grave 140, plan and associated grave-goods

away from their original positions). Textile in fine tabby weave is preserved in folds over the loop of the hasp and the hinge loop exhibits additional traces of textile in twill; the finer tabby weave material appears to lie directly next to the hasp. Maple (*Acer* sp.) wood in mineralised form occurs on one side of the hinge plate.

SF.873   Various fragments and broken **nails**, found in association with the hasp and the handle, preserving traces of mineralised maple wood (*Acer* sp.). Not illustrated.

SF.878   Two staple-like **strips**, both incomplete, with mineralised maple (*Acer* sp.) wood on both surfaces. One only, the more complete, illustrated.

Other finds:
Eight sherds of early/middle Bronze Age pottery; one of late Bronze Age pottery; one of medieval pottery (SF.845, 876, 879, 881–884, 891). Five flints.

Grave 144
N–S; 1.76 m, 0.92 m, 0.22 m; 41.39 m OD (north), 41.34 m OD (south). Very gravelly very dark greyish brown sandy clay loam, 79.
No grave-goods; no other finds.

Grave 145 (Fig. 10)
NNW–SSE; 2.06 m, 0.58 m, 0.23 m; 41.34 m OD. Moderately gravelly dark greyish brown sandy silt loam, 42.

Bone:
Small quantity of unidentifiable cremated bone fragments.

Grave-goods:
SF.577   The two items appear to have been tied together with twine and placed in a leather pouch. The underside of the strike-a-light/purse mount is covered with very fragmentary traces of textile, possibly in tabby weave.

Strike-a-light or **purse mount** with mineralised organic material on the underside, possibly the remains of tinder; length 62 mm, maximum width c.28 mm.

Ring with mineralised organic material; external diameter c.30 mm, internal diameter c.20 mm.

SF.1089   (Recovered from sieving; position in grave not known.) Iron **stud** with round flat head, 12 mm in diameter. A thin silver sheet, upon which traces of repoussé decoration are visible, has been applied to the surface.

Other finds:
One sherd of early/middle Bronze Age pottery; two sherds of late Bronze Age pottery; one sherd of Romano-British pottery; (SF. 547, and unnumbered). Five flints.

Grave 146 (Fig. 12; Plate 3)
N–S; 2.10 m, 0.64 m, 0.20 m; 41.49 m OD (north), 41.35 m OD (south). Moderately gravelly very dark greyish brown sandy silt loam, 43.

Bone:
One unidentifiable burnt bone fragment.

Grave-goods:
SF.567   The knife was recovered with the buckle attached to the base of the blade. Mineralised traces of wool, perhaps the remains of the interior of the knife sheath, were observed in the position where the buckle had rested.

Knife of Böhner's type A, preserving its horn handle in mineralised form and with possible traces of mineralised leather sheath; length 153 mm.

Small oval **buckle**; oval, 22 mm x 12 mm.

SF.575   **Spearhead** of Swanton's type C1 (1973), its textile wrapping in tabby weave secured with vegetable twine, well-preserved in mineralised form. Traces of mineralised wood, probably coppiced ash (*Fraxinus* sp.), occur in the socket; length 117 mm.

SF.1090 Small **rod-shaped object** with one broken end and mineralised remains of a possible handle. Twisted fibres are wrapped around the metal part of the object; length 38 mm.

Orientation:
The body may have been deposited with its head at the south, the spearhead, pointing toward the feet, lying at the left side, the knife on the right hand side and the rod-shaped object at the centre.

Other finds:
Three sherds of early/middle Bronze Age pottery; six sherds of late Bronze Age pottery (SF.185, 186, 543, 544, 565). Four flints.

Grave 147
N–S; 1.95 m, 1.06 m, 0.17 m; 41.38 m OD. Moderately gravelly very dark greyish brown sandy silt loam, 80.

Plate 3   Field Farm: Spearhead from Grave 146 (SF.575), showing traces of mineralised textile wrapping and cross binding

Bone:
Unidentifiable cremated bone fragments.

Grave-goods:
No grave-goods.

Other finds:
Two flints.

Grave 148 (Fig. 12)
NNE–SSW; 1.66 m, 0.98 m, 0.12 m; 41.60 m OD. Moderately gravelly dark brown silty loam, 56.

Bone:
Fragment of long-bone shaft.

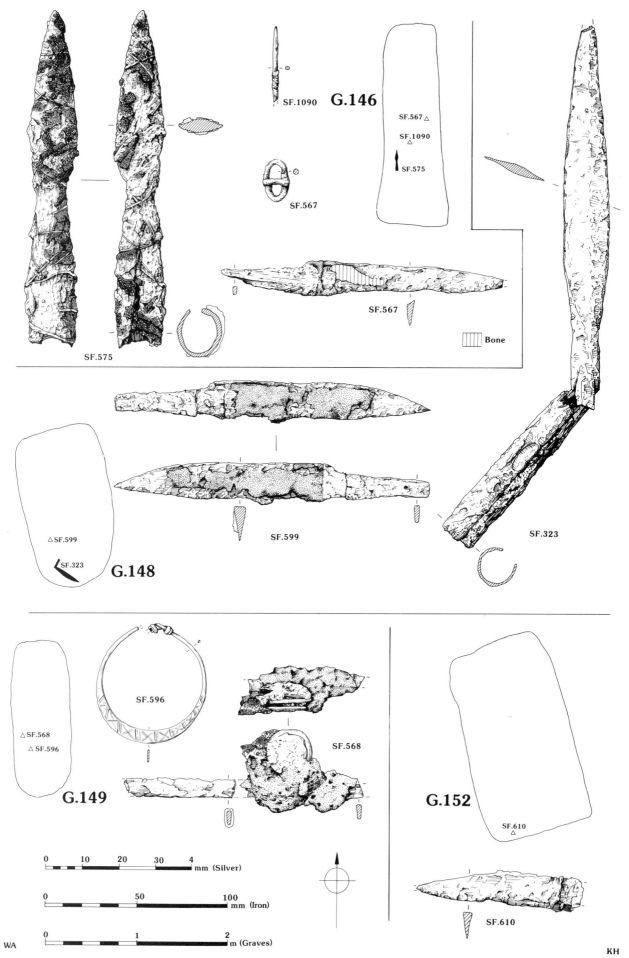

SF.1090

G.146

SF.567 △

SF.1090 △

SF.575

SF.567

SF.567

☐☐☐ Bone

SF.575

SF.323

△ SF.599

SF.323

G.148

SF.599

G.148

SF.596

SF.568

△ SF.568

△ SF.596

SF.568

G.149

G.152

SF.610 △

0   10   20   30   4
mm (Silver)

0   50   100
mm (Iron)

0   1   2
m (Graves)

WA

SF.610

KH

Figure 12   Field Farm: Saxon grave plans and associated finds

Grave-goods:

SF.323 **Spearhead** of Swanton's type C2 with nearly severed socket and tip of blade missing; length *c.* 303 mm. The tip was broken in antiquity but there is uncertainty whether the damage to the socket occurred before burial, since the fracture is relatively uncorroded. Willow (*Salix* sp.) or poplar (*Populus* sp.) wood in mineralised form is preserved in the socket.

SF.599 **Knife** of Böhner's type C with unidentified but possibly mineralised horn on the tang; length 173 mm. A discrete layer of corroded iron is visible on the surface of the blade and separated from it by a thin lens of soil, possibly the remains of the sheath. Two patches of textile in tabby weave are preserved on one surface of the blade.

Orientation:
The body was probably deposited with its head at the south and the knife on the left side of the chest. The position of the spear in relation to the head is uncertain, although it was probably on its left.

Other finds:
Eleven sherds of late Bronze Age pottery (SF.536–538, 549, 562, 563, 573, 574). Three flints.

Grave 149 (Fig. 12)
NNE–SSW; 1.62 m, 0.63 m, 0.23 m; 41.46 m OD. Gravelly dark brown sandy silt loam, 81.

Grave-goods:

SF.568 A group of iron and copper alloy objects corroded together, which appear to be an iron knife and buckle with two copper alloy discs or coins. The whole assemblage is wrapped or caught up in folds of tabby-woven cloth, possibly a container for the set, which obscures the exact relationships of the objects.

Broken **knife**, with bone or antler handle and traces of mineralised leather sheath extending over part of the handle. In order to make the handle firm, wood, probably alder (*Alnus* sp.), has been packed between the bone and the tang; the original size and fixing of the handle can be seen in the corrosion at the shoulder of the blade.

Buckle; in a mass of corrosion, but probably oval.

Two **copper alloy discs** or **coins**, at least one of which may have been perforated.

SF.596 Part of a small **tang**, possibly from a tool, with mineral preserved hazel (*Corylus* sp.) wood. Not illustrated.

SF.596 Crescent-shaped **silver ring** with tightly twisted wire terminals and incised decoration of groups of four parallel lines separating crosses of double parallel lines; diameter *c.* 30 mm.

Orientation:
If the ring was used as an ear-ring, its position in the grave indicates that the head was at the south.

Other finds:
One sherd of late Bronze Age pottery; one sherd of Romano-British pottery (SF.539, 540). Two flints.

Grave 150
NNE–SSW; 1.76 m, *c.* 1.50 m, 0.26 m; 41.44 m OD. Moderately gravelly dark brown silty loam, 82.

Grave-goods:
No grave-goods.

Other finds:
Four sherds of late Bronze Age pottery (SF.541, 612, 613, 633).

Grave 152 (Fig. 12)
NNE–SSW; 2.08 m, 1.12 m, 0.22 m; 41.86 m OD (north), 41.80 m OD (south). Moderately gravelly brown silty loam, 98.

Bone:
Fragments of human bone, mostly skull.

Grave-goods:

SF.610 Small **knife** of Böhner's type A, with the mineralised remains of a horn handle and probable leather sheath; length 89 mm.

Other finds:
One sherd of early/middle Bronze Age pottery; twelve sherds of late Bronze Age pottery (SF.569–572, 598, 605, 609, 614). Eight flints.

Grave 194 (Fig. 13; Plates 4 and 5)
NNE–SSW; 2.0 m, 1.0 m, 0.32 m; 41.32 m OD (north), 41.26 m OD (south). Very gravelly dark brown sandy clay loam, 193.

Grave-goods:

SF.461 **Shale bracelet**, slightly irregular in shape, worn smooth but showing occasional scratches from use (it was not possible to determine the method of manufacture, although very slight traces of facets may be visible); external diameter 73 mm, internal diameter 59 mm.

SF.592 The knife, shears, pin and chain were found in close association; it is possible

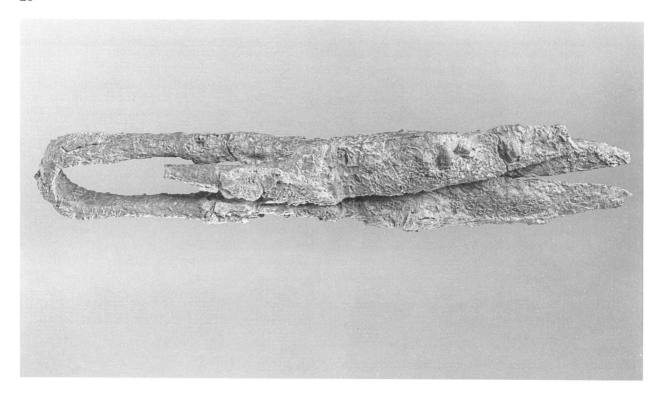

Plate 4   Field Farm: shears and knife 'set' (SF.592) from Grave 194 showing mineralised insect pupae on the knife blade

Plate 5   Field Farm: detail of insect pupae on knife blade (SF.592) from Grave 194

that the knife and shears were parts of a set, contained in a leather bag suspended at the waist by means of the chain.

Knife of Böhner's type C, with a mineralised horn handle, and mineralised insect pupae preserved on one side of the blade, possibly indicating that leather was once present but had been consumed by the larvae before mineralisation could preserve it; length 99 mm.

Pair of shears with possible traces of mineralised wood attached to the curved end and mineral preserved leather on their blades; length 142 mm.

Fragment of a **pin.**

Fragment of a **ring attached to a chain.** Two pairs of coarse S–spun threads preserved in mineralised form on the surface of one of the chain-links may be the remains of a tablet-woven belt, or possibly of a fringe.

SF.593 Iron **pin** with both ends broken.

SF.594 Heavy **copper alloy ring**; external diameter 40 mm, internal diameter 32 mm.

SF.647 Small globular opaque yellow **glass bead**; diameter 7 mm.

Orientation:
The position of the bead in the grave suggests that the head was possibly at the south and all other items, except the bracelet, were placed at the waist.

Other finds:
One flint.

Grave 202 (Fig. 13)
NNE–SSW; 1.35 m, 0.72 m, 0.22 m; 41.42 m OD. Moderately gravelly dark yellowish brown sandy loam, 201.

Grave-goods:
SF.451 **Spearhead** of Swanton's type C2, with traces of a possible holly (*Ilex* sp.) haft preserved in the socket; length 260 mm.

Orientation:
The body was probably positioned with the head to the south, the spearhead at the left shoulder.

Grave 204 (Fig. 13)
NNE–SSW; 2.0 m, 0.84 m, 0.37 m; 41.16 m OD. Moderately gravelly dark brown–dark yellowish brown sandy clay loam, 203, over slightly more gravelly dark brown sandy clay loam, 239, along lower sides and across base of grave; ? possible coffin stain.

Grave-goods:
SF.672 These objects were found in close association.

Knife of Böhner's type C, with the mineralised remains of a horn handle and leather sheath; length 133 mm.

Possible **steel** with unidentifiable mineralised organic material on the tang, probably the remains of a handle; length 130 mm.

Other finds:
Two sherds of late Bronze Age pottery (SF.664).

Grave 206 (Fig. 13)
NNE–SSW; 2.0 m, 0.70 m, 0.28 m; 41.23 m OD. Moderately gravelly dark yellowish brown sandy clay loam, 205.

Grave-goods:
SF.462 Small **knife** perhaps of Böhner's type D, but in poor and worn condition; length 107 mm. The grain of its mineralised horn handle is at an angle to the direction of the tang. The lumps of corrosion on the surface may be the remains of a sheath.

Grave 212
N–S; 1.38 m, 0.50 m, 0.21 m; 41.81 m OD. Moderately gravelly brown silty loam, 83.

Grave-goods:
No grave-goods.

Other finds:
Three sherds of late Bronze Age pottery; two sherds of Romano-British pottery (SF.606, 607). Eleven flints.

Grave 213 (Fig. 14)
N–S; 2.0 m, 1.30 m, 0.25 m; 41.90 m OD (north), 41.78 m OD (south). Moderately gravelly brown silty loam, 84.

Bone:
Fragments of mostly unidentifiable cremated bone (including one fragment each of skull and long-bone).

Grave-goods:
SF.645 These items were found in close association, the curved strip lying on edge round the spear tip, and may have been cloth wrapped although no textile was preserved on the spearhead.

Spearhead of Swanton's type C3, with broken socket; length 441 mm. Mineralised traces of a hazel (*Corylus* sp.) haft are visible inside the socket.

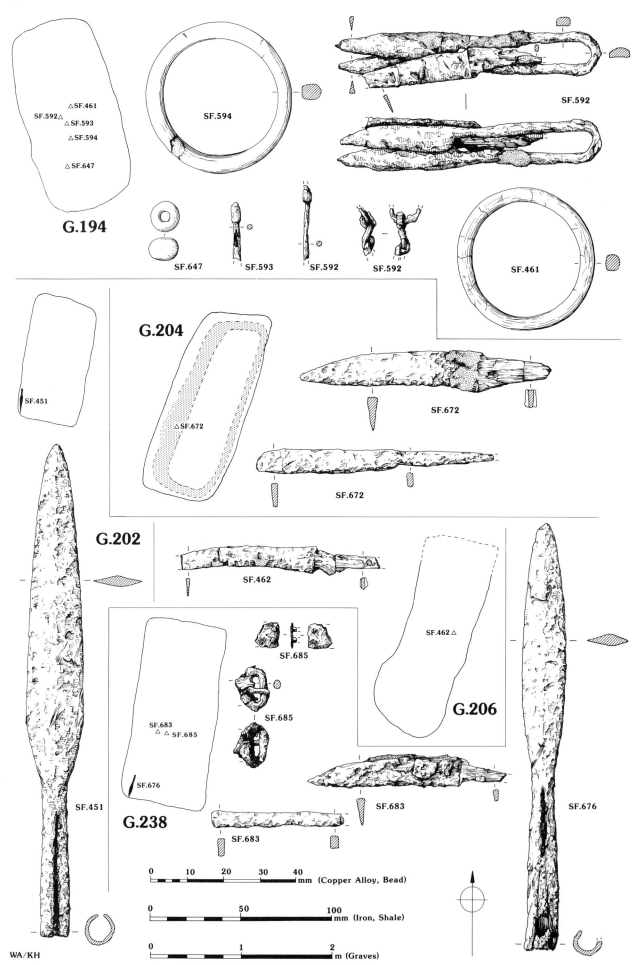

Figure 13   Field Farm: Saxon grave plans and associated finds

Three **hinge pieces**, one with traces of mineralised horn or bone and fibre, one with traces of mineralised textile.

Curved **strip**, tapering to a point at one end, with traces of mineralised textile; length *c.*130 mm. Two small detached fragments not illustrated.

SF.652 **Knife** of Böhner's type C, with mineralised remains of horn handle and leather sheath; length 130 mm. Mineralised insect pupae were present between the sheath and the knife blade.

Orientation:
The body was probably buried with its head at the south, the spearhead at the right shoulder.

Other finds:
One sherd of early/middle Bronze Age pottery; eighteen sherds of late Bronze Age pottery; two sherds of Romano-British pottery (SF.450, 452–454, 618–620, 624, 626, 627, 634–636, 650, 651). Twenty-six flints.

Grave 220 (Fig. 15)
NNE–SSW; 2.20 m, 1.25 m, 0.40 m; 41.44 m OD. Gravelly dark yellowish brown silty loam, 219.

Bone:
One small unidentifiable heated bone fragment.

Grave-goods:
SF.691 **Shield-boss** with five dome-headed rivets *in situ* around the flange and two holes where other rivets may once have been; height 142 mm, diameter of flange 135 mm. Traces of mineral preserved wood, identified as ash (*Fraxinus* sp.), were found in the soil inside the boss and attached to the flange. Slight traces of threads were also seen inside the boss.

SF.691 Incomplete **hand-grip** (without studs or other means of attachment), preserving traces of mineralised ash (*Fraxinus* sp.) wood on the underside at each end, the grain running across the grip probably suggesting that it was part of the shield-board; length 88 mm, width 20 mm. Textile remains in 2/1 twill weave observed on both surfaces of the grip are possibly the remains of a loose binding or wrapping. A small patch of mineralised leather and insect pupae are also preserved.

SF.709 Pair of round-headed **rivets** attached to a tapering plate, with possible traces of mineralised organic material(s) on each shank; shank lengths *c.*13 mm, diameter of heads 13 mm; plate 32 mm x 12 mm.

SF.751 Pair of **rivets** with dome–shaped heads, the opposite ends broken; shank lengths 12 mm and 13 mm, diameters of heads 15 mm and 14 mm. Both shanks are slightly twisted and with mineralised wood running along approximately half their length, mineralised leather on the remainder. The size of the rivets suggests that the shield was 4–6 mm thick. If, however, they secured a leather covering to the shield this would increase its thickness to 11 mm.

SF.704 **Spearhead** of Swanton's type C2, with mineralised traces of an ash (*Fraxinus* sp.) wood haft trimmed from mature timber preserved in the socket; length 267 mm. Vegetable matter in mineralised form is visible on the surface.

SF.728 Small **buckle** with part of a ?round-ended plate folded over one long side; oval, 28 mm x *c.*12 mm; plate width 22 mm. Textile remains, possibly in tabby weave, are visible on the internal surface of the plate.

SF.750 Bent **knife** in worn condition, perhaps of Böhner's type A, bearing mineralised traces of its horn handle and possibly of leather and wool comprising a sheath; length 155 mm.

Orientation:
The body was probably buried with its head at the south, the spearhead at the right shoulder, the shield on the chest and the knife and buckle at the waist.

Other finds:
One sherd of late Bronze Age pottery; one sherd of Romano-British pottery (SF.504, 689).

Grave 236
NNE–SSW; +1.50 m, +0.68 m, 0.26 m; 41.42 m OD (north), 41.37 m OD (south). Not fully excavated. Moderately gravelly dark yellowish brown sandy clay loam, 235.

Grave-goods:
No grave-goods.

Other finds:
Two flints.

Grave 238 (Fig. 13)
NNE–SSW; 1.14 m, 0.94 m, 0.28 m. 41.55 m OD. Moderately gravelly dark yellowish brown loam, 237.

Grave-goods:
SF.676 **Spearhead** of Swanton's type C2, with mineralised but unidentifiable wood preserved in its socket; length 225 mm.

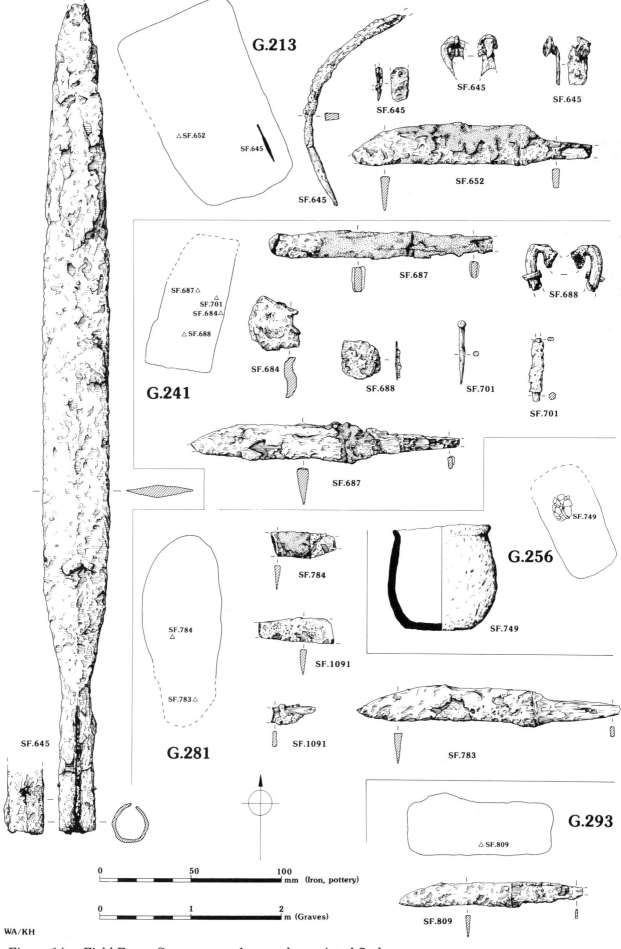

SF.645

G.213

△SF.652

SF.645

SF.645

SF.645

SF.645

SF.652

SF.687

SF.688

SF.687△ △
SF.701
SF.684△

△SF.688

SF.684

SF.688

SF.701

SF.701

G.241

SF.687

SF.749

SF.784

G.256

SF.749

SF.784
△

SF.1091

SF.783△

SF.1091

SF.783

G.281

G.293

△SF.809

SF.809

0   50   100
mm (Iron, pottery)

0   1   2
m (Graves)

WA/KH

Figure 14   Field Farm: Saxon grave plans and associated finds

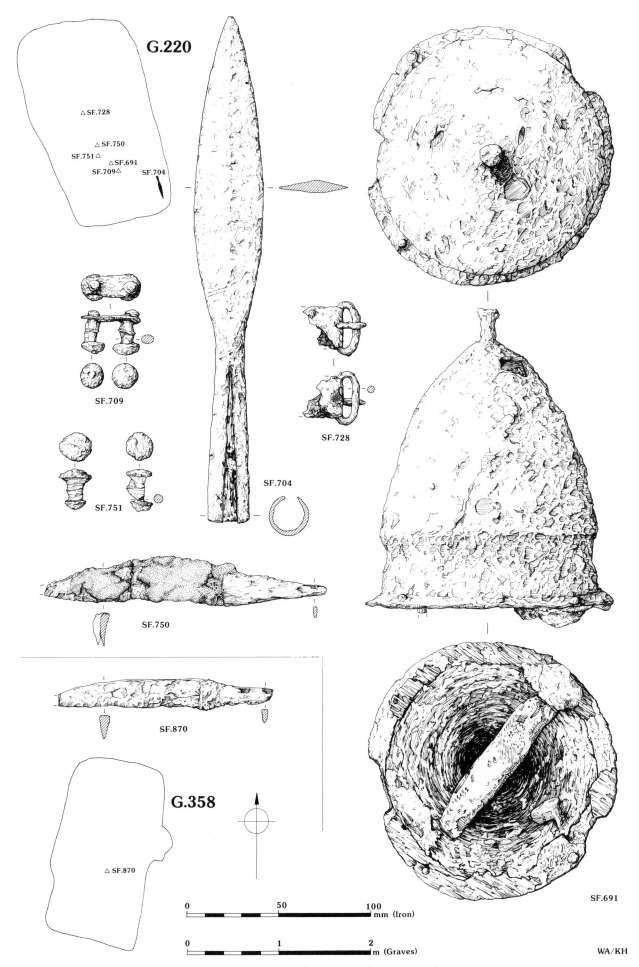

G.220

SF.728

SF.750
SF.751 SF.691
SF.709 SF.704

SF.709

SF.751

SF.750

SF.704

SF.728

G.358

SF.870

SF.870

SF.691

0   50   100
mm (Iron)

0   1   2
m (Graves)

WA/KH

Figure 15   Field Farm: Saxon grave plans and associated grave-goods

SF.679 **Nail** with no head or point. Not illustrated.

SF.683 The knife and steel were found in close association.

Small **knife** of Böhner's type D, with the remains of a horn handle and leather sheath in mineralised form; length 106 mm.

Small **steel**; length 73 mm.

SF.685 Small oval **buckle** with part of a plate and two broken rivets *in situ*; oval, 22 mm x 14 mm. Mineralised traces of tabby- woven cloth are visible on the underside of the buckle. The upper surface of the buckle preserves possible traces of fibres, perhaps wool, in mineralised form.

Orientation:
The body was probably deposited with its head at the south, the spearhead at the left shoulder and the knife at the waist.

Other finds:
One sherd of early/middle Bronze Age pottery; nine sherds of late Bronze Age pottery; three sherds of Romano-British pottery (SF. 667–671, 677, 678, 682, 692, 693). Seventeen flints.

Grave 241 (Fig. 14)
NNE–SSW; 1.40 m, 0.75 m, 0.10 m; 42.14 m OD (north), 42.06 m OD (south). Not fully excavated. Gravelly dark brown sandy clay loam, 240.

Grave-goods:
SF.684 Flattish irregularly shaped **piece of iron with part of a hole** (for nail or rivet?) in one edge; *c.*21 mm x 32 mm.

SF.687 These items were found in close association.

Knife of Böhner's type A with mineralised traces of its horn handle but no securely identifiable sheath; length 147 mm.

Possible **steel**, with part of a leather wrapping preserved in mineralised form; length 122 mm.

SF.688 Fragments of a small **buckle** and **plate**, preserving traces of mineralised textile, identified as twill, on the underside.

SF.701 These items were found in close association.

Small **nail** with flat round head; length 34 mm.

Small **rod-shaped object** broken at both ends with textile or fibre on one face only.

Grave 256 (Fig. 14)
NNW–SSE; 1.20 m, 0.58 m, 0.15 m; 41.29 m OD. Moderately gravelly dark yellowish brown sandy clay loam, 176.

Bone:
Fragments of unidentifiable burnt bone.

Grave-goods:
SF.749 Virtually complete **jar**, hand made in a moderately fine, probably grass-tempered, sandy fabric with patchily oxidised outer surface. The interior bears traces of sooting; maximum height 56 mm, maximum diameter 58 mm.

Other finds:
Five sherds of late Bronze Age pottery (unnumbered).

Grave 279
NNE–SSW; +1.65 m, +0.55 m, 0.30 m; 41.56 m OD (north), 41.29 m OD (south). Not fully excavated. Very gravelly brown sandy clay loam, 278.

Grave-goods:
No grave-goods.

Other finds:
One sherd of Romano-British pottery (SF.786).

Grave 281 (Fig. 14)
N–S; 2.20 m, 1.30 m, 0.60 m; 41.11 m OD. Gravel in sparse brown sandy clay loam matrix, 185, overlying gravelly brown clay loam around sides, 287, and almost stone-free dark brown sandy clay loam 'mounded' in base of grave, 258.

Grave-goods:
SF.783 **Knife** perhaps of Böhner's type D, although the concave cutting edge may be the result of frequent sharpening; length 143 mm. The knife has mineralised traces of a horn handle and some vegetable matter is visible on one side of the blade.

SF.784 Fragment of a **knife**, the junction between the tang and the blade, preserving traces of a leather sheath in mineralised form and of an unidentifiable mineralised organic handle. Traces of mineralised textile, the weave unidentifiable, run over the back and one side of the blade.

SF.1091 From southern half of grave but exact position in grave not known. Two fragments of a **knife** with mineralised horn handle and traces of mineralised textile on one surface.

Other finds:
Nine sherds of late Bronze Age pottery (SF.762). One flint.

Grave 293 (Fig. 14)
WNW–ESE; 1.60 m, 0.65 m, 0.32 m; 41.18 m OD. Moderately gravelly dark brown silty clay loam, 280.

Grave-goods:
SF.809   Small **knife** of Böhner's type A, with mineralised remains of a possible horn (M.B.) handle and of vegetable matter on one side of the blade; length 100 mm.

Other finds:
One sherd of early/middle Bronze Age pottery; two sherds of late Bronze Age pottery (SF.798, 799).

Grave 295
WNW–ESE; 2.30 m, 0.75 m, 0.45 m; 41.13 m OD (west), 41.05 m OD (east). Not fully excavated. Moderately gravelly brown silty clay loam, 283, surrounding a lens of stone-free dark greyish brown clay loam, 294.

Grave-goods:
No grave-goods

Other finds:
Three sherds of Saxon pottery (SFs 807, 808). Six flints.

Grave 320 (Fig. 17)
NNW–SSE; 1.98 m, 0.96 m, 0.40 m; 41.03 m OD. Gravelly brown sandy clay loam, 178/179.

Grave-goods:
SF.707   These items were found in close association.

        Knife of Böhner's type C, possibly with parallel grooves faintly visible on one side of the blade; length 152 mm. Mineralised remains of a horn handle and of a possible leather sheath are visible.

        Buckle; oval, 33 mm x 21 mm.

Other finds:
One sherd of early/middle Bronze Age pottery; one sherd of late Bronze Age pottery (SF.665, 674). Three flints.

Grave 322
N–S; 1.84 m, 0.58 m, 0.40 m; 41.18 m OD. Moderately gravelly dark brown silty clay loam, 243, over similar but less gravelly silty loam, 252.

Grave-goods:
No grave-goods.

Other finds:
One sherd of Saxon pottery (SF.708).Two sherds of late Bronze Age pottery (SF.705,708).

Grave 323 (Fig. 16)
NNE–SSW; 2.0 m, 0.94 m, 0.05 m; 41.54 m OD. Moderately gravelly dark brown silty clay loam, 242.

Grave-goods:
SF.733   Conical **shield-boss** bearing very slight traces of possible wood in mineralised form on the flange and interior when first examined; height 130 mm, diameter of flange 137 mm. Some holes on one side of the boss appear to have turned in edges and may be the result of damage in antiquity. There are also gaps in the flange where two of the five nails or rivets may have been torn out prior to burial and the tip of the boss is missing.

SF.760   **Hand-grip** with nails *in situ* near the slightly splayed terminals, in which one nail preserves slight traces of unidentifiable mineralised wood running across it; length 136 mm, maximum width 21 mm.

SF.734   Pair of **rivets**, each with one dome-shaped and one flat round head, one of which preserves very slight possible traces of mineralised wood running across the shank; length of shanks 17 mm, diameter of heads *c.*12 mm.

SF.735   Pair of **rivets**, each one with one dome-shaped and one flat round head; length of shanks *c.*15 mm, diameter of heads *c.*11 mm. One exhibits traces of unidentified mineralised wood running across the shank (and possibly also a piece of ? grass), whilst the other has a layer of fibrous brown corrosion.

SF.731   Small **rivet**, with one dome-shaped and one flat round head, preserving traces of unidentifiable mineralised wood running across the shank; length of shank *c.*9 mm, diameter of head *c.*9 mm.

SF.757   Small **rivet** with small dome-shaped head and traces of unidentifiable mineralised wood running across the shank; length of shank *c.*9 mm; diameter of head *c.*8 mm.

SF.759   Small rectangular **loop**, possibly a binding hoop which has broken or distorted through stress; external dimensions 25 mm x 12 mm.

SF.732   End of a **pin** or **nail**, with traces of unidentifiable mineralised wood running across it. Not illustrated.

34

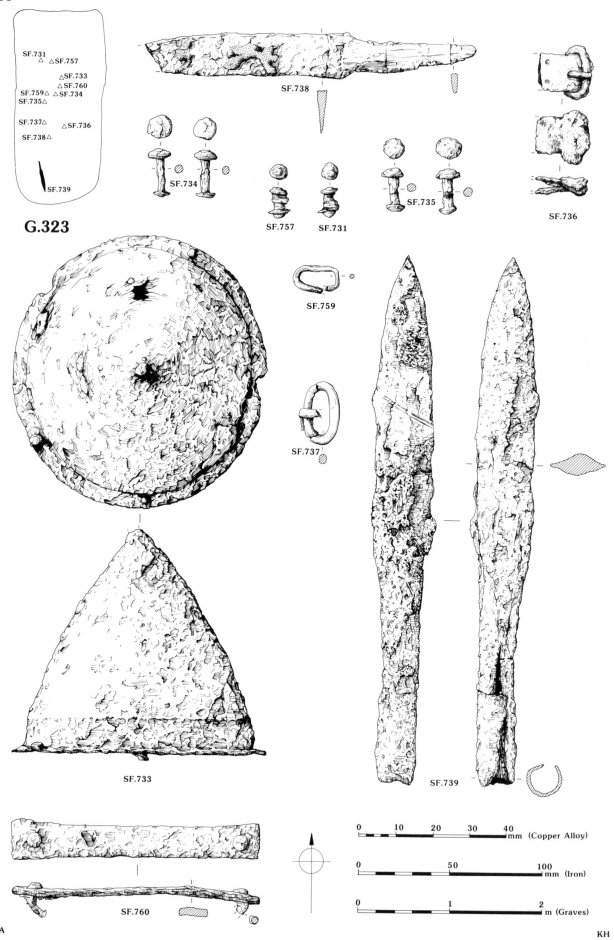

G.323

SF.731
SF.757
SF.733
SF.760
SF.759
SF.734
SF.735
SF.737
SF.736
SF.738
SF.739

SF.738

SF.734

SF.757   SF.731

SF.735

SF.736

SF.759

SF.737

SF.733

SF.739

SF.760

0   10   20   30   40
mm (Copper Alloy)

0   50   100
mm (Iron)

0   1   2
m (Graves)

WA

KH

Figure 16   Field Farm: Saxon Grave 323 plan and associated grave-goods

All of the above items were found in fairly close association and may all be parts of the shield or its attachments. The single rivets were each 9 mm long, the paired ones 14 mm; there is no indication of their original function, but it may perhaps be assumed that the shield thickness fell between these two measurements.

SF.736 Elongated **buckle** with square **plate** folded over one of the long sides and riveted to leather belt (traces of mineralised leather are present between the folds of the plate); oval, 28 mm x c.12 mm; plate width, 20 mm. Textile, possibly tabby-woven, is present in mineralised form on the underside of the buckle and plate.

SF.737 Very small **copper alloy buckle** with a fragment of **plate**, detached pieces of plate sandwiched with probable mineralised leather and a rivet; oval, 16 mm x 10 mm. Buckle only illustrated.

SF.738 **Knife** of Böhner's type C, preserving mineralised traces of a horn handle and possibly of a leather sheath (M.B.); length 180 mm.

SF.739 **Spearhead** of Swanton's type C2, with intermittent mineralised traces of textile, the weave unidentifiable, on both sides of the blade; length 278 mm. Mineralised organic material, possibly straw (J.W.), or an indication of binding (M.B.) survive on the blade. Traces of mineralised willow (*Salix* sp.) or poplar (*Populus* sp.) wood preserved in the socket.

Orientation:
The body was probably buried with its head to the south, the spearhead at the left shoulder, the knife and buckles at the waist and the shield on the legs.

Other finds:
Three sherds of late Bronze Age pottery; two sherds of Romano-British pottery (SF.740, otherwise unnumbered). Five flints.

Grave 325
WNW–ESE; c.2.0 m, 0.35 m, 0.60 m; 41.48 m OD. Moderately gravelly brown sandy clay loam, 187, within gravel in fairly sparse dark yellowish brown silty loam matrix around sides of grave, 324; ? possible coffin stain.

No grave-goods; no other finds.

Grave 349
NNE–SSW; +0.90 m, 0.65 m, 0.15 m; 41.40 m OD. Gravelly brown sandy clay loam, 348.

No grave-goods; no other finds.

Grave 350 (Fig. 17)
NNE–SSW; 1.95 m, 0.95 m, c.0.24 m; 41.94 m OD (north), 41.84 m OD (south). Gravelly dark brown–dark yellowish brown sandy loam, 251, over almost stone-free dark yellowish brown silty clay loam, 260.

Grave-goods:
SF.785 **Spearhead** of Swanton's type C2, perserving traces of unidentifiable mineralised wood in the socket; length 222 mm.

Orientation:
The body was probably positioned with its head at the south, the spearhead at the left shoulder.

Other finds:
Two sherds of early/middle Bronze Age pottery; fourteen sherds of late Bronze Age pottery (SF.729, 730, 748, 754–756, 787–795). Two flints.

Grave 358 (Fig. 15)
N–S; 1.92 m, 1.08 m, 0.19 m; 41.77 m OD (north), 41.84 m OD (south). Moderately gravelly dark brown sandy loam, 141, over similar but almost stone-free soil, 356.

Grave-goods:
SF.870 Small **knife** of Böhner's type C, preserving mineralised traces of a horn handle and possible leather sheath (M.B.); length 116 mm.

Other finds:
Fifteen sherds of probable Saxon pottery (SF.797, 840, 841, 860–863, 866, 867). One sherd of Romano-British pottery (SF.874). Sixteen flints.

Grave 362 (Fig. 17)
NNE–SSW; 1.75 m, c.1.05 m, c.0.18 m; 41.92 m OD (north), 41.74 m OD (south). Moderately gravelly brown–dark yellowish brown sandy silt loam, 85/361.

Bone:
Four unidentifiable burnt bone (shaft) fragments.

Grave-goods:
SF.880 **Knife** of Böhner's type A, with mineralised remains of a horn handle; length 142 mm. The knife was found broken and with its tip missing; both breaks may have occurred in antiquity.

Other finds:
Six sherds of late Bronze Age pottery; two sherds of Romano-British pottery (SF.888–890).

Grave 365 (Fig. 17)
WNW–ESE; +1.60 m, 0.70 m, 0.18 m; 41.79 m OD. Brown silty clay loam with a little gravel, 364. This grave cut an earlier feature.

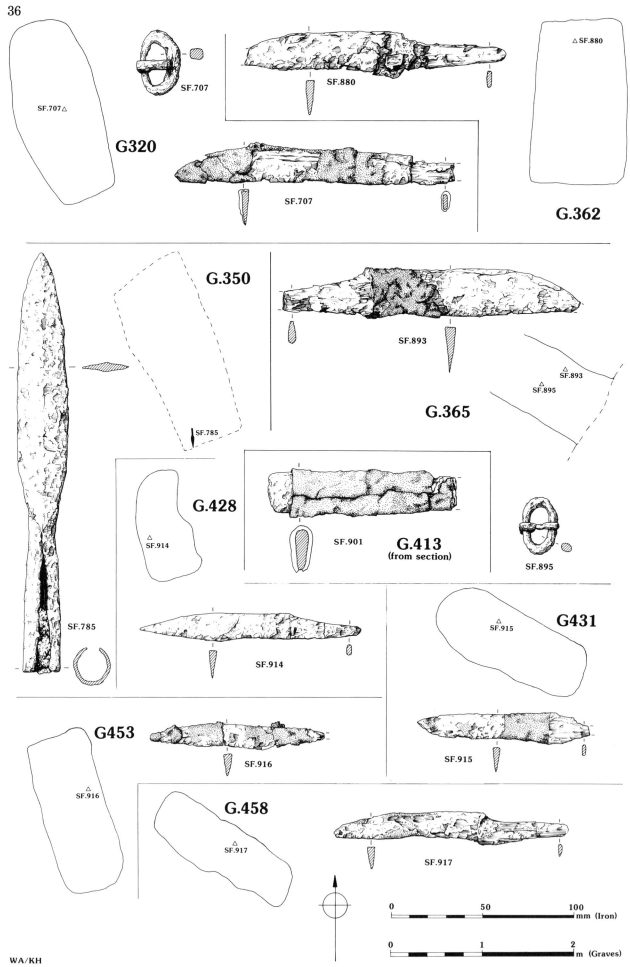

Figure 17   Field Farm: Saxon grave plans and associated grave-goods

Bone:
Fragments of both tibiae only; head at the west.

Grave-goods:
SF.893 **Knife** of Böhner's type C, with the mineralised remains of a horn handle and possible leather sheath; length 162 mm.

SF.895 **Buckle**; oval, 30 mm x 19 mm. No evidence of mineralised leather or textile.

Other finds:
Twenty-two sherds of early/middle Bronze Age pottery (SF.894).

Grave 413 (Fig. 17)
?NE–SW; only recorded in section; length not known, *c*.0.90 m, *c*.0.32 m. Not fully excavated. Moderately gravelly brown silty loam, 412.

Grave-goods:
SF.901 Broken **knife** blade of uncertain type with well-preserved mineralised leather sheath; the handle of the knife was missing when the object was buried.

Grave 428 (Fig. 17)
NW–SE; 1.14 m, 0.58 m, 0.25 m. Gravelly dark orange brown sandy loam, 441.

Grave-goods:
SF.914 Small **knife** of Böhner's type C, with the mineralised remains of a horn handle; length 122 mm.

Other finds:
Two sherds of late Bronze Age pottery (unnumbered).

Grave 429
W–E; 1.97 m, 0.60 m, 0.27 m. Gravelly reddish brown sandy loam, 442.

No grave-goods; no other finds.

Grave 430
WNW–ESE; 2.14 m, 1.08 m, 0.43 m. Light orange brown sandy loam with a little gravel, 443.

Grave-goods:
No grave-goods.

Other finds:
Three sherds of late Bronze Age pottery (unnumbered). Two flints.

Grave 431 (Fig. 17)
WNW–ESE; 1.74 m, 0.72 m, 0.30 m. Light orange brown sandy loam with a little gravel, 448.

Grave-goods:
SF.915 Small **knife** of Böhner's type A, with the mineralised remains of a horn handle and

possible leather sheath; length 94 mm. The knife was found broken and may have been broken in antiquity; the sheath was more clearly preserved on the tanged fragment.

Other finds:
One flint.

Grave 432
?NNE–SSW; length not known; 0.56 m, 0.20 m. Not fully excavated. Very gravelly light brown sandy loam, 444.

No grave-goods; no other finds.

Grave 453 (Fig. 17)
NNE–SSW; 1.70 m, 0.70 m, 0.25 m. Light brown sandy silt loam with a little gravel over a grey outer fill, 454; ? possible coffin stain.

Grave-goods:
SF.916 Small **knife** perhaps of Böhner's type D, with unidentifiable mineralised organic remains of a handle and sheath, possibly leather (M.B.); length 95 mm.

Grave 455
WSW–ENE; 1.50 m, 0.65 m, 0.23 m. Dark brown sandy loam with a little gravel, 456.

Grave-goods:
No grave-goods.

Other finds:
One sherd of early/middle Bronze Age pottery; two sherds of late Bronze Age pottery (unnumbered).

Grave 458 (Fig. 17)
WNW–ESE; 1.66 m, 0.60 m, 0.18 m. Very gravelly light brown–orange brown sandy loam, 459.

Grave-goods:
SF.917 **Knife** perhaps of Böhner's type C, although the blade has been frequently sharpened, with mineralised remains of a horn handle; length 127 mm. There is no evidence of a sheath, but possibly some indication of a belt near the handle.

Other finds:
Three sherds of Saxon pottery (unnumbered).

Grave 494
WNW–ESE; 1.50 m, 0.50 m, 0.09 m. Orange brown sandy loam with a little gravel, 495.

Grave-goods:
No grave-goods.

Other finds:
Seventeen sherds of late Bronze Age pottery (unnumbered).

6 The Finds

Flint, by P.A. Harding

Excavations 1985–87
A total of 568 pieces of worked flint and a small number of flint chips were recovered. All pieces were identified and details can be found in archive.

Most of the flint came from the large ring-ditch, 417; a small number of pieces were also recovered from the smaller ring-ditch, 418, and only a few from ring-ditch 625. The distribution of worked flint from the site is shown in Tables 2 and 3, by trench and by area.

Material was associated with four phases of activity on the site, although in some cases, the flint may be residual from earlier phases, and, in the middle and later Bronze Age phases, there was little or no technological change. In consequence only two groups of flint have been examined in detail:

A. Hearth 262 and the central area of ring-ditch 417, including pits 92 and 297;
B. The fills of ring-ditch 418 and feature 419 cut into the top of silted-up ring-ditch 417 in Trench C.

A. Hearth 262 and the interior of ring-ditch 417
This small group of artefacts is associated with activity which pre-dates or is contemporary with the construction of the ring-ditch. The material contains failed pieces, by-products and corrections from an industry producing blanks which include blades. Two refitting flakes show correction of a hinged flake/blade by using an opposed platform. Other pieces from the hearth include twisted blades, trimming flakes, broken pieces, cortical flakes and three rejuvenation tablets.

Platform abrasion was used to remove overhang to strengthen the platform before flakes/blades were removed. The consistent technique of production plus the refitting flakes suggests that the material is from a single industry.

The cores include a bladelet core made on a flake, from the hearth. One edge has been truncated to form a striking platform for the production of blade-lets with faceted butts. This method of producing bladelets can be paralleled in both Mesolithic contexts at Wawcott III, Berkshire (Froom 1976, fig. 27) and late Neolithic contexts at Wilsford Down, near Stonehenge, Wiltshire (Harding 1990).

B. Ring-ditch 418 and feature 419
The dating of the construction of ring-ditch 418 is uncertain but feature 419 is dated by the pottery to the late Bronze Age. The flint does not suggest the manufacture of a predetermined end product. The

group from ring-ditch 418 contains ore preparation flakes of which two pairs refit. As with the material from the earlier group, this suggests that the flint is predominantly part of a single industry. Platform abrasion is present on two elongated flakes from ring-ditch 418. These flakes have narrow butts and were removed by soft hammers.

Technology
A simple analysis of butt width and percussion angle was carried out on the flakes with unbroken proximal ends from each group to determine if any differences could be established. The results of this analysis, plus those of platform preparation and hammer mode, indicate variation in the two groups. The flakes from group A have butts which are narrower and have been removed using a higher angle of percussion than those from group B (Table 4). The number of linear and punctiform butts from group A, which correlate with the use of platform abrasion, do not allow the percussion angle of all flakes to be recorded. The differences would probably be more accentuated if this were possible. There is also evidence of an increased use of harder hammers, indicated by pronounced cones of percussion (Ohnuma and Bergman 1982) from the ditch recuts.

These variations undoubtedly result from different technologies rather than from different phases of production from the same technology. The apparent absence of platform abrasion and the rarity of soft hammers from the later Bronze Age industry suggests that the two flakes with these characteristics from ring-ditch 418 are residual. Comparable results have been recorded from large contrasting early Neolithic and late Bronze Age assemblages on Chalk (Harding 1991) and from smaller assemblages of Mesolithic and late Bronze Age date from Riseley Farm, Swallowfield, Berkshire (Harding forthcoming).

Tools
The scrapers from both groups, which account for most of the retouched tools, show no clear differences of type or of methods of production. All have regular semi-abrupt retouch forming a convex edge at the distal end. Scrapers from the hearth include one discoidal scraper and one tanged scraper. The large concentration (12) around the hearth suggests that they are not residual, although sites dating from the Mesolithic, as at Wawcott III (Froom 1976, fig. 73) through to the late Neolithic/Beaker periods (Smith 1965) have produced scrapers of similar types. Discoidal scrapers have associations with Grooved Ware pottery (Wainwright and Longworth 1971, 257). The provenance of the scrapers and the regularity of the retouch argues against them being of late Bronze Age date.

Additional tools which can be dated more precisely do not clarify the problem. A microlith was found in the interior of ring-ditch 417, a barbed and

Table 2 Field Farm: distribution of flints by trench

Trench	Cores	Core frags	Flakes	Broken flakes	Burnt flakes	Retouched flakes	Tools
A	–	1	40	20	1	2	2
C	5	5	27	19	4	2	2
D	1	2	93	49	4	1	7
F	–	–	6	5	–	–	–
G	–	–	18	11	1	–	–
H	1	–	15	13	–	1	1
J	7	2	48	37	9	–	8
K	1	2	27	14	–	2	1
L	–	–	6	4	–	–	–
N	2	3	15	7	–	–	–
P	–	–	2	–	1	–	–
R	1	–	4	4	–	–	–
Total	18	15	301	183	20	8	21

tanged arrowhead of Green's Sutton E type (1980) in the same area, in the subsoil of area D, and a pressure-flaked knife with invasive retouch along both edges in pit 92. The microlith is undoubtedly residual but may have been associated with debitage and scrapers. The barbed and tanged arrowhead and knife are not out of keeping with the radiocarbon date for the construction of the ring-ditch (3650±80 BP (HAR–9139)).

Conclusion

In conclusion, two techniques appear to be represented. The first apparently pre-dates the construction of the ring-ditch and is associated with the archaeomagnetic date from the hearth of 3900–3000 Cal BC (AJC–63). This industry is marked by some blade production from prepared cores using platform abrasion and soft hammers. It is unclear whether this is representative of the local Neolithic technology or represents residual Mesolithic material.

The tools do not appear to contradict the proposed date for the construction of the monument; however, it is unclear how many tools are residual. The microlith from the area suggests that there was some activity on the site in the Mesolithic period. This technology contrasts strongly with material found in the later Bronze Age feature 419 and ring-ditch 418.

Watching brief 1983/84 (W70)

The flint recovered from the watching brief consisted of 63 pieces from features, many occurring as single pieces. Most of it is undiagnostic and may have resulted from agriculture or natural collision. The only two sizeable groups of material, from contexts 50 (16 pieces) and 65 (36 pieces) are of broadly late Neolithic character.

Table 3 Field Farm: Distribution of flints by area

Context	Cores	core frags	Flakes	broken flakes	Burnt flakes	Retouched flakes	Tools
Hearth 262	4	1	49	27	4	1	9
Pit 297	3	1	4	5	2	–	–
Pit 92	–	–	2	2	–	–	1
Interior of ring-ditch 417	3	2	128	76	7	4	8
Fill of ring-ditch 417	5	6	30	23	1	2	3
Fill of ring-ditch 418	2	2	15	7	–	–	–
Fill of ring-ditch 604	1	–	4	4	–	–	–
Saxon graves	-	3	62	38	4	1	–
Other	–	–	8	2	2	–	–

Table 4 Field Farm: analysis of butt and percussion angle of struck flints

Butt width (%)

		0–1 mm	2–3 mm	4–5 mm	6–7 mm	8–9 mm	10 mm+	Total
A	Hearth 262 Pit 297 Interior 417	28	36	18	8	2	6	154
B	Features 418/419	9	25	35	16	7	7	86

Percussion angle (%)

		50–54	55–59	60–64	65–69	70–74	75–79	80–84	85+	N/R	Total
A	Hearth 262 Pit 297 Interior 417	2	5	6	13	12	14	15	4	27	154
B	Features 418/419	0	12	21	28	16	12	2	2	7	86

Pottery, by L.N. Mepham

The pottery assemblage from Field Farm consists of 3584 sherds (38,263 g), plus the lower half of a Collared Urn recovered intact. This total is derived from all the watching briefs and excavations over the period 1985–1987. Summaries of pottery found in the earlier watching brief (W70) and the later excavation (W267) on the site are in archive.

The assemblage was analysed using the standard WA pottery recording system (Morris 1992). A hand lens (x8 magnification) and binocular microscope (x20 magnification) were used to divide the pottery into four broad Fabric Groups on the basis of the dominant inclusion type: flint-gritted (Group F), grog-tempered (Group G), sandy (Group Q), and grass-tempered (Group V). These groups were then subdivided into 28 separate Fabric Types on the basis of the whole range of macroscopic inclusions.

The pottery was fully quantified, by number of sherds and by weight, both by context and by fabric type. Full records exist in archive. A unique Featured Sherd Number was assigned to each rim, base and decorated sherd (or conjoining groups of sherds), and this record was used to form the basis for the Vessel Type series. All percentages have been calculated by weight.

Some problems were encountered regarding possible residuality and/or intrusion of pottery on the site. In many cases, for example in the ditch fills of ring-ditch 417 and in the features excavated in between the ring-ditches, mixed assemblages of pottery were recovered, with early, middle and late Bronze Age material occurring in the same contexts. Many of the Saxon graves, cut through the earlier features, contained sherds of residual prehistoric pottery. Some limitations are thus placed on the dating of contexts and features on the site by pottery alone.

In addition, it proved difficult in some cases to distinguish between different fabric types, especially within the flint-gritted group, where several fabric types covered a wide range of variation. For example, sherds of Deverel-Rimbury type urns and late Bronze Age vessels are often almost indistinguishable on the basis of fabric type alone; similar decorative techniques also occur on both types. A similar problem was encountered with the sherds of Beaker and Collared Urn in the grog-tempered group.

Pottery totals by fabric type are listed in Table 5.

Late Neolithic (1.64% of the total assemblage)
One fabric type was identified:

F1. Sparse (5–10%), poorly-sorted subangular flint <3 mm, in a moderately fine, slightly micaceous fabric; unoxidised, some oxidisation on exterior surface.

The earliest pottery on the site comprises sherds which appear to belong to a single vessel: a decorated bowl of Mortlake style (Fig. 18, 1 (FSN1088)). The vessel is decorated on the inside and outside of the rim, and below the cavetto neck, with closely-spaced bird-bone impressions.

Early and middle Bronze Age (79.13%)
Six fabrics were identified:

G20. Moderate (10–20%) grog <1 mm in a soft, fine, soapy, iron-rich clay matrix; rare (<5 %) rounded quartz grains <0.25 mm; rare mica; generally oxidised.

G21. Moderate grog <2 mm, in a soft, iron-rich clay matrix; very rare subangular flint <0.5 mm; sparse quartz grains <0.5 mm; sparse iron oxide< 0.5 mm; oxidised with unoxidised core.

G22. Common (20–30%) grog <4 mm, in a soft, soapy, iron-rich clay matrix; rare iron oxide <0.5 mm; unoxidised, generally with oxidised exterior.

G23. Moderate grog <2 mm in a soft, iron-rich clay matrix; moderate iron oxides <1 mm; rare mica; oxidised.

G24. Common grog <3 mm, in a soft, heavily leached, iron-rich clay matrix; rare iron oxide <1 mm; unoxidised. Probably the result of heat/chemical action on another fabric, eg, G22.

F2. Common, poorly-sorted subangular flint <4 mm, in a soft, iron-rich clay matrix; rare rounded quartz grains <0.5 mm; irregularly fired, generally oxidised.

Two comb decorated and one incised body sherd (Fig. 18, 8 (FSN 828)) of Beaker vessels were recovered, all in the fine grog-tempered fabric G20. Sherds in the same fabric, but decorated with twisted cord impressions, were also recovered. While twisted cord decoration is found on Beaker vessels, the surviving rim sherds with this decoration from Field Farm are more suggestive of Collared Urn forms (see below).

Two partial and one complete miniature Collared Urns were found, all in situ. The complete miniature urn (Fig. 18, 3 (FSN 906); Plate 6), 130 mm in height, was found inside one of the full-size urns (Urn 1, not illustrated), of which the upper portion did not survive. This partial urn also contained the base of a small, irregular vessel (Fig. 18, 2 (FSN 907)). The miniature vessel would seem to be an almost exact replica, both in form and in decoration, although in a finer fabric, of the second full-size urn (Urn 919; Fig. 18, 4). The larger vessels occurred in the coarse grog-tempered fabric, G22, the smaller vessels in the finer fabric, G20.

The two full-size examples, and the complete miniature vessel, are all of bipartite form, and the decoration, where visible, occurs above the collar only, the inner, bevelled edge of the rim being decorated as well as the exterior. Urn 1 tapers to an unusually narrow base (c.160 mm in diameter), while Urn 919 has a deep collar with a 'peaked' collar base. All these traits are suggested as late in the chronological ordering of Collared Urns (Burgess 1986, 345, after Longworth 1984).

Miniature Collared Urns are known, though they are generally found as accessory vessels to, rather than within, larger vessels (Longworth 1984, 49, pl. 246). There are thirteen, possibly sixteen, examples known of full-sized Collared Urns containing smaller vessels, usually inverted as a cover for the cremation. Only one example is from southern England, from Cornwall (ibid., no. 181).

In addition, several decorated rim and body sherds were found, with similar twisted cord decoration, in the same grog-tempered fabrics, and these almost certainly derive from Collared Urns (Fig. 18, 9, 11, 12). One further group, apparently in situ in between ring-ditches 417 and 418, and associated with cremated bone, occurred in the

Table 5 Field Farm: pottery fabrics by period

NB. Fabric F4 appears as both EBA/MBA and LBA/EIA, see text.

	No. sherds	Weight (g)	% of phase	% of total
Late Neolithic				
F1	114	628	1.64	
Early / Middle Bronze Age				
G20	115	764	2.52	
G21	2	3	0.01	
G22	938	10,177	33.61	
G23	3	8	0.03	
G24	22	92	0.30	
F2	808	19,154	63.27	
F4	38	78	0.26	
Total	1926	30,276		79.13
Late Bronze Age / Early Iron Age				
F3	508	2942	44.12	
F4	187	728	10.92	
F5	70	540	8.10	
F6	272	1246	18.69	
F7	1	10	0.15	
F8	158	493	7.39	
Q40	8	21	0.32	
Q41	39	78	1.17	
Q42	16	36	0.54	
Q43	43	88	1.32	
Q44	29	47	0.70	
Q45	5	194	2.91	
Q46	3	18	0.27	
Q47	82	227	3.40	
Total	1421	6668		17.43
Romano-British				
Q100	19	42	47.19	
Q101	2	2	2.25	
Q102	14	21	23.59	
Q103	6	24	26.97	
Total	41	89		0.23
Saxon				
G400	14	31	6.30	
V420	57	461	93.70	
Total	71	492		1.28
Medieval				
Q410	5	35	100	0.09
Post-medieval				
	7	75	100	0.20
Overall total				
	3585	38,263		

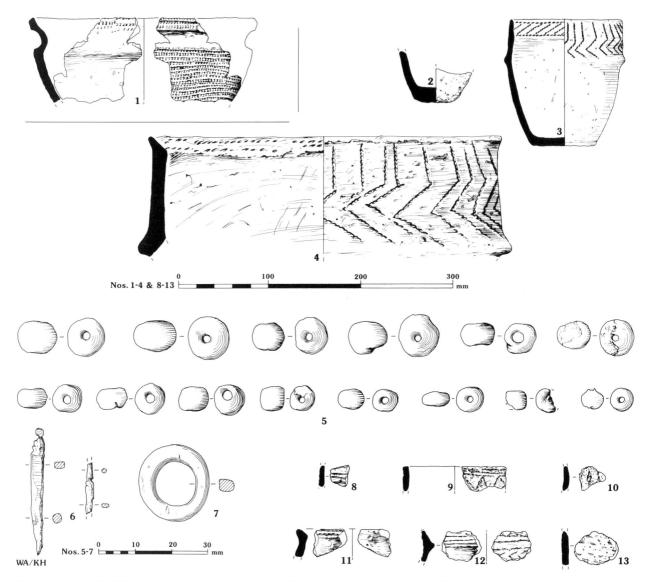

Figure 18   Field Farm: ring-ditch 417, Neolithic and early Bronze Age finds

heavily leached fabric, G24 (Urn 1107). The rim form, though no decoration survived, resembled other Collared Urn rims from the site (eg, Fig. 18, 4), with a characteristic inner bevelling on the rim.

A small group of body sherds is decorated with multiple fingernail impressions (Fig. 18, 10, 13). The dating of this group is particularly ambiguous. Fingernail-impressed decoration is commonly used on Beaker vessels (eg, Gibson 1982, fig. CAS 1), and is also found, though less commonly, on Deverel-Rimbury type material (Needham 1987, fig. 5.8, no. 10). The context in which these sherds occur would indicate a date early in the sequence of activity on the site, and would be consistent with an identification as Beaker. The flint-gritted fabric (F4) is not a typical Beaker fabric, although at least one example of a flint-gritted Beaker vessel with fingernail impressions is known, from Fifty Farm, Suffolk (Cleal 1985, fig. 50 FM:6, P42), and is, in fact, more reminiscent of the flint-gritted Deverel-Rimbury fabrics common in the area.

Sherds in the same fabric are also found on the site in late Bronze Age vessel forms.

Deverel-Rimbury type vessels are represented by a large group of sherds in the very coarse flint-gritted fabric, F2. At least seven urns are represented, none of which are complete (Fig. 19, 15–17, 19 (FSN 1081, 1083, 1986, 584)); two were recovered *in situ* and contained cremated bone. Decoration on these vessels consists of fingertip and fingernail impressions on rims and/or on applied or raised cordons or carinations around the body of the vessels. One vessel has a pair of holes below the rim, drilled through after firing, probably repair holes (Fig. 19, 16).

A further urn was recovered from subsequent excavation on the site (W267). This is a sub-biconical vessel in a moderately coarse flint-gritted fabric (F4), decorated with a double finger-impressed cordon and four sets of vertical double cordons above this, evenly spaced around the rim (Fig. 19, 14 (Urn 1140)). Surface damage at the base of each set of vertical cordons suggests the original presence of lugs or some other protruding decoration, since broken off.

Vessel forms which could be identified appear to belong to the cordoned Bucket Urn or sub-biconical cordoned vessel styles defined for the lower Thames Valley (Ellison 1975, types 5, 7). Both can be paralleled widely in the area (cf. Barrett 1973); the fabric and decoration is also typical, although the double-cordoned urn has no known parallel in the area. A group of urns of very similar form and decoration have been found at the nearby site at Shortheath Lane, Sulhamstead (Woodward, this volume).

Other pottery in the same fabrics may derive from further urns, or from Deverel-Rimbury domestic vessels; no distinction is possible within this assemblage. Two sherds, possibly from the same vessel, had evidence of deliberate perforations made prior to firing, just below the rim (Fig. 19, 18 (FSN 1104)). Drilled holes have been noted on several bucket urns from the lower Thames area, and may have been used to attach some form of cover to the vessels (Barrett 1973, 123).

Given the apparent overlap in use of Collared Urns and Deverel-Rimbury type urns on the site (*see below*), it is interesting to note the dichotomy in fabrics and decorative techniques between these two forms: Collared Urns are found only in grog-tempered fabrics, with twisted cord decoration, whereas Deverel-Rimbury Urns occur only in flint-gritted fabrics, with finger impressed and/or applied decoration.

Late Bronze Age / Early Iron Age (17.43%)
Fourteen fabrics were identified:

F3. Moderate, poorly-sorted, subangular flint <5 mm, in a soft, iron-rich clay matrix; sparse iron oxide <2 mm; sparse grog <2 mm; rare mica; generally unoxidised with oxidised exterior surface.

F4. Common, poorly-sorted, subangular flint <3 mm, in a moderately hard, iron-rich clay matrix; rare grog <1 mm; sparse rounded quartz grains <0.25 mm; rare mica; generally unoxidised with oxidised exterior surface.

F5. Moderate to common, poorly-sorted, subangular flint <5 mm, in a soft, coarse, iron-rich clay matrix; moderate iron oxide <2 mm; rare mica; oxidised.

F6. Common, moderately well-sorted, subangular flint <3 mm, in a soft, iron-rich clay matrix; rare iron oxide <0.5 mm; rare mica; generally unoxidised with oxidised exterior surface.

F7. Sparse, poorly-sorted, subangular flint <1 mm, in a soft, fine micaceous fabric; unoxidised.

F8. Sparse to moderate, moderately well-sorted, subangular flint <3 mm, in a moderately hard, iron-rich clay matrix; unoxidised, sometimes with oxidised surfaces.

Q40. Soft, sandy fabric with moderate red iron oxide <1 mm; sparse grog <1 mm; rare subangular flint <0.5 mm; iron-rich clay matrix; oxidised.

Q41. Sparse, rounded quartz grains <0.25 mm in an iron-rich clay matrix; sparse subangular flint <0.5 mm; moderate mica; unoxidised with oxidised exterior surface.

Q42. Sparse, poorly-sorted quartz grains <1 mm, in a soft, iron-rich clay matrix; moderate iron oxide <1 mm; sparse subangular flint <1 mm; unoxidised.

Q43. Moderate, well-sorted quartz grains <0.5 mm, in a soft, iron-rich clay matrix; rare subangular flint <1 mm; moderate iron oxide <2 mm; unoxidised with oxidised surfaces.

Q44. Common, poorly-sorted quartz grains <1 mm; sparse, poorly-sorted subangular flint <2 mm; hard fabric; unoxidised with oxidised surfaces.

Q45. Moderate quartz grains <0.5 mm, in a soft, iron-rich clay matrix; moderate iron oxide <2 mm; sparse, poorly-sorted, subangular flint <3 mm; unoxidised.

Q46. Common, well-sorted quartz grains <1 mm, hard fabric; unoxidised.

Q47. Rare quartz grains <0.25 mm, in a moderately hard, iron-rich clay matrix; common iron oxide <2 mm; rare subangular flint <1 mm; unoxidised.

The difficulties of distinguishing between Deverel-Rimbury type vessels and sherds of late Bronze Age domestic vessels in flint-gritted fabrics have already been noted. However, four rim forms have been identified, all of which are paralleled in late Bronze Age contexts elsewhere in the area. Three of the rim forms are jars, with everted, upright or hooked rims (Fig. 19, 22–26, 31 (FSN 1100, 1109, 1112, 644, 1099, 1092)), and all three equate to vessel forms found nearby at Aldermaston and Knight's Farm (Bradley *et al.* 1980, fig. 11: types 4, 5, 9/10). Apart from a single example in a coarse sandy fabric (Q45), all the jar rims occur in fabrics with sparse to moderate crushed flint temper (F3, F4, F6). Only one definite bowl form was recovered (Fig. 19, 30 (FSN 406)); this might be due partly to the small number of diagnostic forms present, or it might have some chronological significance. This point is discussed below.

Decoration similar to that found on the Deverel-Rimbury Urns also occurs on the late Bronze Age vessel forms. Fingertip and fingernail impressions occur on rims and shoulders (Fig. 19, 18, 27, 29 (FSN 1104, 614, 1097)), and one large jar has fingernail impressions on an applied neck cordon (Fig. 19, 31). There are two examples of plain raised cordons (Fig. 19, 20 (FSN 481)), and one raised boss (Fig. 19, 21 (FSN 317)). One rim sherd is decorated with incised parallel lines (Fig. 19, 30).

While it is possible that some of this material may derive from Deverel-Rimbury Urns, it is more likely that most, if not all of it can be regarded as late Bronze Age. All of the decorative techniques

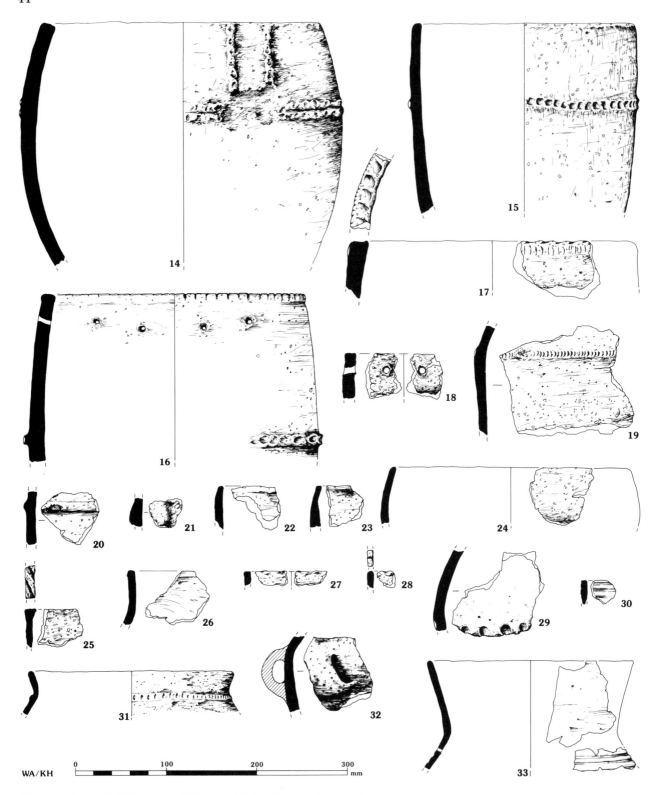

Figure 19   Field Farm: middle and later Bronze Age pottery

described above can be paralleled in the late Bronze Age assemblages from Aldermaston and the adjacent site at Knight's Farm (Bradley *et al.* 1980, fig. 34), and elements appear in the nearby sites at Pingewood (Bradley 1987, fig. 7). The group as a whole belongs to the post-Deverel-Rimbury tradition (Barrett 1980), and the presence of decorated vessels, albeit in small quantities, would indicate a late date in the sequence.

Applied neck cordons, in particular, are considered to be a late innovation at Knight's Farm, where they are directly associated with radiocarbon dates in the 8th and 7th centuries BC (Bradley *et al.* 1980, 270 and fig. 34).

The small quantity of sandy fabrics present in the late Bronze Age assemblage may also have some chronological significance. Sandy fabrics are known in late Bronze Age contexts, for instance, at Runnymede and Petters Sports Field, Egham, Surrey, where they are considered to be a fairly late phenomenon, beginning to supersede flint-tempered fabrics towards the end of the period (Longley 1980; O'Connell 1986). This is supported by the use of a sandy fabric for the decorated bowl rim (Fig. 19, 30), paralleled amongst the latest material at Knight's Farm (Bradley *et al.* fig. 35, no. 41), and also for the furrowed bowls described below.

A small group of sherds from one feature is also indicative of a very late Bronze Age or early Iron Age date. Three vessels of similar form are represented: sharply carinated bowls with upright or slightly everted rims and furrowed decoration on the shoulder, burnished inside and out (Fig. 19, 33 (FSN 1101)). All three vessels are in different fabrics, two finely flint-gritted (F7, F8), and one fine sandy fabric (Q47).

Furrowed bowls are found in early Iron Age contexts at several sites in Wessex, and the examples from Field Farm suggest parallels in the later All Cannings Cross–Meon Hill style of the 5th–3rd centuries BC (Cunliffe 1978, fig. A: 6, nos 1–4). Although furrowed bowls have not so far been found on late Bronze Age sites in the area, such a late date would not be entirely inconsistent with comparable late Bronze Age assemblages; for example, Petters Sports Field has yielded radiocarbon dates in the 6th century BC (O'Connell 1986).

Romano-British (0.23%)
Four fabrics were identified, none of known source:

Q100. Moderately fine fabric with oxidised margins; common, well-sorted quartz grains <0.5 mm; wheelthrown; unoxidised.
Q101. Very fine, soft, sandy fabric; iron-rich clay matrix; rare iron oxide <0.5 mm; wheelthrown; oxidised with unoxidised core.
Q102. Soft, moderately fine fabric; sparse quartz grains <0.25 mm; rare subangular flint <1 mm; sparse iron oxide <1 mm; handmade or wheelthrown; unoxidised with oxidised surfaces.
Q103. Soft, fine, micaceous sandy fabric; rare iron oxide <0.5 mm; handmade or wheelthrown; unoxidised with oxidised margins

Only a very small amount of Romano-British pottery was recovered (89 g), and this consisted of undiagnostic body sherds only.

Saxon (1.28%)
Two fabrics were identified:

G400. Common grog <2 mm, in a soft, leached fabric; sparse iron oxide <1 mm; sparse quartz grains <0.25 mm; handmade; unoxidised.
V420. Moderately fine, soft, slightly micaceous fabric; sparse quartz grains <0.25 mm; moderate to common linear voids; rare grog <1 mm; handmade; unoxidised with oxidised exterior surface.

One complete vessel and a few body sherds in the grass-tempered fabric V420 were found. The complete vessel (Fig. 14, Grave 256) is not of particularly diagnostic form; slack-shouldered jars with weakly everted rims are also found, for example, in late Bronze Age contexts in the area, as at Anslow's Cottages (compare Fig. 42, 3). However, the vessel was recovered from a Saxon grave fill, and other sherds of the same fabric occur almost exclusively in Saxon grave contexts on the site.

One other fabric may be of Saxon date. A small group of body sherds in a coarse, grog-tempered fabric (G400) was found together in a Saxon grave (Grave 358). However, grog-tempered fabrics are unknown on other Saxon sites in the area, and the dating of this fabric remains uncertain.

Medieval (0.09%)
One fabric was identified:

Q410. Common, poorly-sorted quartz grains <1 mm; rare subangular flint <2 mm; oxidised or unoxidised.

There were a few sherds of medieval material, all in the same sandy fabric, including the 'foot' from a tripod pitcher.

Distribution

Late Neolithic
The sherds of the Mortlake Ware vessel (Fig. 18, 1) were recovered from the centre of ring-ditch 417. With the exception of a few sherds, all came from a small area of burnt soil, context 60, bounded by a series of possible stake-holes (Fig. 7). A few sherds, almost certainly from the same vessel, occur elsewhere on the site in residual contexts, for instance in upper fills of the ring-ditch, together with pottery of later date. It would appear that the deposition of this bowl pre-dates the construction of the ring-ditch itself, and may be associated with hearth 262 which produced an archaeomagnetic date of 3900–3000 Cal BC (AJC–63).

Early and middle Bronze Age
Sherds in grog-tempered fabrics, with twisted cord decoration, which almost certainly derive from Collared Urns (Fig. 18, 11, 12), were recovered from the central area of ring-ditch 417, in a scatter adjacent to the Mortlake Ware bowl fragments. All appear to be of similar style to the Collared Urns containing cremations, despite the fact that the latter were apparently deposited at a much later date (*see below*). The scatter also contained sherds

of moderately fine flint-tempered fabrics with fingernail-impressed decoration (Fig. 18, 13), the dating of which is uncertain. The distribution of the grog- and flint-tempered fabrics and the Mortlake Ware is mutually exclusive within this central area (Fig. 7), and it is likely that the later material is associated with the construction of the ring-ditch and pit 297 at its centre.

Pit 297 contained five sherds of finger-impressed, flint-gritted ware (Fig. 18, 10), sixteen sherds of probable Collared Urn (Fig. 18, 9), and a possible Beaker sherd (Fig. 18, 8), as well as one sherd of Mortlake Ware. A radiocarbon date of 3650±80 BP (HAR–9139) was obtained from charcoal from the fill of the pit. The associations of the features in the central area are ambiguous, but it appears that pit 297 cuts through the charcoal-rich context containing the Mortlake Ware bowl.

The large ring-ditch 417 is also the focus for the distribution of Collared Urns containing cremations. Within the interior of the ring-ditch, two cremations were found, 363, 524, both contained in incomplete vessels, and both apparently in situ. One of these, Urn 1, was found in an upright position, and only the lower, undecorated half survived. Subsequent excavation under controlled conditions revealed a complete miniature vessel within the larger urn (Fig. 18, 3), plus the base of another small vessel (Fig. 18, 2). A radiocarbon date of 2890±60 BP (HAR–9143) was obtained from charcoal from the fill of the full-size urn. The miniature vessel would seem to be an almost exact replica, both in form and in decoration, though in a finer fabric, of the second partially complete, full-size urn, Urn 919 (Fig. 18, 4). The latter vessel was found in an inverted position, although the base had been removed by later activity, and contained a number of amber and faience beads, two bronze awls and a shale ring, as well as cremated bone (see below).

A third cremation, 369, had been subsequently disturbed by a Saxon grave (365), the fill of which contained sherds of Collared Urn. All three cremations were located at approximately the same distance (7.5–9.5 m) from the inner edge of the ring-ditch, probably on the edge of the suggested mound. A further cremation on the same line, 505, was contained in a pot too decayed for identification. Outside ring-ditch 417, sherds of another possible Collared Urn, 1107, were found associated with cremation 508.

The urns of Deverel-Rimbury type were concentrated in the small ring-ditch 604. The remains of two urns, 1081, 1082 (Fig. 19, 15), both apparently in situ, were recovered from the interior of small ring-ditch 604, one in an inverted position. Both contained cremated bone. Charcoal from the fill of one produced a radiocarbon date of 3690±100 BP (HAR–9140). Fragments of at least four further urns were found in the fill of the ring-ditch itself (Fig. 19, 16, 17). None of the urns was complete, and sherds of all four vessels occurred mixed together in what appeared to be a deliberate dump, broken before deposition. This deposit occurred immediately above the primary fill of the ditch. There was no associated cremated bone. All the vessels from ring-ditch 604 are of similar form and decoration, and all are in the same coarse, flint-tempered fabric (F2).

One other urned cremation was recovered in situ, from the interior of ring-ditch 417, again on the same approximate line as the Collared Urns described above. Only undecorated body sherds survived of this vessel, though the fabric is similar to that of the urns from ring-ditch 604.

Urn 1140 was recovered in situ from the centre of small ring-ditch 032 (W267) during subsequent excavation in 1988. This double-cordoned, sub-biconical urn is in a different fabric to the other urns on the site (F4), and with decoration not paralleled amongst the other vessels (Fig. 19, 14).

Further sherds of Deverel-Rimbury type vessels, all in the same coarse flint-tempered fabric (F2), occurred also in the upper ditch fills of ring-ditches 417 and 418, in both cases mixed with late Bronze Age flint-tempered material; no pottery was recovered from the primary fills of either ring-ditch.

Late Bronze Age/early Iron Age

A concentration of late Bronze Age flint-tempered pottery (276 sherds; 2203 g), with some sherds of Deverel-Rimbury fabrics, the latter probably residual in this context, was found in a feature cut into the top of the silted-up ring-ditch in Trench C, associated with burnt material.

Ten features excavated in the areas between the three ring-ditches produced late Bronze Age pottery, in several cases mixed with Deverel-Rimbury fabrics; again, the latter occurs in small quantities and is probably residual in these contexts. Diagnostic forms include three indeterminate jar/bowl rims, and six jar rims, one with an applied neck cordon with fingernail-impressed decoration from pit 449 (Fig. 19, 31), which also produced a handle in the same fabric (Fig. 19, 32 (FSN 1093)).

One feature also contained later material: sherds of three furrowed bowls were recovered from pit 482 (Fig. 19, 33). The form is confined to this feature on the site, and may therefore represent a group which extends the period of occupation in the Field Farm/Knight's Farm complex. This feature also contained part of a vessel with finge- impressed shoulder (Fig. 19, 29), and a plain jar rim (Fig. 19, 26), both in the same fabric as one of the furrowed bowls.

Saxon

Thirty-four of the Saxon graves produced pottery (1391 g). More than half of this total consists of sherds in prehistoric fabrics (883 g), which can be regarded as residual in these contexts. Several of the graves can be seen to cut earlier features, and at least one grave (365) disturbed a Collared Urn containing a cremation.

Only one probable Saxon vessel was recovered in situ: a small, slack-shouldered jar from Grave 256 (Fig. 14). Other sherds of the same grass-tempered fabric, not from the same vessel, occur in four other graves (295, 322, 358, 458), though not more than three sherds in any one grave. Fourteen sherds of another possible Saxon fabric were also found in Grave 358.

Discussion

Despite the absence of a clearly stratified sequence of pottery on the site, some observations can be made on the basis of spatial distribution of the pottery of various types, and on the archaeo-magnetic and radiocarbon dates obtained.

The presence of the Mortlake Ware bowl at the centre of ring-ditch 417 could be used to date the construction of the ring-ditch itself. However, this interpretation leads to some problems. The Mortlake Ware is adjacent to, and apparently from the same context as, a scatter of pottery which includes Collared Urn and possible Beaker material, and all would have been sealed by the postulated central mound of the ring-ditch. While Mortlake Ware may have overlapped with the use of Beakers, it is unlikely to have overlapped with Collared Urns. The early date for hearth 262 of 3900–3000 Cal BC (AJC–63) indicates that this too is earlier than the ring-ditch.

If the Mortlake Ware and the hearth are associated, then this date is perhaps earlier than might be expected for this type of pottery, which is generally considered to be a late Neolithic development (Smith 1974, 112); however, an early date (1610±90 bc, 3560 BP; HAR–2498) was obtained for a Mortlake Ware bowl from Eden Walk, Kingston, Surrey (Bird and Bird 1987, 89).

It is more likely, therefore, that the deposition of the other types of pot in this layer is associated with the construction of the ring-ditch, and therefore pit 297, with its radiocarbon date of 3650±80 BP (HAR–9139). This is an acceptable date for the Collared Urn sherds, falling towards the beginning of the range suggested by Longworth (1984, 79); however, taken together with the other date for Collared Urn on the site (2890±60 BP, HAR–9143), this indicates a very long timespan for the use of this pottery style at Field Farm.

The position of the urned cremations around the outside edge of the interior of ring-ditch 417 would indicate their deposition at a time when the ditch and/or any existing mound were still at least visible. The fact that three Collared Urns and one Deverel-Rimbury Urn were found on the same line might suggest that the two types of pottery had at least some period of overlap. Using Barrett's chronology (1976), this is quite possible, and is supported by the late radiocarbon date for one of the Collared Urns. However, this date is particularly late for Collared Urns, and would in fact place the vessel after the end of the date range suggested for Deverel-Rimbury pottery in the area (Barrett 1980, 306), and well after the Deverel-Rimbury Urn from ring-ditch 604, which produced a radiocarbon date of 3690±100 BP (HAR–9140). Moreover, this would imply a period of use for Collared Urns on the site of up to 800 years, and suggesting that their use outlived the Deverel-Rimbury Urns. Two late dates

for Collared Urns are known, both from the north of England (Longworth 1984, 140), but their reliability has been questioned; Burgess prefers a date range extending no later than the 13th century BC (1986, 342).

The early date obtained from one of the Deverel-Rimbury vessels 3690±100 BP (HAR–9140) falls at the beginning of the range of radiocarbon dates quoted by Barrett (1976, fig. 17.1), and is comparable with the date from Worgret Barrow, Dorset (1740±90 Cal BC, NPL–199). One of the Deverel-Rimbury Urns from Shortheath Lane, Sulhamstead (Woodward, this volume), produced a slightly later radiocarbon date of 3340±60 BP (HAR–9141). At Knight's Farm the earliest date associated with Deverel-Rimbury material is 1245±95 bc (3195 BP) (Bradley et al. 1980, 268), although a date of 1290±135 bc (3240 BP) (BM–1592) from Aldermaston was associated with pottery of post-Deverel-Rimbury type (ibid., 248). However, although the date from Field Farm is quite acceptable for Deverel-Rimbury, it raises problems when taken together with the very late date for the Collared Urn.

Deverel-Rimbury material was recovered in several cases from contexts also containing material identified as late Bronze Age, belonging to the post-Deverel-Rimbury tradition as defined by Barrett (1980), for example in features excavated in between the three ring-ditches. The former type may be residual in these contexts, and this is almost certainly the case for the Deverel-Rimbury material from the feature cutting into the upper fill of ring-ditch 417 in Trench C, although at the site of Pingewood, just over 1 km distant, Deverel-Rimbury material was found in the same features and fabrics as plain jars similar to those found at Field Farm (Bradley 1987, 27). In this case, the two appear to be contemporary. The two types are not directly associated at Knight's Farm.

Given the proximity of Field Farm to the excavated site at Knight's Farm, close affinities between the two late Bronze Age assemblages are not surprising; the features excavated at Field Farm are probably an extension of the Knight's Farm complex. However, there are some differences in the two assemblages, which might be explained by a chronological shifting of activities across the site, or possibly a functional differentiation of the two areas.

The quantity of decorated sherds from Field Farm is not as great as that at Knight's Farm, but is comparable to that at Aldermaston (less than 10%); however, the range of decorative techniques is wider than that at either Aldermaston or Pingewood. The examples of incised decoration and the single applied neck cordon may be significant here: both techniques are considered to be later innovations at Knight's Farm (Bradley et al. 1980, 270). The chronological significance of the sandy fabrics has already been discussed. On the other hand, the relative absence of bowl forms is comparable to the situation at Pingewood, where this characteristic is considered to support an early date for the site (Bradley 1987, 28), though at Field Farm this may merely be due to the small size of the assemblage.

The only element in the assemblage which cannot be paralleled at Knight's Farm is the furrowed bowl, three examples of which occur associated with two jars which would otherwise be regarded as late Bronze Age. While the furrowed bowl is regarded as early Iron Age on sites elsewhere in southern England, for instance at All Cannings Cross, Dorset (Cunliffe 1978, 33), the earliest dates for this form would overlap with the latest dates obtained from Knight's Farm (Bradley et al. 1980, 270). The form is confined to one feature, but may represent some survival of activity at Field Farm after the apparent abandonment of Knight's Farm. There is no comparable material from the other late Bronze Age sites in the immediate vicinity.

Objects within Urn 919, by L.N. Mepham

The upper portion of a Collared Urn (Urn 919, feature 524; Fig. 18, 4) was recovered almost intact, and was subsequently excavated under controlled conditions. Apart from cremated human bone, a number of objects were found within the urn. Full details can be found in archive.

Amber beads
Fifteen amber beads were recovered from the urn fill (Fig. 18, 5). Six beads were found together in a linear arrangement, which suggests that they may originally have formed part of a necklace, and this group was also associated with a shale ring (*see below*). The remaining nine beads were scattered throughout the urn fill.

Eight beads are of flattened spherical shape, three are barrel-shaped, and the remaining four are too abraded for their original shape to be identified. The beads range in diameter from 6.5–12.0 mm, and in length from 3.0–8.7 mm. All are pierced with a single central perforation, which range in diameter from 1.7–3.4 mm. Rilling marks were observed within the perforation of one bead.

Two of the beads are badly cracked. This is more likely to be the result of post-depositional decay rather than burning with the body. None of the other objects show any signs of burning, and the linear grouping of amber beads, mentioned above, would have been unlikely to survive burning on the funeral pyre.

Faience beads
One complete faience bead, plus three fragments of a second bead, were found (not illustrated). They probably originally formed part of the same necklace as the amber beads.

The complete bead is of biconical or spherical shape, with flashings at each end of the perforation. The fragmentary bead is probably of spherical or elongated-spherical shape. Both beads are c.5–6mm in diameter, and are mid-turquoise in colour.

Plate 6   *Field Farm: miniature Collared Urn lying* in situ *within full-sized Collared Urn 1*

Shale object
Associated with the group of amber beads was an annular shale ring, 19 mm in diameter, and 3 mm thick, with a sub-rectangular cross-section (Fig. 18, 7). Although the ring was associated with the beads, which are assumed to have formed part of a necklace, the internal diameter (12 mm) is too great for the ring to have acted as a spacer bead in such a necklace.

Copper alloy objects
Fragments of one almost complete copper alloy awl were recovered, together with fragments which comprised part of a tapering rod, possibly part of a second awl (Fig. 18, 6). The larger piece is 34 mm in length, corroded and incomplete at both ends, although it is unlikely that the original length would have been more than c.35 mm. It has a flattened rectangular tang with a circular-sectioned point. The smaller piece is 14 mm long, tapering, and is of circular section, sub-rectangular at the wide end.

Discussion
Accompanying grave-goods, apart from accessory vessels, are not common either within, or associated with, Collared Urns. Copper alloy objects are known from only 75 urns, and trinkets of exotic materials such as amber and shale in only 27 (Longworth 1984, 48). Neither copper alloy objects nor beads of exotic materials have been found exclusively with Collared Urns; amber beads, for example, are known from all periods from the Neolithic to the late Iron Age, though they are most common in the early and middle Bronze Age. They have often been found associated with shale beads, as at Wilsford G16, Wiltshire (Annable and Simpson 1964, 52; 107, nos

Table 6 Field Farm: objects within Urn 919

SF. No.	Description	Shape	Diameter	Length	Perforation
Amber beads (Fig. 18, 5; SF.969 not illustrated)					
929	Complete, 2 frags	Flattened spherical	12 mm	5 mm	–
931	Complete	Flattened spherical	10.5 mm	8.7 mm	2.8 mm
937	Complete	Flattened spherical	9.5 mm	8 mm	2.5 mm
941	Incomplete, 2 frags	Flattened spherical	8 mm	3.3 mm	*c.* 3 mm
956	Complete but deeply cracked	Flattened spherical	8.8 mm	5.3 mm	3.2 mm
957	Complete but deeply cracked	Barrel-shaped	8 mm	5.5 mm	3 mm
958	Complete	Spherical, slightly flattened ends; rilling marks on perforation	9.7 mm	6.7 mm	2 mm
959	Complete, badly decayed	Not identifiable	9 mm	6 mm	3 mm
960	Complete	Not identifiable	9.5 mm	5–6 mm	3–4 mm
961	Complete	Flattened spherical	9.2–9.5 mm	7.5 mm	3 mm
963	Complete	Flattened spherical	7 mm	3 mm	2 mm
969	Incomplete, 3 frags	Not identifiable	–	*c.* 4–5 mm	–
972	Complete	Not identifiable	7 mm	5–6.5 mm	2–4 mm
973	Complete	Barrel-shaped	7 mm	6–6.5 mm	2 mm
974	Incomplete, *c.* 50% surviving, broken	Barrel-shaped	6.5 mm	5 mm	1.7 mm
Faience beads (not illustrated)					
1078	Complete, mid-turquoise	Biconical/spherical; flashings at each end of perforation	6 mm	4.5 mm	2 mm
The perforation has a marked angle, possibly from winding					
1079	Incomplete, 3 frags, mid-turquoise	Probably spherical or elongated-spherical	5 mm	5 mm	2 mm
Shale object (Fig. 18, 7)					
962	Complete	Annular ring			
Perforation slightly off-centre to circumference; smoothed (?wear) facets on 2 opposing edges. External diam. 19 mm; internal diam. 12 mm; thickness 3 mm					
Copper alloy objects (Fig. 18, 6)					
971	Almost complete awl; 4 pieces, corroded and broken at each end; tang of rectangular section, changing to circular at about mid-point and tapering to a point			34 mm, originally max. 35 mm	
968/ 1012	2 frags reconstructed to form part of tapering rod; circular section at one end, rectangular at other. Possibly part of an awl			14 mm	

308–312). A necklace from a primary cremation at Upton Lovell G1, Wiltshire, consisted of eleven shale, eleven amber and ten segmented faience beads (*ibid*. 54; 108, nos 340–342). This included two shale rings of the type found at Field Farm.

There is no known instance of a Collared Urn containing all four of the types of object found in the single urn at Field Farm, although beads of faience, amber and shale were found with a Collared Urn at Collingbourne Kingston, Wiltshire (*ibid*. 1964, 64; 119, nos 515–518). In southern England, a copper alloy awl of similar type to the examples from Field Farm is known only from Winterbourne Stoke, Wiltshire (Longworth 1984, cat. no. 1733); amber beads of similar type from Hengistbury Head, Dorset (*ibid*., cat. no. 375), Lewes, Sussex (*ibid*., cat.

no. 562), Collingbourne Kingston *ibid.*, cat. no. 1673), and Winterslow 21, Wiltshire (*ibid.*, cat. no. 1739); and faience beads from Chalton, Hampshire (*ibid.*, cat. no. 620). Shale beads are known from Collared Urns, but no shale rings; similar objects in jet have been found, for example at Chalton (*ibid.*).

Saxon Grave-Goods, by H. Rees and C.A. Butterworth

Weapons
Eight of the 50 burials investigated at Field Farm contained weapons, 16% of the total (Fig. 20). The weapon burials were all very simply equipped; all eight contained spears, two also had shield-bosses (4%); none contained swords. Because of the absence of bone it is not possible to say what percentage of the male population these burials represent nor whether they were all fully adult males, but it may be that shield-bosses were only buried with those who were fully adult (Pader 1980, 149). All of the weapon burials were within the southern interior of ring-ditch 417.

Shields
The non-organic constituents of two shields were recovered from Graves 220 and 323 (Fig. 20). The bosses are of late 6th/7th century type (Evison 1963) with very narrow flanges, that from Grave 220 being a tall curved cone, more markedly carinated (142 mm tall, 135 mm maximum diameter) than the other, a tall straight cone (130 mm tall, 137 mm maximum diameter). The apex of the larger bears a small spike with a round flat head, a feature that was probably originally present on the other boss.

The bosses were fixed to the shield-boards by means of small dome-headed rivets, the dimensions of which imply a board thickness of 5–6 mm. In the case of the boss from Grave 220 five rivets are extant, but lacunae on the flange suggest the presence of two more which have been lost or removed in antiquity. The flange of the boss from Grave 323 bears similar lacunae together with three extant rivets, and exhibits damage on one side, perhaps in an attempt to remove the boss by force before burial, although the positions of the rivets may deny this.

The bosses were both accompanied by hand-grips, one of which (Grave 323) was independently fixed to the shield-board by means of nails, whilst the other was probably an integral part of the shield-board. The traces of mineralised textile on both surfaces of the latter may be remnants of a loose binding or cloth wrapping. Both bosses were associated with paired and single dome-headed rivets, probably for fixing a covering (or arm-straps), for which, in the case of the shield from Grave 220, there is slight evidence that leather was used. Mineralised wood is present on parts of both shields but is only identifiable, as ash, on the the shield from Grave 220.

As far as can be ascertained in the absence of skeletal material, the shield from Grave 323 was positioned on the chest and that from 220 at or near the feet.

Spears
All eight spearheads are of the leaf-shaped variety, of which seven are proportionally longer in the blade than the socket; blade and socket are of equal length in the eighth (from Grave 146). All have been classified according to Swanton's type series (Swanton, 1974) of which types C1, C2 and C3 seem to be represented.

Details of the spears are given in Table 7. The presence of these types at Field Farm is unexceptional in view of their general distribution and date range. All three types were distributed throughout southern England during the 6th–7th centuries, with type C1 being confined more closely to the central southern area; type C2 is the most commonly found spearhead throughout central and southern England (*ibid.*, 51).

It has been assumed in the absence of skeletal material that the position of the spearhead indicates the orientation of the body as such weapons are usually found placed near the head in Anglo-Saxon graves with extant skeletons (eg. Cook and Dacre 1985, 91; Hirst 1985, 91; Härke 1988, fig. 10). Two were probably placed at the right hand side of the body (Graves 213 and 220), five, probably six, at the left hand side (Graves 146, 148, 202, 238, 323 and 350). This bias to the left hand side is unusual in Wessex, but is paralleled at Portway, Andover, Hampshire (Cook and Dacre 1985, 91) and Market Lavington, Wiltshire (Montague in prep.).

Four were found very close to the edges of graves. Two of the spears may have been deliberately broken or damaged before burial; one (in Grave 146) was carefully wrapped and laid near the centre of the grave, probably pointing toward its foot; the blade of the other (Grave 148) was almost severed from its socket. Although it is uncertain whether the damage to this latter spearhead took place before burial, the slighting of weapons placed with the dead has been noted elsewhere (Evison 1987, 28).

Mineralised wood is present in the sockets of all eight spearheads, although in two cases there is not enough for it to be identified. Of the remaining six hafts, two were ash, two either willow or poplar, one hazel and one probably holly. Although ash has been generally regarded as the wood most commonly used for spear hafts, hazel (or alder) and willow or poplar have been among other woods identified elsewhere (Evison 1988, 7; Hurst 1985, 91).

A textile wrapping which had been secured with twine is extremely well-preserved in mineralised form on the C1 type spearhead from Grave 146. Less well-preserved evidence of a similar covering is observed on the type C2 spearhead from Grave 323.

Knives
As in many other Anglo-Saxon cemeteries, the knife is the most common item of grave furniture at Field Farm. Twenty-six whole or nearly whole knives, together with four fragmentary examples and one which was buried without its handle, were

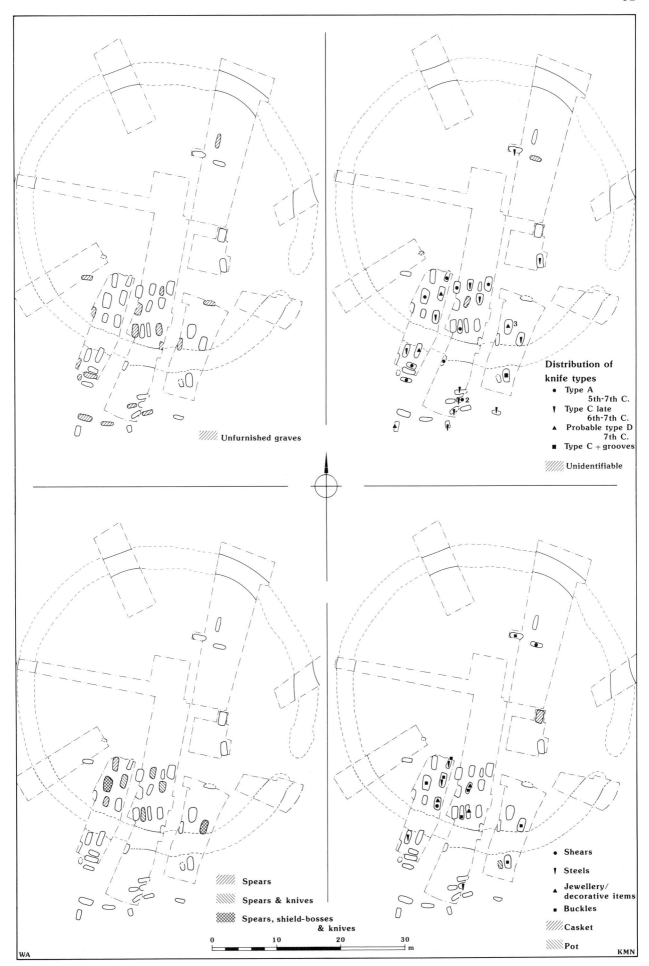

Distribution of
knife types
- Type A
   5th-7th C.
- Type C late
   6th-7th C.
- Probable type D
   7th C.
- Type C + grooves

Unidentifiable

Unfurnished graves

Spears

Spears & knives

Spears, shield-bosses
& knives

Shears

Steels

Jewellery/
decorative items

Buckles

Casket

Pot

0   10   20   30
                    m

WA   KMN

Figure 20   Field Farm: Saxon cemetery, distribution of objects in graves

Table 7 Field Farm: spear types, positions in graves and associated grave-goods

Grave No.	Swanton type C1	C2	C3	Overall length	Haft wood	Position in grave and other comments	Other grave-goods
146	X			177 mm	Ash	Left side, centre, pointing to feet? Cloth wrapped	Knife, buckle, rod
148		X		c. 303 mm (bent	Willow/ poplar	Left side, by head. Spearhead bent	Knife
202		X		260 mm	?Holly	Left side, by head	
213			X	441 mm	Hazel	Right side, by head	Knife, curved strip, 3 hinge pieces
220		X		267 mm	Ash	Right side, by head	Shield-boss, hand-grip and rivets, knife, buckle
238		X		225 mm	Unident.	Left side, by head. ?Cloth wrapped	Knife and steel, buckle, nail
323		X		278 mm	Willow/ poplar	Left side, by head	Shield-boss, hand-grip, rivets, rectangular loop and pin or nail, 2 buckles, knife
350		X		222 mm	Unident.	Left side, by head	

recovered from 28 graves (Grave 126 contained two knives and Grave 281 held three) (Fig. 20, Table 8). Where this could be determined, the knives were constructed by driving the handle on to the pointed tang, usually in the direction of the grain, but in one case (in Grave 206) apparently at an oblique angle to it; this example may represent the use of a horn tip to the handle, however. In all but one of the 26 cases where there is sufficient mineral replacement to allow the identification of these handles, they were of horn (Table 8). One knife (in Grave 149) had a bone or antler handle with mineralised alder wood packed between the tang and the handle, presumably in order to make the handle firm.

Of the two graves, 126 and 281, which contained more than one knife, 126 also held a steel. Three other knives were found in direct association with these tools (in Graves 204, 238 and 241), two with pairs of shears (in Graves 61 and 194) and one with a possible girdle group (in Grave 149). One knife was recovered adhering to a buckle (in Grave 146) (see below). Most of the knives were centrally placed in the graves, although some were near one or other of the long sides. In some of the graves for which the orientation of the body could be assessed, knives appear to have been placed nearer the chest or shoulder than the waist.

All knives of identifiable form have curving backs, but the original shapes of the cutting edges are often difficult to ascertain because of frequent sharpening in antiquity and deterioration after burial. Three of Böhner's (1958) classes seem to be represented, types A, C and D.

One example of type C (Grave 320) exhibits faint traces of grooves near the back edge on both sides,

a feature which has been identified as late elsewhere (Cook and Dacre 1985, 93; Montague in prep.). The typology of the knives thus suggests that the cemetery most probably dates to the late 6th or 7th centuries, which is in keeping with the other datable artefacts.

The distribution of knife types does not appear to follow any significant pattern in terms of the chronology of individual graves (Fig. 20), but some differentiation in terms of the sex of their occupants may be indicated. Four of the six graves with the longest knives have been identified as male burials since they also contained spearheads (Graves 146, 148, 320 and 323); one other has been more tentatively so identified (Grave 126) on the basis that it contained a steel and two knives, the former generally thought to be associated with male burials (Hirst 1985, 89) (Table 8). From this it may perhaps be suggested that the other grave with a similarly long knife (Grave 365) was also that of a man and that indeed all of the graves with longer knives were those of men, though Graves 213 and 238 contained only short–medium length knives associated with spears. The longest knife in the cemetery (in Grave 126) was shorter than the true scramasax and it has been suggested that such knives are only associated with 7th century male burials (Davies 1985, 138). The only measurable knife from a probable female grave was a short example from Grave 194.

Evidence of mineralised sheaths is present on 21 knives. These were identified as leather in eighteen cases, but the other three were too degraded for identification (Table 8). In one case (Grave 146) wool was thought to be present between the blade and

Table 8 Field Farm: knife types, positions in graves and associated grave-goods

Grave No.	Böhner type A	C	D	? type	Length	Handle	Sheath	Additional comments	Associated grave-goods	Other grave-goods
32	?					?		?Leather	Tip only		
61				X	?	Horn	?	Broken; 2 frags leather on blade and shears possibly from bag enclosing both	Shears	
125		X			150 mm	?Horn				Hooked Cu alloy rod
126	X				217 mm	Unident.		Leather on both blades and steel possibly from bag enclosing all 3	Steel (broken)	
		X			115 mm					
127		X			98 mm	?Horn	?Leather			
146	X				153 mm	Horn	?Leather	Wool between buckle and blade (buckle attached to base of blade)	Buckle	Spearhead (wrapped)
148		X			173 mm	Horn		Textile on blade		Spearhead
149				X	?	Bone/ antler	Leather	Broken. Wood packed between tang and handle	Cu alloy discs, part of small tang	Silver ear-ring
152	X				89 mm	Horn	Leather	Tang broken		
194		X			99 mm	Horn		Tip missing. ?In bag with shears. Fly pupae on knife and shears	Shears, pin frag., ring and chain frags	Shale bracelet, Cu alloy ring, glass bead and pin
204		X			133 mm	Horn	Leather		Steel	
206			?		107 mm	Horn	?	Both tips missing		
213		X			130 mm	Horn	Leather	Both tips missing. Fly pupae between blade and sheath		Spearhead, curved strip, 3 hinge pieces
220	X				155 mm	Horn	Leather and wool	Tip missing, bent		Shield-boss, hand-grip, rivets; spearhead, buckle
238			X		106 mm	Horn	Leather		Small steel	Spearhead, nail, buckle
241	X				147 mm	Horn	?		Steel (leather wrapped)	Buckle, nail, rod, flat pierced plate
281			?		143 mm	Horn	Leather	Vegetable matter on blade		
			X		?	Unident	Leather	Broken; junction between blade and tang		

Grave No.	Böhner type A C D	? type	Length	Handle material	Sheath material	Additional comments	Associated grave-goods	Other grave-goods
281	X		?	Horn		2 frags. Textile on one surface		
293	X		100 mm	Horn		Vegetable matter on blade		
320	X		152 mm	Horn	?Leather	?Grooved blade	Buckle	
323	X		180 mm	Horn	?Leather	Tip missing		Shield-boss, hand-grip, rivets, rectangular loop, pin or nail; spearhead, 2 buckles
358	X		116 mm	?Horn	Leather	Tip missing		15 sherds Saxon pottery
362	X		142 mm	Horn		Tip missing		
365	X		162 mm	Horn	?Leather	Both tips missing	Buckle	
413	X		?		Leather	Handle missing when buried. Tip missing		
428	X		122 mm	Horn				
431	X		94 mm	Horn	?Leather	Broken		
453	?		95 mm	Unident	?Leather	Broken		
458	?		127 mm	Horn		?Indication of belt near tang		

the sheath, perhaps as part of an inner lining. There was not enough mineralised leather remaining to indicate how the sheaths were made.

Buckles

Nine buckles were recovered, eight of iron and one of copper alloy. Six, possibly seven, of these were associated with male grave goods (Graves 146, 220, 238, 323: two buckles, 241 and 365) and only one with female (Grave 149) (Table 9). The burial in Grave 320 was accompanied only by a knife in addition to a buckle and its sex therefore remains unidentified. Seven were quite centrally placed within the grave, although two were slightly nearer to one of the grave edges.

The buckle in Grave 241 was near the (southern) end of the grave but this was one of the shallowest surviving graves and the buckle may not have been *in situ* (the orientation of the burial is not known). The buckle in Grave 149 was caught up in a group of objects comprising a knife and two copper alloy discs or coins, the whole wrapped or otherwise surrounded by cloth and lying in the southern half of the grave.

Both buckles in Grave 323, one of iron and one of copper alloy, were centrally placed, one on each side of a knife and may have attached it to a belt

(although no recognisable belt fittings were found). Another, in Grave 146 was found adhering to the junction of a knife tang and blade (and preserves traces of possible mineralised wool sheath interior), perhaps as if the knife had been thrust through the belt at the point where it buckled. Two buckles preserve mineralised remains of belts or straps, one of woven textile (Grave 238) and one of leather (Grave 323).

All of the buckles are oval and have, where extant, simple square or, in one case (Grave 220), possibly round-ended, riveted plates. The dimensions of three indicate a belt thickness of substantially less than 20 mm (12 mm, 15 mm and 16 mm respectively), whilst the internal lengths of four others are not greatly larger, at between 20–23 mm. The remaining examples are either too fragmentary or too obscured by corrosion and other objects to be measured accurately.

It has been noted elsewhere that buckles from later cemeteries were usually very plain (Meaney and Hawkes 1970, 45–6). In addition, they were much less likely to occur in female graves during the 7th century than hitherto, and tended to become very much smaller late in that century (Hirst 1985, 86). The typology of the buckles from Field Farm thus contributes further evidence toward the late dating of the cemetery.

Table 9 Field Farm: buckles, attributes, positions in graves and associated grave-goods

Grave No.	Material	Overall length	Overall width	Associated objects, position in grave	Additional comments
146	Iron	22 mm	12 mm	Adhering to knife; near centre (east side)	
149	Iron	Not measurable		In a corroded group with a small knife and 2 Cu alloy discs; south of centre (west side)	
220	Iron	28 mm	c. 12 mm	Shield-boss, hand-grip and rivets in grave but not directly associated; north of centre	Plate attached
238	Iron	22 mm	14 mm	Near knife; near centre	
241	Iron	Not measurable		With unidentifed iron frag.; south of centre	
320	Iron	33 mm	21 mm	With knife; near centre	
323	Iron	28 mm	c. 12 mm	Shield-boss, hand-grip and rivets, spearhead and knife in grave but none directly associated; near centre	Plate attached
	Cu alloy	16 mm	10 mm	As above; south of centre	
365	Iron	30 mm	19 mm	Knife nearby; ?near centre	

Girdle groups and 'sets'

Several classes of objects were recovered in close association, in some cases adhering to each other through the action of corrosive processes. Such sets often gave evidence of having been wrapped or contained in some way, through the presence of mineralised organic remains on their surfaces.

The most common of these were the knife and steel sets, which accompanied four burials, one positively identified as male by the presence of a spearhead (Grave 238) and three of uncertain sex but also thought to be male (Graves 126, 204 and 241). The set from Grave 126 comprises a long knife of Böhner's type A, a small knife of type C and a steel, all of which were probably originally wrapped in a leather covering. One other set (Grave 241) may also have been wrapped in this way.

Metallographic examination of a steel from Sewerby in Yorkshire found that the its hardness was less than that of the accompanying knife and it was suggested that these objects may have been used more as hones rather than true steels (Hirst 1985, 88–9). Whatever their function, they seem to have been more frequently associated with male than female burials (*ibid.*, 89), and it is possible that the knife and shears sets were their feminine counterparts.

In Grave 194, thought to be that of a female since it also contained a shale bracelet and yellow glass bead, shears were associated with fragments of an iron pin and chain, whilst another pin and a heavy copper alloy ring were all disposed along a similar alignment nearby. Here it is likely that the ring functioned as a girdle ring from which the bag was suspended by means of the pins and chain. This arrangement suggests that the body was orientated with the head to the south. A combination of shears and knife (with a leather covering) was the sole furniture from Grave 61, which has also been therefore tentatively suggested as a female burial, although shears have been associated with both male and female 7th century graves (Hawkes 1973, 198).

The strike-a-light/purse mount and ring from Grave 145 were apparently tied together with twine and both objects wrapped or otherwise contained in leather. The possible remains of tinder are preserved on the underside of the strike-a-light and were presumably also held in the leather container. This class of grave-good has been found with both male and female burials (Hawkes 1973, 195) and there were no other grave-goods present here which might have helped to establish sex. It has been suggested that the objects could have functioned as dual purpose items, as both strike-a-light and purse mount, but it is not clear why the ring should have been tied to such an item, as was the case here. The iron stud with soldered silver decoration recovered from sieved soil from the grave may originally have been associated with these objects but its function is also not clear. The objects were found near the centre of the grave and close to its western side, suggesting that they were carried at the waist.

The objects from Grave 149 are so lodged in a mass of corrosion that full identification is difficult but they are thought to be a small knife, two copper alloy discs and a buckle. The whole group is apparently wrapped or caught up in a coarse textile, possibly a bag, which obscures the items' relationship to each other and makes it difficult, except in the case of the knife, to establish their function. The copper alloy discs, one of which appears to be perforated, may be very worn coins; Roman coins have frequently been found in female Anglo-Saxon graves (it has been suggested that they were kept as amulets), often occurring in pairs and, during the 7th century, more usually unperforated, suggesting that they were carried in bags (White 1988, 99–101). The group of items was found south of the centre of the grave near the western side and may have been carried at the waist. However, it should be noted that a small, broken tang and a possible ear-ring were lying (together) quite close nearby, suggesting perhaps that some displacement of either or both groups occurred after burial or that the bag, if such it was, was placed in the grave separately.

Jewellery

Two of the three items of jewellery, the shale bracelet and the glass bead were from the same grave, 194, and were associated with one of the knife and shears sets. Shale bracelets are not common in Anglo-Saxon graves, but a Roman shale bracelet is known from a possible Anglo-Saxon grave at Girton (White 1988, 109). The bracelet is plain, and bears no clear evidence of the method of manufacture which might indicate its date, although very slight traces of facets may survive. The smooth, worn appearance of the bracelet may indicate that it was already of some antiquity when buried.

The opaque yellow glass bead was found near the southern end, thought to be the head, of Grave 194. It may have been worn at the neck or perhaps as an ear-ring, but there was no indication of how it might have been suspended. It would seem to be too small to have been used as a fastener, as has been suggested for single beads (in children's graves) at Alton, Hampshire, where similar beads were found (Evison 1988, 13, 18).

The remaining object is the incised silver ring from Grave 149, which was also associated with part of a small tang and possible girdle group. The ring is decorated with crosses of double parallel lines, separated by groups of four parallel lines. Plain silver rings with knotted terminals have been widely found in Anglo-Saxon graves of all periods, with those of the 7th century more tightly knotted as in this instance (Meaney and Hawkes 1970, 37–38). Its position in the grave indicates that it may have been worn as an ear-ring, but it could also have been worn suspended at the neck.

Containers

Both objects classed under this heading are the sole accompaniment to the body in each of the graves in which they occur. The pot in Grave 256 is in an undiagnostic very simple rounded form, with flat

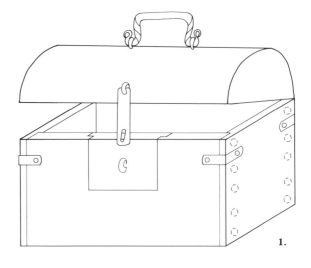

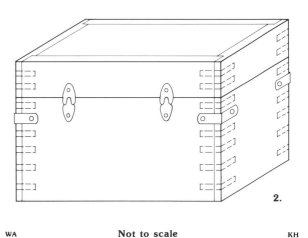

WA   Not to scale   KH

Figure 21   Field Farm: suggested reconstructions of the casket in Grave 140

base, short neck and plain, slightly everted rim and bears no decoration. The traces of sooting on parts of its inner surface suggest that it was used as a domestic cooking pot before its deposition in the grave.

The casket in Grave 140 (Figs 11 and 21) was its sole item of grave furniture. It appears to have been made from flat, sawn maple timber as tangential surfaced boards predominate, with thicknesses in the region of 14–15 mm. From hinge SF.858, the sides of the lid may have only been 11 mm thick, which could indicate that the base had an inner lip to ensure a close fit with the lid. The lid had a minimum depth of 41–45 mm (31 mm length of wood preserved on hinge + 11–14 mm thickness of top), but there was no indication as to the depth of the base. Slight curvature on the hinges and the hasp may indicate that the casket originally had a curved lid. Possible reconstructed shapes are illustrated in Figure 21.

There is no evidence of the type of joints used, except that the front and back pieces sat in recessed butt joints with the sides. This type of joint would not have been adequate to hold the casket together even with glue, and the joints may have been held together with pegs or tenons, although none of the corner brackets were positioned over these. The base was probably held in place using tongue and groove joints, although there was no evidence on the fittings to support this.

The provision of boxes or caskets has been identified as a feature of 7th century female graves (Meaney and Hawkes 1970, 46); they were usually placed at the foot of the grave (Evison 1987, 103) which suggests that the head of Grave 140 was to the south. The casket from Field Farm may be similar to two other fairly local examples, one from Swallowcliffe, Wiltshire (Speake 1989) and one from Finglesham, Kent (unpublished); both of these were also made from maple wood. (Information about the construction of the casket was provided by Jacqui Watson of the Ancient Monuments Laboratory.)

Miscellaneous metal objects
A number of pins, nails or otherwise rod-shaped objects and other miscellaneous items, largely of iron, but including one of copper alloy and another with applied silver, were recovered from graves. Most are of uncertain function. None have been positively identified as coffin fittings but the objects were so few in number that, although the idea should not be completely disregarded, this seems unlikely.

Lying quite close to the knife in Grave 146, was part of a possible small tool. It has mineralised remains of an unidentified wooden handle and fibres wrapped around the metal part, but unfortunately the operational end is missing; it may perhaps have been an awl. A broken fragment of a second small tang was found with the decorated silver ring in Grave 149.

Two pins, a ring and chain fragments from Grave 194 were associated with the copper alloy ring and shears and knife set in that grave and were probably the means of their suspension from a belt.

Three fragmentary objects were recovered from Grave 241, including a small nail, a rod-shaped piece broken at both ends with fibre or cloth wound around it and an irregular flat piece of iron possibly with part of a hole in one edge. The first two items were lying together near the centre of the eastern side of the grave with the third nearby but right at the grave's edge. All may have been parts of a container (or its contents), the rest of which did not survive; this grave was very shallow and it is possible that some of the objects in it may have been destroyed or at least displaced.

A small rectangular loop from Grave 323 was lying between two pairs of rivets probably associated with the shield-boss in the grave and may also have been similarly associated. The loop had apparently been distorted and broken through stress, but its function was not known.

A silvered iron stud was recovered from sieved soil from Grave 145 and may have been associated with the possible girdle group from that grave. A short (broken) nail or pin fragment was found lying close to the knife and buckle in Grave 238.

The hooked copper alloy rod from Grave 125 preserves traces of mineralised flax, and may have been used to pin items of clothing. It was found near the centre of the grave, at its western side; the knife, the only other object found in the grave, was at the same side but nearer to the south-western corner.

Dating
The cemetery at Field Farm displays many of those characteristics which have been identified by Hawkes as late within the pagan Anglo-Saxon period, characteristics which more particularly suggest a 7th century date (Meaney and Hawkes 1970, 45–6). Of these features, two which are most clearly evident at Field Farm are the high number of unfurnished graves, 16, or 32% of the total (Fig. 20), and the paucity and simplicity of grave-goods when these are present. Very striking is the total absence of brooches and the near absence of beads. The single item of metal jewellery, the silver ear-ring, is typical of the late style of small ornament in its unostentatious and delicate taste. The shale bracelet might, if contemporary rather than antique, also be viewed as evidence of the return to 'classical' simplicity in the 7th century. The dating of the more common and functional artefacts such as the shield-bosses, spears, knives, buckles and the casket, is in agreement with this. Any attempt to define more precisely the dating for individual graves is, however, frustrated by the lack of closely datable objects, even in the more richly furnished graves.

It has been noted both by Arnold (1980, 84–90) and by Hawkes (Meaney and Hawkes 1970, 45) that burials accompanied by weapons decrease in number throughout the pagan Anglo-Saxon period, perhaps as a result of increasing political stability in relations between the Anglo-Saxon kingdoms through time. Viewed in this light, the proportion of weapon graves at Field Farm is quite high, at 16% of the total number of graves, when compared to figures of under 10% at other sites such as the 7th–8th century cemetery at Polhill, Kent and none at the 7th century cemetery at Winnall, Hampshire. This might serve as an indication that at least some of the graves at Field Farm were dug in the earlier part of this late period or that the cemetery was in a less politically and socially stable area, one where the ability to defend territory was still desirable or necessary.

Textile remains, by Margaret Brooks

Only a few of the graves produced textile evidence. This was generally in a mineral-preserved condition and seen on small areas of iron objects, though two bast fibres were obtained from threads in contact with copper alloy. There seems no obvious reason why survival should be so limited among graves with similar artefacts, but seasonal groundwater conditions may be a factor.

58

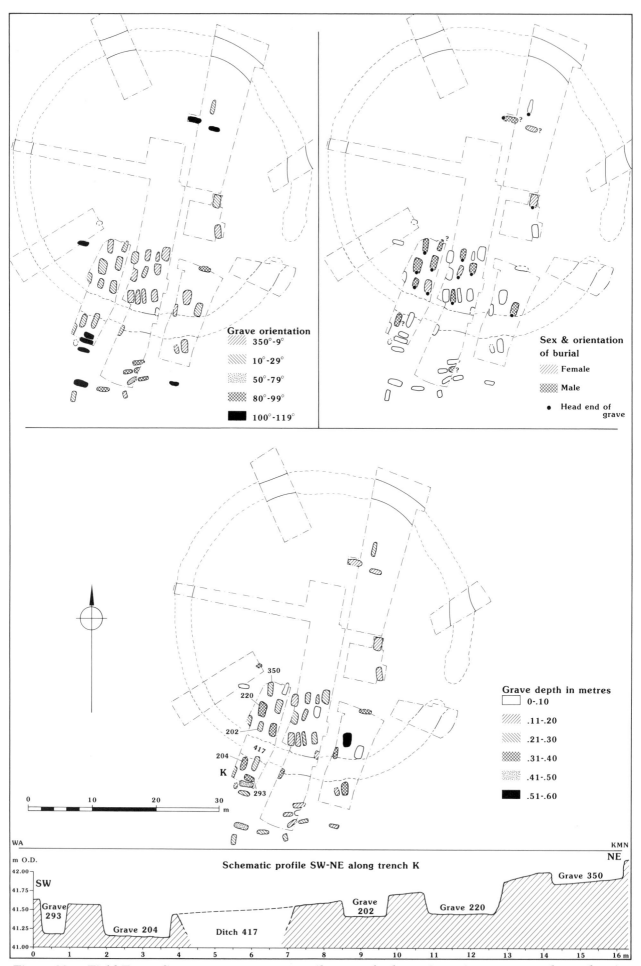

Grave orientation

- ⬚ 350°-9°
- ⬚ 10°-29°
- ⬚ 50°-79°
- ⬚ 80°-99°
- ■ 100°-119°

Sex & orientation
of burial

- ⬚ Female
- ⬚ Male
- ● Head end of
  grave

Grave depth in metres

- ☐ 0-.10
- ⬚ .11-.20
- ⬚ .21-.30
- ⬚ .31-.40
- ⬚ .41-.50
- ■ .51-.60

350
220
202
417
204
K
293

0   10   20   30 m

WA   KMN

NE

m O.D.

Schematic profile SW-NE along trench K

42.00
41.75   SW
41.50   Grave   Grave   Grave 350
41.25   293   202
41.00   Grave 204   Ditch 417   Grave 220

0   1   2   3   4   5   6   7   8   9   10   11   12   13   14   15   16 m

*Figure 22   Field Farm: Saxon cemetery, grave attributes and schematic section across north–south axis
of cemetery in Trench K*

The exact location of the objects worn on the clothing at burial is a problem in the absence of skeletal remains. Much of our information on early Anglo-Saxon women's dress comes from association with brooches and objects placed near the neck and wrists. However, by the 7th century the style of dress had changed and here these artefacts are no longer present (Owen-Crocker 1986). Little is known of men's dress in this period.

Remains of fourteen woven fabrics were found at Field Farm, of which ten could be identified. The types of weave are those widespread at this period; tabbies (one over one) and twills (two over two and two over one). Surviving examples are very small, however, and may not show the range of decorative patterns which could be present. Nor, of course, is there any indication of colour. Details are summarised in Table 10; full details are in archive.

Tabby weaves (Z/Z and Z/S)

The majority of fabrics were in plain tabby weave. Three buckles from men's belts (Graves 220, 238 and 323) had traces of fine Z/S and Z/?Z spun material, probably from shirts. Two of these were seen to be in a bast fibre. Another fine Z/S spun cloth lay against the fittings of a small chest (Grave 140) and may be a woman's veil or head covering. The linen Z/Z tabby around the objects in Grave 149 may be a bag or represent the folds of a garment gathered at the waist. Another Z/Z tabby on a knife placed at one end of Grave 148 could be from a blanket or cloak.

The neatly wrapped spearhead (Grave 146) has an example of Z/S 'spin-patterning' in which threads spun in opposite directions are used in bands to give a self pattern or possibly a check. One system has bands each six threads wide, 6Z6S, etc, the other has only one or two threads of opposite spin in a much wider spacing which could not be established. 'Spin-patterning' was an old tradition, and occurs occasionally in Saxon and Anglian cemeteries (Crowfoot 1985a; 1985b).

Twill weaves (Z/Z and Z/S)

2/2 twill: one piece of Z/S twill was found in Grave 220, apparently wrapped around the hand-grip of a shield, and fragments of a Z/Z twill were seen on an object in Grave 241, possibly from a blanket or cloak.

2/1 twill: lying next to the possible head covering in Grave 140 is a Z/Z twill which may belong to a woman's dress or tunic. The threads in this fabric were much finer in one system than the other, giving a decorative surface effect (Plates 7 and 8).

Tablet weave

Tablet woven bands are often found on the edges of Anglo-Saxon garments, but here there are no metal artefacts in the appropriate positions. However, there is a chatelaine chain in Grave 194 which has two sets of paired S spun threads running over one link, and this may be part of a tablet-woven belt or possibly a fringe.

Single threads

Z spun yarn was found wound around two pin-type objects (Graves 125, 146). The function is unclear. A short length of sewing yarn is visible on the spearhead wrapping (Grave 146), where an S plied Z spun thread runs for 6mm in and out of the material.

Several loops of coarse Z spun twine linked a purse mount (Grave 145) to a bag, probably of leather. A two ply bast twine had been used to bind the fabric round the spearhead in Grave 146.

Fibre identification

Using transmitted light and x100 magnification, two fibres extracted from the yarn round a pin from Grave 125 and the cloth in Grave 149 showed the typical cross markings of flax (Luniak 1953).

It was decided to use the high level of resolution given by the scanning electron microscope (SEM) to look at the surface structure of the fibres preserved as negative casts in the iron corrosion (Janaway 1983). A series of SEM photographs were taken of small samples by Duncan White at the Ancient Monuments Laboratory, London. These were mainly at x600 magnification. Although the poor state of mineral preservation did not give vey clear detail, it was possible to divide the fibres into two groups on their cross-section dimension, taking into account also the occasional appearance of cuticle scales and longitudinal striations.

Plate 7   Field Farm: casket hasp from Grave 140 (SF.873) showing mineralised remains of two different textiles

Table 10 Field Farm: mineralised textile remains from the Saxon cemetery

Note: the abbreviation 'm–p' is used for the term 'mineral-preserved fibres'. The spinning direction of the yarn (/ and \) is shown by the letters Z and S. Weave counts are given in threads per cm unless otherwise stated and overall measurements are from the more well-visualised fragments. All objects are made of iron unless otherwise stated.

Grave No.	SF. No.	Object	Textile position	Measure-ments	Fibre	Spin	Count	Weave comments
125	654	Cu alloy rod	around angle	–	bast	Z	–	single thread
140	873	Hasp	1) top of loop	0.81x1.5	m-p ?animal	Z/Z	14x20–24 on 0.5 mm	uneven 2/1 twill
			2) along hasp under twill	0.7x1.0	m-p ?bast	Z/?S	24x22	fine, even tabby
	875	Bracket	over corner	1.4x3.0	m-p	Z/S	24x20	same as 2) above
	877	Bracket	over corner	1.2x2.5	m-p ?bast	Z/S	24x22	same as 2) above
145	577	Purse-mount	1) on mount front	0.4x0.2	m-p ?bast	Z/?Z	c.17x17	fragmentary, ?tabby
			2) through mount	–	m-p ?bast	Z	–	coarse, single threads
146	575	Spearhead	1) wrapped round	1.6x1.2	m-p ?bast	Z(S) S(Z)	20x18	spin-patterned tabby, folded
			2) on torn edge	0.6	m-p	Z, S plied	–	sewing thread 2 ply
			3) criss-cross binding	4.0	m-p ?bast	S plied	–	2 ply twine
	–	Rod	around shank	1.0x0.2	m-p	?Z	–	single thread
148	599	Knife	on blade	0.7x0.4	m-p	Z/Z	15x15	tabby
149	568	Iron and Cu alloy	around objects	0.8x0.6	bast fibre	Z/Z	14x14	tabby, lying in folds
194	592	Chain	over one link	0.4x0.1	m-p ?animal	S	–	?tablet weave or fringe; coarse threads
213	645	Strip	over one edge	0.4x0.4	m-p ?animal	Z/Z	?18x20	weave indistinct
220	691	Shield-boss	around grip and in boss	0.4x0.5	m-p ?animal	Z/S	12x12 on 0.5 mm	2/2 twill, pulled ?wrapping
	728	Buckle	on back of plate	1.0x0.5	m-p ?bast	Z/?Z	c.17x17 on 0.2	?tabby, poorly preserved
238	685	Buckle	on back	2.4x1.0	m-p	z?s	c.22/? on 0.3 mm	tabby, poorly preserved
241	688	Loop	on one side	0.5x0.6	m-p	Z/Z	16–18/16 on 0.5 mm	2/2 twill
	701	Rod	on one face	2.0x1.0	m-p	Z?	c.12x12 on 0.4 mm	weave indistinct
281	784	Knife	over blade	4.0x1.2	m-p	Z/?	c.15/?	weave indistinct, in folds
323	736	Buckle	over back of buckle and plate	2.5x2.4	m-p ?bast	Z/S	c.24x24 on 0.1mm	fine tabby
	739	Spearhead	over both faces sporadically	1.2x0.5	m-p ?animal	?Z/?S	?12x?12	threads very broken, weave indistinct

Plate 8   Field Farm: detail of uneven 2/1 twill on hasp from Grave 140 (SF.873)

Taking all the woven yarns from the site, the evidence suggests that four are wool and six are bast, presumably linen. Three are not identified.

Eight of the textiles may be identified as garments worn at the time of burial (if the tabby in Grave 149 is a garment). Five of these, including the suggested head covering, are interpreted here as linen. Only one garment is a wool twill. The use of linen in three or four of five garments, some possibly shirts (Graves 140, 145, 149, 220 and 323) is noticeable although it is such a small group.

Summary
The textiles surviving in this small group were produced in the normal range of Anglo-Saxon weaves, but preservation has been limited by the type of artefacts in association. The wrapping of two spearheads and a shield hand-grip in textile is unusual, although isolated examples occur (Crowfoot 1953; 1985c). Fine linen seems to be used for garments which are probably shirts.

Human remains

The 1985–87 investigations, by Lynne Bell
Human bone from the 1985–1987 investigations consisted mostly of cremated material with some inhumation material. At a macro level, bone preservation is generally poor, with surfaces exhibiting considerable post-mortem damage, and this has necessarily placed limitations on the interpretation of the material. However, wherever possible, age (Suchey 1979; Katz and Suchey 1986; Stewart 1979; Warwich and Williams 1980; Brothwell 1981; van Beek 1983; Bass 1985), sex (Stewart 1979; Brothwell 1981 and Bass 1985) and stature (Trotter and Gleser 1952 and 1958) have been documented alongside any biometrical, nonmetrical (WEA 1980, English Heritage nd) and pathological findings (Steinbock 1976; Ortner and Putschar 1985).

Bone was recovered from three main groups of contexts: those pre-dating the construction of ring-ditch 417; middle Bronze Age cremations; and Saxon inhumations. The preservation of bone from all three groups was very poor. The inhumation material is scanty as only two partial inhumations had survived and these were in a highly degraded and fragmented state.

The cremated material is also scanty, surviving best as interpretable material when contained within an urn before excavation. The cremated material which was not urned, including the bulk of the catalogued material, was present often as a total weight of less than 5 g, quantities too small to make any meaningful comments on individual collections.

However, a qualitative impression gained from the colouration and cracking present in all periods represented is that bone has been exposed to a vartiety of temperatures but has not always been well calcined. There is little curling deformation, although some darkly charred material is present. A wide range of maximum fragment lengths is recorded in all three phases (25–45 mm), suggesting both selective retrieval for large fragments and deliberate pounding for small fragments (Gejvall 1969 and Brothwell 1981).

Despite the small quantities recovered it can be stated that the urned Bronze Age cremations all appear to be single cremations, with only one urn (1082, feature 627, ring-ditch 604) containing two individual adults.

Ring-ditch 417 and associated features
Less than 30 g of cremated bone was recovered from the central area of ring-ditch 417, from hearth 262 and associated soil 10, pre-dating the construction of the monument. These fragments were mostly unidentifiable apart from a small collection of cremated skull fragments.

Bronze Age cremations
Cremated bone was recovered from five urns (Urn 919, 776.5 g; Urn 1, 377 g; Urn 1081, 210 g; Urn 1082, 1407.5 g; and Urn 1107, less than 5 g) and two unaccompanied deposits (369, and 520, both less than 5 g). At least six individuals were identified: three single urned cremations comprising two adults (Urns 919 and 1081) and one sub-adult (Urn 1); one unaccompanied sub-adult cremation (369) and one double cremation (Urn 1082).

No other information on age, sex, stature, morphology or pathology was obtainable. The cremated bone from 520 was too fragmented to provide any further information.

Saxon graves
Only two partial inhumations survived. Grave 87 contained a poorly preserved and poorly represented supine inhumation which was considered to be 17–25 years old, of unknown sex with no apparent morphology or pathology. Grave 365 contained tibial bone fragments of a possible adult of unknown sex and no apparent morphology and pathology. Unburnt bone was also recovered from Grave 148, which contained a fragment of a long-bone shaft, and Grave 152 contained a small amount of skull fragments.

Cremated material, all less than 5 g in weight, was recovered from Graves 140, 145, 146, 147, 213, 220, 256, 322, 350, 362, and 453, and from layers above and around graves. The bone from Grave 140 consisted of four enamel crowns and enamel fragments which indicated a possible age range of 17–25 years.

These many small amounts of cremated material may be residual in the Saxon contexts, possibly originating from Bronze Age cremations.

The 1988 excavation (W267),
by Jacqueline I. McKinley
The cremation was recovered from a large, inverted Bronze Age urn, 1140, which was inserted into pit 041 at the centre of ring-ditch 032. The bone was excavated (not by the writer) from the urn, still inverted (base damaged), in 30 mm spits, all other debris being removed at this stage. Quantities of burnt flint were removed and a very small quantity of pale fuel ash slag, both products of the cremation pyre and reflecting the soil-type on which the cremation was conducted. As the site was on sandy gravel with a high flint content this would fit the area indicated by the pyre debris. Pyre debris, charcoal, etc, had been dumped in the pit around the urn, apparently when cool; this would also support the idea that the cremation was conducted in the vicinity of the ring-ditch.

The cremation was examined within spits for any significant variation in deposition. Each spit was passed through a series of 10, 5 and 2 mm mesh sieves, weighed and presented as a percentage of the total weight in order to assess fragmentation. Identifiable fragments were then removed for further examination in order to ascertain number of individuals, age and sex. Weights of body areas represented were presented as percentages of total weight in order to ascertain any bias in collection. Age was assessed from bone fusion (Gray 1977; McMinn and Hutchings 1985) and degree of degenerative disease. Sex was assessed from the diamorphic traits of the skeleton (Bass 1985).

There was a total of 1585.3 g of cremated bone. The maximum fragment size for skull was 82 mm and for long-bones 80 mm. Most (73.8%) of the bone was extracted from the 10 mm sieve, 20.3% was between 5 and 10 mm and 5.8% between 2 and 5 mm. Of the 52.2% of bone which was identifiable 31.7% was skull, 20.7% axial, 20.7% upper limb and 27.0% lower limb). There was no evidence for more than one individual, a mature (30–45 years) adult, probably female. A fragment of unidentified cremated animal bone was also recovered.

Notable pathology included: 1. Slight mild osteophytes on surface margins of thoracic and lumbar vertebrae (age-related degeneration). 2. Degenerative disc disease, as evidenced by pitting of vertebral surfaces in upper thoracic. 3. Schmorl's nodes in several thoracic vertebrae (disc degeneration). 4. Osteoarthritis of the thoracic and lumbar vertebrae, as evidenced by pitting and marginal osteophytes in several of the articular process facets of thoracic and lumbar vertebrae. 5. Osteophytes on proximal articular margins of several distal finger phalanges (age-related). 6. Fusion of middle and distal (fifth) foot phalanges (morphological variation). 7. Slight peridontal disease around mandibular molars as evidenced by alveolar bone resorbtion and new bone formation (indicative of poor dental hygiene).

The bone was well oxidised, ie. the organic component had been burnt away. Fragmentation was not heavy and there is no reason to assume any deliberate fragmentation took place after cremation. Collection of bone for burial was good, with between 65–80% of the expected weight of an adult cremation being present. There was no apparent bias in areas of the body collected and no specific distribution within the urn was observed.

The bone was clean (no charcoal staining) and the urn contained little other pyre debris except for a few fragments of burnt flint and fuel ash slag. Deliberate separation of the bone from other debris had taken place. Collection was probably *en masse*, with cleaning perhaps by some winnowing or water process (McKinley 1989; forthcoming).

This report was submitted in September 1988.

7 Environmental Evidence

Plant remains, by W.J.Carruthers

Soil samples were taken during the excavation for the recovery of carbonised plant remains. The samples were subjected to manual flotation on site and in the laboratory using a 25µ meshed sieve for the recovery of the flot. In several cases it was necessary to add hydrogen peroxide to the sample to help to disaggregate the cohesive soil. The final volumes of soil processed varied according to the initial results and type of context, but samples were generally taken in multiples of five litres. The total volumes processed for each phase are given at the bottom of the species list (Table 11).

Only seventeen out of 36 soil samples produced carbonised plant remains. The total number of fragments recovered from the site as a whole was small, and in many cases the cereals were in a poor state of preservation, being badly eroded. The carbonised plant remains are summarised in Table 11.

Neolithic
The hearth (feature 262, context 261) and associated charcoal spread (contexts 55, 57–60) within ring-ditch 417 produced a few cereals of which emmer/spelt (*Triticum dicoccum / spelta*) was the only identifiable taxon. The range of weed seeds present includes taxa which could have grown as arable weeds, such as black bindweed (*Bilderdykia convolvulus* (L.) Dumort.) and fat hen (*Chenopodium album* L.), but can also be found in a variety of other disturbed habitats. Amongst the other weed seeds recovered, sheep's sorrel (*Rumex acetosella* L.), cf. marsh bedstraw (*Galium* cf. *palustre* L.) and indeterminate grass seeds indicated that the local vegetation type might have been damp grassland.

The recovery of carbonised hazelnut shell fragments is typical of deposits of this period, indicating the continued use of woodland/scrub resources alongside areas of arable cultivation. Evidence from early prehistoric sites in England and Wales summarised by Moffett *et al.* (1989) shows that gathered foodstuffs such as hazelnuts and apples remained important components of the diet up to the late Bronze Age.

The presence of grassland taxa in the Neolithic samples may reflect small-scale localised clearance in areas of oak/hazel woodland, as suggested by the charcoal evidence (Gale, this volume), or more widespread events.

Plant macro- and microfossil studies undertaken by Holyoak (1980) in the Kennet Valley indicate the survival of alder woodland in some areas of the floodplain into the post elm-decline period. However, Mesolithic and Neolithic activities at Field Farm suggest some degree of clearance, as does the presence of charcoal from the light-demanding tree, *Prunus* sp. (Gale, this volume).

Early Bronze Age
An early Bronze Age pit (297, fill 267) cutting through the hearth deposits contained a range of taxa similar in nature to the Neolithic assemblage. This included two caryopses of barley (*Hordeum* sp.), hazelnut shell, fat-hen and sheep's sorrel seeds. Although the quantity of material was too small to draw useful conclusions concerning the local economy and environment of the site in the early Bronze Age, the presence of hazelnut shell again suggests a continued reliance on wild food sources. The construction of the ring-ditch and layer of oak charcoal (Gale, this volume) in the ditch suggest that further clearance took place in this period.

Middle Bronze Age
The features and cremations associated with four middle Bronze Age urns (416, 625, 627, 919) produced similar remains to the Neolithic samples. In addition, several tuberous culm bases of onion couch grass (*Arrhenatherum elatius* var.*bulbosum*) were recovered. These remains are often associated with Bronze Age cremations, possibly because they are useful as tinder (Robinson 1988). Jones (1978 101) suggests that the onion couch tubers recovered from a Bronze Age cremation pit at Ashville Trading Estate, Abingdon, Oxfordshire were 'purposely gathered and added to the cremation fire', although no reason for this action is given. The good state of preservation of the tubers at Field Farm indicates that they may have been dried out prior to burning. Onion couch grass is characteristic of abandoned arable or abandoned pasture.

Late Bronze Age
A late Bronze Age feature (419, context 22) cutting ring-ditch 417 produced a few carbonised remains, including a possible spelt (*Triticum* cf. *spelta* L.) glume base. As the state of preservation was poor this identification is tentative, based mainly on the width at the point of attachment of the glume to the rachis (1.08 mm), a criterion which is not totally reliable on its own. However, evidence for the

Table 11 Field Farm: summary of carbonised plant remains

Taxa	Neolithic hearth	EBA pit	MBA cremations	LBA features	Saxon graves	Habitat
Triticum cf. spelta (cf. spelt glume bases)	–	–	–	1	–	
Triticum spelta/dicoccum (spelt/emmer caryopses)	1	–	–	–	–	
Triticum spelta/dicoccum (spelt/emmer glume bases)	–	–	–	3	1	
Triticum aestivocompactum s.l. (bread club wheat caryopses)	–	–	–	–	2	
Hordeum sp. (barley caryopses)	–	2	–	–	–	
Avena sp. (oat caryopses)	–	–	–	–	4	
Indeterminate cereals	8	–	2	1	4	
					–	
Arrhenatherum elatius var. *bulbosum* (onion couch grass tubers)	–	–	6	–		G
Atriplex hastata/patula	2	–	–	–	–	AD
Bilderdykia convolvulus (L.) Dumort.	3	–	3	–	–	AD
cf. *Bromus* sect. *Bromus*	–	–	–	–	1	ADG
Carex sp.	–	–	1	–	1	GM
Caryophyllaceae	–	–	–	–	1	
Chenopodiaceae	2	–	–	–	–	
Chenopodium album L.	8	2	–	–	–	AD
Corylus avellana L. (hazelnut shell frags)	22	12	–	–	–	HSW
Galium cf. palustre L.	1	–	1	–	–	BMw
Galium sp.	–	–	–	–	3	
Gramineae gen. et sp. indet.	9	–	–	–	5	G
Gramineae gen. et sp. indet. (culm frags & culm bases)	1	–	73	–	202	G
Leguminosae	–	–	2	–	–	
Plantago lanceolata L.	–	–	–	–	15	G
Polygonum aviculare agg.	–	–	–	1	–	AD
Polygonum sp. (minus seed coat)	–	1	–	–	–	
Ranunculus acris/bulbosus/repens	–	–	–	–	9	DG
Rumex acetosella L.	22	1	–	1	–	CEGa
Rumex sp.	12	–	2	–	–	
Stellaria graminea L.	–	–	–	–	1	EGWl
Totals	91	18	91	6	249	
Total volume of soil processed (litres)	495	65		70	275	

Habitat preferences: A= arable, B = ditch/stream banks, C = cultivated soils, D = disturbed land, E = heath, G = grassland, H = hedgerows, M = marsh, S = scrub, W = woodland

a = acid soil, l = light soil, w = wet soil

cultivation of spelt during the late Bronze Age has now been recovered from other sites, including Potterne, Wiltshire (Straker, pers. comm.) and Runnymede (Greig, pers. comm.).

As with the cereal remains from earlier samples, arable cultivation may not have been occurring locally on the gravel terraces of the River Kennet. The adjacent site at Knight's Farm (Bradley *et al.* 1980) produced little pollen or plant macroscopic evidence to indicate the cultivation of cereals in the immediate area, although it could not be ruled out, and the site at Anslow's Cottages downstream produced very few carbonised cereal remains (*see below*). The local vegetation at Anslow's Cottages appears to have been primarily grassland, and it was suggested that clearance was probably widespread.

The paucity of carbonised plant remains at Field Farm appears to be typical of funerary monuments, although few large-scale sampling programmes have been carried out on such sites. In her discussion of carbonised remains from a Bronze Age cairn at Manor Farm, Lancashire, Van der Veen (1987) cites three other examples; Whitton Hill, Northumberland (Van der Veen 1985), Trelystan, Powys (Hillman 1982) and Abingdon, Oxfordshire (Jones 1978). These sites range in date from late Neolithic to middle Bronze Age. None was sampled extensively and none produced large quantities of material. In comparison with these sites Field Farm produced a similar low concentration of cereals and similar range of weeds of arable/disturbed ground.

The round barrows at Trelystan (early Bronze Age) are notable for the lack of cereal remains but culm bases were found which, it was said, might have originated from burnt turf below the funeral pyre or dry grasses used to light it. This might also apply to the relatively frequent grassland remains recovered from the middle Bronze Age cremation urns at Field Farm, since culm bases, culm fragments and onion couch tubers were present.

From the small amount of evidence recovered from these monuments, it would appear that domestic and arable activities were not occurring in the vicinity. It should be remembered that carbonised plant remains are generally infrequent on sites of early prehistoric date (Moffett *et al.* 1989). Nevertheless, it is likely that ring-ditches would have been set in a grassland clearing and that the reason for recovering small quantities of grain at these sites may be due to their transportation to the site for ritual purposes (Balkwill 1978).

The Saxon cemetery
Of the eight Saxon graves sampled, only two produced carbonised plant remains, most of which came from Grave 145. The large number of grass culm fragments, ribwort plantain seeds (*Plantago lanceolata* L.) and buttercup seeds (*Ranunculus acris/bulbosus/repens*) indicated that burnt turves or hay may have been present. As carbonised culm bases were recorded, the former explanation seems likely. Some cereal caryopses but few arable/disturbed land weed seeds were recovered. Although some redeposition of carbonised material is possible on such a multiperiod site, the bread/club wheat (*Triticum aestivocompactum* s.l.) and oat (*Avena* sp.) caryopses identified are most likely to have been Saxon in date. The good state of preservation of delicate grass culm fragments also indicates that this assemblage was not redeposited. It is not possible to determine how the remains came to be in the grave fill, but they may have originated from domestic fires or bonfires.

Charcoal, by R. Gale

Carbonised woody material from 32 contexts was received for identification using comparative anatomical methods. The material was first examined using a hand lens and sorted into groups based on the features visible on the transverse surface. Representatives from each group were then pressure-fractured to reveal clean surfaces in the transverse, tangential longitudinal and radial longitudinal planes and mounted in plasticine on microscope slides. These were examined using an epi-illuminating stereo microscope at magnifications up to x400, and compared to authenticated reference material.

Although much of the charcoal was very fragmentary, the cellular structure was generally well-preserved and only a few samples (in which insufficient diagnostic features were present) could not be positively identified. In these instances tentative names have been given. A summary of the identification is presented in Table 12.

Neolithic
The carbon-rich layer associated with hearth 262 (contexts 10, 57 and 59) within ring-ditch 417 contained a mass of twig or stem material mainly of oak, but with a small representation of hazel and *Prunus*.

Early Bronze Age
Pit 297 at the centre of ring-ditch 417 presented a quantity of small fragments of charcoal, predominantly *Prunus* with a small sample of oak. Context 34, the spread of burnt soil within the fill of ring-ditch 417, contained a large amount of oak fragments. These appear to be mainly of mature timber, of which approximately half originated from very fast-growing trees, the annual ring width measuring as much as 75 mm. Post-hole 291 produced small slivers of oak.

Middle Bronze Age
The fill of pit 363, containing Urn 1, was associated with a mass of mature oak wood fragments; the urn also contained fragments of mature oak. Within ring-ditch 604, cremation pit 625 produced roughly equal proportions of *Prunus* and hazel, and charcoal from the sieved contents of Urn 1081 in pit 627 was mainly hazel but with some *Prunus* and buckthorn.

Charcoal from layer 23 within the fill of ring-ditch 417 produced only a small quantity of charcoal in very poor condition, the only positively identified sample being oak. Other species tentatively identified included ash and alder. Charcoal from layer 7 in the top fill of the ditch was predominantly oak, probably from large stem or branch wood rather than mature timber. Also present were small samples of *Prunus* and Pomoideae.

The small sample of charcoal from the top layer of ring-ditch 418 (context 307) contained fragments of mature oak and stem of buckthorn. The fill of pit

Table 12 Field Farm: summary of charcoal identifications

Context/description		Weight	Ac	Al	Co	Fr	Il	Qu	Po	Pr	Rh
Neolithic											
10	burnt layer around hearth 262	10 g	–	–	xs	–	Xs	Xs	Xs	xs	–
57	part of 10	3 g	–	–	–	–	X	X	–	–	–
59	part of 10	20 g	–	–	–	–	X	X	–	–	–
Early Bronze Age											
267	layer in pit 297	13 g	–	–	–	–	x	x	X	X	–
34	burnt layer in fill of ditch 417	18+ g	–	–	–	–	Xm	Xm	–	–	–
Early/middle Bronze Age											
3	cremation pit within 417	17 g	–	–	–	–	Xm	Xm	–	–	–
23	layer in ditch 417	5 g	–	?x	–	?x	–	x	–	–	–
7	top fill of ditch 417	10 g	–	–	–	–	–	Xs	x	x	–
416	fill of Urn 1 in ring-ditch 417		–	–	–	–	–	Xm	–	–	–
290	fill of burnt post-hole 291	27 g	–	–	–	–	–	Xm	–	–	–
625	cremation pit within ring-ditch 609		–	–	x	–	–	–	–	x	–
627	cremation pit within 609		–	–	X	–	–	–	–	x	x
307	layer in upper fill of ring-ditch 418	3 g	–	–	–	–	xm	xm	–	xs	xs
367	fill of pit 366 within ring-ditch 418		x	–	–	–	x	x	X	X	–
Later Bronze Age											
21	layer in pit 419	8 g	Xm	–	–	–	x	Xm	–	–	–
22	layer in pit 419	22 g	x	x	–	x	–	x	–	–	–
154	layer in pit 419	21 g	–	–	x	–	–	–	–	–	–
165	layer in pit 419	9 g	–	–	X	x	–	–	–	–	–
477	fill of post-hole 475	9 g	?x	–	–	x	–	x	–	–	–
479	fill of post-hole 478	7 g	–	Xm	–	–	–	–	–	–	–
466	fill of ?cremation pit 465	4 g	–	?xs	?xs	–	–	–	–	xs	–
484	fill of pit 483	2 g	–	–	Xs	–	–	–	–	–	–
467	layer in pit 499	18 g	–	–	–	–	–	X	–	–	–
486	fill of pit/post-hole 485	14 g	–	x	x	–	–	x	–	–	–
489	fill of pit 488	8 g	–	–	–	–	–	?x	–	–	–
Saxon											
42	fill of Grave 145	10 g	–	–	–	–	–	Xm	–	–	–
80	fill of Grave 147	10 g	–	–	xs	–	–	xm	–	–	–
164	layer in Grave 140	11 g	–	–	x	–	–	x	x	–	–
201	fill of Grave 202	7 g	–	–	–	–	–	Xm	–	–	–
219	fill of Grave 220	116 g	–	–	–	–	–	xm	–	x	–
242	fill of Grave 323	3 g	–	–	–	X	–	–	–	–	–
53	fill of Grave 61	4 g	–	–	–	–	–	Xm	–	–	–

Ac = *Acer*, Al = *Alnus*, Co = *Corylus*, Fr = *Fraxinus*, Il = *Ilex*, Qu = *Quercus*, Po = Pomoideae, Pr = *Prunus*, Rh = *Rhamnus*

x = species present, X = dominant species, m = mature wood, s = stem wood

367 within this ring-ditch yielded a large quantity, possibly of stem material, of field maple, *Prunus*, and the Pomoideae group, with one fragment of oak.

Later Bronze Age
Feature 419, cut into the upper fill of ring-ditch 417, contained large quantities of charcoal. Layer 21 included a small quantity of oak and maple charcoal, both from mature wood, and in addition, a small sliver of holly. A large amount of charcoal from layer 22 included a mixture of oak, alder and maple. Two further contexts (154 and 165) contained almost exclusively hazel and one small fragment of ash from the latter.

Small amounts of charcoal were retrieved from several other features, notably post-holes and pits to the west of ring-ditch 417 and a pit adjacent to ring-ditch 457. Post-hole 475 contained a mixture of oak, ash and ?maple; post-hole 477 produced a few large fragments of mature alder; layer 467 in pit 449 contained oak; pit 483 contained stem material of hazel (incomplete but showing a minimum of ten annual rings); post-hole 485 contained oak, hazel and alder; pit 488 contained very small slivers probably of oak but they were too small to confirm. The fill of pit 466 included young stem or twig material of *Prunus* and hazel/alder.

Saxon
Several graves produced charcoal, mostly of oak (Graves 61, 145, 147, 194, 202, 220). Grave 147 also produced some incomplete hazel stems, with 5–11 annual rings visible; hazel was also present in Grave 140, together with Pomoideae. Some *Prunus* sp. was present in Grave 220 and ash in Grave 323.

Discussion
Oak, the species occurring most commonly throughout all phases, is a dominant woodland tree thriving in damp acidic situations, often in association with hazel as understorey. The frequency of hazel charcoal on the site suggests that the floodplain terrace did indeed support a primary woodland of oak/hazel. Initial tree clearance during the Neolithic prior to the construction of ring-ditch 417 is confirmed by the presence of *Prunus*, most probably blackthorn, a shrubby species which will not tolerate heavy shade.

The subsequent phases of the Bronze Age show the sporadic evidence of other large woodland species such as ash and field maple. The former is a ready coloniser but light-demanding and probably became established after the clearance of the primary woodland. The field maple is generally considered to be a late arrival in Britain and its absence before the Bronze Age at Field Farm conforms with records from other contemporary sites. The Pomoideae, a sub-family of the family Rosaceae, is also present as charcoal during the Bronze Age and later phases. Anatomically, the members of this group are very similar and it is not possible to separate them with any certainty. However, bearing in mind the floodplain environment and the immediate proximity of the

river, the most likely species would seem to be hawthorn which grows prolifically as scrub on cleared land.

Buckthorn, a calciphile, is a puzzling find on the flooplain terrace. Its occurrence in two distinct contexts (fill of ring-ditch 418 and within the cremation urn in pit 627 in ring-ditch 604) suggests that its presence is more than accidental. It is of little value as fuel, but the black berries and bark have long been used as a purgative and laxative. It is possible of course that this shrub was surviving in a somewhat hostile environment, or alternatively it may have been sought out from local chalklands and brought onto the site for medicinal, symbolic or even ritual purposes. Holly, present in only one context (late Bronze Age pit 419), is a ubiquitous tree or shrub that tolerates both light and heavy shade and acid or alkaline soils. The river banks would have offered the ideal habitat for alder, as also for poplar and willow, both of which are conspicuously absent in woody form from the site.

The burnt layer (context 34) in the lower fill of ring-ditch 417 in Trench F, might have been thought, by analogy with other ring-ditches in the region (Bradley and Richards 1979–80) to indicate secondary land clearance of regenerated scrub. However, the mass of charcoal retrieved from this context was exclusively oak and made up of roughly equal proportions of slow grown and very rapidly grown mature timber. Two possible interpretations are that either the material originated from trees which had experienced a phase of very fast growth during unusually moist conditions for a short period of time, or that it came from trees exposed to differing habitats, that is, one relatively dry and the other very much wetter. In the former case the tree(s) may have been on the site and thus cleared by burning. If the latter is correct then this layer is most unlikely to represent a clearance horizon. The absence of other woody species that were evidently growing in the locality also throws doubt on the possibility of secondary woodland or scrub clearance.

Woodland management
As can be seen from Table 12 much of the wood apparently selected for specific purposes, such as that associated with cremations in the earlier periods and inhumation burials in the later phase, was mature stem (trunk) or branch wood. In some contexts young stem wood was present but not in any great quantity and the incomplete nature of the samples negated any significant annual ring counting. There was, therefore, insufficient evidence to comment on woodland management.

Selection of timber
A fairly consistent pattern of the selection of oak wood emerges particularly during the Neolithic, early and middle Bronze Age and Saxon periods. Interestingly, two Bronze Age cremation features are curiously opposed in the selection of wood. In ring-ditch 417 the wood associated with the cremation pit and Urn 1 is mature oak, whereas a

similar feature in ring-ditch 604 contains hazel, *Prunus* and buckthorn. The radiocarbon dates indicate that nearly a millennium separates the two urns; suprisingly, perhaps, the earlier of the two (from ring-ditch 604) contains no oak and a greater diversity of species than the urn from ring-ditch 417. Woods associated with features in this period show a range of species including field maple, alder, hazel, ash, oak and *Prunus*. Possibly oak was less readily available by this period due to excessive clearance and usage.

Conclusion

The natural woodland on the floodplain terrace of the River Kennet in the immediate vicinity of the site was oak/hazel, with alder on the river banks possibly extending into the margins of the wood where the ground was marshy. Following the intervention of man during the late Neolithic the clearance of the primary woodland encouraged species such as ash and field maple and shrubs such as hawthorn and blackthorn to recolonize. However, the oak still appears to have flourished until the late Bronze Age, when the increased use of other woody species suggests a possible decline in the oak population.

A long period of abandonment of the site appears to follow, during which the site would have reverted to woodland. Evidently by the Saxon period mature oak is once again plentiful enough to be used almost exclusively.

8 Discussion

Prehistoric features

The search for evidence of prehistoric activity at Field Farm concentrated on probable areas of activity already suggested by cropmark evidence; other more dispersed features were recorded where time and opportunity allowed, but the view of the area presented is an incomplete one.

Mesolithic

The evidence for activity in this period at Field Farm is slight; a few pieces of worked flint diagnostic of this period were recovered from what was probably a buried soil preserved at the centre of the later monument defined by ring-ditch 417. The gravel knoll on which these finds were located offered a probably drier patch of ground by the side of a stream, as a temporary resting place. Other similar sites may have existed in the area, as indicated by the small flint scatter of this date found during fieldwalking at SU 674 706, on the edge of the peat in the north-west corner of the site (Fig. 4).

Neolithic

Two small pits recorded during the 1983–84 watching brief (W70), containing flint and pottery of early Neolithic types, provide rather isolated indications of activity in this period. These pits were so shallow that it is quite possible that other features may have existed in the immediate vicinity which were not observed or recorded. Further evidence for this period is provided by hearth 262 and stake-holes encircling a Mortlake Ware bowl (Fig. 7), pre-dating the construction of ring-ditch 417 and preserved by the buried soil at the centre of the monument. These were associated with a small flint industry dominated by blade production. The hearth produced an archaeomagnetic date of 3900–3000 Cal BC (AJC–63), which is perhaps earlier than might be expected for Mortlake Ware, although it is possible that the two features were not associated. There did not appear to be any other substantial associated features and it is not clear whether this group of features represents domestic or ritual activity.

The local vegetation at this time was predominantly mature oak woodland with damp grassy clearings, perhaps resulting from small-scale clearance for arable cultivation; the fragment of polished flint axe (SF.66) found during fieldwalking may be a reflection of this. Further confirmation of the wooded nature of the area may be suggested by the presence of *Prunus* in the charcoal-rich layer sealing the hearth at the centre of ring-ditch 417, although it is possible that this may relate to the construction of the monument.

The nature of the evidence for human activity at this period is both fragmentary and ephemeral but suggests initial colonisation of territory which had previously been exploited only in a transitory manner and on a small scale.

Late Neolithic–Early Bronze Age

Ring-ditch 417 was probably constructed in a small grassy clearing in the oak woodland; the small number of barley, emmer/spelt and weed seeds indicate some arable cultivation, while the number of carbonised hazelnut shells suggest continued exploitation of woodland/scrub resources.

The construction of the ring-ditch and associated central pit 297 is dated by radiocarbon to 3650±80 BP (HAR–9139) for charcoal from the pit. Although no central mound or evidence of inner or outer banks survived (or were recognised) it seems probable from the surviving arrangement of later features that some visible earthwork, probably a mound, was constructed from the material quarried out of the ditch. This suggestion is supported by the preservation of a soil in the central area of the monument which would otherwise have been open to erosion or destruction by later activity.

All the later Bronze Age features in the interior of the ring-ditch were located within a circle up to 9.50 m from the inner edge of the ditch, and the Saxon graves extended only a further 2 m (11.50 m in from the ditch) towards the centre. In addition, the graves were cut in a stepped sequence, rising across Trenches D and K from south to north, suggesting that the ground occupied by the cemetery rose as it approached the centre before falling again toward the northern arc of the ditch (*see below*). From these observations it seems fair to assume that some form of central mound did exist and stood at least until Saxon times, when it provided a focus for the cemetery; the berm between the edge of the ditch and the edge of the postulated mound suggests that the barrow would have been bell-shaped.

The buried soil and pit 297 contained small sherds of Collared Urn and Beaker pottery, apparently distributed randomly although avoiding the Mortlake Ware bowl, which may still have been visible at the time of the construction of the ring-ditch, the area around it possibly still defined by stakes. There was no evidence for associated human bone, although this may not have survived in the acid soils which appear to have prevailed at the time; even the cremated bone of some of the later burials was not very well preserved. The lack of deliberate deposition of both grave-goods and human remains suggests that if this pit did serve a burial function the ritual must have been in the nature of a token gesture, perhaps with greater emphasis on the visible memorial provided by the mound.

Soon after the initial silting of the ditch, there appears to have been some burning within the northern arc of the ditch, charcoal from this layer producing a radiocarbon date of 3569±70 BP (HAR–9142). The charcoal was all of mature oak and may represent further clearance of the primary woodland for settlement or agricultural purposes.

Middle Bronze Age
This period is marked by at least eleven cremation burials located in and around several ring-ditches. Most of the burials were contained in urns which had been deposited in pits, but several unaccompanied deposits of cremated bone were also recorded. They occurred in primary contexts within small ring-ditches 418, 604 and 032, in secondary contexts around the edge of the putative mound of ring-ditch 417, and between the monuments.

Five cremations in urns were inserted as secondary burials probably around the edge of the mound within ring-ditch 417 (Fig. 6); finds of prehistoric pottery and cremated bone from some of the Saxon graves suggest that other burials may previously have existed. Three of the cremations, 363, 369 and 524, were associated with Collared Urns (fragments only in the case of 369) and the other two were in Deverel-Rimbury Urns. In ring-ditch 418 two possible cremations, 366 and 520, both unaccompanied and in shallow pits, were identified (Fig. 8). Two cremations in Deverel-Rimbury Urns, 625 and 627, and another possible unaccompanied cremation, 626, were found in the interior of ring-ditch 604 near the southern arc of the ditch (Fig. 8).

Sherds of at least four Deverel-Rimbury Urns, broken before deposition, were also found in the bottom of this ditch; no associated bone was recovered and it is not certain whether their deposition in this context was part of a burial ritual

or they were simply discarded as surplus to requirements. Ring-ditch 032 (W267) contained a primary cremation burial, 041, in a Deverel-Rimbury Urn at the centre of the monument and a possible second cremation, 051, outside the ring-ditch to the south-west (Fig. 9). Two other possible cremations were identified between ring-ditches 417 and 418, one unaccompanied, 507, and the other, 508, associated with Collared Urn fragments (Fig. 5).

The original number of cremations cannot be estimated, as large areas of the site were not investigated. Only four of the six ring-ditches within the field were partially investigated and additional unmarked burials not directly associated with these monuments may have existed, as possibly indicated by the recovery of a few sherds of Collared Urn during fieldwalking some distance from the ring-ditches (Fig. 4).

The dating of the cremations at this site raises several questions (Mepham, this volume). Collared Urns occur alongside Deverel-Rimbury type urns in secondary contexts within ring-ditch 417. In addition, small fragments of Collared Urn were found beneath the putative mound of ring-ditch 417, the construction of which has been dated to 3650±80 BP (HAR–9139) providing a *terminus post quem* for the use of this type of pottery on this site; this date falls at the beginning of the range for Collared Urns (Longworth 1984).

A very late date for the use of Collared Urns is indicated by the radiocarbon date of 2890±60 BP (HAR–9143) from charcoal associated with the cremation within one of the secondary urns. While Longworth suggests that Collared Urns might continue in use after c.2900 BP (1984), Burgess positively disputes this, suggesting a more likely date for their demise in the 13th century BC (c.3200 BP) (1986). There is no obvious reason to doubt the authenticity of the Field Farm date and, unless one argues for reuse of the urn, for which there is no discernible evidence, it clearly lends some support to the former thesis, al- though, taking account of the calibrated range at 2σ, the point might just be stretched. This late date also falls outside the latest date suggested for the decline of the Deverel-Rimbury material (Barrett 1976).

While the Collared Urn date appears to push the use of this type of urn beyond the end of the Deverel-Rimbury period, the date for the urn of Deverel-Rimbury type from ring-ditch 604 (3690±100 BP (HAR–9140)) indicates a very early date for the use of the latter (Barrett 1976). The large standard deviation suggests that the date should be treated with some caution but, even taking the extreme of the calibrated range at 2σ, the date is one of the earliest known for this type of pottery and is comparable only to the date from the cremation urn beneath Worgret Barrow, Dorset of 3690±90 BP (NPL–199).

Both types of urn appear, therefore, to have been in use throughout the period of cremation burial at this site. Generally, the distribution of these two urn types is thought to be mutually exclusive even in the same cemetery (Barrett 1976; Bradley 1984), and on the whole this pattern holds true at Field Farm. Collared Urn sherds are found beneath the postulated barrow mound of ring-ditch 417 and around the edge of the mound, while the middle Bronze Age urns are found as secondary burials in the side of the mound, but also exclusively associated with the smaller ring-ditch monuments.

Some differences in burial practices are evident. The Collared Urn fragments from beneath the barrow, possibly associated with a small amount of cremated bone, suggest less emphasis on containing the burial.

This contrasts with the later secondary burials which both contained cremated bone within urns, one inverted and the other upright, and were also accompanied by other grave objects. In all cases, based on the weight of bone present, there appears to have been some sorting and selection of bone prior to burial with only a sample being included. The inclusion of grave-goods appears to be unusual with Collared Urns, especially exotic objects such as those from Urn 524.

The Deverel-Rimbury cremations vary in quantity of bone and represent mostly single burials, except in the case of cremation 627 from ring-ditch 604 where two individuals were identified. There does not appear to be any discernible difference between those cremations in urns and un-accompanied cremations, which may have been buried in bags or simply placed in holes in the ground. A third type of ritual may perhaps be inferred from the apparently deliberate deposition of four broken urns without associated bone in the base of ring-ditch 604.

In the middle Bronze Age the area appears to have been more open, although some oak woodland still survived. The plant remains suggest grassland characteristic of abandoned grazing or arable, while the increased range of wood species represented in the charcoal samples indicates further clearance of the oak forest with some scrub regeneration.

Later Bronze Age
The environment of the Late Bronze Age period appears unchanged from the earlier phase of occupation. Evidence for activity at the site in this period is patchy and incomplete and is characterised by a number of pits and post-holes. These features are perhaps best seen in the context of the adjacent Knight's Farm settlement (Bradley *et al.* 1980), which may have formed the nucleus of the settlement, while the features recorded in the Field Farm investigations may represent more marginal activities.

While it is not possible to be certain about the overall distribution of features at this site they do appear to be in more widely distributed clusters than at Knight's Farm, the greatest concentration, including the feature or recut in the silted-up ditch, occurring near the south and east side of ring-ditch 417.

The Saxon cemetery, by C.A. Butterworth and H. Rees

Extent and arrangement of the cemetery
Although there is common observation and agreement that Anglo-Saxon cemeteries were frequently sited on or near earlier prehistoric ritual monuments, usually barrows (eg. Dickinson 1973, 248), and that this may be regarded as a way of defining territorial rights (Jarvis 1983, 132), there seems to be no consistent arrangement of the cemeteries in relation to those earlier monuments. In some cases the burials have respected the earlier structure and been set around or outside it. In others, as at Field Farm, the cemetery has apparently extended across the earlier barrow mound, often, as also probably happened in this case, with later loss of graves through erosion of the monument (*see below*). Whether the earlier barrow may have suffered some alteration to adapt it for reuse could not be determined in this instance.

No evidence was discovered of posts, ditches or other structures which might have enclosed the cemetery. The probable western and eastern limits of the cemetery may, however, have been indicated by the excavated graves; 494, 279, 432 and 453 at the west and 358, 325, 323, 320 and 458, possibly with 61 and 140, to the east. The southern and, more particularly, the northern limits were less clearly indicated, but a roughly rectangular area approximately 60 m long and 22 m wide, would be formed by the addition of east–west boundaries immediately south of Graves 453 and 423 and north of Grave 87. No graves were found beyond these limits during the excavation nor during the watching brief as the surrounding area was stripped.

There is reason to suppose that the 50 graves recorded may not represent the original number of graves in the cemetery, however, since the plan of the excavated graves reveals a large central area empty of burials. The schematic section demonstrates the rising grave bases from the inner southern edge of the ditch toward the centre (Fig. 22), an arrangement which suggests that the graves were cut into a central mound extant at the inception of the cemetery. From this, the presence of further burials in the centre of the ring-ditch may be inferred, although their disposition may not necessarily have been on the closely-spaced and well laid-out basis of those surviving graves excavated within the southern arc of the ditch.

If the graves were arranged across the centre of the ring-ditch in similar density to those excavated, at least another 30, perhaps as many as 50, may have existed. This assumes that the cemetery did not extend beyond the limits already suggested; although no boundaries or other signs of enclosure were recorded there seems no reason to suppose that the cemetery was indeed more extensive.

The absence of graves from the rest of the inner perimeter of the ditch, that is from the area between the limits of the cemetery as suggested above and the inner edge of the ditch, is difficult to explain. If the earlier monument was recognised as a place suitable for Saxon burials it would seem reasonable for the whole of the enclosed area to be favourably regarded, unless, perhaps, there was some change of opinion as to the suitability of burial inside or outside the ditch or some choice was offered to individuals as to where they were to be buried.

The cemetery was not a large one and it would easily have been possible for the graves outside the ditch to have been placed inside it, even if the central area was not available (either because it was already occupied or because it was not to be disturbed) and had this remained an acceptable choice for all people at all times.

Unfortunately one way by which this difficulty might have been resolved, that is by establishing a relative chronology for individual graves and thus determining the area(s) of the earliest graves, is not available because of the lack of securely datable grave-goods. If it may be assumed that the earliest were placed inside the ditch, on the still upstanding barrow mound, then one reason for a move outside it might be a change in the religious beliefs of those responsible for the cemetery (*but see below*).

Orientation

The graves at Field Farm followed two main orientations, approximately north–south and east–west; the deviation of the grave in degrees from north is shown in Figure 22. Although the orientations of the burials remain unknown in most cases they were sometimes indicated by the positions of the grave-goods; in the ten approximately north–south graves where this was possible the heads were at the south (Fig. 22). Most of the north–south burials, 22 out of a total of 33, were in the southern interior of the ring-ditch, the most well-ordered part of the cemetery.

Whilst the idea of a precise one-to-one correlation between grave orientation and the religious beliefs of its occupant may have been discredited (Rahtz 1978), it is possibly of some significance that the east–west orientated graves are more peripheral, both inside and outside the ditch; even the four east–west graves within the ditch and nearest to the centre of the monument, 61, 365, 194 and 325, are also close to the suggested cemetery boundaries.

It remains possible that such a change in orientation, together with the simplicity of the grave-goods and their generally low numbers may indicate that the occupants were Christian but were only slowly relinquishing former burial practices. The inner peripheral graves at Field Farm might represent the earliest converts to the new beliefs, perhaps not yet too concerned that they were buried inside a pagan monument or content to be buried there since other family members were. The graves outside the ditch might then be the result of a deliberate decision of disassociation from the inner area, placed close to the other graves but not within the earlier monument, the north–south graves outside the ditch perhaps belonging to those who still held to the old beliefs.

The presence of grave-goods would not necessarily invalidate any proposition that the cemetery may have been in part Christian; it has been suggested elsewhere (Meaney and Hawkes 1970, 53) that many of the so-called grave-goods from later cemeteries were only such items as might have been generally worn or carried when the person was alive. It may be of significance to an argument for a partly Christian cemetery to note that all of the spear burials are inside the ditch, that is in the postulated 'most pagan' part of the monument, and are orientated north–south.

Patterning within the cemetery

Without the evidence of skeletal material, identification of the sex and age of the occupants of the graves is totally reliant on the associations of the grave-goods. Eight graves, 146, 148, 202, 213, 220, 238, 323 and 350 (that is, those containing spears), of the 50 can be identified as male and another four, 126, 204, 241 and 365, may be added if steels and long knives are regarded as diagnostic. Of these only the two graves containing shield-bosses are necessarily those of fully adult males (Pader 1980, 149). In this connection, it is worth noting that the spearhead, knife and steel from Grave 238 are rather small in size and could have belonged to a juvenile (eg. Cook and Dacre 1985, 91); the grave itself is of average size.

Only three graves, 140, 149 and 194 were identified as those of females, with possibly one other, Grave 61, which contained a knife and shear set. All of the eleven sexed burials (eight males and three females) were within the ring-ditch, together with four of those less securely identified (two males and two females); only two graves outside the ditch were tentatively identified, both thought to be male burials.

Unfortunately this may reveal more about Anglo-Saxon customs concerning the deposition of grave-goods than it does about the sex/age structure of the Anglo-Saxon population at Field Farm, but it may be of some significance that the richer and therefore more sex-diagnostic graves are clustered towards the middle of the cemetery, within the boundary of the ring-ditch. Whilst it is possible that this may reflect a difference in social status between the burials in the centre and those on the periphery (Arnold 1980), it is also possible that it may indicate a later date for the peripheral burials (*see above*).

The generally well-ordered arrangement of the graves in the southern interior of the ditch may be an indication that these were more closely contemporary burials than the smaller, more isolated groups elsewhere. It is notable that no two graves were superimposed anywhere in the cemetery and it must be assumed either that they were individually marked or that they remained clearly visible, perhaps as mounds, during the life of the cemetery. Within this area the cluster of identifiable male burials inside the ditch (Fig. 22) may represent a more closely linked group, perhaps of physically related individuals or an otherwise distinct group; since spears were buried only with free men (Swanton 1973, 3) this indicates at least one area shared in common by the group.

Within this broad group occurred a smaller sub-group of three, possibly four, graves, 145, 146, 147 and 144, the last a little to the east of the first three, all four set close inside the southern edge of the ditch. These graves were very similarly aligned and all four were orientated rather more directly north–south than were the other graves of the larger group. Grave 146 was the only positively identified burial of this sub- group (a male). These graves may have been a family group.

Other small and less coherent groups lay outside the southern perimeter of the ditch. The largest of these consisted of three approximately east–west orientated graves, 124, 126 and 127, with a possibly related pair, 125 and 455 aligned slightly differently just to their south. Grave 126, in the centre of the group, has been suggested as a possible male burial since it contained two knives, one a long knife of a type of 7th century date. A pair of north–south graves, 256 and 320, in Trench L, one a male burial with a spear and shield-boss and the other unidentified but containing a small ceramic vessel, lay close together in an otherwise relatively deserted part of the cemetery.

Finally two rather 'ragged' possible groups occurred toward the south western corner of the cemetery, one of three east-south-east– west-north-west graves, 293, 295 and 431, the other of two, possibly three, graves almost exactly at right angles to the first three, Graves 204, 206 and 279. Only Grave 204 of the second group, which contained a knife and steel set, was identified as a possible male grave. These grave-groups may also have held family groups.

The graves
Throughout the cemetery the graves varied considerably in size and shape. Although most graves were approximately rectangular in plan, in only a few were the corners sharply defined, in some one end was well-formed and the other less so and in the remainder irregular, often almost oval outlines prevailed. In a very few instances (eg. Grave 146 and possibly Grave 87) the graves appeared to taper toward the foot. There was little differentiation through depth, shallow graves were as well- or ill-shaped as deeper ones. It has been suggested that more regular, square-cut graves may have held coffins (West 1988, 6), on which basis graves such as 238 and 362 might have contained them, although no evidence of wood stains or coffin fittings was found in either. There were indications of possible coffins in four of the graves, however, Graves 204, 281, 325 and 453, but only in 204 and 325 was the evidence anything more than nebulous, taking the form of darker soil along the lower sides and across the base of the graves (Grave 204 was well-defined, trapezoid in plan; 325 was not fully excavated but appeared oval in plan as far as could be seen). No recognisable evidence of coffin fittings was recovered from any grave, regular in outline or otherwise, although a few unidentifiable iron fragments in some graves may have been such. There was no evidence of any structural features within the graves.

The graves ranged in size from the largest, 281, at 2.20 m x 1.30 m to 428, the smallest at 1.14 m x 0.58 m; the size and shape of some graves suggests that not all inhumations were extended. The depths of the graves generally decreased the nearer they were to the centre of the ring-ditch, although this was not always the case; Grave 323, the shallowest grave at only 0.05 m deep, was next to the inside edge of the ditch (and to the deepest grave, 281, 0.60 m deep). The bases of some graves were not level; this usually occurred inside the ring-ditch where the lower end of the grave was always at the south, toward the ditch, but an uneven base was noted in Grave 279 outside the ditch, where the southern end of the grave was again lower.

3 Excavation at Shortheath Lane, Abbotts Farm, Sulhamstead

by S.J. Lobb

1 Introduction

In April 1985, while digging out a trench to connect a new water pipe to a trough at the edge of a field adjacent to Shortheath Lane, several large sherds of a Bronze Age urn were found by the farmer, Mr Richard Massey. The finds were reported to Reading Museum and Art Gallery and the Museum archaeologist, Leslie Cram, visited the site. It was clear that the sherds had come from a vessel which was still largely intact and visible in the section of the trench. An area large enough to remove the urn intact was excavated and a second urn was noted in the section of the excavated trench. Lack of time prevented further excavation, at that stage, to remove this second urn.

Because of the small area around the urns, about 5 m between the road and the fence line, and because of the possibility of more disturbance to the area, it was decided that further excavation should be carried out to establish the extent of the urns and their state of preservation. Accordingly, a small excavation was mounted over one weekend by the Trust for Wessex Archaeology and the Berkshire Field Research Group, as part of the Kennet Valley Survey.

The land around the site has been entirely extracted for gravel leaving only the roads and buildings intact, with little or no archaeological observation and recording (Fig. 23); consequently the immediate context of the site remains largely unknown. Stray finds from the gravel workings suggest a background of Neolithic activity in the area and a ring-ditch was exposed during topsoil stripping in the field adjacent to the site, about 400 m away from the excavated area. This feature was destroyed without further archaeological investigation, but, in this location, it is likely to have been the remains of a barrow. There is an extant barrow and a ring-ditch on the same contour as the site, in Poors Allottments less than 1 km to the south-west, and a small barrow cemetery in a similar locality on the Plateau Gravels about 2 km to the south. A few sherds of Bronze Age pottery are recorded from the churchyard 400 m to the east.

2 The excavation

An area of about 3 m by 4 m was excavated on each side of the water trench in the available area between the road ditch and the fence line (Fig. 23). A low bank (0.50 m high), created by the upcast from the road ditch, covered most of this strip and sealed the burials. The road verge was covered in scrub growth and several tree stumps indicated that large trees had been growing along the road edge in the past. Both the bank and the vegetation cover had clearly provided suitable habitat for rabbits and there was much evidence of burrowing both within and below the bank.

There were no indications of burials in the area to the west of the water pipe but seven further urns (making eight in total) and two possible unaccompanied cremations were identified in the eastern half of the trench, in an apparent linear arrangement running in an east west direction along the contour. A large tree stump at the eastern edge of the trench prevented further excavation in this direction but pottery from another probable urn, 71, was found under the section suggesting that the line of burials continued in this direction. It was not possible to excavate fully the eastern end of the trench in the time available.

The burials were found in an area about 3 m long and 2 m wide. The whole area had been severely disturbed by tree root activity and by burrowing and, in many cases, pottery and soils had been dislodged and the edges of features obscured. In addition, it was clear that the uppermost levels of the urns had been removed in antiquity, possibly by ploughing, which may also account for the fragmentary nature of one or two of the urns. Urns 42, 51, 59 and 72 were all inverted and the bases of the pots had been removed, although some base sherds were found in the fill of Urn 72. Urn 41 was upright and about half of the rim had been lost; this vessel was apparently a later insertion as it had truncated and pushed aside the sherds of Urn 59. Urn 50 was rather fragmentary with only the very top of the vessel represented (about half of the rim circumference) perhaps suggesting that it had originally been inverted. This vessel apparently contained a very abraded small cup. Urns 70 and 71 appeared on the surface to be fragmentary but both were left unexcavated.

Most of the urns had been inserted into shallow pits and all contained cremated bone. Small quantities of cremated bone were also found in the soils around and below some of the inverted urns (72, 59 and 51). The cremated bone, 15, adjacent to Urn 51 may be surplus bone which could not be fitted into the urn, or it is possible that it represents a separate burial. Similarly the cremated bone, 29, around the northern edge of Urn 50 may be an earlier burial truncated by the insertion of the urn, or it is possible that it had been packed around the edge of the vessel at the time of burial.

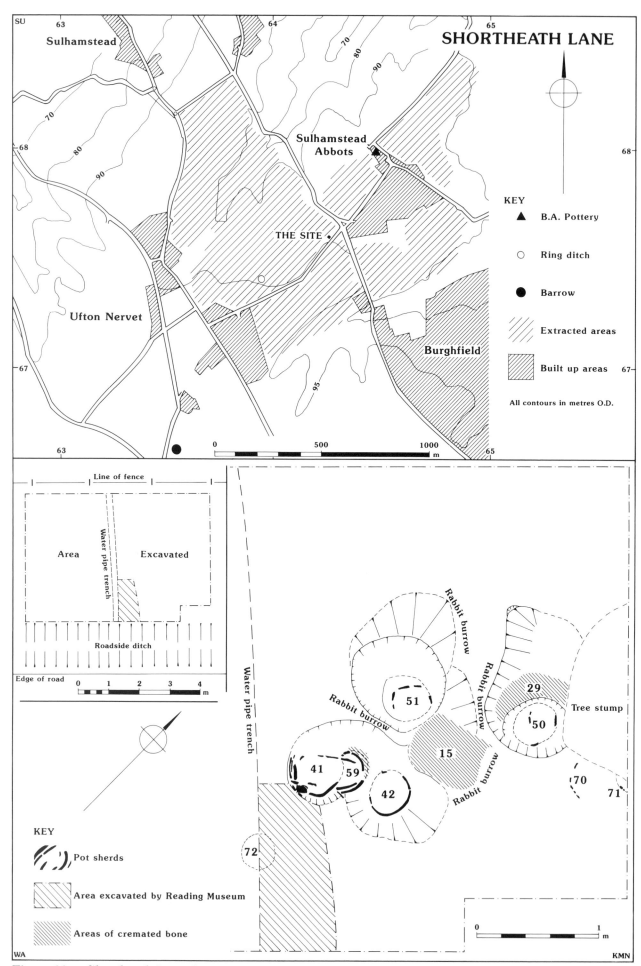

Figure 23   Shortheath Lane: location of site and trench plan showing features excavated

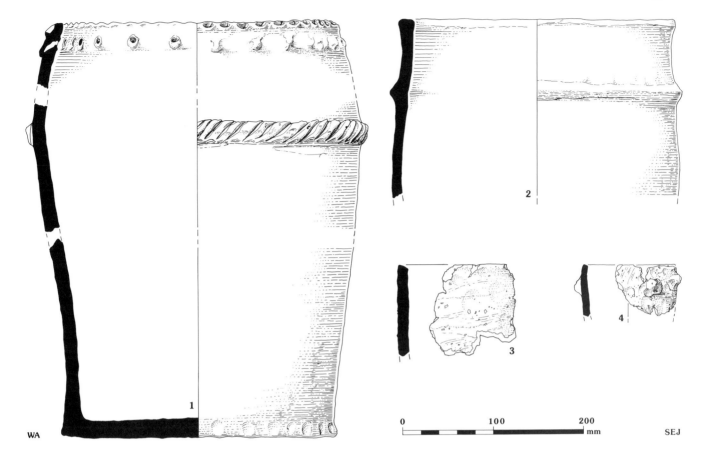

Figure 24   Shortheath Lane: pottery

Patches of ashy soil and burnt flint, as well as small quantities of charcoal, were noted in and around some of the urns although there was no indication of burning *in situ*.

3   The Finds

The Urns

A total of 680 sherds, including the urns, weighing 35.69 kg were recovered and four fabrics were identified by Lorraine Mepham. Details of the weights can be found in the archive.

Fabric 1 Soft, moderately coarse fabric. Moderate (10–15%), poorly-sorted, subangular, burnt flint grits <5 mm; sparse (5–10%) rounded quartz grains <0.5 mm; rare (<5%) mica. Dark brown to dark brown/grey matrix. Surfaces smoothed to disguise inclusions.

Fabric 2 Moderately hard, very coarse fabric. Common, poorly-sorted, subangular burnt flint grits <7 mm; sparse rounded quartz grains <0.5 mm. Dark brown to dark brown/grey matrix. Surfaces smoothed.

Fabric 3 Hard, very coarse fabric. Common (20–25%), poorly-sorted, subangular burnt flint grits <6 mm; rare rounded quartz grains <0.5 mm. Dark grey to black matrix. Surfaces smoothed.

Fabric 4 Moderately hard, coarse fabric, oxidised throughout. Common, poorly-sorted, subangular burnt flint grits <6 mm; rare rounded quartz grains <0.5 mm. Surfaces smoothed.

Fabrics 1–3 were used for the identifiable urns. Fabric 4 is represented by a few sherds (thirteen sherds; 212 g), found in the vicinity of Urns 70 and 71, and may indicate a further vessel possibly disturbed by subsequent burials.

Discussion, by Ann Woodward

Five burial urns could be reconstructed in part and are illustrated in Figures 24 and 25, 1, 2, 5–7. The vessels belong to the lower Thames Valley series of middle Bronze Age ceramics defined by Ellison (1975). These equate to Ellison fabric codes 2/3LF and 2MF.

1.   Urn 41 (Fig. 24, 1). Large upright urn with slightly curving body profile and a wide applied shoulder cordon decorated with broad diagonal incisions to form a cabled effect. The rim is slightly expanded externally and bears a row of spaced fingertip impressions on the outer top surface. Below the rim is a row of

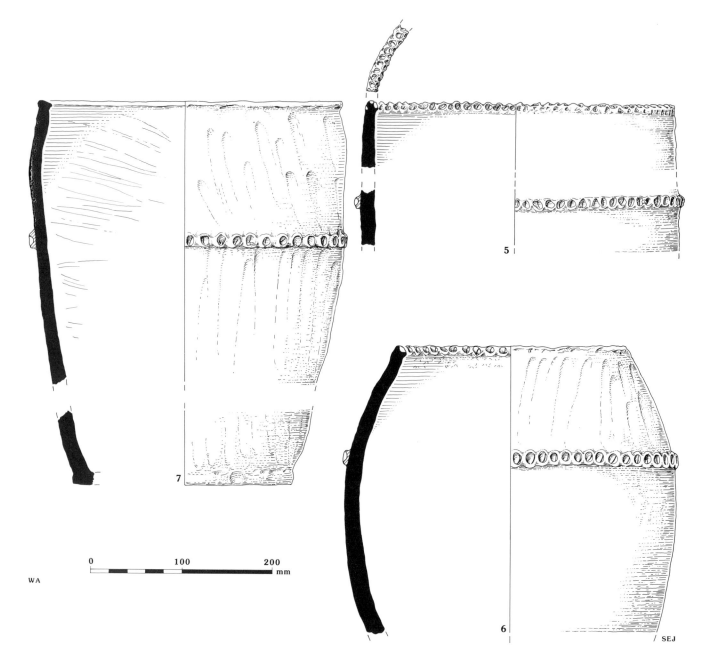

WA

0   100   200
mm

Figure 25   Shortheath Lane: pottery

circular holes, pierced from the inside before firing, not quite penetrating the body but giving rise to a row of irregular protrusions on the outer surface of the vessel. Fabric 1; Ellison fabric 2 S/MF. Lower Thames Valley type 3.

2. Urn 42 (Fig. 24, 2). Upper portion of a plain urn of slightly biconical profile with a flat externally expanded rim and a raised plain cordon a short way below the rim. Fabric 3; Ellison fabric 2/3LF. Lower Thames Valley type 5.

3. Urn 51 (Fig. 25, 6). Upper portion of an urn with smooth ovoid profile. The simple rim bears a row of closely-spaced fingertip impressions while, above the point of

maximum diameter, there is an applied horizontal cordon decorated similarly with fingertip impressions. Fabric 3; Ellison fabric 2/3LF. Lower Thames Valley type 5.

4. Urn 59 (Fig. 25, 5). Upper portion of a straight-sided urn. The slightly inturned rim is decorated with three rows of fingertip impressions located on the outside of the rim, the top of the rim and on the slight internal bevel. A short way below the rim is an applied fingertip-impressed horizontal cordon. Fabric 2; Ellison fabric 2/3LF. Lower Thames Valley type 7.

5. Urn 72 (Fig. 25, 7). Straight-sided urn, almost complete, with slightly inturned neck and a T–shaped rim with very slight internal bevel.

Some way down the vessel is an applied horizontal cordon decorated with spaced fingertip impressions. Fabric 2; Ellison fabric 2/3LF. Lower Thames Valley type 7.

The three styles of urn represented at Sulhamstead, cordoned Bucket Urns (LTV type 7), sub-biconical cordoned vessels (LTV type 5) and an urn with a row of perforations (LTV type 3) are all common within the middle Bronze Age assemblages of the lower Thames and the fabric types represented are also quite typical.

Of particular interest are the two sub-biconical urns, one plain and one decorated. The decorated vessel (Urn 51, Fig. 25, 6) can be matched at Ashford, Middlesex (Barrett 1973, fig. 1,3) and by a series of remarkably similar vessels which remain unpublished. These include stray single urns from Woking, Surrey (Ellison 1975, pl. 61) and Frindsbury, Kent (*ibid.*, pl. 63).

Further examples come from the Sunningdale, Berkshire, cemetery (*ibid.*, pl. 47) and from Kimpton (Dacre and Ellison 1981, fig. 18, E2), both in assemblages of middle Bronze Age date. The form also occurs, albeit in an assemblage of smaller domestic vessels, at Pingewood, in contexts which have been ascribed to the Deverel-Rimbury/post-Deverel-Rimbury tradition of *c.* 11th century bc (Bradley 1985, 28 and fig. 7,1 and 4).

The plain sub-biconical vessel (Urn 42, Fig. 24, 2) can be paralleled from Hammersmith (Ellison 1975, pl. 56,2) and Sulham, Berkshire (*ibid.*, pl. 45,7) but is more closely matched in the middle Bronze Age assemblages of the upper Thames Valley such as Standlake, Oxfordshire (Atkinson 1947, vessel E).

Throughout the Thames Valley, slack biconical and sub-biconical urns form a major component of the middle Bronze Age assemblages, quite distinct from the Biconical Urns of the later early Bronze Age, and often characterised by cordons located above the point of maximum girth.

The forms of the Bucket Urns (Urns 59 and 72) are standard, as are the features of their applied fingertip cordons. However, aspects of their rim forms are quite unusual. The rim of Urn 59, decorated with multiple rows of fingertip impressions cannot be paralleled in known middle Bronze Age assemblages, although the general undulating 'pie-crust' effect is reminiscent of some late Bronze Age rim forms, for instance from Runnymede (Longley 1980, fig. 23, 87–9; fig. 32, 276; fig. 29, 228).

On the other hand, multiple rows of fingertipping at the rim is also a common characteristic of the earlier middle Bronze Age Barrel Urns of South Lodge type in Wessex. The slightly T–shaped rim of Urn 72 is seen on Barrel Urns too but also occurs in late Bronze Age vessels, as at Kimpton (Dacre and Ellison 1981, fig. 21, G2) and, in a more exaggerated form, in the plain ware assemblage from Furze Platt, Berkshire (Lobb 1980, 16, and fig. 25, 11).

The vessel with a row of part perforations, Urn 41, resembles no. 8 from Sunningdale (Ellison 1975, pl. 46), except that the cordon on the Sunningdale urn is decorated with fingertip impressions rather than diagonal incisions, and that the part perforations have been effected from the exterior rather than the interior. A vessel combining a row of (full) perforations and a diagonally-incised cordon was found at Acton, Middlesex (Barrett 1973, fig. 4,3), whilst a similar sharply-indented cordon may be found on an urn from Weybridge, Surrey (Ellison 1975, pl. 60).

Both the perforations and the massive cordon bearing diagonal incisions are found sporadically throughout south-eastern England in the middle Bronze Age and these features occur particularly in some of the East Anglian assemblages such as that from Grimes Graves, Norfolk (Longworth *et al* 1988).

Other vessels, by L.N. Mepham

In addition to the urns, the remains of at least three other vessels were identified (Urns 50 and 70).

1. Urn 70 (*not illustrated*). Represented by seven sherds of Fabric 3 (260 g), including one plain rim sherd, and the traces of an applied horizontal cordon, possibly finger-impressed (as Urns 51, 59 and 72). This vessel may belong to the cordoned Bucket Urn group (cf. Urns 59, 72).

2. Urn 50 (Fig. 24, 3). This urn was very fragmentary and abraded. It consisted of 48 sherds of Fabric 1 (705 g), including fourteen rim sherds indicating a diameter of 300±20 mm. There was no trace of a cordon or any decoration although only the top of the vessel survives; the vessel may belong to the cordoned Bucket Urn group.

Within the vessel was found the remains of a second, miniature vessel also in Fabric 1 (Fig. 25, 4), comprising ten sherds (94 g). This smaller vessel, with a rim diameter of 100 mm, was decorated with a row of irregular protuberances or bosses, just below the rim. A radiocarbon date of BP 3340±60 BP (Har–9141) was obtained from charcoal from the fill of the larger urn. Comparable early dates were obtained from two urns from Kimpton, although the validity of these dates is slightly questionable (Dacre and Ellison 1981, 201).

A few bossed cups are found amongst the Surrey Deverel-Rimbury material, in fabrics similar to the Bucket Urns, to which they appear to have been accessory vessels (Needham 1987, 111, fig. 5.8: 1). Two examples come from Farnham, where one was associated with a stapled disc (*ibid.*, 116).

Table 13 Shortheath Lane: cremated bone, sample weight, and results for sex and age

Context/ SF No.	Sample weight	Sex	Age
15/–	4.5 g	–	–
37/41	745 g	–	Adult
38/59	450 g	–	Adult
43/42	14.5 g	–	–
44/51	37 g	–	Adult
–/60	107.5 g	–	Adult
–/72	800 g	–	Adult

Cremated bone, by Janet Henderson

Seven samples from in and around urns were examined. One (context 12) contained residue only, one might or might not have been human (from Urn 42) and the remainder were a group of small collections of cremated human bone. All were poorly preserved and present in very small quantities. Analyses were attempted for bone identification, sex, age and details of cremation practice but very few conclusions could actually be made. A catalogue of the results obtained for each sample can be found in the archive.

The results for sex, age and sample weight are summarised in Table 13. A 'minimum number of individuals' estimate was not considered justifiable on the available samples.

Details of the bones present, the colour and size of the bone fragments may yield information concerning cremation practice. With this group, however, it should be noted that there were only two samples of sufficient weight for assessment (contexts 37, Urn 41 and Urn 72) and therefore any comments apply to them alone, not to the whole sample.

In both cases insufficient bone could be identified for a categorical statement to be made to the effect that 'elements of all parts of the skeleton were found'. Thus there were no indications of discrimination (in favour of the skull for example).

Most of the fragments were white in colour, with some pieces of blue-grey. This suggested that the cremations had been fairly complete.

4 Discussion

While it is impossible to draw many conclusions from such a small excavated area, it seems likely that the excavated urns were placed in a linear arrangement running along the ridge. However, other contemporary cremation cemeteries in the area tend to be more clustered in plan (Barrett 1973) and it is possible that this cemetery may have been of similar type. The extent of the cemetery was not determined but is unlikely to have been very extensive. Ellison's study of Deverel-Rimbury cemeteries has indicated that burials tend to occur in discrete clusters of 10–50 burials, although more than 25 is rare (Ellison 1980, 122).

Contemporary settlement can be found nearby on the lower ground of the gravel terraces about 4 km to the north-east and to the north-west of the site. However, because of the lack of fieldwork in the immediate vicinity of the site, it is not known if there was a settlement closer to the cemetery, although the few sherds of Bronze Age pottery from the churchyard about 400 m to the north-east may suggest more domestic activity.

In general, the stray finds from the plateau suggest very little occupation in the Bronze Age and the known monuments are all ring-ditches and barrows with assumed burial functions. This appears to differ from the pattern for the region where a close association between settlement and cemetery in the Deverel-Rimbury period has been suggested (Barrett and Bradley 1980, 251). In southern Wessex, the evidence suggests that there is a consistent distance between cemetery and settlement ranging between 50 and 100 m (Bradley 1981, 100). However, the Sulham cemetery, on the opposite side of the valley, appears to occupy a similarly isolated location and it is possible that these more marginal agricultural areas, but still prominent situations, were preferred for burial, relieving some of the pressure on the lower more fertile lands.

4 Archaeological Investigations at Anslow's Cottages, Burghfield

1 Introduction

In the autumn of 1984 Tarmac Roadstone (Southern) Ltd submitted a planning application for permission to extract sand and gravel from 20 hectares of land at Anslow's Cottages, Burghfield. At the time Berkshire County Council was formulating new policies towards archaeology, seeking assessment of sites of known or potential archaeological value as part of the planning process. There was little known archaeological information from the site itself but its potential was indicated by the density of finds and sites of prehistoric and Romano-British date from the neighbouring areas. Limited funds for archaeological evaluation of the site were provided by Tarmac Roadstone after the application was approved in the spring of the following year and the work began in May 1985, at the same time as site clearance for gravel extraction began.

Evaluation excavation was carried out in advance of and during removal of the overburden in the southern part of the application area. A small area adjacent to the railway was fieldwalked. In one of the evaluation trenches part of a well-preserved late Bronze Age timber structure was discovered, interpreted as a small landing-stage or jetty, built at the southern edge of a river channel. Signs were also found of possible associated occupation features on the adjoining river bank. Because of the potentially excellent state of preservation afforded by the wet ground conditions and the imminent threat of the site's destruction, it was clear that further excavation should be carried out.

Preservation *in situ* was neither practical, since the removal of gravel from the surrounding area would lower the water table thereby destroying the conditions which had preserved the site, nor economically viable because of the likely cost of compensation for the loss of income from the gravel. Further evaluation work was also carried out in the northern part of the site during the first season in order to assess the archaeological potential of the floodplain area.

A large-scale excavation was carried out between October and December 1985, followed by a second season in July and August 1986, unexpectedly made possible by the rescheduling of the gravel extraction programme. Both seasons of excavation focused on the river channel and occupation areas.

Situation

The site, located 3 km south-west of Reading, lay mostly within Reading Borough, but 5 hectares were in Burghfield parish in Newbury District. The area of the quarry was bounded by the River Kennet to the north, by the Reading to Basingstoke railway line to the east, by a CEGB transformer station to the south and by worked out gravel pits to the south-west (Fig. 26). The fields in the northern part of the site, closest to the Kennet, had been used as pasture; those to the south as arable land. The junction between the floodplain and the gravel terrace was broadly defined on the surface by a modern drainage ditch, 1575, running east-west across the site. Excavation revealed an old river channel beneath this ditch.

In the northern area, on the floodplain adjacent to the river, the gravel was covered by alluvial deposits. An auger survey carried out by Tarmac Roadstone showed that the gravel surface undulated considerably (Fig. 26). The positions of former river channels were indicated by deposits of deeper alluvium and peat between higher gravel islands; minor undulations were still visible on the surface in the northern fields, some of which were undoubtedly the result of changes in the course of the river. One abandoned loop of the river to the north survived as a lower-lying, marshy area; the north-eastern boundary of the site was also marked by an abandoned loop. Some of these changes may have been caused by the construction of the Kennet and Avon Canal and more recent management by the water authorities.

There was no significant variation in ground level between the northern and southern areas, although the edge of the terrace was indicated by the higher level of the gravel surface, generally 0.50–1.00 m above the floodplain gravel. The northern area was poorly drained; until recent times flooding, especially in the winter months, was common and in rainy weather the land soon became waterlogged, in part due to the high water table (0.50–1.00 m below ground surface, although it has probably varied over the years as a result of more rigid control by the water authorities).

On the floodplain, the deposits overlying the gravel varied between 0.35 m and over 2.50 m in depth and consisted predominantly of mixed clays; some peat was encountered in old river channels and more organic horizons were sometimes discernible amongst the clays. To the south, on the terrace, the gravel was overlain by a mottled yellowish loam (0.30 m deep) into which the archaeological features were cut. This layer was sealed by a dark brown humic silt (0.20 m deep) which also sealed the archaeological features and the silted-up river channel; this was subsequently interpreted as an old land surface. The area around

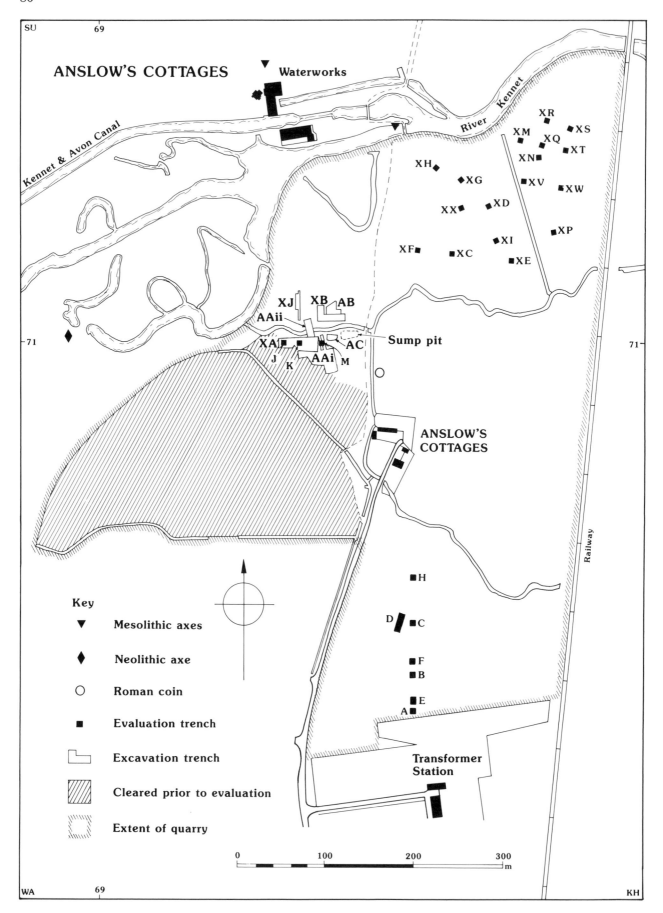

Figure 26   Anslow's Cottages: location of investigations

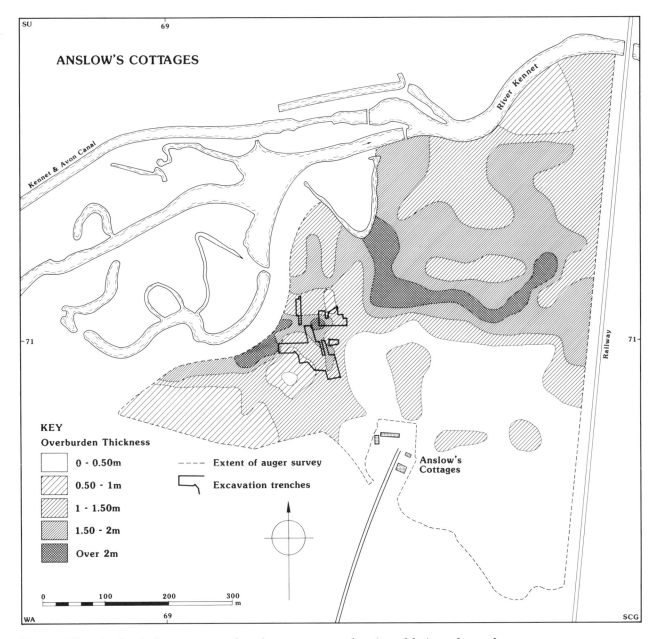

KEY

Overburden Thickness

☐	0 - 0.50m
▨	0.50 - 1m
▨	1 - 1.50m
▨	1.50 - 2m
▨	Over 2m

- - - - Extent of auger survey

⌐ Excavation trenches

0   100   200   300
m

Figure 27   Anslow's Cottages: results of auger survey showing old river channels

the excavation trenches was subsequently covered in a silty clay deposit, varying between 0.30 m and 0.70 m in depth, thought to have been laid down across watermeadows, traces of which were visible on the surface prior to topsoil stripping; this layer did not extend into the area to the east and south of Anslow's Cottages.

In more recent years the floodplain had been used largely as pasture for cattle grazing, while the drier ground to the south was used for arable agriculture from time to time.

Archaeological background

Direct evidence of archaeological activity from the site was previously limited to stray finds of a Roman coin, several Mesolithic flint axes from the river's edge and a single Neolithic flint axe (Fig. 26). This scarcity of evidence reflects earlier landuse, with no major disturbances and soil conditions which were not suitable for the formation of cropmarks. Much of the area immediately surrounding the site has been destroyed by gravel extraction without archaeological observation. However, a Bronze Age spearhead, an Iron Age cremation burial and Romano-British occupation material within and adjacent to old river channels have been found within 600 m of the site to the west and south-west (information from Berkshire SMR; Boon and Wymer 1958). Less than 1 km to the east, a burial in a hollowed-out tree trunk, radiocarbon dated to the 5th century AD, was found during gravel extraction (Chadwick 1981–2, 104). The intensive occupation of the gravel terrace further to the south in the Bronze Age and Romano-British periods has already been summarised in the introduction to this volume.

2 The Evaluations

Trenches A–H; XC–XI, XN–XT, XV–XX

Archaeological evaluation was carried out to establish the date, nature and extent of any archaeological activity on the site and to assess the nature of the alluvial deposits on the floodplain. Access to the site was allowed only after planning permission was granted and site clearance and gravel extraction had already commenced; initially, work was concentrated in areas under immediate threat of destruction. Fieldwalking was carried out over the southern part of the site, but very little artefactual material was recovered.

Shortly before the overburden was removed in the southern area eight small trenches, A–H, were excavated. Three trenches, J, K and M, were also excavated in the field to the north-west of Anslow's Cottages (Fig. 26). Subsequently, seventeen trenches, XC–XI, XM–XT, XV–XX, were dug in the nothern part of the site, on the floodplain adjacent to the river (Fig. 26). A brief summary of the evaluation results is given below; details are in archive.

Four ditches of Bronze Age and Romano-British date were excavated in Trenches C, D, E and G and two possible post-holes (undated) in Trench H.

One probably Romano-British ditch was identified in Trench XC. Two other ditches and a possible feature, all undated, were recorded in Trenches XN, XW and XX. No recognisable evidence of archaeological activity was recorded in the other trenches in the northern area, although high ground water levels were a problem during excavation. It may, however, perhaps be assumed that the area was always too wet for intensive use.

Trenches J, K and M

In the area north-west of the cottages three 2 m squares (Trenches J, K and M) were excavated on an east–west alignment at 25 m intervals (Fig. 26); Trench K was almost immediately enlarged by machine, the larger area renamed Trench L. The topsoil had already been stripped from the field in preparation for gravel extraction. A brief description of the trenches is given here but, since they formed the focus of the subsequent excavations, details of the archaeological features and deposits investigated are also integrated with the description of the main trenches.

Trench J, the eastern trench, contained no archaeological features, although a mixed assemblage of finds was recovered, including seventeen sherds of middle/late Bronze Age pottery, three sherds of late Iron Age or early Romano-British pottery, three knapped flints, some burnt flint, two pieces of fired clay and a few fragments of animal bone. All came from a single layer of greyish brown clay with sand lenses lying between 0.30 m and 0.60 m above gravel. Altogether up to 1.05 m of pale brown clays and silts, some with dense concentrations of mollusc shells, were present above gravel.

In Trench *K/L* (extended to an area approximately 9 m x 7 m) the removal of 0.35–0.70 m of greyish-brown silty clay subsoil revealed a number of post-holes, three ditches and the southern edge of a river channel. A darker coloured silt layer, almost entirely removed by machine but seen clearly in section, sealed the archaeological features south of the channel and the channel itself; this layer represented an earlier land surface and was more closely examined in the later excavation. Beneath this layer, but over the southern part of the trench only, was a pale yellow – brown silty clay into which the features were cut.

Excavation of a 2 m-wide section into the river channel led to the discovery of eight well-preserved upright wooden stakes *in situ* against the southern bank. The stakes formed two parallel rows about 0.50 m apart and the structure, as then visible, was apparently less than 2 m long overall (Plates 11 and 12). Horizontal timbers, irregular in size and shape and not apparently worked, were lying in and around the uprights and may have formed part of the structure, although there was no clear evidence of this. A small but almost complete late Bronze Age jar was found in dark organic silt sealing the stakes.

The deposits further out in the channel consisted of interleaved layers of tufaceous sand and gravel interspersed with occasional deposits of organic material (wood, from large branches to small twigs and/or roots, occurred throughout the channel). A ditch and an alignment of ten post-holes were identified, running parallel with the river channel and 2–3 m south of it. Cutting through the uppermost deposits at the extreme southern edge of the river channel (but also sealed by the old land surface) were two intersecting ditches. A late Bronze Age date was indicated for all of these features, although they were not all contemporary.

In *Trench M* three ditches were recorded, two of these being continuations of ditches in Trench K/L. The third ditch lay at the southern side of the trench and was not fully excavated. All were sealed by just over one metre of greyish brown silty clays. The southern edge of the river channel was also visible in this trench.

3 The Excavations

Strategy and method

The discovery of the river channel and the associated timber structure, together with the occupation features on the southern bank, dictated to a considerable extent the nature of the first season of excavation. The fact that planning permission had been granted and extraction was proceeding rapidly was a major influence on the excavation strategy, limiting the southward extent of the area available for excavation. Consequently, the two seasons of excavation concentrated on the area of the river channel and associated timber structures and the adjacent occupation features. The aims of the excavations were to establish:

1. The nature, extent and function of the timber structure identified in the evaluation
2. The nature of the river channel and the surrounding environment
3. The nature of the occupation features on the river bank.

Part only of the north-east corner of the field in which Trenches J–M had been located was available for excavation, most of the land to the south having been stripped down to the gravel shortly after the end of the first evaluation and the gravel subsequently extracted. Further restriction was placed on the location of trenches by the presence of an operational drainage ditch a few metres north of the evaluation trenches. In 1985 Trench XA was excavated in the area between evaluation Trenches J and M, encompassing Trench K/L (Fig. 26; Plate 9). Trench XB, which was some 20 m north-east of XA, and Trench XJ, approximately 21 m west of XB, were opened in the area to the north of the drainage ditch to allow further examination of the river channels.

The 1986 excavation aimed to investigate further the occupation features south of the river channel and more of the river channel deposits to the north in Trench XB. It was also hoped that stratigraphical and chronological relationships could be established between Trenches XA and XB, which had previously been separated by the modern drainage ditch. New trenches, AAi, AAii and AAiii, were all extended from XA: AAi and AAiii were to the south and east; AAii ran northwards from XA, across the former course of the drainage ditch (Fig. 26). Trench AC was opened to the east of Trench AAii. A sump pit dug by Tarmac in the extreme north eastern corner of the field was also examined. Trench AB extended northwards from Trench XB (Plate 10). Altogether about 2490 m² was opened for excavation during the two seasons.

The evaluation trenches in this area had identified an old land surface sealing the features and the river channel deposits. In Trenches XB, AB and AC, 0.50–1.10 m of soil, down to and including the old land surface, was excavated mechanically. Topsoil had already been removed from XA and AA before machining was started. In the south-western corner of XA all of the overburden and some of the gravel had previously been removed in preparation for gravel extraction.

Approximately 158 m² of the old land surface, 869, in the south eastern corner of XA, was left for excavation by hand. The trenches were all cleaned and planned before excavation started. All features were sectioned; sections were generally 1–5 m apart in the case of linear features and had a maximum width of 4 m in the case of the river channel. Smaller features such as pits or post-holes were usually completely excavated, although some features, thought to be patches of naturally occurring variable soil or animal disturbance, were only half-sectioned. Within Trenches XB/AB only small sample areas were excavated by hand.

Phasing and dating

Although a number of phases could be recognised while excavation was taking place within the river channel, considerable difficulty was experienced in establishing an overall sequence of events. This difficulty lay mainly in the nature of the deposits. There had clearly been numerous episodes of downcutting and deposition in many small channels within the main river channel; all of these small channels were shallow, discontinuous and inconsistent over short distances, with many separate episodes of erosion and deposition occurring within limited areas, often within depths of one metre or less. The length of time available for excavation limited the area that could be excavated, perhaps adding to the confusion by over-emphasising minor variations and obscuring the broader sequence which might have been more apparent in larger area excavation.

Attempts were made to dig the channel deposits stratigraphically in Trenches XA, XB, AAi and AC, but with only limited success, and any further such attempts did not appear to justify the amount of time they would have required. Even within the excavation trenches it was not possible to examine all of the channel deposits and this may, in some cases, may have compounded the problem. Finally, the drainage ditch and its precursors separating Trenches XA/AA and XB/AB appeared to lie at the junction of different soil types and obscured crucial relationships, making it difficult to link the two areas satisfactorily.

Samples from eight timbers, seven of which were *in situ*, were submitted for radiocarbon determination at the AERE Harwell Isotope Measurements Laboratory in an attempt to both clarify and date the sequence identified; the lack of artefacts from the river channel meant that there were no other means of dating. The resulting dates indicated more phases of water-related activity than had previously been identified. An additional sample from the wicker basket (SF.1093) in Trench AAii was submitted to the Oxford Accelerator for dating. Details can be found in Table 14.

On the basis of the pottery, radiocarbon dates and the stratigraphy, several phases were identified and are summarised below. These phases relate to recognisable archaeological activity, and it is acknowledged that alluviation within the river channel and on the floodplain began prior to the Bronze Age.

Plate 9   Anslow's Cottages: general view of Trench XA looking north-west, showing the very wet conditions experienced in 1985

Plate 10   Anslow's Cottages: general view of Trench AB looking south-west, 1986

Table 14 Anslow's Cottages, summary of dating evidence

| Ref. No. | Timber No. | Age BP | Calibrated date ranges | |
			1s	2s
HAR–9186	T94	2570±70	810–610 BC	840–510 BC
HAR–9179	T26	1670±60	AD 260–425	AD 230–540
HAR–9182	T366	1370±60	AD 630–675	AD 565–770
HAR–9183	T139	1390±60	AD 610–670	AD 550–760
HAR–9184	T77	1300±60	AD 660–775	AD 640–880
HAR–9186	T31	1030±70	AD 960–1030	AD 880–1160
HAR–9180	T358	930±60	AD 1020–1170	AD 990–1230
HAR–9181	T345	1030±60	AD 970–1025	AD 890–1155
OxA–2126	SF.1073	1060±80	AD 880–1035	AD 785–1160

The Harwell dates have been calibrated according to Pearson and Stuiver and Pearson (1986). The date from the Oxford Accelerator was calibrated using the program of CIO Groningen.

Phase 1: Bronze Age
1a: Track/hollow way 1091 leading to the edge of the river (Trench XA, AAi)
1b: Landing-stage 873 at edge of river channel radiocarbon dated to 2570±70 BP (HAR–9186); with possible associated post-hole alignment and interrupted ditches 93, 714 and 848 on the adjacent bank; burnt flint concentration 809 at edge of the river channel; occupation features to the south of the river channel (Trench XA, AAi)
1c: Infilling of southern river channel 871 (Trench XA)
1d: Ditch 874; ditch 362 (Trench XA)
1e: Ditch 875 (Trench XA)
1f: Ditch 908 (Trench XJ)

Phase 2: Romano-British
2: Stakes in hollow 688 within river channel (Trench XB); associated radiocarbon date of 1670±60 BP (HAR–9179)

Phase 3: mid Saxon (6th–7th centuries)
3a: Silting in base of river channel 648 containing unstratified timbers including T77 which produced a radiocarbon date of 1300±60 BP (HAR–9179)
3b: Shallow hollow 690 in channel 648 with sloping stakes (Trench XB)
3c: Stake-/post-settings 1595=1647, 1648; 1601=1644, 1645; 1602 (Trench XB/AB); associated radiocarbon date 1390±60 BP (HAR–9183)
3d: Stake-setting 1523 (Trench AAii); associated radiocarbon date 1370±60 BP (HAR–9182)
3e: Further infilling of part of northern channel 648 with coarse ?flood deposit of calcareous sand and gravel (Trench XB/AB), sealing timber structures

3f: Old land surface 869 with associated ploughmarks 870 (Trench XA, AAi) (*possibly Romano-British, see text*)
3g: Ditch 1019; pit 1176 (Trench AAi) (*possibly Romano-British, see text*)

Phase 4: late Saxon (10th–11th centuries)
4a: Wicker basket SF.1073 (Trench AAii) dated by radiocarbon to 1060±80 BP (OxA–2126)
4b: Stake-/post-settings 1594, 1646 (Trench XB/AB; associated dates 1030±70 BP (HAR–9186), 930±60 BP (HAR–9180), 1030±60 BP (HAR–9181)
4c: Final infilling of northern river channel (Trenches XB/AB, XJ)
4d: Peat formation sealing the river channels and extending onto the floodplain

Phase 5: medieval
5: Ditch 611 (Trench XB/AB)

Phase 6: post-medieval
6: Watermeadow system

Many of these phases were not stratigraphically related and the overall sequence is therefore extrapolated from the dates. Within all the phases of river channel activity there are areas of uncertainty. The phasing represents a broad sequence; some episodes of erosion and deposition were recognised in some areas; many went unrecognised. Only those linked to timber structures or features (eg, ditches) are included.

Within Phase 1 the sub-phases represent a sequence with 1a earliest and 1e latest; all sub-phases have been assigned to the later Bronze Age. It is possible that Phase 1a might be earlier, although there is no evidence for any associated earlier activity.

Phase 1f cannot be directly related to the other sub-phases but is thus assigned on the basis of a few sherds of pottery. It might, however, be later; its

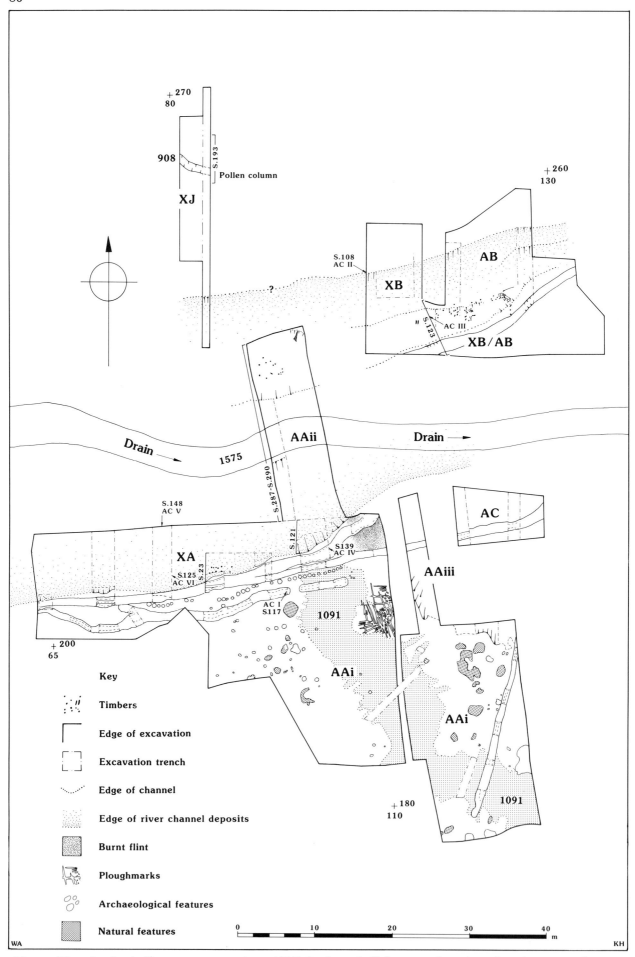

Figure 28   Anslow's Cottages: excavations 1985–6, plan of all features, location of environmental samples and illustrated sections

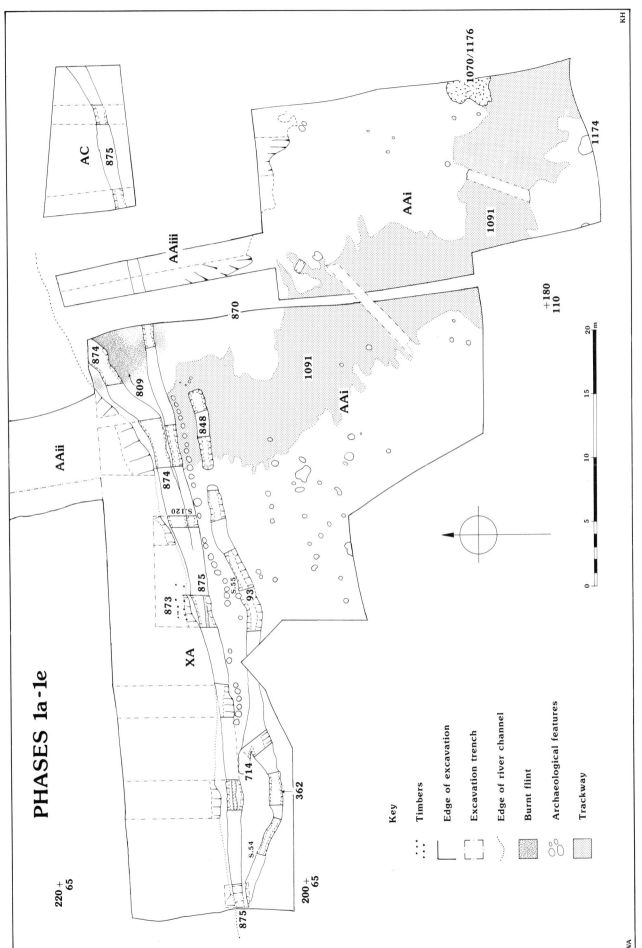

Figure 29 Anslow's Cottages: Phases 1a–1e, plan of features

stratigraphic location indicates that it is earlier than the channel containing the Roman timber, and the layer through which it is cut contained four sherds of later Bronze Age pottery.

Within Phase 3, sub-phases 3c and 3d may well be contemporary (Table 14) but they are not directly associated. Sub-phase 3a is stratigraphically earlier, but the radiocarbon date is very similar to those of 3c and 3d. Sub-phases 3e – 3g represent sequential phases post-dating sub-phases 3c and 3d.

The site: excavated features

The modern drainage ditch 1575, and a wide predecessor 1570, 1.15 m deep and 6.90 m wide (Figs 28 and 39, S.288), were located at the junction of higher, drier and better-drained gravel to the south, and the floodplain to the north, where the land was wetter and marginally lower-lying. The ditches appeared to follow the southern edge of a former river channel which was approximately 35 m wide and directed the course of a number of smaller channels, of which probably only one was in use at any one time. The edges of the small streams were difficult to define but they appeared to migrate within the overall channel. Other former river channels were identified in the gravel surface across the floodplain to the north.

Alluviation on the floodplain appears to have begun prior to the Bronze Age. Two channels in the gravel surface were identified at the base of the sequence in Trenches XB and XJ; these were both filled with silty sand and may represent the same channel. In Trench XJ approximately 0.40 m of fine clay silts had accumulated above the gravel, sealing the earlier channel and predating the cutting of ditch 908. These represent overbank flood deposits. Within the river channel, the lowest deposits were redeposited gravel and sand, indicative of fast flowing water.

Phase 1: Bronze Age

Phase 1a: Feature 1091
Terminating at, or interrupted by, the southern edge of the river on the eastern side of Trench XA was a band of dark brown clay, between 5–6 m wide, filling an irregular, shallow (0.27 m deep) feature, 1091, which curved south and eastwards out of the excavation trench (Figs 28 and 29); it was cut by all other features in the area. The edges of the feature were very irregular, showing as extending 'fingers' of dark, mineral-stained clay. The sides sloped gently down to a fairly level base, barely reaching the underlying gravel. Finds were few but included a number of small fragments of sandstone, not otherwise very common on the site; there were no datable artefacts. The primary fill in the deepest, central part of the depression was a thin layer of sand, not recorded in any other feature and the heavy iron-staining of the overlying clay suggests impeded drainage. The feature has been interpreted as a trackway leading to the edge of the river channel, the full extent of which is not known.

Phase 1b: Timber structure 873.
Ten, possibly eleven, vertical pointed wooden stakes were found forming part of a structure at the southern edge of the river channel (Figs. 29 and 30; Plates 11 and 12). The stakes were sealed by sands and gravels filling the upper levels of the channel (Fig. 40, S.23). They were set in two parallel rows, following the line of the bank. Four were set into the lower part of the bank (a possible fifth stake was found in an appropriate position to have formed part of this group but appeared to be a root, dividing as it entered the gravel); the other six stakes were c. 0.50 m further out in the base of the channel (Fig. 30). The overall span of the surviving stakes was 2.70 m, with distances between of 0.15–1.15 m. It is likely, however, that the widest gap, which was between pairs of stakes excavated in different trenches and at different times, may have been the result of an interposed pair having been lost by damage to the site in the period between the two excavations. West of the surviving stakes the bank

Plate 11   Anslow's Cottages: timber structure 873 (Phase 1b) at the southern edge of the river channel, with ditches 874 (Phase 1d) and 875 (Phase 1e) cutting the top of the bank

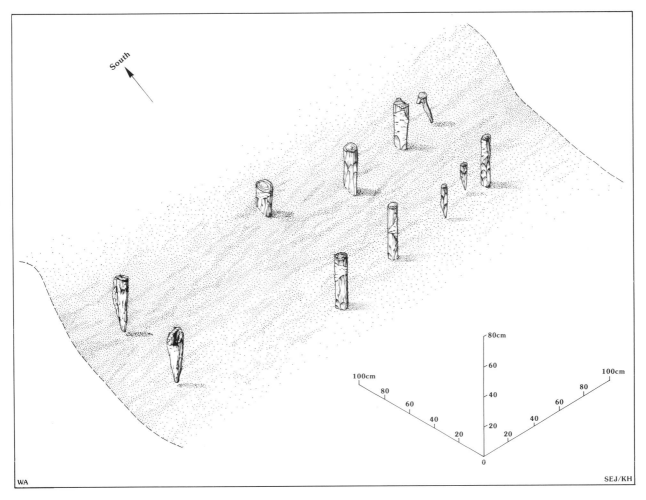

Figure 30   Anslow's Cottages: isometric drawing of timber structure 873 (Phase 1b)

curved southward, away from the apparent line of the structure, suggesting that some erosion may have occurred.

Two of the stakes were shorter and smaller in diameter than the remainder and were set in a mixed deposit of shelly sand, gravel and fibrous organic material which surrounded all of the larger stakes and filled the base of the channel. Except for the two short stakes, all of those found during the evaluation were damaged by vandals before they could be properly excavated; the other two, excavated later, were found to penetrate only 0.15 m into the gravel, which suggests that the mixed deposit described above may have already accumulated before these stakes (if not all of them) were inserted.

Some pieces of wood were found lying horizontally between and close by the vertical stakes, but these appeared to be neither worked nor attached to the uprights. Around the upper portions of the stakes, and more noticeably toward their eastern (downstream) side, was an organic, almost peaty, silt, probably the result of material accumulating in the slower moving water around the structure. This organic layer extended approximately 7 m to the west and 10 m to the east of structure 873, although there were no indications

of further stakes. One of the stakes (Timber 94) produced a radiocarbon date of 2570±70 BP (HAR–9168).

Post-hole alignment
On the river bank south of the landing-stage was a line of 31 irregularly spaced post-holes running roughly parallel with the channel (Fig. 29). Most of the post-holes were cut down through the silt overlying the gravel and were occasionally deep enough to cut into the gravel; ten post-holes at the eastern end of the alignment cut trackway 1091. The post-holes were set approximately 2 m back from the river's edge at the west side, the distance increasing to almost 4 m at the east. The post-holes were as little as 0.10 m apart in some instances, although more usually there was 0.20–0.40 m between them; wider spaces of slightly less than 1 m and 1.50 m were also noted and a large gap of c. 3.50 m occurred south and slightly west of timber structure 873. The post-holes extended approximately 8 m west and 14 m east beyond the surviving timbers, but the two westernmost post-holes were cut by ditches 874 and 875, and the alignment may originally have been longer.

The post-holes were usually 0.25–0.35 m in diameter (Table 15), with vertical sides and flat

Plate 12   Anslow's Cottages: timber structure 873 (Phase 1b); the horizontal timbers are not thought to be an integral part of the structure

bases. Three were slightly larger; two, 731 and 762, at the western end of the alignment, were 0.45 m and 0.50 m and a third, 769, 0.47 m in diameter; this last post-hole was near a terminal of interrupted ditch 93. All were filled with similar dark grey silty clay, sometimes charcoal-flecked and containing burnt flint fragments.

Ditches 93, 714, 848
Between 0.70 m and 0.90 m south of the post-holes and following the same alignment were at least two sections of an interrupted ditch, 23 m (west – 93 and 714) and slightly over 6 m (east – 848) long respectively (Fig. 29). The longer western section may have been further interrupted, but there was not sufficient space to investigate this. The ditches were cut down to the top of the gravel. The break between the ditches 93 and 848 occurred toward the eastern end of the post-hole alignment and was *c.* 1.20 m wide. There was no gap corresponding to the wide interval in the post-hole alignment. The western end of ditch 714 extended 3.60 m beyond the last post-hole, but the post-hole alignment appeared to have been truncated (*see above*). The eastern ditch terminal and the eastern end of the post-hole alignment coincided.

Both sections of the ditch were steep-sided and generally flat-bottomed (Fig. 38, S.55; Table 15).

The excavated ditch sections were all similarly filled with dark grey silty clay, although thin primary fills of darker, slightly organic silty clay were recorded in the base of some sections of 93 and of 848; burnt flint was also present in the base of 848.

Burnt flint concentration 809
In the north-east corner of Trench XA, adjacent to the edge of the river channel, was a dense spread of burnt flint and charcoal up to 0.20 m deep (Fig. 29). This deposit was sealed by the clean alluvial silt and clay layers which also extended over and beyond the edge of the channel in this area. The burnt material was interrupted by two later ditches, 874 and 875, but would originally have covered an area of at least 28 m^2; it did not extend as far east as Trench AAiii, but a similar patch of dense burnt flint was observed in the sump trench excavated by the gravel company about 12 m to the east and may represent a similar feature. There were no associated artefacts or features.

Other post-holes
Three groups of post-holes were found in the area south and east of the river channel; the largest group, 36 features, lay south of the post-hole alignment, the second, a smaller cluster of ten

Table 15 Anslow's Cottages: dimensions of aligned post-holes and related features in Trench XA

Feature No.	Type	Width (m)	Depth (m)
87	post-hole	0.38	0.29
93/714/848	ditch	0.90–1.30	0.50
95	post-hole	0.33	0.16
99	post-hole	0.39	0.21
101	post-hole	0.30	0.23
116	post-hole	0.40	0.26
118	post-hole	0.37	0.30
120	post-hole	0.43	0.29
122	post-hole	0.30	0.31
124	post-hole	0.30	0.27
165	post-hole	0.28	0.20
728	post-hole	0.36	0.38
729	post-hole	0.40	0.39
730	post-hole	0.31	0.43
731	post-hole	0.50	0.47
761	post-hole	0.29	0.39
762	post-hole	0.45	0.31
763	post-hole	0.32	0.27
764	post-hole	0.24	0.26
769	post-hole	0.47	0.22
774	post-hole	0.23	0.20
775	post-hole	0.30	0.31
776	post-hole	0.38	0.24
855	post-hole	0.35	0.17
856	post-hole	0.30	0.16
857	post-hole	0.33	0.10
858	post-hole	0.37	0.06
860	post-hole	0.33	0.15
861	post-hole	0.27	0.20
862	post-hole	0.23	0.23
863	post-hole	0.28	0.27
864	post-hole	0.24	0.20

features, was at the eastern side of AAi, and the third, an arc of four very shallow features, was recorded to the east of the terminal of ditch 848 (Fig. 29). Fifty-six possible post-holes were excavated, although at least five of these were probably the result of natural soil variations or animal disturbance. A number of other possible features were noted in the area south of Trenches XA/AA before the subsoil was stripped ready for gravel extraction but there was no opportunity to examine these before they were destroyed.

All of the post-holes were sealed by the old land surface (Phase 3f) as far as could be determined, but the fill of some was very similar to that layer and these could have cut it; some may have been truncated by it. In 1985, however, when part of the old land surface was excavated by hand, no features could be seen to cut it; in 1986 only two large features were thought to do so, a ditch and a pit (Phase 3g).

The post-holes ranged in diameter from 0.08 m to 0.40 m and in depth between 0.04 m and 0.34 m (Table 16). No obvious structural groups were discernible, although at least three possible lines of three/four regularly-spaced features could be recognised in the largest group. However, only an incomplete plan could be recorded, the area to the south and south-west having been destroyed by soil stripping in advance of gravel extraction. The second group was too small and too diffuse to show any evidence of coherent structures. The crescent of four very shallow features at the eastern end of ditch 848, all probably truncated, may represent a single structure. Fills, as with almost all features on the site, were dark grey or greyish brown silty clays, sometimes with gravel or burnt flint, and contained very few artefacts.

Pits
A number of possible pits were also examined; on excavation most of these appeared to be natural, sometimes mineral-stained, variations in the pale silty clay covering the southern parts of Trenches XA/AAi (Figs 28 and 29). Most were shallow, less than 0.25 m deep (Table 16), irregularly shaped and extremely poorly defined. (Where a feature was thought to be 'natural' it was not fully excavated). All of the features, natural and man-made, were filled with grey silty clay, usually stone free, occasionally with a few fragments of burnt flint. There were no finds from fifteen of 23 excavated features.

Pit 1174 contained an almost complete late Bronze Age upright jar, apparently *in situ*. The contents of the jar were excavated and sieved but disclosed nothing to signify its purpose. This pit extended beyond the trench section and was not fully excavated; the fill was not markedly different from the fills of features classed as natural.

Pit 1070/1176, an amorphous feature at the eastern edge of Trench AAi, may belong to this phase, if the character of the finds recovered from it is considered. The finds included large quantities of burnt flint and fired clay, the latter apparently burnt *in situ*. Pottery and some animal bone also were recovered, the fabric of the former being very similar to both that of Bronze Age pottery from elsewhere on the site and to the fired clay found in the pit. Stratigraphically, however, the feature is considered to be much later since it appeared to cut the old land surface, 869, of Phase 3f.

Phase 1c: infilling of river channel 871
Deposition of sand and gravel continued around and above timber structure 873 to a maximum depth of 0.70 m (Fig. 39, S.287; Fig. 40, S.23, S.148). Thereafter increasingly fine silts, with occasional

Table 16 Anslow's Cottages: dimensions of other excavated features in Trenches XA, XB and AAi

Feature No.	Trench	Type	Width (m)	Depth (m)	Feature No.	Trench	Type	Width (m)	Depth (m)
362	XA	ditch	1.40	0.40	1101	AAi	post-hole	0.36	0.22
611	XB	ditch	0.70	0.26	1102*	AAi	?pit	0.95x0.40	0.10
745	XB	pit	1.80	0.20	1103*	AAi	?pit	0.50	0.06
765	XB	post-hole	0.12	0.10	1104*	AAi	?pit	0.60	0.08
766	XB	post-hole	0.32	0.13	1106*	AAi	?pit	1.05x0.65	–
767	XB	post-hole	0.17	0.12	1110	AAi	post-hole	0.32	0.17
768	XB	post-hole	0.25	0.23	1112	AAi	post-hole	0.28	0.17
777	XB	post-hole	0.26	0.24	1114*	AAi	?pit	0.90	0.20
778	XB	post-hole	0.30	0.26	1116*	AAi	?pit	0.42	0.04
779	XB	post-hole	0.30	0.28	1118	AAi	pit	1.30x0.80	0.16
781	XB	post-hole	0.40	0.04	1120	AAi	post-hole	0.21	0.12
849	XB	post-hole	0.13	0.02	1122	AAi	post-hole	0.21	0.08
850	XB	post-hole	0.13	0.03	1124	AAi	post-hole	0.16	0.08
851	XB	post-hole	0.12	0.02	1126*	AAi	?post-hole	0.18x0.12	0.05
852	XB	post-hole	0.11	0.02	1128*	AAi	?post-hole	0.06	0.07
854	XB	post-hole	0.30	0.32	1130	AAi	?post-hole	0.23	0.12
859	XB	pit	0.62	0.09	1132	AAi	?post-hole	0.33	0.08
874	XB	ditch	1.0–1.50	0.36	1135	AAi	?post-hole	0.14	0.07
875	XB	ditch	0.60–0.70	0.60	1137	AAi	?post-hole	0.24	0.04
1019/1108	AAi	ditch	0.62–1.20	0.48	1138	AAi	?post-hole	0.20x0.15	0.07
					1140	AAi	?post-hole	0.20	0.15
1036*	AAi	?pit	1.40x1.20	0.04	1142	AAi	?post-hole	0.18x0.15	0.09
1038*	AAi	?pit	0.95x0.60	0.07	1144	AAi	post-hole	0.34x0.20	0.14
1040	AAi	?pit	1.0x0.45	0.04	1146	AAi	pit	0.60	0.18
1042	AAi	post-hole	0.08x0.06	0.04	1152	AAi	post-hole	0.33	0.29
1044	AAi	post-hole	0.15	0.07	1156	AAi	post-hole	0.17	0.14
1046	AAi	post-hole	0.30x0.23	0.18	1160	AAi	post-hole	0.23	0.06
1049*	AAi	?pit	1.40x1.0	0.14	1166	AAi	post-hole	0.31	0.22
1051	AAi	post-hole	0.23x0.18	0.05	1170	AAi	post-hole	0.18	0.26
1053	AAi	post-hole	0.18x0.16	0.14	1174*	AAi	pit	1.30	0.22
1055*	AAi	?pit	0.95x0.88	0.22	1182	AAi	post-hole	0.35	0.18
1065#	AAi	pit	0.58x0.30	0.23	1184	AAi	post-hole	0.30	0.10
1070/1176	AAi	pit	c.3.50	0.04	1185	AAi	post-hole	0.30	0.34
					1187	AAi	post-hole	0.24	0.28
1074	AAi	post-hole	0.40	–	1189*	AAi	?pit	0.72	0.18
1082	AAi	post-hole	0.24	0.13	1193	AAi	post-hole	0.28	0.18
1083*	AAi	post-hole	0.30	0.07	1234*	AAi	?pit	0.50	0.22
1084*	AAi	?pit	1.05x0.70	0.11	1244	AAi	pit	0.22	0.11
1085*	AAi	?pit	1.75x1.0	0.09	1251*	AAi	?pit	0.31	0.28
1086*	AAi	?pit	1.30	0.02	1258*	AAi	?pit	0.95x0.70	0.06
1087*	AAi	?pit	1.40x0.65	0.09					
1088*#	AAi	?	1.10	0.17					
1089	AAi	post-hole	0.30	0.20					
1090*	AAi	?post-hole	0.35	0.08					
1092*	AAi	?pit	1.90x1.25	0.12					
1099	AAi	pit	0.40	0.30					

* = natural feature (soil variation/animal disturbance)

= not fully excavated

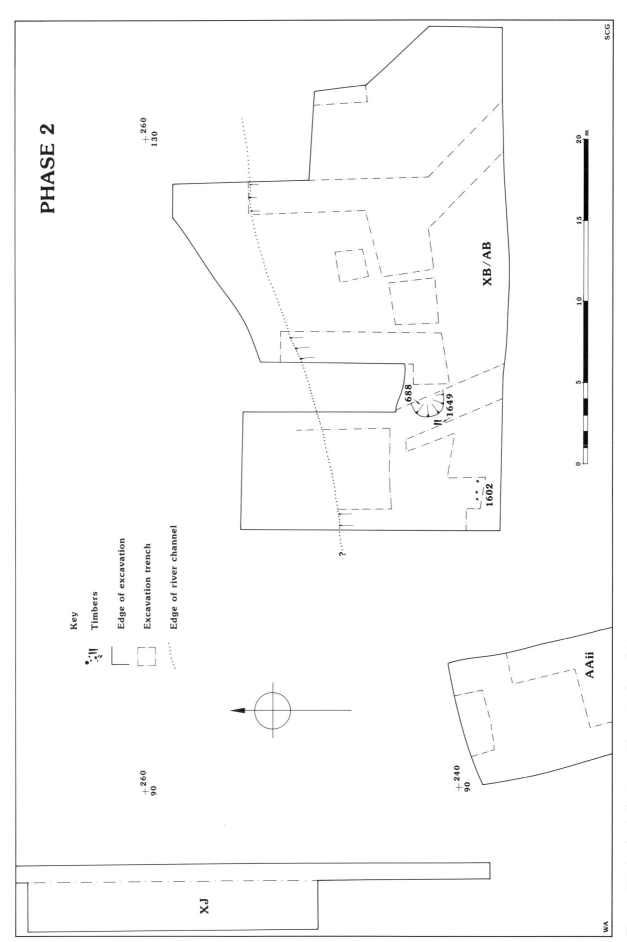

Figure 31 Anslow's Cottages: Phase 2, plan of features

lenses of coarse material, sealed the upper levels of the channel, suggesting a much slower flow of water. A possible northern edge to the channel was seen, in section only (Fig. 39, S.288), beneath the drainage ditch 1570, suggesting it had an overall width of about 17 m.

Phase 1d: ditch 362
A short length of ditch, 362, curved across the south-western part of Trench XA and cut the western end of the interrupted ditch 714/93 (Fig. 29); it was not seen to continue north of that ditch, however, and may either have terminated there or veered south-eastward out of the excavation area. It was cut by ditches 874 and 875. This feature was in an area very much disturbed by machine activity, but the deepest surviving section showed gently sloping sides and a rounded base (Fig. 38, S.54). The ditch was filled with greyish brown silty clay which became increasingly gravelly toward the base.

Phase 1d: ditch 874
North of the post-hole alignment, ditch 874 cut across the silts filling the upper levels of the southern edge of the earlier river channel; it also cut the burnt flint concentration 809 in the north-east corner of XA (Fig. 29). The line of the ditch curved from west to north-east across site, closely following the former course of the river. The ditch had a broad, flat base with quite steeply sloping sides (Fig. 38, S.120; Table 16). The primary fill was pre-dominantly dark, slightly gravelly silt; above this lay paler silty clays, occasionally interspersed with lenses of weathered material from the ditch sides. Some sections showed evidence of a possible recut toward the north side of the ditch, but this was not consistently recorded in all of the excavated sections.

Phase 1e: ditch 875
Cutting ditch 874 was a second ditch, 875, which followed a much straighter course across XA, diverging from 874 at the eastern side of the trench, through Trench AAiii and into AC, where it started to curve slightly to the north-east (Fig. 29). The ditch was narrower and more steep-sided than 874 (Fig. 38, S.120; Table 16) and was filled with homo-geneous dark grey silty clay, slightly darker and with some organic content toward the base in some sections. A shallow slot, 0.05 m deep and 0.12 m wide was recorded in some of the western sections of the ditch.

Phase 1f: ditch 908
Towards the northern end of Trench XJ a single ditch, 908, with an associated gravel bank, 910, was recorded (Figs 28 and 39, S.193). The ditch and bank curved from north-west to south-east, the bank on the northern side of the ditch; the ditch was 2.50 m wide and 0.70 m deep, the bank not more than 0.13 m high. This ditch, which contained no artefactual material, cut through fine floodplain deposits into the underlying gravel which contained three abraded sherds of pottery, possibly of late Bronze

Age date, suggesting a *terminus post quem* in this phase, but a later date (Roman) is not impossible. The fill was a humic silty clay, becoming more silty in its upper levels, indicating slow-flowing water, and was sealed by two peaty horizons separated by a thin silty layer; these are assumed to equate to the stable horizons defined as Phases 3f and 4d. A number of other small ditches similarly sealed by peat were observed but not recorded during soil stripping in advance of extraction in 1987.

Phase 2: Romano-British

Timber structure 1649
The earliest dated timber (Timber 26) in the northern channel complex, for which a radiocarbon date of 1670±60 BP (HAR–9179) was obtained, was one of two stakes lying parallel and almost horizontal in shallow depression 688 in Trench XB/AB (Figs 31 and 40, S.123; only one of these is on the section); another more steeply angled, unnumbered, timber is also shown in the section and may have been associated with the other two. The feature was not fully excavated because of the high water table, but appeared to be a discrete hollow in the base of the river channel, roughly circular in plan, with gently sloping sides and a flat base, 0.40 m deep and 2.30 m wide. The two parallel stakes may not have been strictly *in situ* in view of the angle at which they were lying, but their position relative to each other may have been maintained. The third timber may indicate the more likely original position of the stakes. All were in the upper fill of the feature, a shelly sand, above a similarly shelly silt filling the base.

Phase 3: Mid Saxon

Phases 3a and 3b: silting in channel 648
Partly sealing the southern edge of feature 688 was a layer of silty sand, truncated by another shallow sand-filled feature, 690, 2.12 m wide and 0.27 m deep, almost directly above 688 (Fig. 40, S.123). Sealing the northern half of 688 and also cut by 690, was a silty deposit in which an apparently random horizontal spread of large pieces of timber was found (Fig. 32). Some of the wood was worked and one of the timbers, a plank (Timber 77), provided a radiocarbon date of 1300±60 BP (HAR–9184). No worked timbers were recovered from feature 690 although an angled stake was visible in the section (Fig.40 S.123).

Phase 3c: timber structures 1644, 1645, 1647, 1648, ?1602
To the east of features 688 and 690 further groups of at least 35 possibly related timbers were found *in situ* (Fig. 33). One timber (Timber 366) from group 1647 produced a radiocarbon date of 1370±60 BP (HAR–9182). A row of three *in situ* timbers, 1602, none of which were dated, was recorded to the west of feature 690 and may belong to this phase. All except one of the eastern timbers were driven into gravel along what may have been the base of a

95

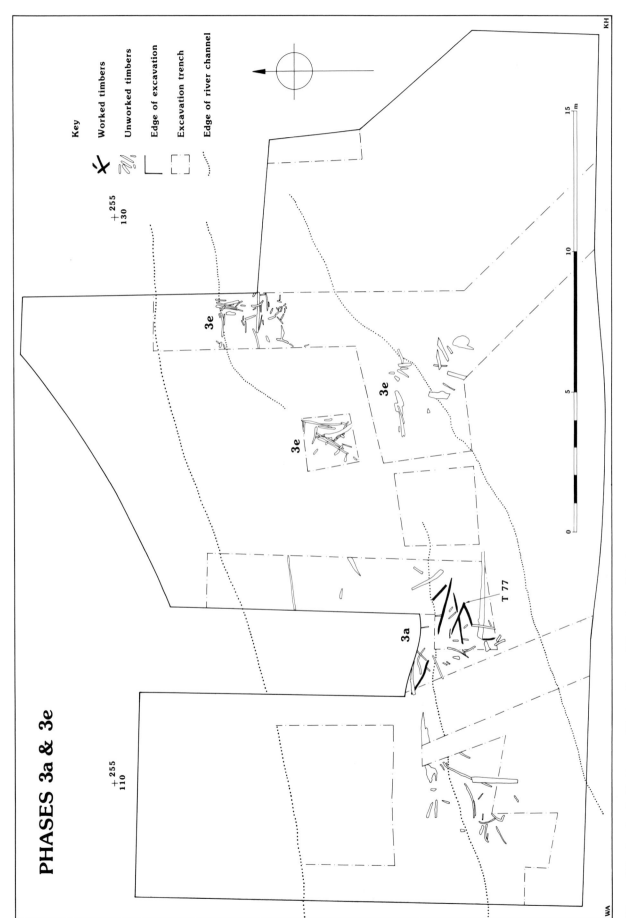

Figure 32 Anslow's Cottages: Phases 3a and 3e, plan of features

96

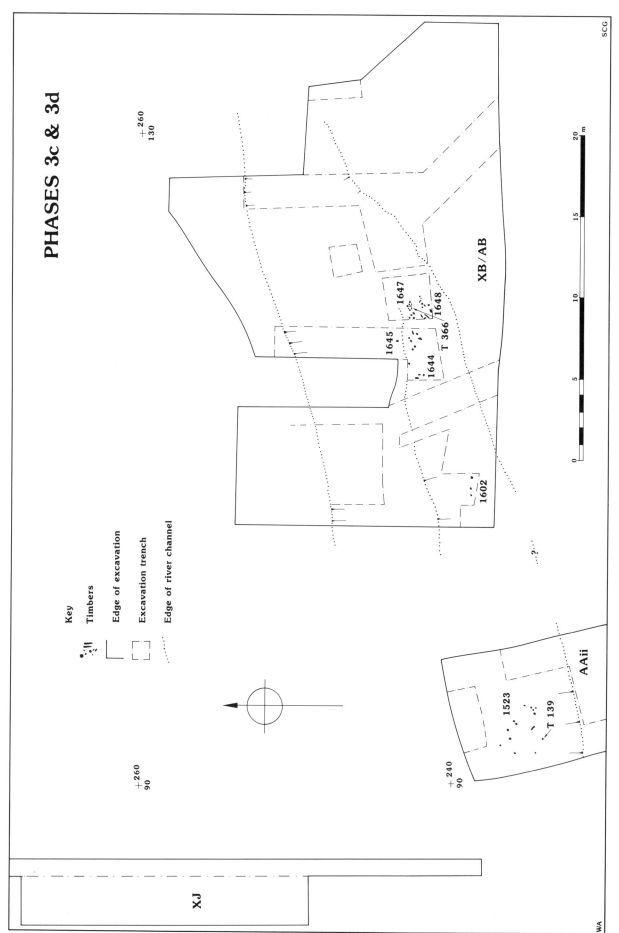

Figure 33 Anslow's Cottages: Phases 3c and 3d, plan of features

shallow channel, with the remaining single timber on a possible low gravel bank to the north of the main clusters. No clear pattern or arrangement of the groups could be discerned, and it is possible that they may represent several structures, not all of which were contemporary. Some timbers were set in pairs or clusters which may indicate repair or rebuilding of the structure(s).

Phase 3d: timber structure 1523
In Trench AAii an almost circular setting of fourteen vertical stakes, 1523, *c.* 3 m in diameter, was recorded in an amorphous shallow hollow, not more than 0.50 m deep (Fig. 33). One of the stakes (Timber 139) was radiocarbon dated to 1390±60 BP (HAR–9183). The hollow was filled with a layer of dark greyish brown silt and organic material which also surrounded the timbers. Some of the stakes were in pairs or groups, suggesting that repair or reinforcement of the structure may have been undertaken.

Phase 3e: infilling of northern river channel
Sealing the features and structures of Phases 3a–3d were variable deposits of very shelly sand and gravel. These gravels and sands were localised in the central part of Trench AB/XB (Fig. 40, S.123). On the northern edge of the channel, and apparently separated from the coarser material by large horizontal timbers, were finer sandy silts (which also sealed 690). The wood lay in a random spread of both worked and unworked timbers, some of the latter over 2 m in length (Fig. 32). Most of the timbers were aligned approximately north-east/south-west, following the direction of the channel, but no other pattern was evident (none of the wood was apparently *in situ*).

Phase 3f: old land surface 869
A layer of dark grey brown, humic clay, darker in colour than the silty clay layers both above and beneath it was, present across the whole of the area south of the modern drainage ditch, in Trenches XA, AAi, AAiii, AC and part of AAii (Figs 34 and 39, S.287). The layer was 0.15–0.20 m deep over most of the area and sealed the southern edge of the river channel and the features of Phase 1. Although the modern drainage ditch obscured crucial stratigraphic relationships, it is thought that this layer was equivalent to a similar, though more humic, deposit sealing timber structure 1523 in Trench AAii which dates to the mid Saxon phase (3d) (Fig. 39, S.288–290). A similar humic horizon was identified in the northern part of the river channel in Trenches AAii and XB/AB (Phase 4d) (Fig. 40, S.23).

In the first season of excavation 144 m^2 of the layer were dug by hand (as separate 1 m squares in the eastern part of Trench XA) to establish whether the distribution of finds followed any pattern. (In 1986 there was not enough time to allow further manual excavation of this layer and almost all of it was removed by machine.) The number of finds of all types was noticeably less in the area above the former river channel, probably reflecting the distribution of features on the drier ground to the south. Burnt flint was most common in the area immediately south of ditch 875, where amounts of pottery and knapped flint were also slightly greater; quantities of all categories of finds diminished marginally eastward, but increased over the central and southern parts of the trench. The layer included finds both from preceding phases, presumably brought to the surface by ploughing, and of Romano-British date; the latter provides a *terminus ante quem* for the onset of drier conditions on the higher ground to the south. By this time the Bronze Age river channel had silted up, forcing a slightly northward shift in the water course.

A small area of ploughmarks, 870, was recorded beneath the layer at the eastern side of Trench XA (Fig. 34). These showed as intercutting irregular lines of dark grey in the lighter coloured surrounding silty clay. It is likely that the ploughmarks originally extended over a wider area, but difficult soil conditions made it impossible to separate the old land surface cleanly from the layer beneath, and only faint traces of the marks were seen in Trench AAi. The best-preserved marks were *c.* 0.05 m wide (wider ones were probably overlapping lines) and 0.02–0.03 m deep. Two main alignments were recorded, one approximately north-north-west–south-south-east, the other east–west.

Phase 3g: ditch 1019/1108, pit 1070/1176
Two features, ditch 1019/1108 and pit 1070/1176, appeared to cut the Phase 3f old land surface in Trench XA, although there is some doubt about the inclusion of the latter feature in this phase.

Ditch sections 1019 and *1108*, separate stretches of an interrupted ditch, ran from north-north-east to south-south-west across the whole length of the eastern side of Trench AAi, continuing southwards beyond the excavation area. The sections were separated by a gap of about 2 m (Fig. 34). The northern section of ditch 1019 was 24 m long; some difficulty was experienced in defining the terminal where it cut the dark clay fill of trackway 1091. Only 1.10 m of 1108, the southern ditch, extended into the trench.

The ditches were U–shaped in profile (Fig. 38, S.261; Table 16) and were filled mainly with dark grey or greyish brown silty clays, with occasional lenses of weathered material from the sides and of burnt flint (the latter usually in the upper fills). A few sherds of residual Bronze Age pottery were recovered from the excavated sections.

Pit 1070/1176 was an amorphous feature near the south eastern corner of Trench AAi (Fig. 34). It extended beyond the excavated area and was difficult to define against the dark fill of trackway 1091, although clearly defined elsewhere. The base was very uneven, formed by a number of shallow scoops and ridges (Fig. 38, S.258; Table 15). The pit was filled with dark grey clay and silty clay.

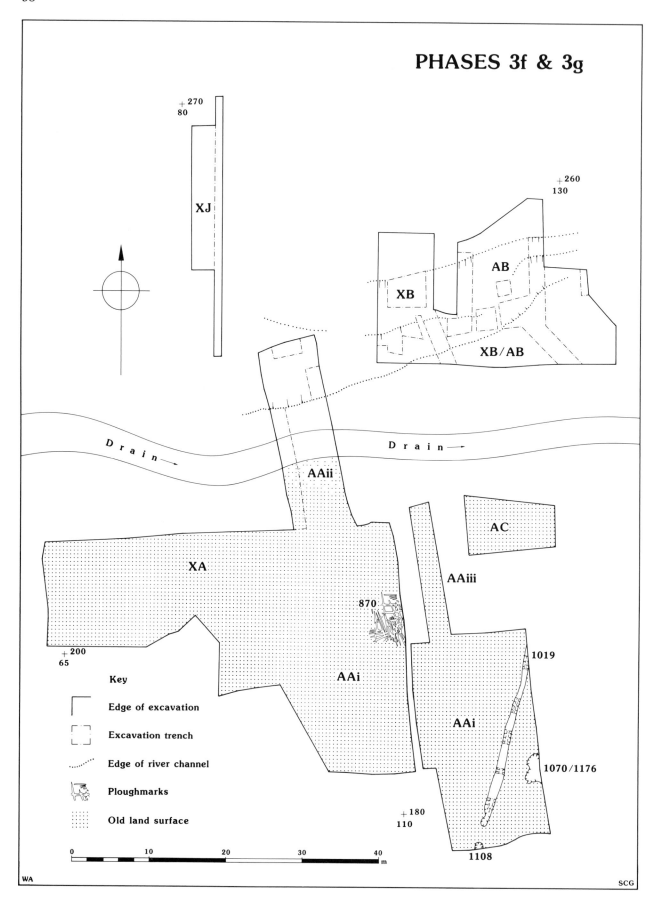

Figure 34   Anslow's Cottages: Phases 3f and 3g, plan of features

Plate 13   Anslow's Cottages: Timber structure 1594 (Phase 4b)

A large deposit of fired clay, apparently fired *in situ* was found in the top of this feature. Burnt flint occurred throughout the fill in large quantities (7255 g); the lower part of the feature also contained some animal bone and a quantity of pottery, but most of the finds were recovered from the upper 0.15 m of the fill in the northern part of the feature. It has been suggested that this feature might have been associated with pottery manufacture (Mepham, this volume). The fabric of the fired clay, containing burnt flint temper, was very similar to the fabric of the Bronze Age pottery found in the feature and elsewhere on the site. A large quantity of pottery (456 g) was found in the pit and the fired clay has every appearance of being *in situ*. However, as the feature appears to be later than the old land surface, a date no earlier than the Roman period is implied and this material must all be residual, unless there was some superstructure which survived to sufficient height to avoid being totally buried by the old land surface.

Phase 4: Late Saxon

Phase 4a: feature 1555 containing wicker basket SF.1073
In the north-east corner of Trench AAii was evidence of a late feature or channel, 1555, possibly the latest of the whole series (Fig. 35). The full extent westward and southward of this feature was not securely established; the southern side may have been truncated by an even later feature, but its northern edge cut the silt which sealed all channel deposits and the Phase 3d structure in this area. It was 0.60 m deep and at least 1.35 m wide, filled with dark sandy silts. From the latest of these silts a wicker basket or net, SF.1073, (Figs 35 and 43) was recovered; it was found lying against the northern edge of the feature, probably not *in situ*. A radiocarbon date of 1060±80 BP (OxA–2126) was obtained for the object.

Phase 4b: timber structures 1594, 1646
Set probably across the line of a channel east of the earlier Phase 3c structures was a cluster of vertical planks and stakes, 1594, reinforcing a possible low gravel bank and anchoring a horizontal beam (Figs 35 and 36; Plate 13). To the east, beyond 1594, the channel appeared to widen out or turn to the north; it was not possible to examine the area fully. Thought to be associated with this structure were other stakes, 1646, possibly placed along a shallow gravel bank forming a northern edge to the channel, and extending west from 1594 (Fig. 35). Radiocarbon dates of 1030±60 BP (HAR–9181) and 930±60 BP (HAR–9180) were obtained from one timber of the northern group (Timber 345) and a plank from the cluster across the channel (Timber

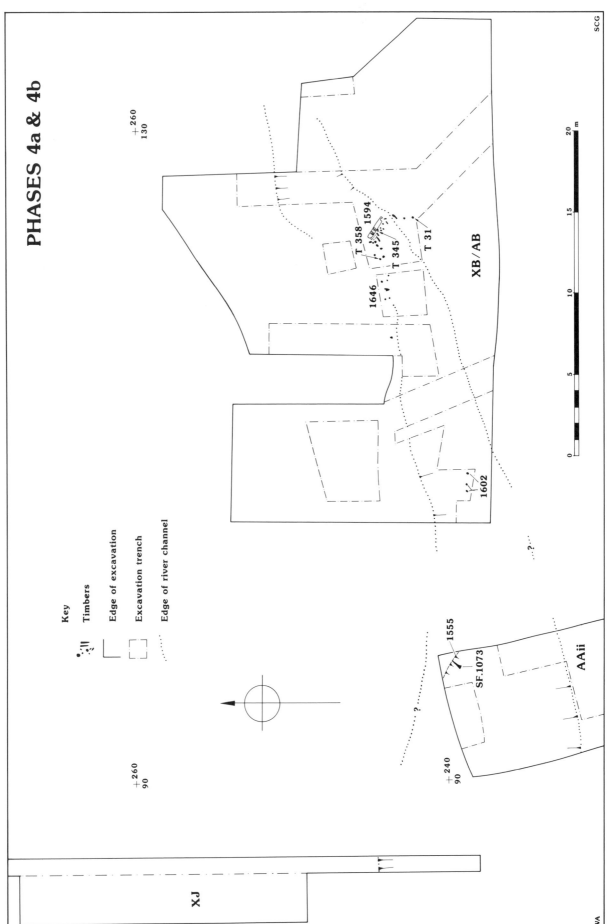

Figure 35 Anslow's Cottages: Phases 4a and 4b, plan of features

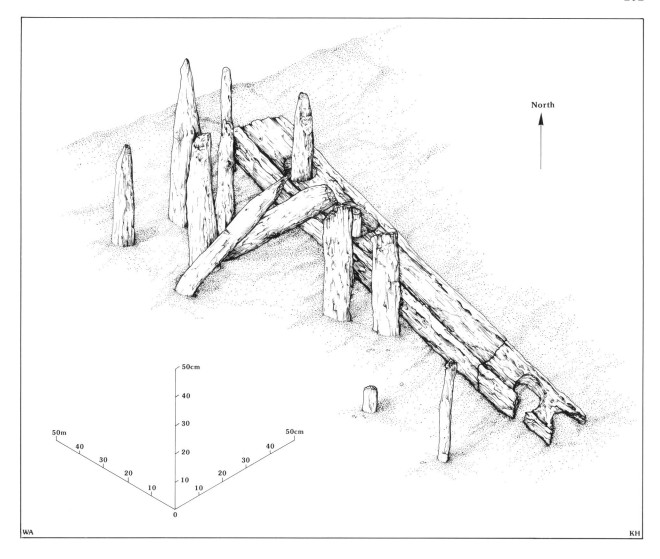

North

50cm
40
30
20
10
0

50m
40
30
20
10

50cm
40
30
20
10

WA

KH

Figure 36   Anslow's Cottages: isometric drawing of timber structure 1594 (Phase 4b)

358). South of 1594 three additional stakes were found, two *in situ*, which may also have been part of the same complex; a radiocarbon date of 1030±70 BP (HAR–9186) was obtained for one of these (Timber 31). The full width of this channel was not ascertained but a slight gravel bank visible in some sections may represent the southern edge.

If this assumption is correct, then structure 1594 appears to have been located at the narrowest part of this channel. The substantial size of some of the timbers and the depth to which they were driven into the gravel suggests they were intended resist a considerable force of water.

Amongst the sands and gravels which surrounded the highest surviving parts of the timbers were small twigs and other larger pieces of driftwood, some of which may have become trapped within or behind the structure. There was no evidence of any horizontal structural timbers having survived other than the single beam retained by the vertical pegs.

Phase 4c: further infilling of the river channel
Further deposits of silty sand with lenses of gravel and some organic material accumulated around and to the east of structure 1594.

Phase 4d: development of peat horizon
The river channel was sealed by a a distinctive peaty layer which also extended on to the floodplain to the north and north-east (Fig. 40, S.123, S.193). This was similar to the old land surface (Phase 3f) which sealed the river channel to the south and marks a change in the environment and landuse in the area.

Phase 5: medieval
The only feature dating to this period was ditch 611, the base of which cut into the the coarse deposits filling the upper level of the channel in Trench XB/AB (Figs 37 and 40, S.123). The ditch crossed the trench from south-west to north-east, following the line of the silted up river channel. The ditch was

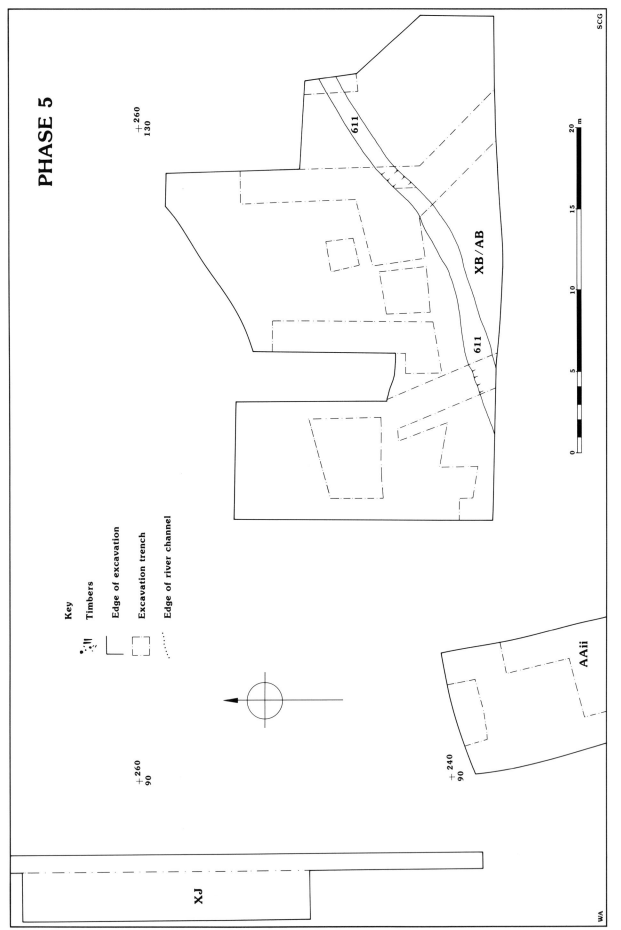

Figure 37 Anslow's Cottages: Phase 5, plan of features

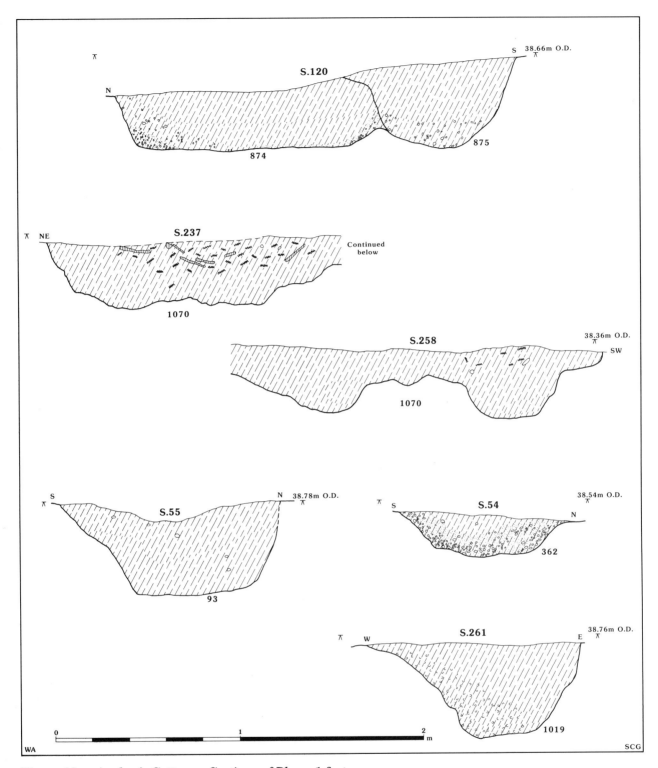

Figure 38   Anslow's Cottages: Sections of Phase 1 features

shallow with gently sloping sides and a rounded base; filled with dark greyish brown silty clay and contained a few sherds of pottery. The upper level may have been truncated when the site was cleared prior to excavation. A ditch in a similar stratigraphic position was observed during the evaluation (Trench XN) and may also date to this period.

Phase 6: post-medieval
A shift northwards of the active river system and the slow deposition of silt during seasonal flooding gradually increased the height of the land. A maximum accumulation of up to 1.80 m was recorded across the area of the river channels and on the floodplain to the north; to the south of the

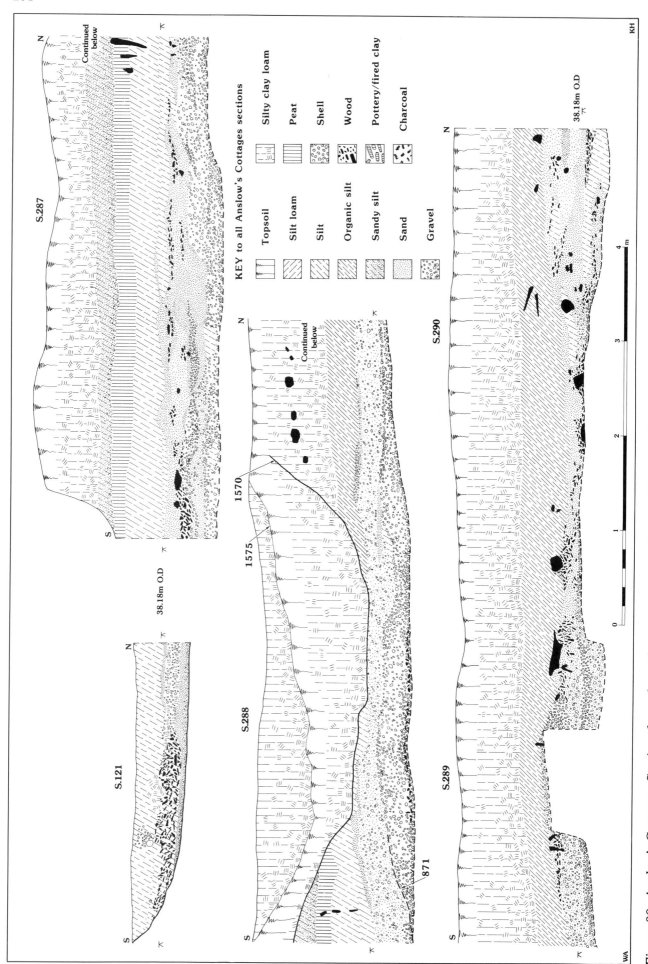

Figure 39 Anslow's Cottages: Section through southern part of river channel (Trenches XA and AAi) (see Fig. 28 for locations)

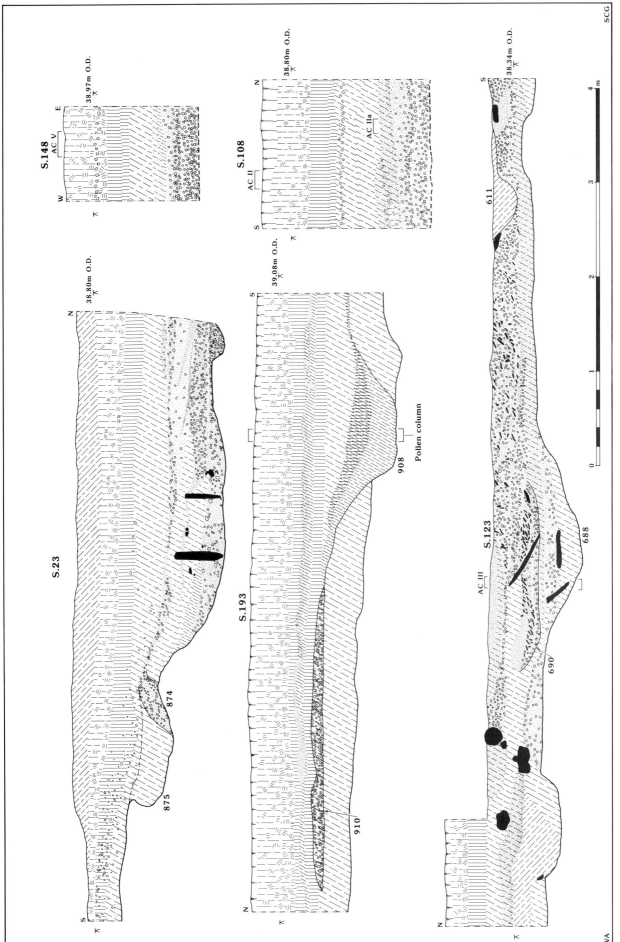

Figure 40 Anslow's Cottages: sections through river channel deposits (see Fig. 28 for location)

Table 17 Anslow's Cottages: distribution of worked flint by trench

Trench	Cores	Core frags	Flakes	Broken	Burnt flakes	Retouched	Scrapers	Others	Total
J–M	–	2	13	8	1	–	–	–	24
AA	15	6	65	43	3	5	6	1	144
AC	–	1	6	3	–	–	–	–	10
XA	11	8	230	138	16	13	9	3	428
XB	–	–	1	–	–	–	–	–	1
XF	–	–	–	1	–	–	–	–	1
XG	–	–	1	1	–	–	–	–	2
Totals	26	17	316	194	20	18	15	4	610

channels the build up of silt was much shallower. Indications of ditches across the northern fields, in the form of still visible depressions, suggest that the area may have been managed as watermeadows, although the normal regular layout of ditches was not apparent. There was no sign of any intensive landuse. The area above the silted up river channel clearly continued to present a drainage problem, with ditches 1570 and 1575 dug through the upper fills of the channel (Figs 28 and 39, S.288), the latter continuing in use until recent years.

4 The Finds

Flint, by P.A. Harding

The distribution of the 610 pieces of worked flint from the excavation is shown by trench and by phase and location in Tables 17 and 18. These show that, in common with other finds from the site, the worked flint is more commonly found in areas south of the river channel. Most of it came from the Phase 3f old land surface and is therefore unsuitable for dating the features. In the second season of excavation, most of the old land surface was removed by machine and a proportional decrease in the recovery of flint from this horizon is reflected in the totals from Trench AA in Table 17.

Diagnostic material consists of a Mesolithic microlith and a Levallois flake of probable late Neolithic date. Occasional flakes with abraded butts are also present but less closely dated. The remaining flint includes probable late Bronze Age material associated with the main period of activity on the site.

The cores are undiagnostic and are mainly multi-directional unprepared flake cores. Most are unsystematic, although crude discoidal and biconical cores are also present. One core has been made on a flake, but most used small nodules of poor quality gravel flint which is often thermally

Table 18 Anslow's Cottages: distribution of worked flint by phase and location

Phase	Location	Cores	Core frags	Flakes	Broken	Burnt flakes	Retouched	Scrapers	Others	Total
0	South river channel	–	–	7	3	–	–	–	–	10
1a	Trackway 1091	–	–	4	2	1	1	1	–	9
1b	Post-holes	2	–	7	5	1	–	–	–	15
1b	Ditches 93/714/848	1	1	12	6	–	3	–	–	23
1b	Burnt flint 809	–	1	2	4	1	–	–	–	8
1c	Channel	–	1	14	10	–	1	2	1	29
1e	Ditch 875	–	1	10	3	–	–	1	–	15
3f	Old land surface 869	15	9	209	145	5	10	7	3	403
3g	Features	4	3	26	12	1	2	2	–	50

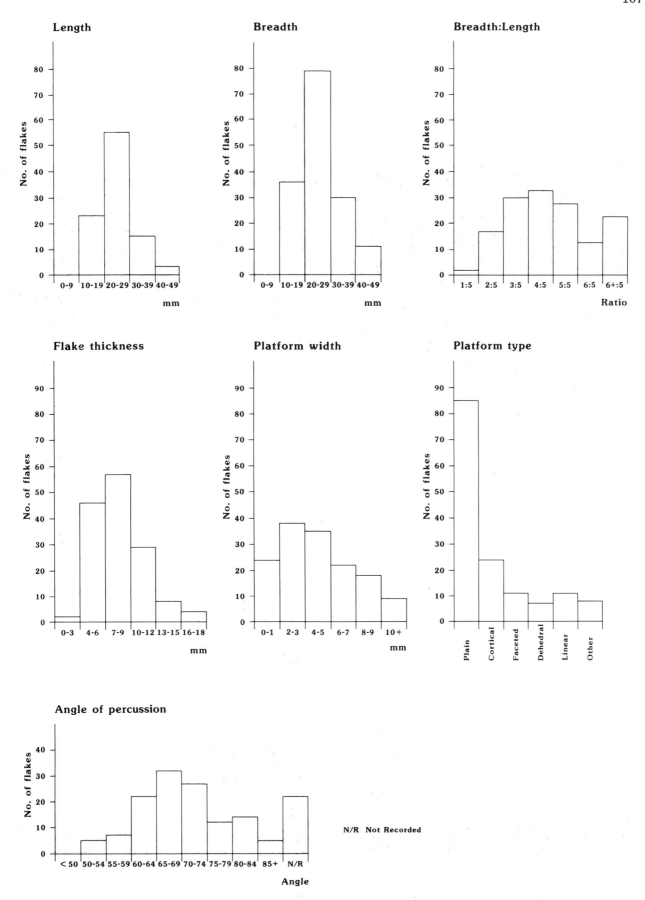

Figure 41   Anslow's Cottages: histograms showing attributes of worked flints from Phase 3f contexts

fractured. There are no blade or bladelet cores, nor is there evidence of platform abrasion or faceting to prepare the core before flakes were removed. The edges of the cores are often irregular, which indicates that the point of percussion has been set well back onto the striking platform. Incipient cones of percussion which indicate mis-hits are also common.

The flakes from the old land surface have been analysed to establish their characteristics and the main results presented in Figure 41. Most flakes are small, squat or broad in shape and were removed by hard hammer percussion. Flake butts are predominantly plain and percussion angles low. Flakes of this type are normally associated with material dating from the 2nd millennium BC, continuing into the late Bronze Age (Ford *et al.* 1984; Pitts 1978). An earlier date seems unlikely; the early Neolithic assemblage at Staines, Middlesex, utilising similar raw material, demonstrated the trend for more elongated flakes (Healey and Robertson-Mackay 1983).

The retouched pieces can be divided into three categories: denticulates and notches, those with the bulb removed, and scrapers. Twelve flakes with denticulate retouch or Clactonian notches (Bordes 1961, 53, pl. 39.10) were found, of which four occurred in the old land surface. Denticulate retouch was normally direct and on a straight edge. Clactonian notches were also made by direct retouch on one or both edges of the flake. A flake removed during the manufacture of a Clactonian notch was found in Trench AA. These pieces recur with sufficient regularity to indicate that the technique was deliberate.

Five bulb removal (Janus) flakes (Tixier *et al.* 1980, 90) and three flakes from which the bulb has been removed were found, of which seven came from the old land surface. One Janus flake has been retouched with a Clactonian notch. Bulbs were removed from across the butt or from a flake edge (Harding 1992).

The fifteen flake scrapers have a similar distribution to the other retouched material, only four being found in the old land surface. Two scrapers, one of which may have been retouched by pressure flaking, were found in the river channel deposits and are probably derived. Most are end scrapers retouched by abrupt or semi-abrupt retouch into a convex scraping edge. A scraper from the old land surface was retouched on the proximal end and one from pit 1070/1176 has the proximal end removed by a notch.

Discussion

The flint from Anslow's Cottages does not form a homogeneous group; however, certain observations can be made about the material from Phase 3f. The known Mesolithic component on the site consists of one microlith from an ill-defined feature, 1069. Blade debitage which normally characterises this period in the Kennet/Thames valleys is restricted to one blade with an abraded butt and several rejuvenation/faceting flakes. These pieces and

several flakes with abraded butts may also belong to a Neolithic component.

The late Neolithic is represented by a derived atypical Levallois flake (Bordes 1961, 31) with a plunged distal end found in the pre-Bronze Age river channel deposits. It has centripetal preparation, irregular edges, a faceted butt and was probably removed by hard hammer percussion. The axis of percussion does not however correspond to the axis of morphology.

The ridges between the flake facets are worn and the edges damaged by gravel abrasion. This flake and two others with which it was found were made from nodules of good quality flint which are larger than the cores found on the site. A scraper with pressure-flaked retouch which was also found in the river channel deposits must also be considered residual.

The remaining material, which comprises small waste flakes, cannot be dated with certainty. The flint from Phase 3f dates from some time after the 2nd millennium BC and, on the basis of the associated pottery, could date to the later Bronze Age. The retouched flakes do not contradict this. Denticulate retouch and notches have been associated with late Neolithic industries (Alexander and Ozanne 1960, 295, Saville 1981, F568 and F571). However 'bold' retouch has also been associated with Deverel-Rimbury contexts (Stone 1941, 131). Refitting denticulate retouch flakes were found at Rowden, Dorset, from a late Bronze Age deposit (Harding 1991, fig. 47.96 and 97).

The technique of removing the butt is similarly not unique to the late Bronze Age but has been noted on contemporary sites from the Marlborough Downs, Wiltshire (Harding 1992) and South Dorset Ridgeway (Harding 1991). The concentration of these pieces in the old land surface at Anslow's Cottages contrasts with the diffuse spread of scrapers. Despite the limited stratification at Anslow's Cottages, there is no reason why the flint assemblage cannot be considered contemporary with the later Bronze Age pottery from the site.

Pottery, by L.N. Mepham

The pottery assemblage from Anslow's Cottages comprises 2022 sherds (10,316g). This material was recovered from hand-dug and machine- excavated, small-scale evaluation trenches; and also from larger-scale trenches excavated by hand after topsoil stripping by machine. The majority of the pottery is of late Bronze Age date; there is also a small group of Romano-British material, and smaller amounts of early Bronze Age, Iron Age, medieval and post-medieval material.

The pottery was analysed using the standard Wessex Archaeology recording system (Morris 1992). A hand lens (x8 magnification), and a binocular microscope (x20 magnification) were used to divide the pottery into four fabric groups on the basis of the dominant inclusion type: flint-gritted (Group F), grog-tempered (Group G), sandy (Group

Q), and 'established' wares of known source (Group E). These four groups were then subdivided into 28 fabric types on the basis of the range and coarseness of the macroscopic inclusions.

The assemblage was fully quantified, both by number and weight of sherds, by fabric type within each context. Details of vessel form, surface treatment and decoration were also recorded, and this information can be found in archive. In the relative absence of recognisable profiles (only one complete and three partial profiles were recovered), vessel types have been defined largely on the basis of rim forms or other diagnostic sherds. All percentages given are calculated by weight.

In the descriptions of the fabric types below, the following terms are used to define the proportion of visible inclusions: rare (1–3%), sparse (3–10%), moderate (10–20%), common (20–30%). The pottery is discussed by period below; pottery totals by fabric type are given in Table 19. References to equivalent fabric types at Field Farm are given (*see above*).

Early Bronze Age (0.26% of the total assemblage)
Two fabrics were identified:

G1. Moderately hard, fine, iron-rich clay matrix, slightly soapy; moderate grog <1 mm. Oxidised with unoxidised interior.

G2. Soft, fine, iron clay matrix, soapy; sparse grog <0.5 mm; very rare, subangular flint <2 mm; sparse calcareous inclusions <2 mm; rare black iron oxide. Oxidised.

Three sherds in fabric G2 derive from Beaker vessels, decorated with twisted cord or comb impressions, and other undecorated sherds in the same fabric are likely to derive from similar vessels. The slightly coarser fabric G1, both sherds of which are decorated with twisted cord impressions, can be broadly dated to the early Bronze Age.

Late Bronze Age (86.17%)
Twelve fabric types were identified:

F2. Moderately hard, iron-rich clay matrix; sparse, poorly-sorted flint, both subangular and rounded, <3 mm; sparse, rounded quartz <0.5 mm. Unoxidised; burnished on both interior and exterior surfaces.

F3. Soft, moderately fine clay matrix; sparse to moderate, poorly-sorted, subangular flint <1 mm; rare grog <1 mm. Unoxidised.

F4. Moderately hard, fine, iron-rich clay matrix, slightly laminated; moderate, poorly-sorted, rounded quartz <1 mm; sparse to moderate, poorly-sorted, subangular flint <2 mm, concentrated on exterior surface; moderate red iron oxide; rare mica. Unoxidised with oxidised exterior.

F5. Soft, moderately coarse, iron-rich clay matrix, laminated; common, poorly-sorted, rounded quartz <3 mm; sparse to moderate, subangular flint <3 mm. Irregularly fired.

F6. Soft, fine, iron-poor clay matrix, slightly soapy; sparse to moderate, poorly-sorted, sub-angular flint <3 mm; rare calcareous inclusions <1 mm; sparse to moderate red iron oxide; sparse mica. Irregularly fired. This group includes a wide range of variation both in firing and inclusions, and is sometimes difficult to distinguish from Fabric F7. (Field Farm F3)

F7. Soft, fine, iron-rich clay matrix; moderate to common, poorly-sorted, subangular flint <5 mm; sparse to moderate red iron oxide <3 mm; sparse mica. Irregularly fired but generally wholly or partially oxidised. Again this group includes a wide range of variation. (Field Farm F5)

F8. Soft, fine, iron-poor clay matrix; common, subangular flint <3 mm, better sorted than F6 and F7; some examples have rare iron oxide <2 mm. Generally unoxidised. (Field Farm F6)

F9. Soft, fine clay matrix; common, very poorly-sorted, subangular calcined flint <4 mm (rarely <6 mm); sparse red iron oxide. Unoxidised; very irregular.

F10. Heavily leached fabric, very light, sandy, unoxidised; rare subangular/subrounded flint <1 mm; sparse flecks of calcareous matter <1 mm; common poorly-sorted voids, irregularly shaped, <2 mm; sparse grog, poorly sorted, <1 mm. Possibly the result of heat/chemical action on one of the other fabrics.

Q1. Soft, fine, iron-poor clay matrix; sparse subrounded quartz <1 mm; rare rounded and subangular flint <3 mm; rare grog <2 mm; sparse iron oxide. Unoxidised with patchy exterior surface.

Q2. Soft, coarse, iron-rich clay matrix, laminated; common, fairly well-sorted, rounded quartz grains <1 mm; rare, rounded flint in some examples; rare red iron oxide. Irregularly fired; both oxidised and unoxidised examples.

Q3. Soft, very fine, clay matrix; sparse mica; very rare subangular flint <0.5 mm. Unoxidised, sometimes with oxidised surfaces.

Although no diagnostic Deverel-Rimbury style material was identified within the assemblage from Anslow's Cottages, the coarse flint-gritted fabric F8 includes some thick-walled body sherds which may have derived from a Deverel-Rimbury urn. The fabric is comparable to fabrics found in Deverel-Rimbury urns elsewhere in the Kennet valley, for instance at Sulhamstead (Woodward, this volume), though it is also found at Anslow's Cottages in late Bronze Age vessel forms.

The majority of the late Bronze Age assemblage comprises flint-gritted fabrics (91.6%); sandy fabrics form only a very small proportion of the group. Of the rim forms which could be recognised, all fall within the range of vessel forms known from assemblages in the area of the Kennet Valley, particularly at Aldermaston Wharf which includes parallels for nearly all the later Bronze Age rim forms from Anslow's Cottages (Bradley *et al.* 1980, types 2–5, 8, 9).

Although the sample of diagnostic sherds is very small, there appears to be an emphasis on jar forms; fourteen jars (Fig. 42, 1–9, 11, 12), compared with three bowls (Fig. 42, 10). Two complete profiles were recovered: a small, slack-shouldered jar in sandy fabric Q3 (Fig. 42, 3), and a small, straight-sided, bucket-shaped vessel in flint-gritted fabric F6 (Fig. 42, 5). Similar straight-sided vessels have been found at Pingewood (Bradley 1987).

There was one example of a sharply carinated bowl in sandy fabric Q1 (Fig. 42, 10). This form is paralleled amongst the late Bronze Age material from Knight's Farm (Bradley *et al.* 1980, fig. 31, 36), but also continues into the early Iron Age (cf. Cunliffe 1978, fig. A:6). It occurs at Petters Sports Field, Surrey, where it is considered to be a late phenomenon within the late Bronze Age/early Iron Age assemblage (O'Connell 1986, 72). The same comments apply to the high-shouldered, burnished jar in fine flint-gritted fabric F2 (Fig. 42, 11). Similar vessels have been found at Petters Sports Field (*ibid*, fig. 56, 260), and the form also has parallels within the All Cannings Cross, Wiltshire, assemblage, dated 5th–3rd centuries BC (Cunliffe 1978, fig. A:6.5).

Apart from the carinated bowl described above, the sandy fabrics are restricted to jars with upright or slightly out-turned rims and rounded profiles (Fig. 42, 3, 6, 8); there is also one example of this form in a fine flint-gritted fabric (F2). Coarse flint-gritted fabrics are found mostly in roughly biconical or straight-sided jar forms.

Decoration amongst the late Bronze Age group is very sparse. Incised chevron decoration was recorded on two conjoining sherds in coarse flint-gritted fabric F8, and one rim sherd in sandy fabric Q1 is decorated with impressed dots (Fig. 42, 6). The two latter examples are both paralleled amongst the late Bronze Age assemblage from Knight's Farm (Bradley *et al.* 1980, fig. 35).

Iron Age (0.08%)
One fabric was identified, represented by two sherds only:

F1. Soft, moderately fine clay matrix; common, well-sorted, rounded quartz grains <0.5 mm; sparse, subangular, flint <1 mm. Unoxidised.

Only one diagnostic form was recognised: a saucepan pot rim. This plain form, with characteristic groove below the rim, is typical of the St Catherine's Hill/Worthy Down style, dated 2nd–1st centuries BC (Cunliffe 1978, fig. A:15).

Romano-British (8.10%)
Ten fabrics were identified, including four of known type or source:

E100. Samian. No distinction has been made between samian from different sources, ie. Central or Southern Gaul.

Table 19 Anslow's Cottages: pottery fabric types by period

	No. sherds	Weight (g)	% of period	% of total
Early Bronze Age				
G1	2	9	33.3	
G2	5	18	66.7	
Total	7	27		0.26
Late Bronze Age				
F2	13	174	1.96	
F3	35	114	1.28	
F4	6	72	0.81	
F5	41	358	4.03	
F6	473	2228	25.06	
F7	440	1937	21.79	
F8	716	3016	33.93	
F9	13	230	2.59	
F10	5	12	0.13	
Q1	20	288	3.24	
Q2	37	181	2.03	
Q3	26	280	3.15	
Total	1825	8890		86.17
Iron Age				
F1	2	8		0.08
Romano-British				
E100	5	4	0.48	
E170	6	18	2.16	
E151	6	46	5.51	
E250	2	3	0.36	
F100	2	17	2.04	
G100	35	111	13.29	
G101	24	198	23.71	
Q100	59	362	43.35	
Q101	1	12	1.44	
Q102	11	64	7.66	
Total	151	835		8.10
Medieval				
Q400	7	270		2.62
Post-medieval				
E600	28	259	90.56	
E770	2	27	9.44	
Total	30	286		2.77
Overall total	2022	10,316		

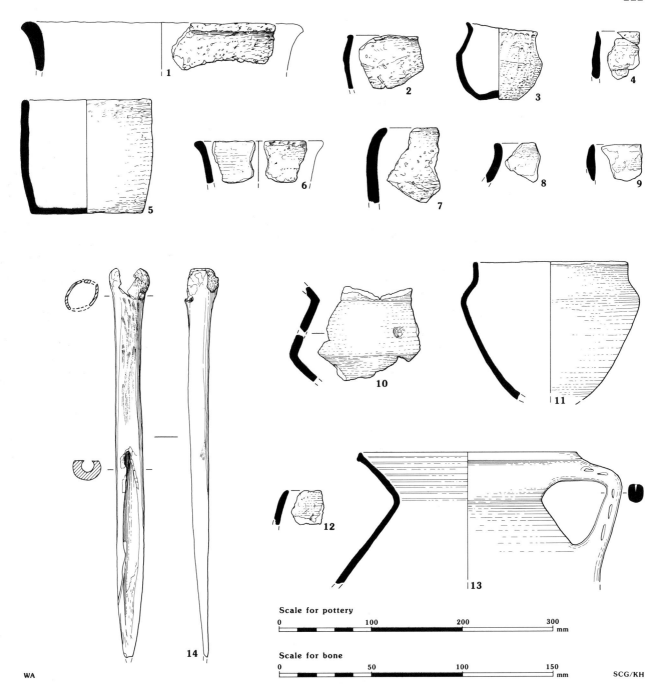

Figure 42   Anslow's Cottages: pottery and worked bone

E151. Silchester ware: very coarse fabric; common, poorly-sorted, subangular flint <4 mm; sparse red iron oxide. Early to late 1st century AD (Charles 1979). It can be difficult to distinguish this fabric from late Bronze Age flint-gritted fabrics, especially in the absence of diagnostic sherds.

E170. Oxfordshire oxidised ware: very fine, soft, sandy fabric, sometimes with red iron oxide (Young 1977).

E250. Lyons ware: very fine, soft, creamy fabric, no visible inclusions. Traces of brown/purple colour coat. *c.* AD 43–70 (Greene 1978, 15).

F100. Soft, moderately coarse, iron-rich clay matrix; common, fairly well-sorted, sub-angular flint <1.5 mm; sparse to moderate rounded quartz <1 mm; rare iron oxide; sparse grog <1 mm. Unoxidised with oxidised surfaces; handmade.

G100. Soft, fine clay, iron-rich clay matrix; sparse grog <1 mm; sparse red iron oxide; rare sub-angular/subrounded flint <1 mm; some mica. Unoxidised, oxidised surfaces; wheelthrown?

G101. Soft, moderately coarse, iron-rich clay matrix; common, poorly-sorted grog <3 mm; rare calcareous inclusions; rare red iron oxide. Irregularly fired; unoxidised with partially oxidised surfaces; handmade.

Q100. Soft, moderately fine clay matrix; moderate to common, well-sorted, rounded quartz grains <0.5 mm; some mica. A 'catch-all' group for Romano-British unoxidised sandy wares, probably mostly of local or regional manufacture. Generally unoxidised; wheel-thrown.

Q101. Soft, moderately coarse, iron-poor clay matrix; common, poorly-sorted, rounded quartz grains <3 mm. Unoxidised with oxidised surfaces; wheelthrown? Vessel form suggests 1st century AD.

Q102. Soft, moderately coarse clay matrix; common, well-sorted, rounded quartz grains <1 mm; rare subangular flint <1 mm. The group may include some late Iron Age material. Unoxidised; generally handmade.

The small group of Romano-British material includes a bead rim in Silchester ware (E151) and two cordoned jar rims (F100, Q101), all of which can be dated to the 1st century AD. In addition, several everted rims were found, one from a large, coarse grog-tempered storage jar (G101), plus two samian bowl rims and a flanged bowl rim (Q100). The latter form is the only sherd which is demonstrably 3rd/4th century AD.

Medieval (2.62%)
One fabric was identified:

Q400. Hard, moderately coarse, iron-rich clay matrix; common, well-sorted, rounded quartz <0.5mm. Unoxidised with oxidised margins; wheelthrown.

Nearly all the sherds of this fabric derived from a single vessel: a glazed jug/pitcher, heavily sooted on the exterior, with partially glazed interior and handle with stabbed decoration, probably of 14th century date (Fig. 42, 13). Similar examples of pitchers with very constricted necks, in very similar sandy fabrics, were found at Reading Abbey (Slade 1973, fig. 11, no. 1).

Post-medieval (2.77%)

E600. Red earthenware.
E770. Salt-glazed stoneware.

Most of the sherds were of red earthenware, probably from a variety of sources. The salt-glazed stoneware is of 19th/20th century type.

Distribution

Phase 1 features
No pottery was recovered from contexts in Phase 1a. The feature fills of Phases 1b–1e, south of the river channel, and sealed by the Phase 3f old land surface, produced an homogeneous group of pottery (1964 g), consisting largely of three coarse flint-gritted late Bronze Age fabrics (F6, F7, F8). These fabrics made up 85.1% of the total from the ditches, and 100% of the total from other features. The remaining pottery can also be regarded as late

Bronze Age, apart from two possibly later sherds from sections across ditch 874 (Fabrics F2, F3).

Diagnostic material comprised two jar rims, from ditch 874, and feature 781 (Fig. 42, 4), and sherds of a complete pot (Fig. 42, 5) in a coarse flint-gritted fabric (F6), apparently deliberately deposited in a small pit (1174). All these vessel forms are paralleled at late Bronze Age sites in the area, for instance at Aldermaston (Bradley *et al.* 1980, fig. 11). The radiocarbon date of 2570±70 BP (HAR–9186), obtained from the timber structure in Phase 1b, indicates a date between the 9th and 6th centuries BC for this pottery.

In Trench XJ, four sherds (10 g), in a very fine, micaceous sandy fabric (Q3) were recovered from context 905, which was cut by ditch 908 and by the northern edge of the river channel complex. The sherds were undiagnostic, but were in a fabric also found within the channel deposits and a late Bronze Age date is probable.

Phase 1c: the river channel deposits
The river channel deposits produced a fairly small amount of pottery (1230 g), of which nearly half (496 g) comprises coarse flint-gritted fabrics F6, F7 and F8. These fabrics were recovered from contexts throughout the sequence of channel deposits, though they appear to be concentrated at the eastern end of the excavated channel sequence, in Trenches AAii and AC, where they occur almost to the exclusion of other fabric types.

The remaining pottery from the river channel deposits consists mainly of single large sherds (Fabrics Q1, F5, F9) or groups of sherds of the same fabric (Fabric F5). One complete pot was recovered; a small, slack-shouldered jar in the sandy fabric Q3 (Fig. 42, 3). Neither the form nor the fabric are particularly diagnostic; the vessel is presumed to be late Bronze Age, and indeed, similar forms have been recorded from local late Bronze Age sites such as Aldermaston (Bradley *et al.* 1980, fig. 17, 144).

Other diagnostic material comprised three jar rims (Fig. 42, 1 and 2), all in coarse flint-gritted fabrics (F8, F9), one of which was recovered from context 753, the earliest context excavated within the channel.

The pottery from the channel deposits of Phase 1c is indistinguishable from that from other Phase 1 features. Two sherds were recovered in fabrics which occur in overlying layers in vessel forms which may be slightly later than the rest of the diagnostic material from the channel deposits; however, these were undiagnostic body sherds and as such cannot be closely dated.

One small sherd (2 g) of Romano-British pottery was found in context 738, near the southern edge of the river channel in Trench XA but can be regarded as intrusive.

Phase 3f: old land surface
Just over one-third of the whole pottery assemblage (3659 g) was derived from layers sealing the channel deposits and the area to the south of the river channel.

Flint-gritted fabrics F6, F7 and F8 again form the largest proportion of the group (70.7%), however, these contexts also contain a higher proportion of later material. Late Bronze Age diagnostic material included jar rims in forms similar to those found in the river channel deposits and dry-land features (Fig. 42, 6–9), all but one in flint-gritted fabrics F6 and F8.

Sherds forming the partial profile of a high-shouldered jar (Fig. 42, 11) in a sparsely flint-gritted fabric (F2), which is burnished on both surfaces, were recovered from context 572, a silt sealing the river channel deposits. One other partial profile was recovered, from context 580, a sharply carinated bowl (Fig. 42, 10) in a relatively fine sandy fabric (Q1). The affinities of these two vessels have already been discussed. Neither fabric occurs in other demonstrably late Bronze Age forms on the site; both in fact are markedly poorly represented on the site apart from contexts overlying the river channel deposits and dry-land features. These two vessels, therefore, may represent isolated deposits after the main period of late Bronze Age activity on the site.

The majority of the pottery from these contexts was derived from the area to the south, in Trenches XA/AA; however, four sherds (79 g) were also recovered from Trench XB/AB, to the north, from cleaning layer 1600/1611. These comprised one hooked rim in Fabric F9 (Fig. 42, 7), one upright jar rim in Fabric Q1, decorated with impressed dots (Fig. 42, 6), and two small body sherds in Fabric F7. The decorated rim is in the same fabric as the sharply carinated bowl described above, and both form and decoration can be paralleled amongst the latest material from the Knight's Farm assemblage (Bradley *et al.* 1980, fig. 35).

Seventy-seven sherds (411 g) of Romano-British material were recovered from these contexts, including a bead rim in Silchester ware, which can be dated to the 1st century AD, before *c.* AD 70 (Charles 1979).

Phase 3g: features
Two features on the southern side of the river channel appeared to cut through the Phase 3f land surface. Ditch 1019 contained only five very small sherds of late Bronze Age pottery (14 g), all in Fabrics F7 and F8. To the east of this ditch, feature 1070/1176 again produced a very similar range of pottery to that recovered from the features sealed by the old land surface. The feature contained a large quantity of pottery (456 g), almost all in coarse flint-gritted fabrics F7 and F8, including one jar rim of a type also found in the ditches sealed by the old land surface (Fig. 42, 12).

The distinction between the two fabrics in this case is very unclear, and they may in fact represent one fabric type only with a wide range of variation in firing and temper. The feature also contained large amounts of fired clay (7762 g). The fabric of the pottery closely resembled the fabric of the fired clay from the feature, and it is suggested that this feature may have been associated with the production of pottery on the site (*see below*).

Phase 5: ditch 611
Ditch 611 contained sherds of a partially glazed medieval jug/pitcher, probably of 14th century date (Fig. 42, 13).

Discussion
The majority of the pre-Roman pottery from the site appears to fall into Barrett's post-Deverel-Rimbury tradition (Barrett 1980), with an emphasis on plain bowls and jars in both coarse and fine fabrics and generally smaller vessels than were produced in the Deverel-Rimbury tradition. The only possible group of Deverel-Rimbury material on the site came from the evaluation Trench D, *c.* 300 m to the south of the river channel; thick-walled sherds in the coarse flint-gritted fabric F8 were recovered, but these included no diagnostic sherds. The only other earlier material from the site comprises three Beaker sherds from an unstratified context in Trench AA, and two grog-tempered sherds with a general early Bronze Age date, again from Trench D.

The post-Deverel-Rimbury material is paralleled closely at the nearby sites of Aldermaston and Knight's Farm, particularly so at the former, where there is a comparable emphasis on undecorated vessels. The settlement at Aldermaston is dated to the 11th–9th centuries BC. There are at least two examples of vessels which might fall into a slightly later date range, more comparable with the later elements amongst the assemblage from Knight's Farm, dated to the 8th–7th centuries BC; these are not securely associated with the rest of the late Bronze Age material, and it thus seems reasonable to propose a date range for the majority of the assemblage within Barrett's plain post-Deverel-Rimbury tradition in the early part of the 1st millennium BC (Barrett 1980, 307). This would be consistent with the radiocarbon date of 2570±70 BP (HAR–9186) obtained for the Phase 1b timber structure.

The range of diagnostic material from Anslow's Cottages is very small, and only seventeen late Bronze Age rim forms could be identified. When these are assigned to Barrett's five vessel classes, there appears to be a definite emphasis on coarse jar forms (class I), which is not unexpected, since these form the major element in domestic assemblages of this period throughout southern England (Barrett 1980, 302–3). There are fourteen jars represented compared to only three bowls, and a similar rarity of bowls was observed within the late Bronze Age assemblage from the nearby site at Pingewood, where it was suggested that this might indicate a date slightly earlier than the settlement at Aldermaston Wharf (Bradley 1987, 28).

A relatively early date within the post-Deverel-Rimbury sequence is also suggested by the low incidence of decoration at Anslow's Cottages. Elements within the assemblages from Runnymede Bridge and Petters Sports Field (Longley 1980; O'Connell 1986) which have been considered to indicate a fairly late date within the post-Deverel-Rimbury tradition, such as the increased use of decoration, the tendency towards sandy rather than flint-gritted fabrics, and the appearance of carinated vessel forms, are not apparent at Anslow's Cottages, except in some isolated examples which are not associated directly with the rest of the late Bronze Age material.

The relatively small amount of pottery recovered from Anslow's Cottages, and the generally homogeneous nature of the material derived from features suggests that the pottery represents a fairly short-lived occupation during the late Bronze Age (Phase 1). Although there appears to be more than one phase of activity on the site, most of this activity would seem to have taken place within a relatively short time-span.

That there was some activity in the vicinity during the Roman period (Phase 2) is indicated by the small amounts of Roman pottery recovered. This material was largely recovered from layers sealing the river channel, including the Phase 3f old land surface, in Trenches XA/AA, but was also concentrated in the area to the east, where a small amount was collected by fieldwalking, and in the evaluation Trenches A–H to the south. No dryland features could be definitely dated to this phase. The evaluation Trenches A–H also produced the only two Iron Age sherds from the site, including a rim sherd from a saucepan pot, which was found together with sherds of late Bronze Age pottery in Trench D.

Fired clay, by L.N. Mepham

A large deposit of fired clay (SF.1018/1054) was found in the top of feature 1070/1176 (Phase 3g), which appeared to cut the old land surface. Burnt flint occurred throughout the feature fill, in large quantities (7255 g); the lower fill of the feature also contained some animal bone and a quantity of pottery (456 g). The fired clay was concentrated in the top 0.15 m of the fill.

The fired clay recovered from the feature weighed over 7.5 kg. The fabric was homogeneous throughout, a very friable, iron-rich clay matrix, largely oxidised, with moderate subangular calcined flint inclusions <5 mm and moderate rounded quartz grains <1 mm, with no sign of any deliberate sorting of the inclusions. This fabric resembled the coarse flint-gritted pottery fabrics F6 and F7, sherds of which were contained in the same feature. Fragments of the upper surface of the deposit survived; these had been smoothed. No lower surfaces could be recognised.

The material bore the appearance of having been plastered over the interior of the feature after it had been almost completely filled, and then burnt or fired in situ. Several very similar late Bronze Age deposits were found at Knight's Farm, where they were interpreted as pit linings used to consolidate the sides of storage pits (Bradley et al. 1980, 244–5). However, the deposit occurred at the very top of the feature, and the resulting clay-lined depression would surely have been too shallow for any form of storage. In any case, clay with flint inclusions would not have been waterproof.

The crushed flint inclusions would not have occurred in the clay naturally, and must have been deliberately added. The most obvious reason for this would have been the intention of firing the clay, the flint inclusions serving to help stabilise the clay during firing. A large quantity of burnt flint was found associated with the fired clay, and could represent the raw material used for tempering the clay, calcined to aid crushing. Deposits of calcined flint, associated with stone pounders, have been found at the late Bronze Age site of Runnymede Bridge, where they have been interpreted as part of the process of pottery manufacture on the site (S. Needham, pers. comm.).

These observations, and the close resemblance of the fabric of the fired clay to the fabric of some of the coarse flint-gritted pottery found on the site, might suggest that this deposit represents part of the process of pottery manufacture. The fired clay could be part of a larger deposit, part of which was employed to line a shallow depression which may then have been used for a simple bonfire kiln, while the remainder formed the raw material for the pottery itself. Whilst most of the fired clay is oxidised, the interior, smoothed, surface of the deposit is fired to a lighter buff-grey colour, partially unoxidised in places, which would suggest that it was fired in unoxidising conditions.

However, despite these observations, which imply that this feature is associated with late Bronze Age pottery manufacture on the site, stratigraphic evidence would suggest that this feature should be placed no earlier than the Roman period. The in situ appearance of the fired clay would argue against this material being residual, and unless, as has been suggested, there was some surviving superstructure which prevented burial by the old land surface, this feature must be of Roman or later date, and as such is unlikely to be associated with pottery manufacture. Flint-gritted pottery is known in the early Roman period in the area, such as Silchester ware, but is almost completely absent from the site.

Objects of worked bone, by L.N. Mepham

Two pieces of worked bone were recovered, both from Phase 1c river channel deposits. The bones were identified by Jennie Coy. The more complete example (SF.270, context 582, Trench XA) (Fig. 42, 14) comprises a long-bone, possibly a large roe deer tibia (250 mm in length), with an oblique diagonal cut across the shaft, and a sharply pointed tip, which is broken. The shaft has been hollowed, and the butt is perforated through both sides. The whole piece has a high overall polish, particularly at the tip. A second fragment of worked bone (SF.314, context 759, Trench XA) (not illustrated), from a small ungulate, appears to derive from a tool of very similar form to SF.270. Only a short length survives (70 mm), showing part of an oblique diagonal cut. As in the more complete example, the shaft has been hollowed and the fragment has a high overall polish.

Objects of this type are known from late Bronze Age contexts, for example at Runnymede Bridge, Surrey, and Eldon's Seat, Dorset, (Longley 1980, fig. 14; Cunliffe and Phillipson 1968, 225), and throughout the Iron Age, for example at Danebury, Hampshire (Cunliffe 1984, fig. 7.34). They are generally classified as 'gouges', though a number of different functions have been suggested for them, including use in weaving, and in the dressing of hides. Many examples have been found with perforated butts, as is the more complete example from Anslow's Cottages, perhaps for some form of attachment.

Basketry, by J. Watson

Fragments of basketry were recovered which probably constituted part of an eel or fish trap (Fig. 43). It appears to have been made using a twined basketry technique and this has been recorded using the analysis form from Adovasio (1977, 21–2). Essentially a close plain weave has been employed, using split hazel (*Corylus* sp.) stems for both the warp and weft components. The basket seems to have been started around a tapered alder post (*Alnus* sp.) with the warps arranged tightly together. From this starting point the trap has then been enlarged by splaying the warps while continuing the plain weave arrangement with the wefts.

Both systems are unequal in size. The warps range from 6.4 mm to 11 mm in width, an average of 7.3 mm, and the wefts range from 4.2 mm to 9.1 mm, to give an average of 6.7 mm. The basketry is so closely woven that there is no measurable gap between the weft elements. When required, additional wefts appear to have been laid in under exhausted ones, but it is not obvious what method was used for warp splices. Bark has been retained on both systems; on the warps this is arranged towards the inside of the basket, while the wefts are woven with the bark on the outside. Possibly this arrangement increased the durability of the trap.

This fragment of basketry seems to be the last chair of a putt type fish trap (Jenkins 1974, 60) or an eel pot like the closely woven Fenland grig type (*ibid.*, 278). The latter seems more likely because of the presence of the wooden plug.

This trap was found in a stream channel, but it is not known if it was deliberately placed in this position or accidentally caught there. Often eel traps were placed in stream channels and mill races with the open mouth pointing upstream in order to catch eels on the ebb-tide (see Salisbury 1991, fig. 11.1 and table 11.1 for examples).

Archaeological examples from Denmark, Sweden, and the Netherlands, appear to have a more open structure than this trap (Brinkhuizen 1986), but otherwise the shape appears very similar. In terms of basketry technology there are few differences between prehistoric and recent examples, only local variation. This means that it is impossible to suggest a date for this basket based on typology alone. Known examples of fishweirs and eel traps incorporating baskets are quite widely known in northern Europe, from as early as the Mesolithic, as at Bergschenhoek in the Netherlands (Louwe Kooijmans 1985, 92–9), but again the form of construction has remained remarkably consistent (see Salisbury 1991 for summary). For these reasons a fragment of the basketry was submitted to the Oxford Radiocarbon Accelerator and produced a date of 1060±80 BP (OxA–2126).

A 9th century Saxon fishweir at Colwick, Nottinghamshire, consisted of a closely spaced double row of round-sectioned posts 115–140 mm in diameter and c. 1.4 m long, driven into the gravel bed of the River Trent. The gaps between the posts were filled with wattle panels, mostly of hazel. The eel basket did not survive but the reconstruction in the Canal Museum, Nottingham, incorporates a basket very similar to the original form of the example from Anslow's Cottages. The type is still widely used on the Severn Estuary where it is now usually made from willow. The earliest illustrated example of this type of eel basket, in use in a mill race, is in the *Luttrell Psalter* (Jenkins 1974, 282).

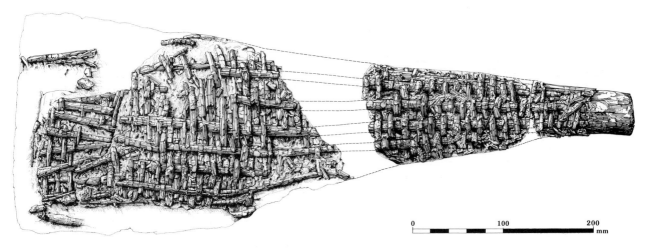

Figure 43   Anslow's Cottages: wicker basket (SF.1073), Phase 4a

Worked Timbers, by L.N. Mepham

A total of 398 pieces of waterlogged wood was recorded from Anslow's Cottages, and of these 191 showed signs of utilisation. Selection of wood for recording was made on site, on the basis either of visible signs of working, and/or position suggesting utilisation, since time and resources did not permit the recording of every piece of wood. The recorded sample represents *c.* 25% of the total amount.

Methodology

Each piece of wood recorded was allocated a unique number. Details of dimensions, position, and visible tool marks were recorded. Samples were taken for identification of wood species, and selected worked pieces were also sampled for radiocarbon dating. Full details of all recorded wood are held in archive.

A basic terminology has been adopted to describe the recorded pieces. The term 'timber' is used to refer to all wood which shows signs of conversion from the parent tree, by cutting, splitting or shaping, ie. all possible 'structural' pieces. Apart from simple 'cut timbers' and 'split timbers', which show no other signs of working, the worked timbers have been divided into 'stakes' and 'planks'. In this instance, 'stakes' are all roundwood timbers which have been sharpened to a point at one end. 'Planks' can be either radially split (with the grain), or tangentially split (across the grain). There is some unavoidable ambiguity in the distinction between simple radial splits and radially split planks; in this instance, radially split planks are defined as less than a quarter section of the parent branch. There is some obvious functional overlap: some planks as defined here have also been sharpened at one end, and were found in upright positions, and several timbers with a simple diagonal cut had been utilised as stakes.

The dangers of using a blanket term such as 'stakes' to cover all pointed timbers have been pointed out (Crone and Barber 1981, 513); it should be noted that the diameters of stakes from Anslow's Cottages range from 30–150 mm, with one anomalously small example of 15 mm diameter, and as such all fall within the range defined by Crone and Barber for 'stakes' (*ibid.*, 513).

Table 20 Anslow's Cottages: timber types by phase

Phase	Stakes	Planks	Split	Diag. cut	Util.	Total
1	15	–	1	–	10	26
2	2	–	–	–	–	2
3	43	2	1	2	4	52
4	21	8	–	1	–	30
UP	27	15	4	34	–	80
Total	108	25	6	37	14	190

Util = unworked but utilised
UP = unphased

Although the majority of timbers from Anslow's Cottages were not *in situ* when excavated, and the position and nature of the structures from which they derived are unknown, it was possible to define several groups of timbers which were *in situ*. On the basis of a series of radiocarbon dates, and limited stratigraphic evidence, a tentative phasing has been constructed for these timber groupings. Most of the timbers came from mid or late Saxon groups (Phases 3 and 4) from the northern edge of the river channel, although the dating suggests that at least one group in the same area dated to the Roman period, and the possibility of residual timbers cannot be ruled out. The Bronze Age timber structure was located on the southern bank of a river channel which was probably distinct from that in which the other timbers were found. There appears to be little or no distinction in the woodworking techniques throughout the collection; for this reason the timbers have been discussed altogether in the first instance and subsequently by phase. A list of the various timber types by phase is presented in Table 20.

Primary working

A limited amount of evidence was recovered of the methods of primary working used on the site. Thirty-eight timbers had been cut diagonally, though in some cases it was difficult to distinguish between deliberate working and post-depositional damage; 27 can be said, with reasonable certainty, to represent original working. In addition, two stakes had been cut diagonally at the end opposite the point. One timber showed signs of cutting by chopping and then tearing; one timber had been cut to a chisel-shaped point, with facets on two opposing sides (not illustrated) and ten timbers showed faceted diagonal cuts (eg. Fig. 47, 15); the remainder were either cut with a single stroke (eg. Fig. 47, 16), or any existing tool marks have been subsequently eroded. It is not possible to say whether these cuts resulted from the original felling of the timbers or from subsequent preparation of timbers by cutting into lengths. Of the seventeen timbers where the angle of cut was recorded, all had shallow angles of 40° or less to the stem (cf. Coles and Orme 1985, 26). The shallow angles and the fact that more than half the timbers appeared to have been cut by a single stroke would suggest that a metal axe was used rather than a flint or stone axe.

Some of these cut timbers were certainly intended for use as stakes. Ten otherwise unworked pieces were found *in situ*, that is, in an upright position, the diagonally cut end forming the point of the stake, and at least some of the remainder may have been similarly utilised, or they may represent the debris left after secondary working had taken place, ie. pieces felled and/or cut but not selected for further use. Certainly the diameters of many of these pieces fall within the range of recorded diameters of the worked stakes (*see below*), and diagonal cuts have been recorded on a small number of worked stakes, on the end opposite the point (eg. Fig. 48, 17). However, the dimensions of some pieces

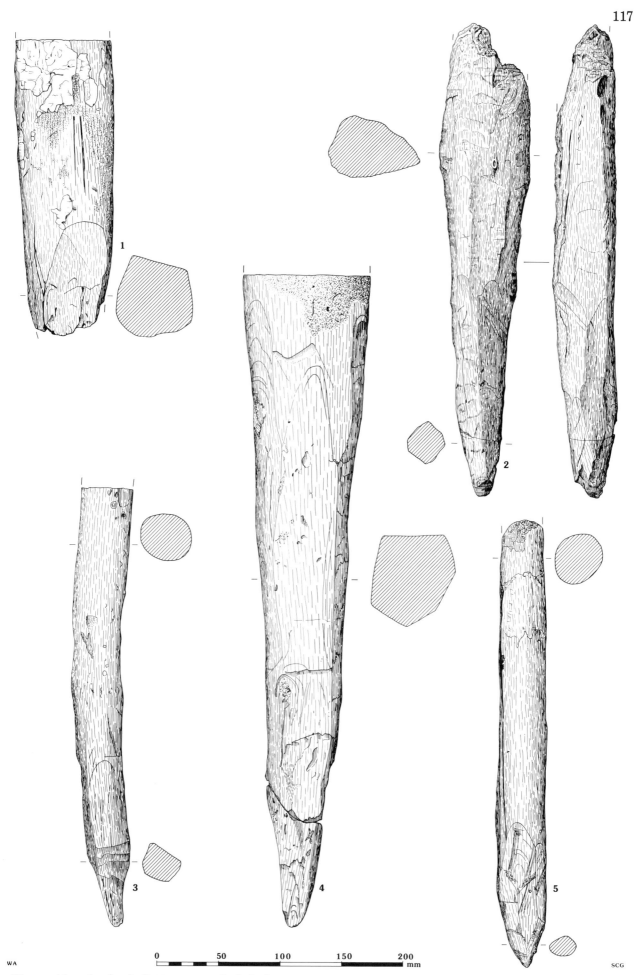

0   50   100   150   200
mm

WA

SCG

Figure 44   *Anslow's Cottages: worked timbers*

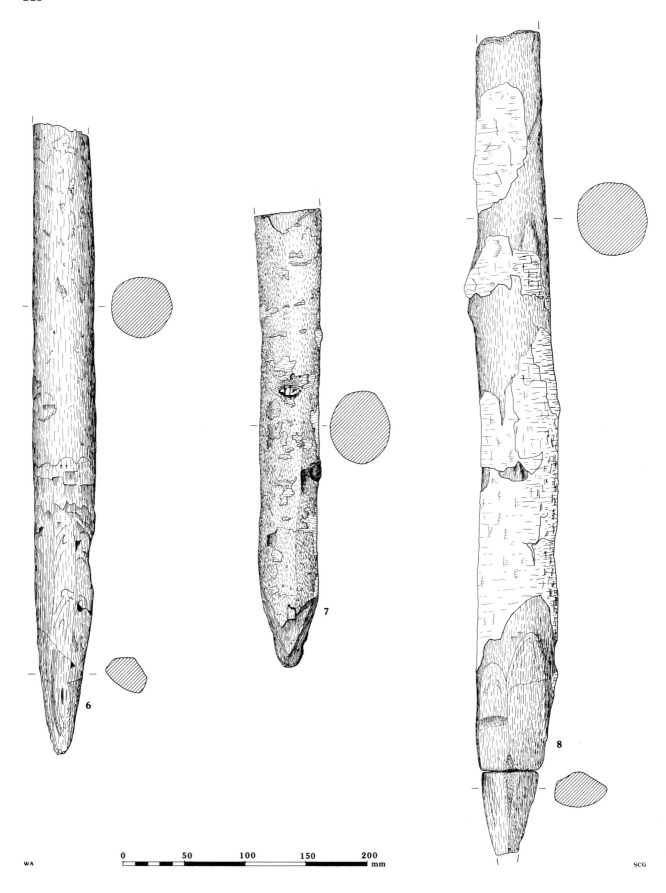

WA

0   50   100   150   200
mm

SCG

Figure 45   Anslow's Cottages: worked timbers

suggest that they were selected for some other use; this point is discussed below. Several timbers had been deliberately split, and probably represent the first stages in the preparation of planks, of which a number were recovered on the site (*see below*). One half-section and two quarter-sections were recorded.

There was no evidence for any working of timber on the site itself. Sites such as Etton (Pryor *et al.* 1985) and Flag Fen (Pryor *et al.* 1986), both in the Cambridgeshire Fens have produced woodworking debris such as small wood chips; and on the Somerset Levels wooden mallets and wedges used for splitting timbers have been recovered (Orme and Coles 1985, 22). No such evidence was found at Anslow's Cottages, although the absence of wood chips may be due to post-depositional removal by water action. A more likely reason is that the woodworking took place on the riverbank, perhaps at the site of felling.

Secondary working
Stakes
A total of 111 pieces of timber was recovered which were considered to represent partial or complete stakes; there were in addition ten diagonally cut timbers utilised as stakes, which have been discussed above. Most had been worked to a 'pencil' point at one end; a few were merely short, broken, sections of timber which had been roughly squared or otherwise shaped along the length, from which the points had been broken off. Only one stake had been made from a deliberately split timber; all the rest were roundwood, although three stakes had been roughly squared or otherwise shaped along most of their surviving length.

Nearly all the stake points had been worked on at least three sides or in three planes, many being faceted all round the point (eg. Figs 44 and 45, 2–7); however, there were thirteen examples which had facets in only two planes. About two-thirds of the stakes retained no bark at all on their surviving outer surfaces; the remainder retained 5–75%, and one example retained 100% bark on the outer surface. This information may be misleading, as bark can be removed by post-depositional processes rather than by deliberate action, but it can give some indication of the methods of timber preparation. It appears that there was some variation in the amount of time spent in preparing the various stakes, and there seemed to be little or no standardisation in form. Some had been shaped along part of their length as well as having worked points (Fig. 48, 17), whereas other timbers obviously underwent the minimum of preparation necessary to produce a usable stake (Fig. 45, 8).

One stake was considerably smaller than the rest of the stakes (diameter 15 mm), although it had been shaped in the same way, with facets on two sides forming a pencil point (Fig. 47, 14). This piece might be regarded rather as a peg; similar pegs have been found at the Bronze Age site at Flag Fen, where they held a brushwood layer in place (Pryor *et al.* 1986, 8). The remaining stakes, where mea-surable, range in diameter from 30–150 mm, with 86% falling within the range 35–80 mm. There appears to be no correlation between diameter and wood species.

Several stakes survive to a considerable length; 24 are over 0.70 m long and five are over 1 m in length. One survives to a length of 1.55 m and may be complete; there is a diagonal cut, possibly original, at the end opposite the point. Not all the stakes were originally this long, however; three other possibly complete stakes are around 0.70 m in length and another example with a diagonal cut was 0.53 m in length. Many of the stakes and other timbers found *in situ* had quite badly eroded upper ends, and this was probably due to water action (see Fig. 36).

Planks
Twenty-six planks and possible planks were recorded. Those which could be positively identified comprised eight radial splits (eg. Figs 50 and 51, 19–21) and seventeen tangential splits (eg. Fig. 46, 9–11; Fig. 49, 18). Of the two methods, radial splitting is the easier; trunks are split in half, then in half again, and finally slices are taken off the radial sections. Tangentials require carefully controlled splitting across natural planes of weakness. In only four cases could the original diameter of the parent branch be determined; all were radial splits and came from branches with diameters ranging from 0.10–0.18 m.

Five planks were sharpened at one end, by faceting to a pencil point (eg. Fig. 46, 11) and it appears that these were meant to be driven into the ground vertically; three were recovered *in situ* in such a position, all tangentials, from Phase 4b, group 1594 (*see below*). The five planks ranged in breadth from 0.09–0.17 m, and in length from 0.51–1.31 m. Another plank was of a particularly small size compared to the other planks, measuring 0.16 m x 0.03 m x 0.02 m, and this piece might better be described as a lath (Fig. 47, 13). Alternatively, it might be interpreted as a tub stave. Such vessels have a wide date range; tub staves of similar dimensions are known from the late Iron Age at Glastonbury Lake Village, Somerset (Earwood 1988, fig. 84), and from a 10th century AD rath in County Antrim (Lynn 1978). Of the remaining planks, the tangentials had surviving lengths ranging from 0.15–1.59 m, breadths 0.05–0.19 m and thicknesses 0.015–0.12 m. The radials covered a narrower range of dimensions, with surviving lengths of between 0.40–1.53 m, breadths 0.05–0.10 m and thicknesses 0.03–0.08 m. Again, there appears to be no correlation between dimensions and wood species.

A deep (0.17 m), V–shaped notch had been cut in the end of one of the radial planks (Fig. 50, 19). The timber was quite eroded, but some faceting did survive around the notch, which was probably axed out with a fairly thin blade. The plank was 1.5 m in length, and its function is uncertain, but it may have been used as a kind of pronged peg to hold another timber in position.

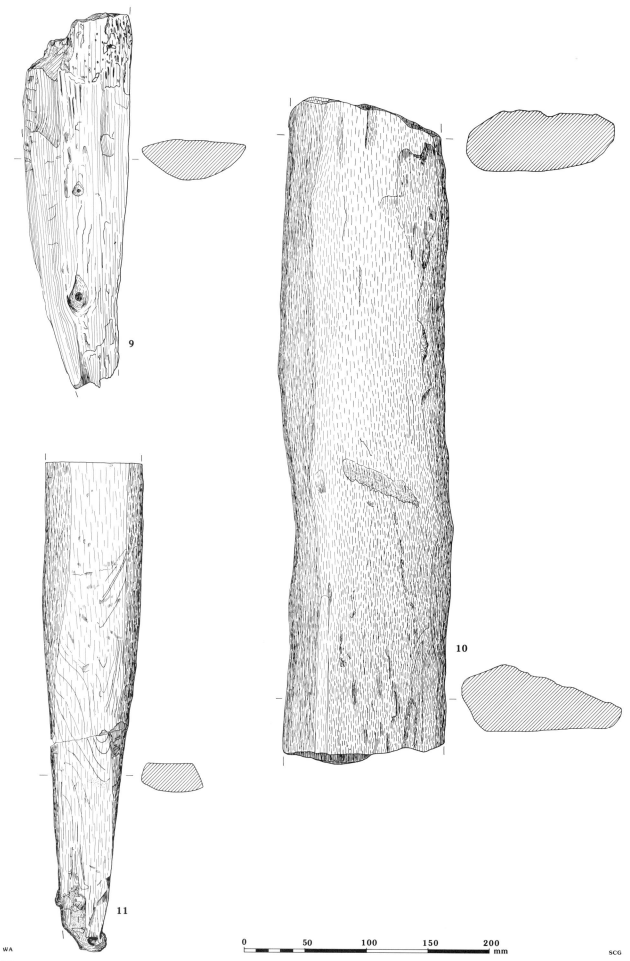

Figure 46   Anslow's Cottages: worked timbers

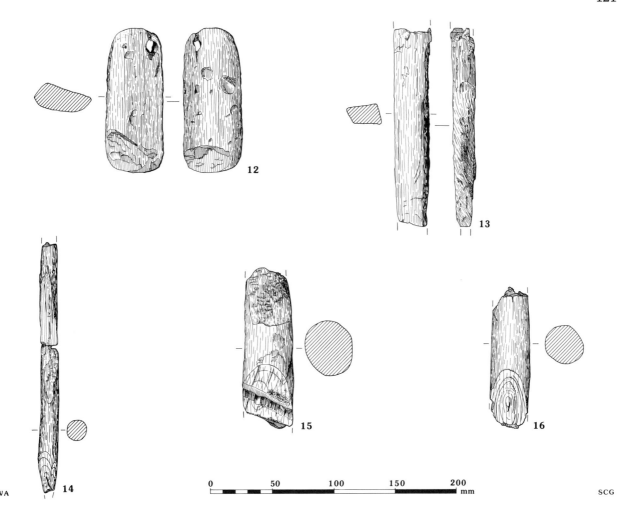

WA

0 50 100 150 200
mm

SCG

Figure 47   Anslow's Cottages: worked timbers

Another plank from Phase 4b, a squared tangential split, was perforated by four sub-rectangular holes, two at each end (Fig. 49, 18), the whole plank measuring 1.59 m in length, but was not quite complete as the timber had broken across the fourth hole. The holes had been axed out from one side. A slight lip was observed running along both longitudinal edges of the upper side of the plank; it is not certain whether this was intentional or what purpose it might have served. Although this piece has been radiocarbon dated to the late Saxon period (1030±70 BP, HAR–9186) it is interesting to note that similar pieces have been recovered from prehistoric sites in the Somerset Levels (Orme and Coles 1983, figs 38–41) and the Bronze Age site at Flag Fen (Pryor *et al.* 1986, fig. 12).

Other worked timbers
One other timber had a deep V–shaped notch cut lengthwise in one end, though this example was far more crudely executed than the notched plank described above, and may in fact be fortuitous.

Wooden object
One wooden object was recovered from a late Bronze Age ditch (Phase 1e): a small, flattish, sub-rectangular fragment, 0.115 m x 0.05 m x 0.025 m,

similar in shape to a small axe-head (Fig. 47, 12). A similar object, described as a tomahawk has been found in the Somerset Levels, wedged in the split end of another piece of timber (Orme and Coles 1983, fig. 29); its function is unknown. The piece from Anslow's Cottages may have been used as a wedge for splitting timbers, although its regularity suggests careful shaping, which would not have been necessary for such a wedge.

Timbers by phase
It should be stressed that only the timbers for which radiocarbon dates have been obtained are securely dated; the other timbers described below have been assigned to the various phases on the basis of association with the dated timbers, and by limited stratigraphic evidence. The possibility of the reuse of timbers is discussed below.

Phase 1
Along the southern bank of the river channel, a double line of ten, or possibly eleven, stakes was discovered (873, Figs 29 and 30). The overall span of the surviving stakes was *c.* 2.7 m, with gaps between ranging from 0.15–1.15 m, though some stakes may be missing. All of the stakes were set into the gravel of the river bank, with the exception

of two, which were shorter and smaller in diameter. Some horizontal lengths of wood, apparently unworked, were recorded between and close to the vertical stakes. None appeared to have been attached to the stakes. These horizontal pieces may have formed part of the overall structure; alternatively they may have lodged in the silt which accumulated around the stakes during or after use of the structure. It has been suggested that the line of stakes may originally have been more extensive. The structure was interpreted as a revetment of the river bank and may have operated as a small jetty or landing stage.

The stakes range in diameter from 0.035–0.08 m, none survived to a length greater than 0.33 m, largely due to vandalism before they could be recorded. Where the lower end survives, all stakes have been worked to a pencil point, with facets on more than two faces (Fig. 44, 1 and 2). Apart from one oak stake, and a possible horizontal piece of *Prunus* sp. (sloe/wild cherry, etc.), all the wood was either ash or alder. A radiocarbon date of 2570±70 BP (HAR–9185) was obtained from Timber 94.

Two additional alder stakes were found unstratified in the river silts above this structure (Phase 1c). In addition to these worked timbers, the wooden object, possibly a wedge (Fig. 47, 12), was recovered from ditch 875 (Phase 1e) adjacent to Timber structure 873. The function of this object cannot be suggested and the reason for its location in the ditch fill is unclear.

Phase 2

Towards the northern edge of the river channel, two stakes were found *in situ, c.*0.2 m apart, driven into the gravel at an angle of about 45°, pointing towards the northern bank (1649, Fig. 31); a third stake observed in the section may belong to the same structure. They were both of alder with diameters of 40 mm and 50 mm and have both been worked to a pencil point at the lower end (Fig. 44, 3). A radiocarbon date of 1670±60 BP (HAR–9179) was obtained from one stake (Timber 26). Both stakes were associated with a depression in the bed of the river channel (688), and may have formed part of a fish trap. One unstratified willow/poplar stake, of similar diameter to the other stakes, may also belong to this phase. Three alder stakes, an ash stake and an alder plank were found in the channel deposits below the group described above.

Phase 3

The lower deposits of the northern side of the river channel in this period (Phase 3a) contained a relatively large number of unstratified timbers (Fig. 32). Of the worked timbers recorded from this phase, one (Timber 77) of two alder planks (Fig. 51, 20–21) produced a radiocarbon date of 1300±60 BP (HAR–9184). Other worked timbers in this phase included two ash and one willow/poplar stake and one alder notched split timber. A deep, V–shaped notch (170 mm) had been cut in the end of one of the radial planks (Fig. 50, 19); the timber was quite eroded, but some faceting did survive around the notch. The plank is 1.5 m in length, and its function is uncertain, but it may have been used as a kind of pronged peg to hold another timber in position.

In Phase 3c 37 pieces of wood were recorded *in situ* along the base of a small channel, including groups 1644, 1645, 1647 and 1648, immediately to the east of the Phase 2 stakes (Fig. 33). They comprise 32 stakes, two radially split planks, one diagonally cut timber and two unworked pieces. The two unworked pieces and one of the planks had all been utilised as stakes, driven into the gravel in an upright position. The whole group covered an area of *c.*5.5 m x 3.0 m.

The stakes range in diameter from 0.035–0.11 m. Apart from one chisel point, all had been worked to pencil points (eg. Fig. 44, 4). Six stakes were of willow/poplar, and one of birch; the remaining timbers and unworked pieces were either of ash or alder. A radiocarbon date of 1370±60 BP (HAR–9182) was obtained from Timber 366. This group of timbers showed no coherent patterning or structure. Not all the timbers were necessarily contemporary, and it may be that this group represented a series of structures, repaired or replaced over a period of time.

The timbers from Phase 3e which sealed the Phase 3c timbers included four planks of ash and alder and an alder stake (Fig. 45, 8) and may include timbers from the collapsed structure of the earlier phase.

Towards the southern edge of the Phase 3 river channel a roughly oval setting of timbers was recorded (1523, Fig. 33) (Phase 3d). This consisted of thirteen worked timbers, and one apparently unworked piece, all driven into the gravel in upright or slightly angled positions. The whole setting measured *c.* 0.3 m x 0.2 m. The worked timbers comprised eleven stakes (eg. Fig. 45, 6), one tangentially split plank (Fig. 46, 9) and one timber diagonally cut at one end but otherwise unworked. The diameter of the stakes ranged from 40–75 mm. One stake had been worked to a chisel point with facets on only one face (Fig. 44, 5); the others were all worked to a pencil point. Apart from one willow/poplar stake, all the wood was either alder or ash. A radiocarbon date of 1390±60 (HAR–9183) was obtained from Timber 139.

In the silts around and sealing the Phase 3d timbers an additional 35 worked timbers were recorded including diagonal cuts (eg. Fig. 47, 15 and 16) stakes/pegs and planks in alder, ash and willow/poplar; seven of these were *in situ* but did not appear to form part of the structure. These timbers presumably derive from structure 1523 or from replacement structures. One of the stakes was of particularly small size, with a diameter of only 15 mm, although shaped in the same way as the other stakes, with a pencil point (Fig. 47, 14). While this example falls within the size range of stakes as already defined (cf. Crone and Barber 1981, 513), it could be regarded rather as a peg. Likewise, it has been suggested above that one of the tangentially split planks of alder might originally have been a lath (Fig. 47, 13) or part of a wooden tub.

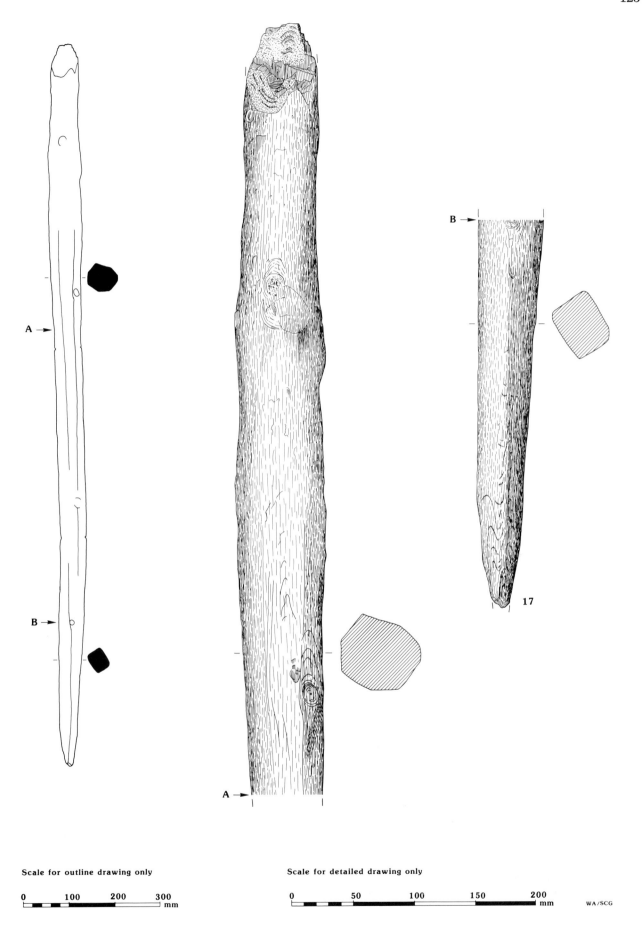

17

Scale for outline drawing only

0   100   200   300
                    mm

Scale for detailed drawing only

0   50   100   150   200
                                              mm

WA/SCG

Figure 48   Anslow's Cottages: worked timbers

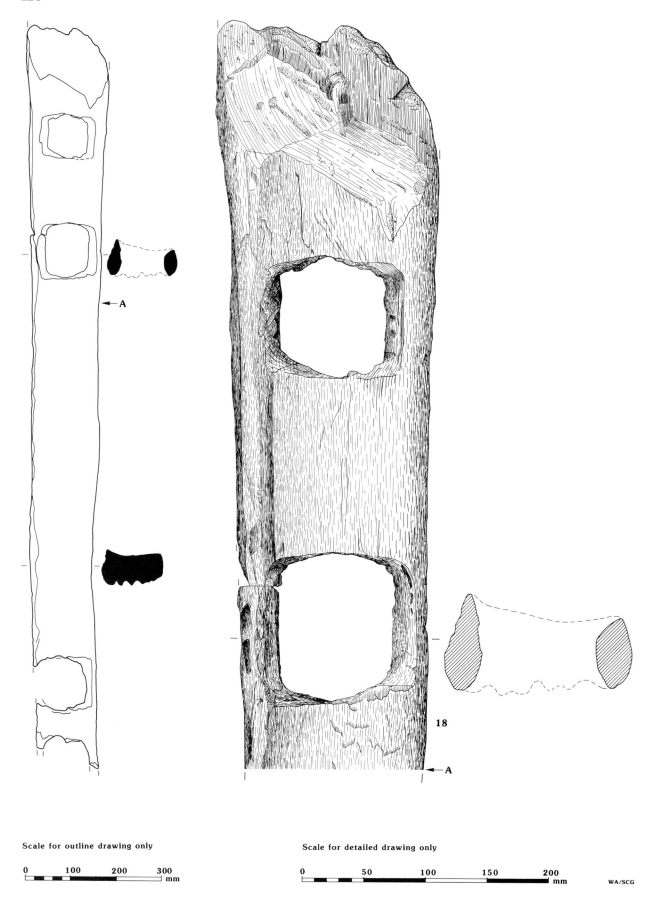

← A

18

← A

Scale for outline drawing only

0   100   200   300
                      mm

Scale for detailed drawing only

0   50   100   150   200
                                            mm

WA/SCG

Figure 49   Anslow's Cottages: worked timbers

Phase 4
Thirty-one timbers (groups 1646, and 1594, Fig. 35) were recorded in Phase 4b along the northern edge of the river channel, and in a multiple line across the channel, consisting of 21 stakes (including Fig. 45, 7; Fig. 48, 17), four radially split and four tangentially split planks (eg. Fig. 46, 11; Fig. 49, 18), and one diagonally cut timber utilised as a stake.

The stakes ranged in diameter from 0.035–0.12 m. One stake, 1.55 m long, is likely to have survived to its original length, since it had been diagonally cut at the end opposite the point (Fig. 48, 17). Apart from one chisel point, all stakes had been worked to a pencil point. All stakes were of either ash or alder.

One of the tangential planks was perforated by four sub-rectangular holes, two at each end, and had been pegged in place horizontally at one end by two stakes (Fig. 49, 18). The opposite end was probably also originally pegged in a similar fashion. This timber does not seem to have been prepared specifically for this structure; the four holes are regularly shaped, and are all of similar size, while the stakes inserted through them are of varying diameter and much smaller, and it is possibly a reused door-sill. Similar pieces have been recovered from the late Bronze Age settlement at Flag Fen (Pryor *et al.* 1986, fig. 12) although the example from Anslow's Cottages was part of a structure of much later date.

Of the remaining seven planks, three were found in an upright position, and all of these had been worked to a point at one end. One more was found in a horizontal position. These planks ranged in breath from 0.05–0.095 m, in thickness 0.02–0.070 m, and in length 0.17–0.89 m. All were of either ash or alder. Radiocarbon dates of 1030±60 BP (HAR–9181), 1030±70 BP (HAR–9186), and 930±60 BP (HAR–9180), were obtained from two stakes and one tangential plank from this structure (Timbers 31, 345 and 358). A further four alder timbers including stakes and a plank were recovered from the channel deposits sealing this structure.

This group of timbers may represent a more formal arrangement of water control than the structures in earlier phases. The arrangement of timbers across the channel, with the horizontal pegged plank may have supported a shuttering of some sort. The line of timbers along the northern bank, one of which yielded the latest radiocarbon date, perhaps marked the edge of the channel.

Wood species
The wood species of 340 of the 398 pieces of wood recorded were identified by Wendy Carruthers and are listed in Table 21 by timber type. If it is assumed that the unworked wood from the site is a fair representation of the range and relative abundance of species to be found in the near vicinity, a comparison with the worked/utilised wood might provide evidence of any deliberate selection that was taking place to provide structural timbers for the site.

However, a comparison of the species of worked and unworked wood from the site shows a close correspondence between the proportions of the various species used. Alder is the most common species (50.5% of the worked and 57.2% of the unworked wood), followed by ash (29.5% and 11.1% respectively) and willow/poplar (12.1% and 7.7% respectively). Oak, hazel, birch, apple/pear and *Prunus* sp. are each represented by one or two examples. All these species could have been found locally; the three most common species, in particular, are often found on slightly damp ground near running water. The evidence would suggest that only timbers easily available were being used, and that no deliberate selection for particular species was taking place. The evidence is insufficient to indicate whether any coppicing for timbers was taking place at any time, but the quantities of timber recorded would suggest that such a practice would not have been necessary for the provision of timber for the site.

The species used for the various types of worked timber generally reflect the relative proportions for the overall total of worked timbers. However, the numbers of ash and alder stakes are equal, and there is a particularly large number of willow/poplar timbers with diagonally cut ends. While the

Table 21 Anslow's Cottages: wood species by type

	Stakes	Planks	Split	Diagonally cut	Unworked, utilised	Unworked	Total
Alder	45	19	4	19	9	119	215
Ash	45	5	1	4	1	23	79
Willow/poplar	12	1	–	10	–	16	39
Oak	1	–	–	–	–	–	1
Hazel	1	–	–	–	–	1	2
Birch	1	–	–	–	–	–	1
Pomoideae	–	–	–	1	–	1	2
Prunus sp.	–	–	–	–	1	–	1
Unidentified	3	–	1	3	3	48	58
Total	108	25	6	37	14	208	398

Table 22 Anslow's Cottages: wood species by phase (worked and utilised pieces only)

Phase:	1	2	3	4	UP	Total
Alder	13	2	20	17	44	96
Ash	5	–	24	13	14	56
Willow/poplar	–	–	7	–	16	23
Oak	1	–	–	–	–	1
Hazel	–	–	–	–	1	1
Birch	–	–	1	–	–	1
Pomoideae	–	–	–	–	1	1
Prunus sp.	1	–	–	–	–	1
Unident.	6	–	–	–	4	10
Total	26	2	52	30	80	190

mean diameter of alder diagonally cut timbers (44 mm) is roughly comparable to the mean diameter of alder stakes (56 mm), the mean diameter of willow/poplar diagonally cut timbers (29 mm) is considerably less than that of the stakes (56 mm). This could indicate that willow/poplar was being cut not only for use as stakes, but also for some other function. Its flexibility would make it suitable for use in basketwork or hurdle-making, for example. A similar difference can be seen in the diameters of ash stakes and cut timbers, though in this case it is not so marked.

Wood species by phase are listed in Table 22. Numbers are insufficient to indicate any major differences in the use of various species through time. It can be noted that willow/poplar is only used in Phase 3; this might be due to its unsuitability for the more robust structures in Phases 1b and 4a.

Discussion

From an examination of the worked timbers by phase, it can be seen that very similar woodworking techniques were in use on the site from the late Bronze Age to the late Saxon period, and it has proved impossible to date timbers merely on the basis of methods of preparation. Although tool-marks survive, in the form of faceting across cut surfaces, little information can be derived as to the nature of the tools used. The long, relatively flat facets visible indicate the use of metal blades (Coles and Orme 1985, 27), but experimental work in the Somerset Levels has shown that surfaces worked with bronze and iron blades are often indistinguishable (Orme and Coles 1983, 27).

It appears that the majority of timbers in all phases underwent minimal preparation before utilisation. Primary working is demonstrated by a number of timbers which have been diagonally cut at one end, though it is uncertain whether this was a result of initial felling, or the preliminary cutting of felled timbers into the required lengths.

Some of these cut timbers were utilised as stakes with no further preparation, as were several

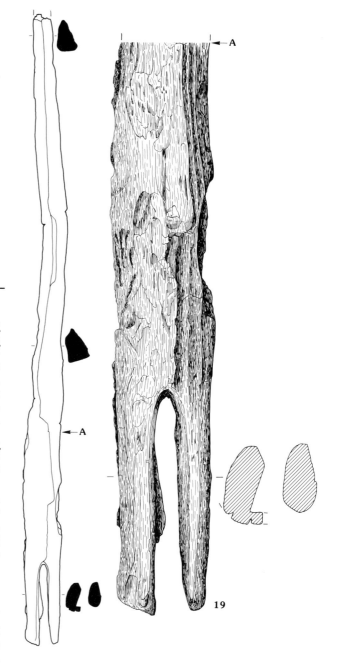

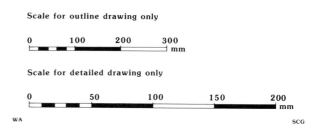

Scale for outline drawing only

Scale for detailed drawing only

Figure 50   Anslow's Cottages: worked timbers

apparently unworked pieces. However, most of the stakes were worked to a point by means of repeated cuts, resulting in a faceted chisel- or pencil-point.

Although the stakes in all phases were apparently prepared in much the same way, it seems that

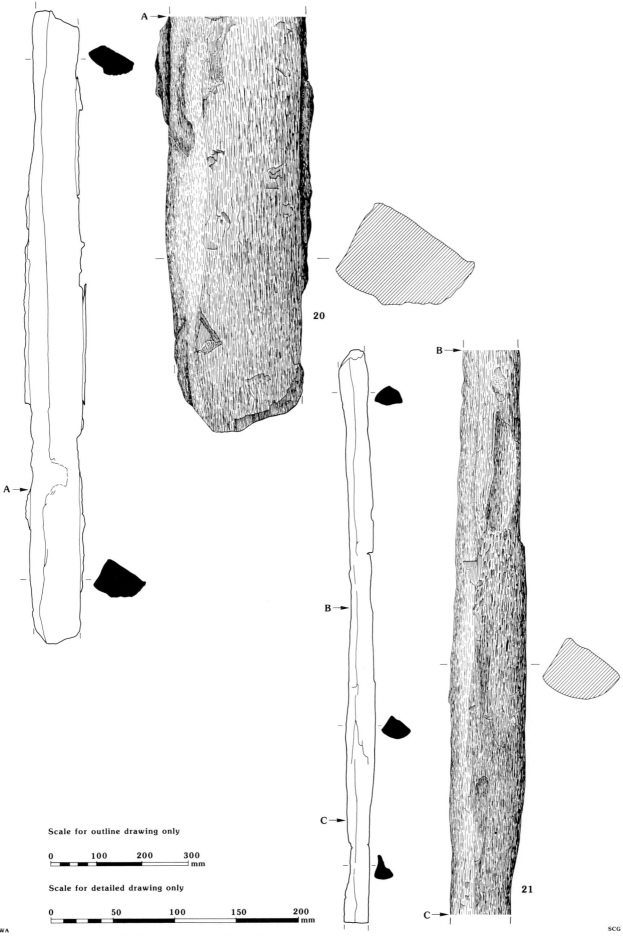

Scale for outline drawing only

0   100   200   300
━━━━━━━━━━━━━━━━━ mm

Scale for detailed drawing only

0   50   100   150   200
━━━━━━━━━━━━━━━━━ mm

WA

SCG

Figure 51   Anslow's Cottages: worked timbers

some selection for size took place, and this is probably related to the function of the various structures. The mean diameters of stakes in Phases 1b (55.7 mm) and 4a (62.1 mm) are greater than those in Phases 2 (45 mm) and 3c/3d (52.8 mm). The structures in Phases 2 and 3c/3d have been provisionally interpreted as fishtraps, and as such would not have required timbers of any great size. The bank revetment of Phase 1b and the possible water-sluice in Phase 4b would have required more sturdy structural timbers to withstand the force of fast flowing water. The possible selection of particular species in different phases has already been discussed.

The structure in Phase 4b is the only one in which plank shuttering has been found, and both this and the use of the pegged horizontal plank indicate a more substantial and more sophisticated structure than the earlier timber settings. Several of the stakes had been quite carefully prepared, and one had been shaped along two-thirds of its length. This contrasts with the more *ad hoc* nature of the possible traps, where simply cut timbers and even unworked pieces were utilised.

Even with this limited evidence for selection for size, and perhaps by species, it is clear that there was little standardisation amongst the timbers from any one phase. Stakes with carefully prepared points, a few also shaped along part of their length, are found beside stakes which obviously underwent the minimum of preparation. This lack of standardisation might be a result of several factors. Either the timber settings were constructed on an *ad hoc* basis, in which any timber readily to hand was used, with the minimum of preparation; or the structures underwent a certain measure of repair or reinforcement through time, with odd timbers used at different times; or a certain amount of reuse of timbers was taking place. These factors are not mutually exclusive.

Reuse of timbers is a possibility, and is suggested by the apparent re-use of a door-sill in structure 1594. The series of radiocarbon dates indicates a date range for the timber settings along the northern edge of the river channel from the late Roman to the late Saxon period. However, it should be noted that these dates relate to the timbers themselves, rather than to the timber settings in which they occur.

Catalogue of illustrated timbers

Fig.44
1. Part of oak stake, partially squared at one end. Damaged subsequent to excavation. Timber 92 (SF.479); context 873; Phase 1b
2. Part of alder stake, worked to pencil-point; multiple facets. Damaged subsequent to excavation. Timber 94 (SF.481); context 873; Phase 1b
3. Alder stake worked to pencil-point; multiple facets; possible original cut at other end. Timber 26 (SF.361); context 1649; Phase 2
4. Alder stake worked to pencil-point; multiple facets. Timber 337 (SF.1142); context 1647; Phase 3c

5. Willow/poplar stake, worked to pencil-point at one end; multiple facets on one side only. Timber 135 (SF. 1040); context 1523; Phase 3d
Fig. 45
6. Ash stake, worked to pencil-point at one end; multiple facets. Timber 139 (SF.1028); context 1523; Phase 3d
7. Alder stake, worked to pencil-point; three facets. Timber 385 (SF.2004); context 1646; Phase 4b
8. Alder stake, worked to pencil-point at one end; two facets. Timber 52 (SF.381); context 615; Phase 3e
Fig. 46
9. Ash tangential plank, flattened on one side only; tapering naturally to point at one end. Timber 128(SF.1047); context 1523; Phase 3d
10. Alder tangential plank, shaped to roughly rectangular section. Timber 155 (SF.2010); context 1525; Phase 3
11. Alder tangential plank, shaped to roughly rectangular section, worked to point at one end. Timber 345 (SF.1172); context 1594; Phase 4b
Fig. 47
12. Shaped wooden object; sub-rectangular with rounded ends. Timber 120 (SF.488); context 584; Phase 1e
13. Alder plank of very small dimensions, possibly a tub stave. Roughly rectangular and slightly curved in section. Timber 193 (SF. 2015); context 1504; pre-Phase 3f/post-Phase 3d
14. Willow/poplar stake/peg, worked to pencil-point at one end; two facets. Timber 280 (SF.1005); context 1503; pre-Phase 3f/post- Phase 3d
15. Willow/poplar timber with diagonal faceted cut at one end. Timber 279 (SF.1034); context 1505; pre-Phase 3f/post-Phase 3d
16. Alder timber with diagonal cut at one end. Timber 292 (SF.1010); context 1503; pre-Phase 3f/post-Phase 3d
Fig. 48
17. Ash stake, shaped along two-thirds of length and worked to pencil-point at one end; multiple facets. Possible original diagonal cut at opposite end. Timber 346 (SF.1178); context 1594; Phase 4b
Fig. 49
18. Alder tangential plank, shaped to roughly rectangular section. Two sub-rectangular holes through each end. Timber 341 (SF.1176); context 1594; Phase 4b
Fig. 50
19. Alder radial split; roughly triangular section. One end has deep V–shaped notch cut lengthwise across timber. Timber 69 (SF.375); unstratified; Phase 3a
Fig. 51
20. Alder radial split; roughly triangular section; possibly cut at one end. Timber 77 (SF.376); context 625; Phase 3a
21. Alder radial split; quarter section of branch. Timber 67 (SF.378); context 608/625; Phase 3a

5 Environmental Evidence

Faunal Remains, by J. Coy

Material and methods
The small collection of animal bones from Anslow's Cottages is generally well-preserved, although the type of preservation noted varies considerably according to the context type. Table 23 presents the quantities by species and by phase; quantities of

Table 23 Anslow's Cottages: animal bone by phase

Phase	Horse	Cow	Sheep	Sheep/ goat	Pig	LAR	SAR	Dog	Red deer	Roe deer	Vole	Bird	Other	Total
Pre-1	–	–	–	–	–	1	–	–	–	–	–	–	–	1
1a	–	1	–	1	1	11	1	–	2	–	–	–	–	17
1b	–	8	–	2	3	20	24	1	–	–	–	–	3	61
1c	11	20	3	8	4	11	9	2	10	3	2	1	4	88
1d	–	1	–	–	3	2	2	–	–	–	–	–	1	9
1e	–	1	–	–	–	3	–	–	–	–	–	–	–	4
1f	–	–	–	–	–	–	–	–	–	–	1	–	–	1
pre-2	–	–	–	–	–	–	–	–	–	–	–	1	–	1
3a	–	–	–	–	–	–	–	–	–	–	–	1	–	1
3c	–	3	–	–	–	–	–	–	1	–	–	–	–	4
3d	–	1	–	–	–	4	1	–	–	–	–	1	–	7
3f	3	30	1	10	3	109	37	–	2	–	1	1	7	204
3g	1	11	1	2	1	43	1	–	–	–	–	–	–	60
4a	–	–	–	–	1	–	–	–	–	–	–	–	–	1
5	1	–	1	–	–	–	1	–	–	–	–	–	–	2
Total	16	76	6	23	16	204	76	3	15	3	4	5	15	461

LAR = large ungulate (horse, cattle, deer); SAR = small ungulate (sheep, goat, pig, deer); Other = unidentified fragment

bone from sieving were very small and insignificant and have not been included. Phase 3 produced the largest quantity of animal bone although comparison with the second largest collection from Phase 1 does suggest that some of the former may be residual.

The data from the bones were recorded using Method 86 of the Faunal Remains Unit which is based on methods developed with the Ancient Monuments Laboratory. Full details can be found in the archive.

Initially it was intended to take 10 litre soils samples from all definable layers and primary fills of all features. Many of these were wet-sieved through 1 mm and 250µ sieves and sorted on site but it soon became apparent that they were barren or contained nothing that was well-preserved. In view of this and the limited time available for the excavations, subsequent samples were selected on the basis of high charcoal content or other burnt material, organic contents and relatively undisturbed layers.

In addition, some contexts associated with special finds (stakes, timbers and a possible fishtrap) were analysed. River channel layers, where they were judged likely to have been disturbed or redeposited, were regarded as being of low priority. As a result of this programme seventeen sieved samples examined for botanical material produced small bones. These were scanned and results can be found in the archive.

Phase 1: Bronze Age (181 bones)
Many of the bones are well-preserved, especially those from the river channel. Those from the burnt

flint spread (809) are eroded and some gnawed, probably by dogs.

Most of the bones were from probable domestic species. Animals represented include a small type of horse, comparable in size with the modern New Forest Pony. The cattle, sheep (no goat was identified), and pig bones were probably all from domestic animals but were largely fragmentary and unmeasurable. In ditch 874 (Phase 1d) there were the remains of an articulated immature pig hindleg with proximal tibia unfused.

Dog is represented by a mandible from a Phase 1b post-hole and a humerus from the channel silts. These represent large animals but the relatively small canine in the former specimen shows that this at least was a domestic dog and not a wolf. The humerus is just larger than a modern comparative specimen with a shoulder height of 0.58 m, which would just be within the range of Bronze Age domestic dogs (Harcourt 1974). Over 100 of the total fragments from this phase are unidentifiable but probably also derived from these species.

Wild species represented in this phase are the native red and roe deer. There are several fragments of red deer from various features; two of these, a scapula in a Phase 1b post-hole, and a humerus from the trackway of Phase 1a (1091) indicate large individuals; the latter gives the largest distal breadth yet recorded for Wessex archaeological material (63.4 mm; details in archive). Two fragments of roe deer tibiae came from the channel silts of Phase 1c, which also produced a jaw of the short-tailed vole and femur of water vole, and a carpo-metacarpus of duck which compares well with a wigeon.

Table 24 Anslow's Cottages: location and percentages of eroded, stained and gnawed bones (all phases)

Location	No. frags	% eroded	% stained	% gnawed
South river channel	97	21	69	23
Trackway 1091	31	26	–	13
Ditches	46	69	22	7
Pits	59	80	–	13
Burnt flint 809	35	56	16	32
Old land surface 869	88	52	2	7
Other	174	74	6	3

A narrow range of other wild species was collected by sieving. None of these is surprising in an area of water channels and damp ditches. In addition to the voles already mentioned, sieving revealed immature water vole, immature frog or toad from a peaty layer in ditch 908 (Phase 1f), vertebrae of very small eel and cyprinid (carp family), and an articular of the bullhead. All these creatures would be found in nearby areas today and it is not likely that such small examples were exploited.

Phase 3: mid Saxon (276 bones)

Most of the bones were recovered from the old land surface (Phase 3f) and features cut into it (Phase 3g). Similar species of domestic animal to those in Phase 1 are represented, although there was a higher proportion of cattle-sized long-bones.

A cattle metacarpus large enough to belong to aurochs or wild cattle was found in the old land surface (Phase 3f). The aurochs survived into the Bronze Age in Wiltshire (Jewell 1962) and a number of archaeological excavations in Wessex have yielded remains (Grigson 1965; Harcourt 1971; Jackson 1943). Its presence in such a context suggests that some of the bones associated with Phase 3 material may be residual. Other wild species are roe deer (tibia) from the channel fills which also produced a mallard humerus; and a vole tooth from Phase 3f. Sieving produced evidence for vole, amphibian and very small, but unidentifiable fish vertebrae. There is evidence of a species of mouse from Phase 3d.

Phase 4: Late Saxon

The only bones from this phase came from two contexts. The first was from a sieved sample from the wicker basket of Phase 4a (SF.1073). This contained some fragments of very small fish vertebrae and fish rays, far too small to have been of economic importance. The channel fill in the same area produced a well-preserved skull of a young male, probably domestic, pig.

Phase 5: medieval

Ditch 611 produced two fragments of bone (sheep and horse), and sieved material contained small mammal remains and fragmentary fish bones.

Discussion

Although several phases of activity at this site have been identified, it is likely that some of the bones are residual (see above). However, some general comments may be made. The bones described here must represent only a very small proportion of those originally present. Table 24 shows the contrasting characteristics of the bone from different context types. Whereas bone from channel fills is stained and generally well-preserved, even though a proportion of it has been gnawed, that from other features such as the old land surface, ditches and pits, is often eroded. Occasionally, however, bones are fortuitously preserved against all odds, such as a humerus fragment of a very young bovine from the old land surface. Generally it is likely that these bones have been more in contact with the air and in some cases subjected to disturbance such as ploughing, or it may indicate that some of the bone has survived from an earlier time.

The bone from the burnt flint concentration 809 in Phase 1 is more eroded and gnawed which might suggest hearth clearance.

The low erosion and good preservation of the channel fill bone and its presence in an area subjected to periodic movement may mean that long-term residuality is possible, with some bone perhaps dating back to a time prior to the Bronze Age. A few of the river channel bones are slightly mineralised.

That there are earlier bones around is confirmed by the find of an unstratified and mineralised aurochs skull recovered from the river channel in 1987 during machining close to the excavation trenches. The skull measurements are compared with ranges given by Grigson (1974; 1978) which clearly demonstrate that this skull fits within the upper part of the size range for aurochs is likely to be from a bull (ibid. 1978, 138).

Mollusca, by J.G. Evans

Three columns of samples were analysed for molluscs (see Fig. 28 for locations), two from infilled river channels, AC II (the northern channel) and AC V (the southern channel), and one from features 688 and 690, AC III. Sample weights are for air-dry material. Most of the samples were analysed by Vivian Evans and Annie Milles, the rest by JGE, and all the identifications were checked by JGE. In the tables, *Pisidium* and *Sphaerium* counts are of valves, but in the histograms these are halved.

Stages of Interpretation

Interpretation, stage 1. The main ecological groups
In the histograms, the species are arranged in a number of ecological groups, the aquatic ones being based on Sparks (Sparks and West 1959).

Table 25 Anslow's Cottages: molluscan sequence AC V (air-dry weight of samples, 0.5 kg)

Depth below surface (cm)	110–120	105–110	100–105	95–100	90–95	85–90	80–85	75–80	70–75	65–70	60–65	50–60	45–50	40–45	35–40	30–35	25–30	20–25	15–20
Aquatics: Sparks Groups 2–4																			
Theodoxus fluviatilis	-	5	1	2	3	1	-	-	-	-	-	-	-	-	-	-	-	-	-
Valvata cristata	17	65	55	69	2	4	5	-	-	1	-	-	1	13	1	-	1	-	-
Valvata piscinalis	91	425	329	314	17	11	6	2	-	1	-	-	-	14	5	1	-	1	-
Bithynia tentaculata	9	92	85	122	16	5	4	3	-	-	-	-	-	-	-	1	-	-	-
Bithynia tentaculata operculae	37	152	120	117	23	10	5	1	6	-	-	-	-	6	11	9	1	2	2
Bithynia leachii	4	34	19	57	3	1	-	1	-	-	-	-	-	-	2	-	-	-	-
Bithynia leachii operculae	10	35	36	59	5	1	-	-	-	-	-	-	-	1	-	-	-	-	-
Physa fontinalis	3	9	11	6	2	-	-	-	-	1	-	-	-	-	-	-	-	-	-
Lymnaea palustris	-	-	-	-	-	-	-	-	-	1	-	-	-	-	-	?2	-	-	-
Lymnaea stagnalis	-	2	1	2	-	-	?1	-	-	-	-	-	-	-	-	-	-	-	-
Lymnaea peregra	6	66	70	76	6	11	28	11	5	-	1	-	-	1	1	1	2	1	-
Planorbis carinatus	-	-	-	1	-	-	-	-	-	-	-	-	-	-	-	1	-	-	-
Bathyomphalus contortus	1	5	7	16	-	-	-	4	-	-	-	-	-	-	-	-	-	-	-
Gyraulus albus	1	25	15	28	3	3	1	-	-	-	-	-	-	-	-	-	-	-	-
Armiger crista	7	67	43	66	8	3	2	-	1	-	-	-	-	3	-	-	-	-	-
Hippeutis complanatus	-	-	-	1	-	-	-	-	-	-	-	-	-	-	-	-	-	-	-
Ancylus fluviatilis	21	154	83	90	20	9	-	-	-	-	-	-	-	7	-	1	-	-	-
Acroloxus lacustris	-	1	3	3	-	-	-	-	-	-	-	-	-	1	-	-	-	-	-
Sphaerium corneum	-	-	1	4	-	-	-	-	-	-	-	-	-	-	-	-	-	-	-
Pisidium amnicum	1	21	31	27	-	2	-	-	1	-	-	-	-	-	-	-	-	-	-
Pisidium milium	-	10	14	24	2	-	-	-	-	-	-	-	-	-	-	-	-	-	-
Pisidium subtruncatum	6	72	103	193	43	29	3	-	-	-	-	-	?1	-	-	-	-	-	-
Pisidium henslowanum	-	13	22	36	5	4	-	-	-	-	-	-	-	-	-	-	-	-	-
Pisidium nitidum	14	167	197	345	20	23	7	-	-	-	-	-	-	-	-	-	-	-	1
Pisidium nitidum var. crassa	-	2	1	5	-	-	-	-	-	-	-	-	-	-	-	-	-	-	-
Pisidium moitessierianum	1	6	6	8	-	-	-	-	-	-	-	-	-	-	-	-	-	-	-

132

Depth below surface (cm)	110–120	105–110	100–105	95–100	90–95	85–90	80–85	75–80	70–75	65–70	60–65	50–60	45–50	40–45	35–40	30–35	25–30	20–25	15–20
Pisidium tenuilineatum	5	36	18	26	3	1	-	-	-	-	-	-	-	?1	-	-	-	-	-
Pisidium spp.	10	79	75	138	11	-	1	-	-	-	-	-	-	-	-	-	-	-	-
Amphibious and Land Mollusca																			
Carychium minimum	4	22	14	30	48	290	420	187	3	-	-			15	38	8	2	-	-
Carychium tridentatum	-	4	5	5	8	42	110	42	-	-	-			2	1	-	-	-	-
Aplexa hypnorum	-	-	-	-	-	-	-	1	-	-	-			-	-	-	-	-	-
Lymnaea truncatula	4	35	23	31	10	57	56	50	39	24	23			19	31	26	42	20	5
Anisus leucostoma	-	4	1	-	2	1	1	4	2	-	3		1	32	31	3	1	-	-
Succineidae	1	6	6	11	5	16	37	17	3	2	15	1		4	5	4	8	5	2
Cochlicopa lubrica agg.	5	15	13	4	10	30	104	39	3	-	-			5	9	-	1	-	13
Vertigo antivertigo	-	-	-	-	-	-	1	1	-	-	-			-	-	-	-	-	-
Vertigo pygmaea	-	4	2	-	-	2	8	4	-	1	-			-	-	-	-	-	-
Vertigo spp.	-	-	-	-	-	-	1	1	1	-	-			-	-	-	-	-	1
Pupilla muscorum	1	2	3	1	1	-	1	-	1	1	-			-	-	-	1	1	-
Lauria cylindracea	-	-	1	-	-	-	-	-	-	-	-			-	-	-	-	-	-
Vallonia costata	1	1	-	1	1	33	52	7	-	-	-			-	1	-	-	-	-
Vallonia pulchella	1	7	5	1	1	16	35	6	6	1	-			3	4	3	5	12	31
Vallonia excentrica	-	1	-	1	-	-	-	?1	-	-	-			-	-	-	-	-	-
Vallonia spp.	8	34	26	23	5	142	191	37	23	10	2		1	6	6	13	17	35	48
Punctum pygmaeum	-	-	-	-	1	3	6	10	-	-	-			1	-	-	-	-	-
Discus rotundatus	4	7	5	3	6	49	141	51	4	?1	-			1	6	4	-	-	-
Vitrina pellucida	-	-	-	-	1	1	-	-	-	-	-			-	-	-	-	-	-
Vitrea crystallina	-	2	?1	-	-	2	11	5	-	-	-			-	-	-	-	-	-
Nesovitrea hammonis	1	2	5	4	-	13	43	27	-	-	-			2	13	-	-	-	-
Aegopinella nitidula	-	4	1	5	-	-	19	11	-	-	2			2	17	5	1	-	-
Oxychilus cellarius	1	4	4	1	3	9	30	5	-	-	-			-	-	-	-	-	-
Zonitoides nitidus	1	15	4	6	13	35	40	21	4	-	-		-	39	39	3	-	-	-
Limacidae	3	13	11	4	2	22	36	46	19	16	7		1	14	9	24	16	19	20

Depth below surface (cm)	15–20	20–25	25–30	30–35	35–40	40–45	45–50	50–60	60–65	65–70	70–75	75–80	80–85	85–90	90–95	95–100	100–105	105–110	110–120
Euconulus fulvus seg.	-	-	-	-	6	1	-	-	-	-	-	6	15	15	3	1	-	1	1
Cochlodina laminata	-	-	-	-	-	2	-	-	-	-	-	-	-	-	-	-	-	-	-
Clausilia bidentata	-	-	-	-	-	-	-	-	-	-	-	-	-	-	-	1	-	-	-
Balea perversa	-	-	-	-	-	-	-	-	-	-	-	-	-	-	-	-	-	1	1
Ashfordia granulata	1	-	-	-	3	9	1	-	-	-	6	-	-	-	-	-	-	-	-
Perforatella rubiginosa	-	-	-	-	-	?1	-	-	-	-	-	-	-	-	-	-	-	-	-
Trichia hispida	3	4	6	11	18	21	1	1	3	49	32	87	130	45	3	16	15	28	3
Arianta arbustorum	1	-	-	-	-	-	-	-	-	-	-	-	-	-	-	-	1	-	-
Arianta / Cepaea spp.	-	-	1	1	2	-	-	-	-	-	-	5	4	-	-	-	1	1	2
Pisidium casertanum	-	-	-	-	-	-	1	-	-	-	1	1	5	30	37	37	40	39	2
Pisidium personatum	-	-	-	?1	81	73	-	-	1	-	-	-	-	-	-	1	1	-	-
Pisidium obtusale	-	-	-	1	-	-	-	-	-	-	-	-	-	-	?1	?3	3	-	-
Ova	-	-	-	-	-	-	-	-	-	-	-	-	-	-	-	-	-	-	-

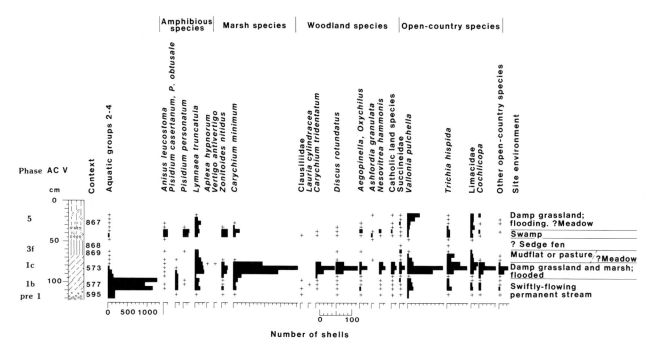

Figure 52   Anslow's Cottages: molluscan sequence AC V. Shells per 0.5 kg sample; Sphaerium *and* Pisidium *counts divided by two. Note the smaller scale used for aquatic groups 2–4*

Sparks group 4. Moving-water species, found in large streams or ponds where currents or wind effect water movement.

Sparks group 3. Ditch aquatic species, mainly occurring in slow-moving plant-rich streams. In the histogram, 'Other group 3 species' are *Planorbis*, *Acroloxus lacustris* and *Pisidium pulchellum*.

Sparks group 2. Catholic aquatic species, tolerating a wide range of conditions, but excluding those tolerated by the amphibious species. 'Other group 2 species' are *Bathyomphalus contortus, Hippeutis complanatus, Lymnaea palustris, Sphaerium corneum* and *Pisidium milium*.

Amphibious species. Slum species, tolerating conditions of poor oxygenation and periodic drought. These are Sparks' group 1 species but I have followed Robinson (1988) in calling them amphibious.

Marsh species. These are confined to habitats that are damp and often flooded, and that botanically are classified as marsh, swamp and fen. They do not live permanently under water, although some such as *Zonitoides nitidus* can tolerate temporary submergence. The two main species at Anslow's Cottages, *Zonitoides nitidus* and *Carychium minimum*, can tolerate shade as in carr although this is not a necessary requirement; by contrast, two other obligate marsh groups, the Succineidae and *Vallonia pulchella*, cannot tolerate shade and are therefore grouped with the open-country species (*see below*).

Woodland species. These live in a wide range of terrestrial habitats, mostly requiring a degree of

shelter and freedom from disturbance. All can live in exposed places such as scree, dunes and short grassland, but the occurrence of more than one of these species in abundance in such habitats at a single locality would be unusual. None is regularly found in such habitats in south-east England.

Catholic land species. The distinction between these and the woodland group is not especially clear. They have been put together as being those of exceptionally wide tolerances and here occurring in low abundance. They are *Punctum, Vitrina, Euconulus, Arianta* and *Cepaea*.

Open-country species. Vallonia pulchella is a wet grassland species and cannot tolerate shade. The 'Other open-country species', *Pupilla, Vertigo pygmaea, Vallonia costata* and *V. excentrica*, are also shade intolerant although not obligatorily so. *Trichia hispida*, the Limacidae and *Cochlicopa* are less tightly confined to open country and could have been grouped with the woodland species; but in this instance they go better in the open-country group.

Interpretation, stage 2. The taphonomy
On the basis of their present-day ecology, the species fall into two main groups, fully aquatic species (Sparks groups 2 to 4) on the one hand and amphibious and land species on the other. The two groups are dealt with separately in Tables 25–7 and Figures 52–4; this procedure is also justified on taphonomic grounds. Thus assemblages made up mainly of aquatic shells are likely to be from permanently aquatic deposits, in the case of Anslow's Cottages fluviatile, with the small terrestrial component being derived. Assemblages that are mainly of amphibious and land shells, with

a small aquatic component, are from floodplain deposits formed by overbank flooding.

There are degrees of allochthony and autochthony, shells in river deposits deriving from a number of habitats such as fast flowing water over a stony bottom and more slowly flowing water over a muddy bottom, shells in over-bank flooding deposits reflecting a slight mixing from microhabitats of varying wetness in addition to incorporating a small aquatic component. Nevertheless, the separate consideration of the two groups is also justified by the results, for all the freshwater species behave more or less synchronously, as well as idependently of the amphibious and land species. Of the four main amphibious species, three behave broadly in sympathy with the land species, only *Pisidium casertanum* perhaps going with the fully aquatic species.

The position at Anslow's Cottages is simple because there is a sharp change between fluviatile channel and over-bank flood deposits in the two main sequences, AC II and V. Towards the top of the fluviatile deposits, one might have expected a situation where the rate of stream flow declined and there was an increase of weed and silt, giving rise to a mixed assemblage of some aquatic and amphibious species but no land species, for example *Valvata cristata*, *Pisidium casertanum* and *Lymnaea truncatula*; but this does not happen.

The implications of these different taphonomies for the interpretation of the land and amphibious sequences are that the assemblages from the fluviatile deposits, being mixed, reflect local and regional environmental conditions, whereas those from the over-bank flooding deposits reflect the conditions of the sampling spot, and that the changing abundances from the one type of deposit to the other are not a reflection of changing abundances in life.

Interpretation, stage 3. The molluscan assemblages
The aquatic assemblages are fairly uniform, the main changes being in the overall abundance of shells. The main species indicate swiftly-flowing, permanent water that was well-oxygenated. The assemblages are diverse and indicate, particularly in the numbers of species of the small pea mussels, *Pisidium*, and in the numbers of group 2 species, a richly-vegetated river with plenty of mud. The river limpet, *Ancylus fluviatilis*, and the nerite, *Theodoxus fluviatilis*, on the other hand, are especially distinctive of stony substrata. The large numbers of *Theodoxus* in the AC III sequence by comparison with its rarity in AC II and V is noteworthy. Presumably this reflects an environmental difference, even though the two groups of assemblages are of widely differing ages, for *Theodoxus* is present in Britain throughout the Holocene.

The absence of *Viviparus* is something that other workers have noted from prehistoric Holocene deposits and probably implies a recent, historic-age, introduction into Britain for the genus. On the other

hand, the absence of the large mussels, *Anodonta* and *Unio*, may be due to the sampling method.

In considering the land and amphibious assemblages we can make only general comments about those from the fluviatile deposits because they are a mixture. The most notable features are that they are broadly similar to those from the over-bank flooding deposits and that open-country species, especially *Vallonia*, are present indicating general open country. There are no significant contributions indicating regional environments different from those of the floodplain, for example dry grassland or old woodland. Notable too, in view of its abundance in some of the over-bank flooding deposits, is the virtual absence of *Pisidium personatum*; this could be a taphonomic effect as the shell is not readily transported.

For the over-bank flooding deposits, five distinct assemblages can be recognised:

1. *Vallonia pulchella*, *Trichia hispida*, Limacidae and *Cochlicopa*. This assemblage indicates relatively dry (absence of *Lymnaea truncatula*), low diversity (low number of species) grassland. Where *Vallonia* exceeds *Trichia*, the grassland was probably short, with the implication of grazing.
2. The above assemblage plus *Lymnaea truncatula*, Succineidae and *Carychium minimum*. This indicates very damp, flooded grassland of a higher diversity and greater three-dimensional structure, for example with substantial tussock development.
3. The above assemblage plus *Zonitoides nitidus* and woodland species. This reflects a more diverse environment than the previous two assemblages, but the question of how much woody vegetation is present is a difficult one to answer. I would suggest, in view of the low diversity of the woodland component and the high abundance of *Vallonia pulchella*, that we are dealing here with unshaded fen of high structural diversity.
4. *Lymnaea truncatula* and Succineidae. This probably reflects mudflat with reeds and other tall monocotyledons such as flag iris.
5. *Anisus leucostoma*, *Pisidium personatum*, *Lymnaea truncatula* and marsh species, with or without a substantial woodland component. This reflects different hydrological conditions from the other assemblages, probably swamp, with more or less permanently-standing water.

It is notable that there are no assemblages which match those detailed by Robinson (1988) for the upper Thames which are from pasture. These are characterised by an abundance of amphibious species and a paucity of land species. The assemblages from Anslow's Cottages which approach these, contain either a high proportion of land species, or a low proportion of amphibious

Table 26 Anslow's Cottages: molluscan sequence AC III

Depth below top of context 667 (cm)	60–70	50–60	40–50	30–40	20–30	10–20	0–10
Air-dry weight of sample (kg)	0.2	0.2	0.2	0.2	0.2	0.3	0.3
Aquatics: Sparks groups 2–4							
Theodoxus fluviatilis	128	69	49	38	117	93	60
Valvata cristata	79	10	61	85	370	104	118
Valvata piscinalis	544	348	315	335	1420	655	546
Bithynia tentaculata	311	200	166	141	420	239	139
Bithynia tentaculata operculae	129	134	99	77	479	367	251
Bithynia leachii	36	20	14	14	75	27	23
Bithynia leachii operculae	8	18	28	16	72	58	38
Physa fontinalis	12	4	1	1	2	14	9
Lymnaea palustris	2	-	1	1	-	-	-
Lymnaea stagnalis	4	1	3	-	10	-	3
Lymnaea peregra	291	201	159	126	491	435	272
Myxas glutinosa	-	-	-	-	-	?1	-
Planorbis planorbis	-	8	6	7	5	8	7
Planorbis carinatus	13	1	-	-	1	-	-
Anisus vortex	3	5	-	-	-	-	-
Bathyomphalus contortus	8	4	5	4	19	7	11
Gyraulus albus	8	-	9	12	51	34	19
Armiger crista	17	4	14	24	103	43	57
Hippeutis complanatus	-	-	-	-	1	-	-
Planorbarius corneus	-	1	-	-	-	-	-
Ancylus fluviatilis	22	7	10	16	68	50	36
Acroloxus lacustris	2	1	-	1	1	8	3
Sphaerium corneum	8	7	7	8	5	4	2
Pisidium amnicum	58	44	26	25	44	42	6
Pisidium milium	4	-	-	1	3	5	-
Pisidium subtruncatum	24	11	5	22	58	-	45
Pisidium henslowanum	3	-	1	-	2	1	2
Pisidium nitidum	35	20	25	24	138	65	86
Pisidium pulchellum	-	-	-	3	7	1	-
Pisidium moitessierianum	3	3	4	1	17	7	8
Pisidium tenuilineatum	3	3	3	5	37	15	36
Pisidium spp.	9	-	6	6	38	20	32
Amphibious and Land Mollusca							
Carychium minimum	24	2	-	16	44	35	41
Carychium tridentatum	9	1	4	4	15	3	2
Lymnaea truncatula	31	10	24	15	87	40	44
Anisus leucostoma	22	7	13	13	40	26	17
Succineidae	29	11	22	9	38	31	7
Azeca goodalli	-	-	-	-	1	-	-
Cochlicopa lubrica agg.	17	9	5	11	30	23	15
Vertigo antivertigo	1	-	-	-	-	-	1
Vertigo pygmaea	-	1	-	-	2	2	4
Vertigo spp.	-	-	-	1	1	-	-
Pupilla muscorum	12	2	2	9	21	9	8
Lauria cylindracea	-	-	-	-	-	1	-

Depth below top of context 677 (cm)	60–70	50–60	40–50	30–40	20–30	10–20	0–10
Vallonia costata	2	-	2	1	3	1	2
Vallonia pulchella	14	-	4	10	28	20	10
Vallonia excentrica	2	1	1	6	-	-	-
Vallonia spp.	27	-	14	16	78	33	36
Punctum pygmaeum	2	1	1	2	2	-	1
Discus rotundatus	6	5	6	4	12	5	8
Vitrea crystallina seg.	-	-	2	-	-	-	-
Vitrea contracta	1	-	-	-	-	-	-
Nesovitrea hammonis	6	3	3	7	6	6	3
Aegopinella nitidula	-	2	1	1	7	7	-
Oxychilus cellarius	3	-	-	5	6	-	7
Zonitoides nitidus	11	9	12	8	35	19	8
Limacidae	2	10	9	12	28	39	16
Euconulus fulvus seg.	4	1	3	2	4	6	2
Cochlodina laminata	1	1	-	-	-	-	-
Clausilia bidentata	-	-	-	-	1	-	1
Balea perversa	-	1	-	-	1	1	2
Helicella itala	-	-	-	-	?2	-	-
Ashfordia granulata	-	?5	-	-	1	3	-
Perforatella rubiginosa	5	?	?2	-	?1	1	-
Trichia hispida	86	47	30	41	119	79	39
Arianta arbustorum	1	3	1	1	-	-	-
Arianta, Cepaea spp.	-	-	2	1	3	1	1
Pisidium casertanum	22	5	18	11	44	16	12
Pisidium personatum	3	2	-	-	3	4	4
Pisidium obtusale	1	-	?2	1	2	1	?1

species, or only one amphibious species, *Lymnaea truncatula*.

The only assemblages which could suggest pasture are those composed of *Lymnaea truncatula* and the Succineidae. For these I have suggested mudflat as the likely environment in view of the low diversity of the assemblage. The distinction between mudflat and pasture as far as the Mollusca are concerned is not great, both being characterised by some unvegetated ground. The basis of the model proposed by Robinson is that pasture cannot support a terrestrial fauna because the vegetation is not continuous or dense enough and the bare surface dries out too much to allow its survival. Mudflat is an environment which takes these characteristics to the extreme so it is likely to have an extreme fauna.

The Sequences

AC V, the southern channel (Table 25; Fig. 52)
In the lower part of the sequence (120–90 cm; contexts 595, 577 and the base of 573; pre-Phase 1–Phase 1c — pre-Bronze Age to Bronze Age), aquatic groups 2 to 4 predominate. These are deposits laid down in a river channel. The land and amphibious component is sparse and allochthonous, washed in from the surrounding land; they

indicate a variety of open and damp ground environments.

Between 95 cm and 90 cm there are few shells of any group, suggesting unvegetated mudflat.

At 90 cm, and continuing to 75 cm (context 573; Phase 1b or 1c — Bronze Age), there is a massive increase in all land groups and *Lymnaea truncatula*, and in practically all species except for the two amphibious species, *Anisus leucostoma* and *Pisidium personatum*. In spite of the diversity of the assemblage, the abundance of *Vallonia pulchella* implies open country, although some woody vegetation could have been present — grassland with trees along the stream edge for example. Whatever the precise details, the environment was structurally diverse.

At 75 cm, this rich assemblage dies out abruptly, and only the familiar components of damp, flooded grassland survive. At the top of the lower alluvium just below the peat (65–60 cm; context 869) the assemblage indicates mudflat. There may be an unconformity at 70 cm, caused by erosion, since context 573 below it is Bronze Age and context 869 above it is Anglo-Saxon. So the sequence cannot be viewed as a continuous one.

Above the peat, which was virtually devoid of shells, the deposits belong to Phase 6, the post-medieval watermeadows. From 45–35 cm,

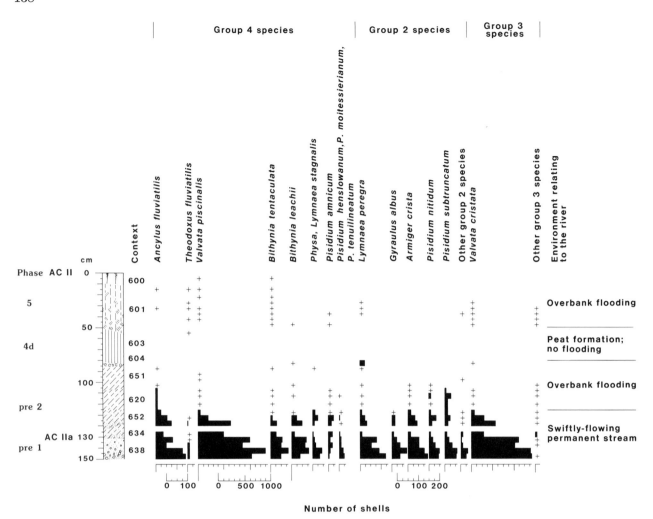

Figure 53   Anslow's Cottages: molluscan sequences ACII and ACIIa. Aquatic mollusca, Sparks groups 2–4; shells per 0.5 kg sample; Sphaerium *and* Pisidium *counts divided by two. Note the smaller scale used for* Valvata piscinalis *and* Bithynia tentaculata

there is an assemblage indicative of swamp, with *Anisus leucostoma* and *Pisidium personatum* characteristic; the swamp was possibly shaded but not especially diverse. This gives way to flooded grassland (35–20 cm) and then drier grassland (20–15 cm) in which only *Vallonia pulchella* is at all abundant, so indicating a reasonably low- diversity and probably short-turved sward.

AC III (Table 26)
The deposits of this pre-Roman feature (Fig. 40, S.123) span pre-Phase 2 (contexts 629–627), the Roman (Phase 2) and Anglo-Saxon (Phase 3a/3e) periods. They therefore occupy the hiatus in the AC V sequence.

Shells are extremely abundant and the assemblages made up largely of aquatic groups 2 to 4; amphibious and land components are sparse. The depositional environment was of swiftly-flowing water throughout. The land and amphibious components are similar to those from the stream deposits of the other sequences, indicating the same general background environments.

In sequences AC V and AC III, therefore, we have two fully aquatic assemblages of different ages, AC V of pre-Bronze Age/Bronze Age date and AC III of mainly Roman to Saxon date. The only difference between them is that the earlier assemblages (AC V) are impoverished in *Theodoxus fluviatilis* by comparison with its later abundance in the AC III sequence; this is unexplained.

AC II, the northern channel (Table 27; Figs 53, 54)
The archaeological contexts and lithostratigraphy are shown in the histograms and Figure 40 (S.108). The samples were taken in two series to obtain a complete sequence, with AC IIa being a downward continuation of AC II at 0.8 m to the north.

The lower part of the sequence, pre-Phase 1 (ie, pre-Bronze Age), contexts 638, 634 and 652, formed in fluviatile conditions as indicated by the very high numbers of aquatic shells and the low numbers of amphibious and land shells. There is a general decrease in shell abundance upwards but otherwise no significant changes. The land assemblages from these contexts indicate a variety of wetland habitats

Table 27 Anslow's Cottages: molluscan sequences ACII and ACIIa

	ACIIa					ACII																					
Depth below surface (cm)	145-150	140-145	135-140	130-135	125-130	135-140	130-135	125-130	115-125	110-115	105-110	100-105	95-100	90-95	85-90	80-85	70-80	60-70	50-60	45-50	40-45	35-40	30-35	25-30	20-25	10-20	0-10
Air-dry weight of sample (kg)	0.2	0.2	0.2	0.2	0.2	0.2	0.5	0.5	0.5	0.5	0.5	0.5	0.5	0.5	0.5	0.5	0.5	0.5	0.5	0.5	0.5	0.25	0.5	0.5	0.5	0.5	0.5
Aquatics: Sparks groups 2–4																											
Theodoxus fluviatilis	5	5	4	2	1	3	1	-	-	-	-	-	-	-	-	-	-	-	2	2	1	-	2	1	-	1	-
Valvata cristata	114	112	82	89	24	47	58	15	4	4	1	-	-	-	1	-	-	-	-	3	4	3	2	1	-	-	-
Valvata piscinalis	411	523	344	397	204	255	197	50	16	9	3	-	2	2	1	-	-	-	-	-	2	1	1	-	1	2	-
Bithynia tentaculata	80	135	79	92	44	47	42	20	24	10	2	2	-	-	1	-	-	-	2	2	5	3	5	3	3	2	2
Bithynia tentaculata operculae	67	87	65	88	56	62	51	21	25	4	7	3	3	2	2	2	54	56	2	6	12	4	4	5	3	3	10
Bithynia leachii	16	33	27	28	7	21	24	5	-	2	-	1	-	-	1	-	-	-	-	1	-	-	-	-	-	-	-
Bithynia leachii operculae	16	21	11	26	14	11	46	14	11	5	-	-	1	1	-	-	-	-	-	-	2	-	-	-	-	-	-
Physa fontinalis	13	14	4	1	-	4	16	10	-	-	-	-	-	-	-	-	-	-	-	-	-	-	-	-	-	-	-
Lymnaea palustris	-	1	-	-	-	-	-	-	-	-	-	-	-	-	-	-	-	-	-	-	-	-	-	-	-	-	-
Lymnaea stagnalis	1	4	2	3	2	-	10	4	-	-	-	-	-	-	1	-	-	-	-	-	-	1	-	-	-	-	-
Lymnaea peregra	49	37	21	32	4	13	22	7	1	3	-	1	-	-	5	23	-	-	-	-	2	-	5	3	-	-	-
Planorbis planorbis	-	-	-	-	-	3	-	-	-	-	-	-	-	-	-	-	-	-	-	-	-	-	-	-	-	-	-
Planorbis carinatus	-	-	-	-	-	-	-	-	-	-	-	-	-	-	-	-	-	-	-	1	-	-	1	-	-	-	-
Planorbis spp.	-	-	-	1	3	-	1	-	-	-	1	1	-	-	-	-	-	-	-	1	2	-	-	-	-	-	-
Bathyomphalus contortus	5	8	2	3	5	3	-	1	-	-	-	-	-	-	-	-	-	-	-	-	-	-	-	-	-	-	-
Gyraulus albus	17	28	17	10	4	7	17	6	-	-	-	-	-	-	-	-	-	-	-	-	-	-	-	-	-	-	-
Armiger crista	38	32	22	22	6	19	33	16	6	4	2	2	-	-	-	-	-	-	-	-	-	-	-	-	-	-	-
Hippeutis complanatus	-	-	-	-	-	-	-	-	-	-	-	-	1	-	-	-	-	-	-	-	-	-	-	-	-	-	-
Ancylus fluviatilis	57	52	19	31	14	29	56	26	10	9	7	3	-	-	2	-	-	-	-	-	-	-	1	-	-	1	-
Acroloxus lacustris	3	-	2	1	1	-	5	4	2	6	1	1	-	-	-	-	-	-	-	-	1	-	1	-	-	-	-

Freshwater Mollusca, then **Amphibious and Land Mollusca** (from *Pomatias elegans* onwards).

Depth below surface (cm)	Sphaerium corneum	Pisidium amnicum	Pisidium milium	Pisidium subtruncatum	Pisidium henslowanum	Pisidium nitidum	Pisidium nitidum var. crassa	Pisidium pulchellum	Pisidium moitessierianum	Pisidium tenuilineatum	Pisidium spp.	Pomatias elegans	Carychium minimum	Carychium tridentatum	Aplexa hypnorum	Lymnaea truncatula	Anisus leucostoma	Succineidae	Cochlicopa lubrica agg.	Vertigo antivertigo	Vertigo pygmaea	Vertigo spp.
0-10	-	-	-	-	-	-	-	-	-	-	-	-	8	8	-	7	1	6	7	-	5	-
10-20	-	-	-	-	-	-	-	-	-	-	-	-	18	-	-	33	5	28	16	-	6	-
20-25	-	-	-	-	-	-	-	-	-	-	2	-	22	-	-	49	13	33	8	-	2	-
25-30	-	-	-	-	-	-	-	-	-	-	2	-	40	1	-	57	4	25	12	-	2	-
30-35	-	-	-	-	-	-	-	-	-	-	-	-	181	11	-	101	67	20	43	3	2	-
35-40	-	2	-	-	-	-	-	-	-	-	-	-	112	13	1	34	32	15	19	-	-	-
40-45	-	-	-	-	-	-	-	1	-	-	-	-	150	10	-	36	14	14	22	-	-	-
45-50	-	-	2	-	-	-	-	-	-	-	-	-	50	2	-	7	16	4	2	-	-	-
50-60	-	-	-	-	-	-	-	-	-	-	1	-	-	-	-	-	-	-	1	-	-	-
60-70	-	-	-	-	-	-	-	-	-	-	-	-	-	-	-	-	-	-	-	-	-	-
70-80	-	-	-	-	-	-	-	-	-	-	-	-	-	-	-	-	-	-	-	-	-	-
80-85	-	-	-	-	-	-	-	-	-	-	-	-	10	1	-	225	9	51	5	-	-	-
85-90	-	-	-	-	-	-	-	-	-	-	-	-	15	-	-	88	3	5	10	-	1	2
90-95	-	-	-	-	-	-	-	-	-	-	-	-	19	-	-	123	5	7	31	1	1	-
95-100	-	-	-	-	-	-	-	-	-	-	-	-	38	-	-	67	2	9	14	-	1	-
100-105	-	8	-	-	-	-	10	-	-	-	-	-	8	-	-	20	2	12	2	-	-	-
105-110	-	5	-	14	-	12	-	-	-	-	-	-	8	-	-	8	3	8	1	-	-	-
110-115	-	9	-	54	1	24	-	-	-	-	-	-	9	-	-	1	2	5	3	-	-	-
115-125	-	1	-	24	-	11	-	-	-	-	-	-	2	-	2	3	2	-	3	-	-	-
125-130	-	8	-	25	4	20	2	-	-	-	11	-	4	1	-	2	3	-	2	-	-	-
130-135	6	45	-	51	3	69	3	-	5	-	-	-	24	7	-	19	7	5	2	-	-	-
135-140	-	10	-	12	-	13	-	-	1	-	-	-	12	4	-	11	16	9	8	-	-	1
125-130	-	8	-	10	-	6	-	-	3	2	-	1	2	-	-	8	4	1	8	-	-	-
130-135	-	8	-	16	2	18	6	-	5	-	6	-	13	1	-	23	6	11	6	1	2	-
135-140	1	13	-	29	-	24	2	-	1	4	-	-	24	8	-	24	12	15	6	-	1	2
140-145	9	10	1	49	1	37	-	-	5	8	-	-	21	1	-	29	13	9	21	-	-	3
145-150	10	4	2	22	2	36	2	-	3	11	-	-	17	5	-	27	7	5	12	-	-	-

Depth below surface (cm)	Pupilla muscorum	Vallonia costata	Vallonia pulchella	Vallonia excentrica	Vallonia spp.	Punctum pygmaeum	Discus rotundatus	Vitrea crystallina agg.	Nesovitrea hammonis	Aegopinella nitidula	Oxychilus cellarius	Zonitoides nitidus	Limacidae	Euconulus fulvus seg.	Euconulus alderi	Cochlodina laminata	Clausilia bidentata	Ashfordia granulata	Trichia hispida	Arianta arbustorum	Arianta/Cepaea spp.	Pisidium casertanum	Pisidium personatum	Pisidium obtusale	Ova
0-10	1	-	18	-	95	-	1	-	-	-	-	1	51	1	-	-	-	2	108	-	-	-	-	-	1
10-20	-	-	41	1	153	-	1	-	1	-	1	1	74	-	-	-	-	-	159	-	1	-	-	1	-
20-25	-	-	39	-	165	-	-	-	1	1	1	1	60	-	-	-	-	1	135	-	4	-	-	1	1
25-30	-	-	23	-	113	-	2	-	1	5	-	2	37	-	-	1	-	1	107	-	4	1	-	4	2
30-35	-	-	9	-	45	-	18	-	28	38	5	45	39	5	1	1	-	14	107	-	1	18	218	-	-
35-40	-	-	-	-	6	4	8	-	29	35	11	26	14	-	1	1	-	17	24	2	4	1	159	-	-
40-45	-	-	-	-	5	3	-	-	22	21	16	35	14	7	-	-	-	26	14	2	2	-	144	3	-
45-50	-	-	-	-	7	2	-	-	7	7	12	17	14	5	-	-	-	7	10	-	-	5	39	3	-
50-60	-	-	-	-	1	-	-	-	-	-	-	-	5	-	-	-	-	-	2	-	-	-	-	-	-
60-70	-	-	-	-	-	-	-	-	-	-	-	-	1	-	-	-	-	-	-	-	-	-	-	-	-
70-80	-	-	-	-	1	-	-	-	1	1	-	-	8	-	-	-	-	-	2	-	-	-	-	-	-
80-85	-	-	2	-	21	-	-	-	1	1	-	10	19	-	-	-	-	-	16	-	-	-	4	-	-
85-90	1	-	21	-	117	-	-	-	1	1	-	1	31	-	-	-	-	-	81	-	-	-	-	-	-
90-95	6	-	43	3	181	-	-	-	2	-	-	1	22	2	-	-	-	-	62	-	1	-	-	-	-
95-100	2	-	19	1	96	-	-	-	1	-	-	5	8	2	-	-	-	-	19	-	-	-	-	-	-
100-105	-	-	5	-	18	-	1	-	-	-	-	6	2	1	-	-	-	-	7	-	-	-	-	-	1
105-110	-	-	-	-	5	-	-	-	-	-	-	10	7	-	-	-	-	-	6	-	2	7	-	-	-
110-115	-	-	-	-	3	-	-	-	-	-	-	12	2	2	-	-	-	-	4	-	-	7	-	-	-
115-125	-	-	-	-	-	-	-	-	-	-	1	2	-	1	1	-	-	-	-	-	-	4	-	-	-
125-130	-	-	-	-	3	-	-	-	-	1	-	2	2	1	-	-	-	-	3	-	-	2	-	-	-
130-135	-	-	2	-	3	2	5	-	-	-	-	6	1	-	1	-	-	-	6	2	-	25	2	-	1
135-140	-	-	1	-	10	1	7	1	1	4	4	12	6	-	-	1	-	-	8	1	-	26	-	-	-
145-150	2	-	6	-	14	-	6	-	2	1	3	7	3	2	-	-	-	-	10	-	2	8	-	-	-
140-145	1	-	6	2	15	-	2	-	2	2	2	10	-	2	-	-	-	-	17	-	2	9	1	-	-
135-140	1	2	-	-	11	1	3	1	3	6	1	3	6	1	-	-	1	-	22	1	-	6	5	-	-
130-135	2	1	4	-	3	2	12	1	10	5	1	12	10	1	1	-	-	-	22	2	-	5	-	1	1
125-130	3	-	-	1	8	-	2	-	1	2	-	3	4	1	-	-	1	-	12	-	-	15	-	-	3

142

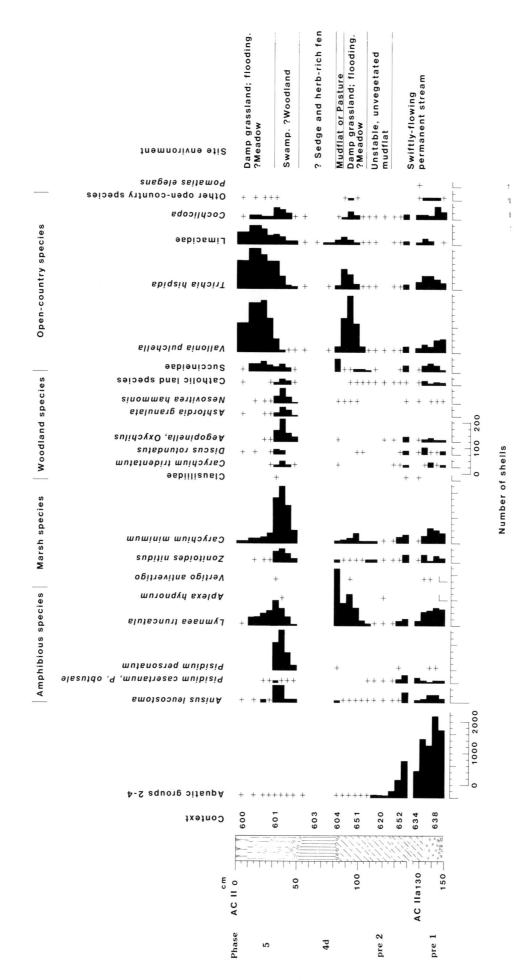

Figure 54 Anslow's Cottages: molluscan sequences ACII and AC IIa. All groups; shells per 0.5 kg sample; Sphaerium and Pisidium counts divided by two.
Note the smaller scale used for the aquatic groups 2–4

in a background of open country. So the situation, and age, are similar to AC V.

Above context 652, and excepting the peat (contexts 603 and 604), the deposits are of over-bank flooding origin, with aquatic shells declining to insignificance and land and amphibious shells becoming abundant. The assemblages are largely autochthonous and specific to the sampling spot. Immediately on the declining influence of the river channel (AC II 125–105 cm; context 620) in pre- Phase 2, ie, pre-Roman, deposits there are practi- cally no shells of any type, land or aquatic, and an environment of unvegetated mudflat can be pro- posed. From 105–85 cm (context 651, also pre-Phase 2), there is an assemblage indicative of damp grassland which at the top (85–80 cm) gives way to one of mudflat. Flooding is indicated by a line of shells at this level, undoubtedly a result of sorting.

The environment of peat formation cannot be determined from the molluscs because they are virtually absent, but a herb-rich sedge fen is likely.

Above the peat, in the lower part of context 601 (50–30 cm), Phase 5b, the medieval and later watermeadows, there is a diverse assemblage, with amphibious, marsh and woodland species all abundant. Initially (50–45 cm), open-country species (including open-country marsh species) are virtually absent, so an environment of wooded swamp of high structural diversity with trees, fallen branches covered with ferns and mosses, perman- ent pools and sedge tussocks in a close mosaic, is likely. Higher in the sequence (35–30 cm), there is an indication of opening, with all the marsh and woodland species declining while the open-country species increase; but the environment was still swampy. In the upper part of context 601, the assemblages indicate grassland, intermittently flooded and similar to that below the peat. Ultimately in the topsoil (context 600) conditions became drier, with *Lymnaea truncatula* and the Succineidae being virtually absent.

Discussion

The molluscan assemblages
There are four basic molluscan components, those of the river channels, those of diverse land/swamp in which woodland species are characteristic, those of swamp in which *Pisidium personatum* and *Anisus leucostoma* are characteristic, and those of grassland. The main interpretational problem is with the woodland component. Do we see this as indicative of woodland *per se* or is it a reflection of highly structured grassland? My inclination is to view the presence of the stenotopic species, *Vallonia excentrica*, as an index of openness, so that where it occurs in an autochthonous context, an open environment is implied, however diverse the rest of the assemblage.

The local floodplain environments
The two main sequences, AC II and AC V, are from two infilled stream channels, the northern and southern channels respectively. The archaeological phasing suggests general contemporaneity al- though the lower fine alluvium and overlying peat are probably slightly earlier in AC V than in AC II.

Environmentally the two sequences are the same but there are slight differences. First, in the fine alluvium below the peat, the environment in AC II was less diverse than that of AC V. Damp, flooded grassland was a major component of both sequences at this level, but in AC V there was greater structural diversity, indicative of aban- doned grassland and possibly some woodland. The second difference is less marked and refers to the swamp horizon above the peat. This time it is the AC II sequence that sees the greater diversity. In both cases, the swamp may have been wooded.

The general floodplain environments
Many questions spring to mind. Why did the stream channel fill up? Or move? Why did alluviation of fine deposits take place? Why did the peat form? None of these questions can be answered by the conchol- ogy but a few relevant observations can be made.

Silting of the river channel was rapid, with no intermediate or transition aquatic stage between fully flowing water to floodplain. Alluviation was presumably caused by ploughing of the valleys sides and the incorporation of eroded material into the stream. In support of this, the Mollusca indicate open country throughout the sequences although there are local episodes when the open-country species decline.

With regard to peat formation, it is notable that there is a change in the water regime just before this begins, with a trend from grassland to mudflat and flooding, or, if one applies the Robinson (1988) model, from meadow to pasture. So there may have been an increase in grazing on the flood-plain which changed the local hydrology and ultimately led to conditions suitable for peat formation.

Insect Assemblages, by M. Robinson

Five samples were successfully analysed for insect remains:

Trench XA, context 820, Phase 1c. 2 kg of grey-brown organic sandy silt with lenses of twig and wood debris associated with the timber structure 873 in the river channel. A fragment of burnt stone was noted from the sample.

Trench AA, SF.1073, Phase 4a. 2 kg of dark grey organic silt associated with a wicker basket.

Trench XB, context 625, Phase 3a. 1.5 kg of grey-brown sandy silt, with many twig fragments and snail shells, within the river channel.

Trench XJ, context 925, Pre-Phase 1, channel fill. 2.1 kg of brown organic silt at the bottom of an alluvial sequence over the Pleistocene gravels.

Trench XJ, context 912, Phase 1f. 2 kg of brown highly organic silt from ditch 908 which cut through a layer containing late Bronze Age pottery which in turn sealed 925 (XJ).

Method
The samples were subjected to the standard paraffin flotation technique and the insect remains were recovered on a 0.2 mm aperture sieve. The insect remains were identified by reference to the Hope Entomological Collections in the University Museum, Oxford and the minimum number of individuals represented by the fragments in each sample for each species are listed in Table 28.

The aquatic and marsh environment
The assemblages of insects from the samples fall into two categories. Samples XA820, AA1073, XB625 and XJ925 share a similar character. Almost 50% of the Coleoptera from them are aquatic, a high proportion being of the family Elmidae, such as *Limnius volkmari* and *Normandia nitens* which cling to submerged stones and plants in clean, well oxygenated flowing water. One of these, *Macronychus quadrituberculatus*, is now extinct in the Thames drainage basin, although it was recovered from Neolithic and late Bronze Age sediments at Runnymede Bridge (Robinson 1991). Trichoptera larvae were abundant in some of the samples and cases of *Ithytrichia* sp., a caddis of running water, were identified from two of them.

The aquatic insects from the first group of samples suggests all these deposits have accumulated in what were active flowing channels for at least most of, and probably throughout, the year. The phytophagous Coleoptera included species of Chrysomelidae which would have fed on the emergent vegetation fringing the channels such as *Donacia clavipes* which feeds on *Phragmites australis*, *D. impressa* on *Schoenoplectus lacustris* and *Prasocuris phellandrii* on aquatic Umbelliferae.

The Carabidae (ground beetles) from these samples were mostly species of damp habitats, particularly marshland including *Bembidion assimile*, which lives in well-vegetated places close to water, *B. doris* which inhabits marshes and riverbanks, and *Elaphrus cupreus* or *uliginosus*, which occurs on mud at the edge of water.

Sample XJ 912 differed from the other samples in that it had a higher proportion of terrestrial Coleoptera and the flowing water element was almost completely absent. Only a single member of the Elmidae, an individual of *Normandia nitens*, was present and it is possible that it had flown into the ditch from one of the nearby river channels. The aquatic beetles comprised a fauna of stagnant or slowly moving water, small species of *Helophorus* and *Ochthebius minimus* being the most numerous. Some of them, such as *O. minimus* and *Dryops* sp. readily leave water and can also be found on wet mud and in damp vegetation alongside water.

About 70% of the Coleoptera were of terrestrial origin but Carabidae of wet habitats were again much in evidence, including *Bembidion gilvipes* and *Chlaenius nigricornis* or *nitidulus*. Some of the weevils from the sample are dependent on marsh and waterside plants such as *Gymnetron beccabungae* on *Veronica beccabunga* and *Notaris acridulus* whose hosts include *Eleocharis palustris*.

The terrestrial environment
The samples from the channel deposits (820, 1073, 625 and 925) did not contain large numbers of Coleoptera from drier habitats, so it is difficult to assess the relative importance of woodland and open country in the landscape. However, faunal elements from both were present in all these samples. In contrast, sample 912 from a stagnant ditch with a high proportion of terrestrial Coleoptera, contained no evidence for woodland or trees. Since the date range spanned by the various deposits was probably about 3000 years and 912 did not represent the culmination of the sequence, the terrestrial environment will be discussed by phase rather than category of fauna.

Pre-Phase 1
The fauna from sample 925 included *Grynobius planus* which bores into dead hardwood, and *Cerylon ferrugineum* which lives under rotten bark. A grassland element was also present, including *Phyllopertha horticola* which has larvae that feed on roots of grassland herbs. Members of the genera *Geotrupes*, *Colobopterus*, *Aphodius* and *Onthophagus*, which feed on the dung of large herbivores, especially domestic animals, were sufficiently abundant to suggest at least a grazed clearing in the vicinity of the deposit. The insect remains, however, do not provide any certain evidence of the proximity of human habitation.

Phase 1c
The evidence from the sediments associated with the late Bronze Age river bank revetment (sample 820) was very similar to that from the previous sample. There were again species associated with wood, such as *Melanotus erythropus* which lives in very rotten wood and scrabaeoid dung beetles. The phytophagous Coleoptera included *Gymnetron labile* and *G. pascuorum* which are dependent on *Plantago lanceolata*. Others of the phytophagous beetles feed on both grassland herbs and weeds of disturbed ground such as *Chaetochnmea concinna* on various Polygonaceae. Despite the archaeological evidence, there was again no indication from the insects of settlement.

Phase 1f
Over 8% of the terrestrial Coleoptera from sample 912 were members of the Scarabaeidae and Elateridae whose larvae that feed on roots of grassland plants, *Agriotes lineatus* being the most abundant. Such a high proportion of this group of Coleoptera strongly suggests grassland to have been a major aspect of the landscape. In contrast, wood and tree-dependent Coleoptera were absent from the sample. The occurrence of the weevils *Apion aethiops* or *pisi* and *Sitona hispidulus*

Table 28 Anslow's Cottages: insect remains

Coleoptera	Minimum No. of Individuals				
	XA820	AA1073	XB625	XJ925	XJ912
Nebria brevicollis (F.)	1	-	-	-	-
Elaphrus cupreus Duft. or uliginosus F.	-	-	-	1	-
Dyschirius globosus (Hbst.)	-	1	-	-	3
Bembidion dentellum (Thun.)	-	1	-	-	-
B. gilvipes Sturm	1	-	-	1	2
B. assimile Gyl.	1	1	-	-	-
B. doris (Pz.)	-	-	-	1	-
B. cf. biguttatum (F.)	-	-	1	-	-
B. guttula (F.)	-	-	1	1	1
Pterostichus anthracinus (Pz.)	1	-	-	-	2
P. cupreus (L.)	-	-	-	-	1
P. diligens (Sturm)	-	1	-	-	-
P. gracilis (Dej.)	-	1	-	-	-
P. cf. gracilis (Dej.)	1	-	-	1	-
P. melanarius (Ill)	-	-	-	-	1
P. cupreus (L.) or versicolor (Sturm)	1	-	1	-	-
Calathus fuscipes (Gz)	-	-	-	-	1
C. melanocephalus (L.)	-	-	-	-	1
Synuchus nivalis (Pz.)	-	-	-	-	1
Agonum albipes (F.)	-	-	-	1	-
A. muelleri (Hbst)	-	-	-	-	1
A. viduum (Pz.)	-	-	-	-	1
Amara sp.	-	-	-	-	1
Harpalus S. Ophonus sp.	-	-	-	-	1
Acupalpas exiguus Dej.	-	-	-	-	1
Chlaenius nigricornis (F.) or nitidulus (Schr.)	-	-	-	-	1
Dromius quadrimaculatus (L.)	-	1	-	-	-
Haliplus sp.	-	-	-	-	2
Hydroporus sp.	-	-	-	-	2
Agabus bipustulatus (L.)	-	-	-	-	2
Agabus sp. (not bipustulatus)	-	-	1	-	1
Orectochilus villosus (Mull.)	-	-	-	1	-
Georissus crenulatus (Ros.)	-	-	-	-	1
Helophorus aquaticus (L.)	-	-	-	-	2
H. grandis Ill.	-	-	-	-	2
H. aquaticus (L.) or grandis Ill.	1	-	1	2	-
H. cf. obscurus Muls.	-	-	1	-	8
Helophorus spp. (brevipalpis size)	1	1	1	1	8
Coelostoma orbiculare (F.)	-	1	-	-	1
Ceryon convexiusculus Step.	-	-	1	-	-
C. pygmaeus (Ill.)	1	-	-	-	-
C. sternalis Sh.	-	-	-	-	1
C. ustulatus (Pres.)	-	-	1	-	3
Cercyon sp.	-	1	-	2	-
Megasternum obscurum (Marsh.)	2	-	-	-	3
Hydrobius fuscipes (L.)	1	-	2	1	1
Anacaena bipustulata (Marsh.) or limbata (F.)	-	-	-	1	3

Coleoptera	Minimum No. of Individuals				
	XA820	AA1073	XB625	XJ925	XJ912
Laccobius sp.	-	1	-	1	-
Hister bissexstriatus F.	-	-	-	-	1
Ochthebius biclon Germ. or *dilatatus* Step.	-	-	-	1	1
O. cf. *bicolon* Germ or *dilatatus* Step.	2	2	2	4	-
O. minimus (F.)	1	-	1	1	7
O. cf. *minimus* (F.)	2	3	-	6	6
Hydraena minutissima Step.	1	1	1	-	-
H. pulchella Germ.	-	1	-	2	-
H. riparia Kug.	2	4	6	7	-
H. testacea Curt.	1	-	-	1	1
Limnebius nitidus (Marsh.)	2	1	1	1	-
L. papposus Muls.	-	-	1	-	1
Ptenidium sp.	-	-	-	1	-
Ptiliidae gen. et sp. indet. (not *Ptenidium*)	1	-	4	1	1
Silpha atrata L.	-	-	-	1	-
Lesteva longoelytrata (Gz.)	-	-	2	-	-
L. cf. *punctata* Er.	-	1	-	-	-
Lesteva sp.	1	-	-	1	1
Carpelimus bilineatus Step.	-	-	-	1	-
C. cf. *corticinus* (Grav.)	-	-	-	-	3
Platystethus cornutus gp.	-	-	-	-	1
P. nodifrons (Man.)	-	-	-	-	2
Anotylus nitidulus (Grav.)	-	-	-	-	1
A. rugosus (F.)	-	2	2	1	4
A. sculpturatus (Grav)	1	-	-	-	-
Stenus guttula Mull.	-	-	1	-	-
Stenus spp.	1	1	-	4	3
Lathrobium longulum Grav.	1	-	-	-	1
Lathrobium sp. (not *longulum*)	-	-	-	-	1
Xantholinus linearis (Ol.)	-	-	-	-	2
X. linearis (Ol.) or *longiventris* Heer	1	-	-	1	1
Philonthus sp.	2	1	-	-	1
Gabrius sp.	-	1	-	-	2
Staphylinus aeneocephalus Deg. or *fortunatorum*(Wol.)	-	-	-	-	2
Tachyporus sp.	-	-	-	-	1
Tachinus sp.	-	-	1	-	-
Aleaocharinae gen. et sp. indet.	1	1	1	2	5
Pselaphidae gen. et sp. indet.	-	-	-	1	-
Geotrupes sp.	-	-	-	1	-
Colobopterus erraticus (L.)	-	-	-	1	-
C. haemorrhoidalis (L.)	-	-	-	-	1
Aphodius contaminatus (Hbst)	-	-	-	-	2
A. distinctus (Mull.)	-	-	-	-	1
A. cf. *fimetarius* (L.)	1	-	-	-	-
A. granarius (L.)	-	-	-	1	-
A. rufipes (L.)	-	-	-	-	1
A. cf. *sphacelatus* (Pz.)	1	-	-	2	5
Aphodius sp.	-	1	1	1	-
Onthophagus ovatus (L.)	-	-	-	1	1

Coleoptera	Minimum No. of Individuals				
	XA820	AA1073	XB625	XJ925	XJ912
Onthophagus sp. (not ovatus)	1	-	-	-	-
Hoplia philanthus (Fues.)	-	-	-	-	1
Phyllopertha horticola (L.)	2	-	-	1	-
cf. Cyphon sp.	1	-	-	-	-
Limnichus pygmaeus (Sturm)	-	-	-	-	1
Helichus substriatus (Mull.)	-	-	-	1	-
Dryops sp.	-	-	2	3	4
Elmis aenea (Mull.)	-	1	-	1	-
Elsolus parallelopipedus (Mull.)	1	1	-	10	-
Limnius volckmari (Pz.)	1	1	2	6	-
Macronychus quadrituberculatus (Mull.)	-	1	2	3	-
Normandia nitens (Mull.)	5	1	9	18	1
Oulimnius sp.	1	-	1	3	-
Agrypnus murinus (L.)	-	-	-	-	1
cf. A. murinus (L.)	-	1	-	-	-
Melanotus erythropus (Gm.)	1	-	-	-	-
Actenicerus sjaelandicus (Mull.)	1	-	-	-	-
Agriotes lineatus (L.)	-	-	-	-	6
A. obscurus (L.)	-	-	-	-	2
Agriotes sp.	-	-	-	1	-
Cantharis sp.	-	-	-	-	2
Grynobius planus (F.)	1	1	-	1	-
Kateretes rufilabris (Lat.)	1	-	-	-	1
Rhizophagus sp.	-	1	-	-	-
Cryptophagidae gen. et sp. indet. (not Atomariinae)	-	1	-	-	-
Atomaria sp.	1	-	1	1	-
Cerylon ferrugineum Step.	-	-	-	1	-
Lathridius minutus gp.	-	1	-	-	-
Enicmus transversus (Ol.)	1	-	-	2	-
Corticariinae gen. et sp. indet.	1	1	-	1	2
Donacia clavipes F.	-	-	1	-	-
D. impress Pk.	-	-	2	1	-
Donacia sp.	1	1	1	1	-
Chrysolina cf. graminis (L.)	-	-	-	1	-
Gastrophya viridula (Deg.)	-	-	1	-	-
Phaedon sp. (not tumidulus)	-	1	-	1	1
Prasocuris phellandrii (L.)	1	1	1	-	1
Chrysomela aenea L.	-	-	1	-	-
Phyllotreta exclamationis (Thun.)	-	-	-	1	1
P. nemorum (L.) or undulata Kuts.	-	-	1	-	-
P. vittula Redt.	2	1	-	1	1
Longitarsus spp.	1	2	1	-	5
Altica sp.	1	-	1	-	1
Chaetocnema concinna (Marsh.)	2	-	1	1	2
Chaetocnema sp. (not concinna)	1	1	2	-	1
Psylloides sp.	-	-	-	1	-
Apion aethiops. Hbst. or pisi (F.)	-	-	-	-	1
Apion spp.	2	-	-	2	4

Coleoptera	Minimum No. of Individuals				
	XA820	AA1073	XB65	XJ925	XJ912
Phyllobius sp.	-	1	-	-	1
Strophosomus faber (Hbst)	-	-	-	-	1
Sitona hispidulus (F.)	-	-	-	-	1
Sitona sp.	-	-	-	-	1
Hypera punctata (F.)	-	1	-	-	1
Hypera sp. (not *punctata*)	-	-	-	-	1
Alophus triguttatus (F.)	-	-	-	1	1
Bagous sp.	1	1	1	2	-
Notaris acridulus (L.)	-	-	-	-	2
N. cf. *scirpi* (F.)	-	-	-	1	-
Ceutorhynchus atomus Boh.	-	1	-	-	-
Ceutorhynchinae gen. et sp. indet.	2	1	-	-	1
Curculio cf. *nucum* L.	-	-	1	-	-
Tychius sp.	-	-	-	-	1
Gymnetron beccabungae (L.)	-	-	-	-	1
G. labile (Hbst.)	1	-	-	-	-
G. pascuorum (Gyl.)	1	-	-	-	-
Total	69	53	67	128	170

Odontata

Agrion sp	-	-	1	-	-
Odontata gen. et sp. indet.	1	1	-	1	-

Dermaptera

Forficula auricularia (Fal.)	-	-	-	-	2

Hemiptera

Stygnorcoris pedestris (Fal.)	1	-	-	-	-
Saldula S. *Saldula* sp.	-	-	-	-	1
Gerris sp.	-	-	1	-	-
Heteroptera gen. et sp. indet.	1	-	1	1	-
Aphrodes cf. *albifrons* (L.)	-	-	-	-	1
A. bicinctus (Schr.)	-	-	-	-	1
Aphidoidea gen. et sp. indet.	-	1	-	-	7
Homoptera gen. et sp. indet.	-	1	-	1	9

Trichoptera

Ithytrichia sp. larval cases	-	7	-	1	-
Trichoptera larvae (not *Ithytrichia*)	35	4	5	21	1

Hymenoptera

Myrmica scabrinodis gp. worker	-	-	-	-	1
Stenamma westwoodi West. worker	-	1	-	1	-
Lasius niger gp. worker	-	2	-	-	3
Lasius sp. (not *fuliginosus*) female and male	-	-	-	-	1 f + 1 m
Hymenoptera gen. et sp. indet.	1	1	-	1	21

Diptera

Chironimod larval head capsules	+	+	-	+	+
Dilophus sp.	-	-	-	-	3
Dipteran puparia	-	-	-	-	1
Dipteran adults (not *Dilophus*)	2	-	-	-	6

suggest clovers and vetches to have been amongst the grassland flora.

The assemblage from sample 912 gave a strong indication of the presence of domestic animals. Scarab dung beetles from the genera *Colobopterus*, *Aphodius* and *Onthophagus* such as *Aphodius contaminatus* comprised over 9% of the terrestrial Coleoptera.

Other beetles which occur in dung included *Megasternum obscurum* and *Anotylus rugosus*. These last two species also occur in decaying domestic refuse, but again there is no evidence from the Coleoptera for the proximity of human settlement.

Phases 3 and 4

The results from samples 820 and 1073 are very similar to those from sample 820. Woodland beetles ranged from *Chrysomela aenea,* which feeds on alder leaves and is now very rare in Britain, to *Curculio* cf. *nucum*, which develops in hazel nuts. Amongst the other phytophagous beetles were *Hypera punctata*, which feeds on *Trifolium* sp. and *Gastrophysa viridula* which is normally assoicated with *Rumex* spp., suggesting some open areas, but there was only a slight presence of dung beetles.

Conclusions

Samples 925 and 820 accumulated in an actively flowing complex of river channels against a background of marsh, grassland and some woodland. In contrast sample 912 accumulated in a ditch containing stagnant or slowly flowing water in an open landscape of grazed marsh and pasture. It is possible that this change represents a transition during the late Bronze Age to a fully cleared landscape. However, the catchment of the ditch deposit would have been more limited than those of the active channels.

It is possible that alder-dominated woodland survived on the small wet islands amongst the back streams of the Kennet after the main areas of gravel terrace and floodplain had been substantially cleared for agriculture. The Saxon samples 625 and 1073 could thus either be indicating post-Bronze Age woodland regeneration or merely reflecting the fact that they were from flowing channel deposits.

The macroscopic plant and insect assemblages from the nearby late Bronze Age settlement on the Kennet gravels at Knight's Farm suggested a landscape of wet pastureland but pollen analysis showed a background presence of at least some woodland (Bradley *et al.* 1980, 278–9).

The occurrence of rich elmid faunas in both the Saxon samples is interesting because it shows that they had been able to survive the effects of the increased sediment load in the waters of the Kennet which would have been consequent upon agricultural intensification from the late prehistoric period onwards.

Plant Remains, by W.J.Carruthers

The excavations exposed waterlogged timbers in good states of preservation. As the site occupied low-lying ground on the Kennet flood plain, it was hoped that other anaerobically preserved plant macrofossils could be recovered by wet-sieving. However, the precise extent of the waterlogging was at first uncertain, since the water table had recently been lowered by gravel extraction. For this reason two types of sample were taken from each of the deposits selected for analysis in order to ensure that both carbonised and waterlogged remains were recovered.

A. Bulk samples of 20 litres of soil were firstly subjected to flotation, ie, the soil was mixed with water and the flot poured off through a 250µ meshed sieve. Since many of the deposits were of a cohesive nature it was necessary to add hydrogen peroxide to the water in most cases to help to disaggregate the soil. If no waterlogged plant macrofossils or fragments of wood were observed in the sample, the flot was dried and examined under the microscope for carbonised plant remains. The residue was discarded.

Where waterlogged plant remains were observed during the flotation process, the residue was retained and sieved in a 1 mm meshed sieve suspended in a large wet-sieving tank until clean of silt. Both the residue and flot were kept wet and sorted for plant remains by eye.

B. In addition to the bulk samples, where waterlogged plant remains were observed, small samples of 500 ml soil were sieved through a stack of sieves (minimum mesh 250µ) and the residues sorted under a binocular microscope. It was necessary to take this second sample in order to recover the complete range of seeds from the deposit, the smaller of which would have been lost through the large meshed sieve in the wet-sieving tank.

The old land surface of Phase 3f, which did not contain waterlogged remains, was excavated in metre squares. In order to recover sparse carbonised plant remains from this deposit three entire metre squares were subjected to flotation (*c.* 140 litres soil each).

Of the 45 contexts sampled, 28 were selected for analysis on the basis of phasing information and conditions of preservation. The carbonised and waterlogged plant remains recovered from these deposits are summarised in Table 29. In an attempt to detect changes in the landscape over the period examined, the plant taxa were placed in habitat groups wherever possible, using information from Clapham *et al.* (1962). The percentages of the total

Table 29   Anslow's Cottages: waterlogged and carbonised plant remains

	Deposit type	c	f	c	d	d	d	cdfl	dl
	Habitat	Phase pre-1	1b	1c	1d	1e	1f	3	5
Ceareals									
Triticum cf. *spelta* L. (glume bases)								[+]	
T. dicoccum/spelta (caryopses)								[+]	
T. dicoccum/spelta (glume bases)								[+]	
T. dicoccum/spelta (spikelet fork)								[+]	
Hordeum sp. (caryopses)			[+]				[+]	[+]	
Indet.			[+]					[+]	
Aceraceae									
Acer campestre L.	HSWc	+		+					
Alismataceae									
Alisma sp.	PR	+		+	+				+
Araceae									
Arum maculatum L.	HW								+
Betulaceae									
Alnus glutinosa (L.) Gaertn. (fruits)	BwSW	+		+	+			+	+
Alnus glutinosa (catkin frags)	BwSW	+		+	+			+	+
Boriganaceae									
Myosotis sp.	CGMW					+	+		
Callitrichaeae									
Callitriche sp.	P						+		
Caprifoliaceae									
Sambucus nigra L.	DHSnWY	+		+	+	+	+	+	+
Caryophyllaceae									
Cerastium sp.	ABDG					+		+	+
Lychnis flos-cuculi L.	wGMW	+				+			
Moerhingia trinervia (L.) Clairv.	Wn	+		+					
Myosoton aquaticum (L.) Moench	BMPwW	+							+
Stellaria graminea L.	EGW					+	+		
S. media (L.) Vill.	AD	+		+		+	+		+
Stellaria sp.					+	+			
Chenopodiaceae									
Atriplex hastata/patula L.	CD	+		+	+	+		+	+
Chenopodium album L.	CDn	+		+	+	+	+	+	+
cf. *C. polyspermum* L.	CD				+	+	+	+	
Chenopodium sp.		+				+		+	
Compositae									
Anthemis cotula L.	ADh								+
cf. *Artemisia* sp.	DH			+		+		+	
Cirsium sp./*Carduus* sp.		+		+	+	+	+	+	+
Eupatorium cannabinum L.	BMwW	+		+	+		+	+	+
Hypochoeris maculata L.	Gc						+		
Leontodon sp.	G						+	+	
Senecio sp.	BCDY					+			
Sonchus asper (L.) Hill	CD			+	+	+			
S. oleraceus L.	CDY					+			
Taraxacum sp.	BDGY			+			+		

	Deposit type	c	f	c	d	d	d	cdfl	dl
	Habitat	Phase							
		pre-1	1b	1c	1d	1e	1f	3	5
Corylaceae									
Corylus avellana L. (nutshell frags)	HSW	+						+	
Cruciferae									
Barbarea vulgaris R. Br.	BwHY								+
Brassica sp./*Sinapis* sp.	ACD						+		+
Rorippa nasturtium-aquaticum (L.) Hayek	PR	+					+	+	+
Cyperaceae									
Carex sp.	GM	+		+	+	+	+	+	+
Eleocharis subg. *Palustres*	MPw			+		+	+	[+]+	+
Schoenoplectus sp.	BPR	+		+			+	+	+
Indeterminate		+		+	+			+	+
Dipsacaceae									
cf. *Dipsacus fullonum* L.	BGY							+	
Fagaceae									
Quercus sp. (acorn cups)		+							
Fumariaceae									
Fumaria sp.	CD	+		+	+	+		+	
Gramineae									
Glyceria sp.	BP	+		+	+	+	+	+	+
Gen. et sp. indet.	CG			+	+	+	+		+
Hydrocotylaceae									
Hydrocotyle vulgaris L.	Ma							+	
Hypericaceae									
Hypericum sp.	GHSW			+	+				
Iridaceae									
Iris pseudacorus L.	BMP			+		+		+	
Juncaceae									
Juncus sp.	wGMR	+		+	+	+	+	+	+
Labiatae									
Ajuga reptans L.	wGW	+							
Galeopsis tetrahit agg.	AWwE	+		+	+				
Lycopus europaeus L.	BM	+		+	+	+	+	+	+
Mentha sp.	ADPW	+		+	+	+	+	+	+
Prunella vulgaris L.	DG	+		+		+	+		
Stachys cf. *sylvatica*	DHW			+	+				
Stachys sp.	ABH	+		+				+	
Indeterminate		+							
Leguminosae									
Vicia sp./*Lathyrus* sp.								[+]	
Linaceae									
Linum cf. *bienne* Mill.	dG							[+]	
L. catharticum L.	EcG					+			
L. usitatissimum L. (capsule frags)								+	
Menyanthaceae									
Menyanthes trifoliata L.	BP			+				+	
Nymphaeaceae									
Nuphar lutea (L.) Sm.	PR	+		+		+		+	

152

	Deposit type	c	f	c	d	d	d	cdfl	dl
	Habitat Phase	pre-1	1b	1c	1d	1e	1f	3	5
Onagraceae									
Epilobium sp.	BDMW	+		+	+	+			
Plantaginaceae									
Plantago major L.	CDGo	+			+	+	+		+
Polygonaceae									
Bilderdykia convolvulus (L.) Dumort.	AD			+					
Polygonum aviculare agg.	AD	+		+				+	+
P. hydropiper L.	P	+		+				+	+
P. lapathifolium/nodosum	BD						+		+
P. persicaria L.	BCD	+		+	+	+	+		+
Rumex conglomeratus Murr.	wG	+		+			+		+
Rumex sp.	wG	+		+	+		+	+	
Potamogetonaceae									
Potamogeton sp.	PR	+		+	+			+	
Ranunculaceae									
Caltha palustris L.	MP							+	
Ranunculus acris L.	wcG						+		
R. flammula L.	wGP	+						+	+
R. sceleratus L.	BPR			+				+	
R. acris/bulbosus/repens	GD	+		+	+	+	+	+	+
Ranunculus subg. *Batrachium*	PR	+		+	+	+	+	+	+
Thalictrum flavum L.	BwG	+		+					
Rosaceae									
Aphanes arvensis agg.	AoG			+	+	+	+		
Crataegus monogyna Jacq.	HSW	+		+				+	
Filipendula ulmaria (L.) Maxim.	wGMW					+			
Potentilla anserina L.	DG	+		+	+	+	+	+	
Prunus spinosa L.	HSW	+		+				+	
Rosa sp.	HSW	+		+					
Rubus fruticosus agg.	DHSW	+		+	+	+		+	+
Rubiaceae									
Galium palustre L.	BMw						+		
Galium sp.						+			[+]
Scrophulariaceae									
Schrophularia sp./*Verbascum* sp.		+							+
Veronica sp.							+	+	
Solanaceae									
Solanum dulcamara L.	DHW	+		+				+	
S. nigrum L.	D	+		+					
Solanum sp.									+
Sparganiaceae									
Sparganium sp.	MP	+		+	+	+	+	[+]+	+
Umbelliferae									
Aethusa cynapium L.	C			+	+				
Apium nodiflorum (L.) Lag.	P	+		+			+	+	+
Berula erecta (Huds.) Coville	P	+		+			+	+	
Chaerophyllum temulentum L.	GH	+		+				+	
Conium maculatum L.	Bw								+

	Deposit type	c	f	c	d	d	d	cdfl	dl
	Habitat	Phase pre-1	1b	1c	1d	1e	1f	3	5
cf. *Oenanthe* sp.	wGMP							+	
Torilis japonica (Houtt.) DC.	GH			+					
Indeterminate				+					
Urticaceae									
Urtica dioica L.	DGHWp	+		+	+		+	+	+
Valerianaceae									
Valeriana officinalis L.	G					+			
Valerianella dentata (L.) Poll.	A			+					
Verbenaceae									
Verbena officinalis L.	DY			+	+				+
Violaceae									
Viola sp.				+					
Zannichelliaceae									
Zannichellia palustris L.	PR	+		+				+	
Indeterminate Characeae	P			+	+			+	+
Number of samples		2	4	6	1	1	2	9	2

+ = waterlogged   [+] = carbonised

Habitat preferences

A= arable	P = ponds, ditches	a = acid soils/calcifuge
B = riverbanks	R = rivers	c= calcareous/basic soils
C = cultivated land	S = scrub	d = dry soils
D = disturbed/wasteland	W = woodland	h = heavy soils
E = heath	Y = waysides	n= nitrogen-rich soils
G = grassland		o = open habitats
H = hedgerows		p = phosphate-rich soils
M = marsh		w = wet/damp soils

Deposit types
c = channel silts
d = ditch fill
f = dry features
l = land surface

seeds represented by these groups have been shown graphically in a series of pie charts which summarise the results from the anlaysis of the waterlogged plant remains (Fig. 55).

It should be noted that only a few of the samples produced sufficient plant remains to be analysed (one or two for each diagram illustrated). The numbers of plant remains in the samples used for the diagrams varied from roughly 100–350 identifiable fragments. It should also be noted that not all of the diagrams are comparable, since some samples came from channel fills and others were from ditch deposits. Because of differences in the 'catchment areas' of these two types of deposit the results cannot be directly compared.

This is shown by the percentages of tree remains, which were dominated in most periods by alder catkins and fruits. These propagules are designed to be dispersed by water and so can float for some distance from their point of origin when growing along riverbanks. Thus, although all of the channel sediments contained large numbers of these remains, the ditch sediments were not likely to do so unless:

a) the river was connected to the ditches;
b) there was some flooding of the ditches from time to time;
c) alder trees overhung the ditches or grew close by; or
d) human activities led to their introduction.

The ditch assemblages, being derived from a more closed system, were generally dominated by the local vegetation type, that is, aquatic and semi-aquatic taxa. The increased percentage of grassland taxa indicates another vegetation type that was obviously local. Therefore, the very low percentages of woodland remains and relatively high occurrence of grassland taxa in comparison with the channel silts does not necessarily demonstrate increased clearance in a wider sense, but is likely to be mainly due to differences in the sources of the material. Only comparisons between sediments of the same derivation can be made with some confidence.

A further difficulty with riverine sediments is that precise sources of material cannot be known and some reworking of earlier silts may occur. In general, though, most of the material is likely to have originated in the immediate vicinity. The above points have been borne in mind in the following discussion of the results by phase.

Pre-Phase 1: Trench XJ

The earliest deposits sampled were river silts 925 and 943 in Trench XJ. Although undated, the presence of lime (*Tilia* sp.) pollen in the uppermost deposit (925) suggests that they may have been Neolithic (Thompson and Allen, this volume). This being the case, pollen and plant macrofossil evidence indicate that there was already some disturbance of the natural alder carr vegetation of the area during this period.

The percentage compositions of the two deposits was almost identical, both samples being dominated by the woodland/scrub component. Large numbers of alder (*Alnus glutinosa* (L.) Gaertn.) fruits and catkins were recovered, in addition to remains from hawthorn (*Crataegus monogyna* Jacq.), sloe (*Prunus spinosa* L.), rose (*Rosa* sp.), hazel (*Corylus avellana* L.), elder (*Sambucus nigra* L.), common maple (*Acer campestre* L.) and the woodland herb three-nerved sandwort (*Moerhingia trinervia* (L.) Clairv.). Both elder and maple are strongly associated with archaeological contexts. Their occurrence in these deposits suggests human disturbance.

Pollen evidence also revealed a high occurrence of alder (*see below*). It is evident that the Kennet floodplain supported an alder carr vegetation type along much of its length in the early prehistoric period, as indicated by plant macro- and microfossil analyses carried out by Holyoak (1980). His study of sites along the Kennet Valley provided evidence of alder woodland from several post elm-decline deposits.

A few acorn cups (*Quercus* sp.) were recovered from the lower of the two silts. Oak pollen and wood fragments occurred at low levels throughout the periods examined and this is probably due to areas of oak woodland occupying the higher ground in the surrounding area (Gale, this volume).

Seeds from aquatic and waterside plants contributed towards a large part of all of the samples examined, as might be expected con-sidering that they would have formed the local vegetation type. Yellow water-lily (*Nuphar lutea* (L.) Sm.), aquatic buttercups (*Ranunculus* subg. *Batrachium*) and pondweed (*Potamogeton* sp.) would have grown in the slow-flowing open water of the main channel, whilst sedges (*Carex* sp.), bur-reed (*Sparganium* sp.) and club-rush (*Schoenoplectus* sp.) may have formed a reedswamp community along the waters edge.

Further evidence of disturbance was provided by the presence of remains from weeds of cultivated and disturbed land. Taxa such as knotgrass (*Polygonum aviculare* agg.), fumitory (*Fumaria* sp.), Chenopodiaceae and stinging nettle (*Urtica dioica* L.) are typical of this habitat group, although stinging nettles also grow naturally in alder woods. No weeds specific to arable crops were recovered, nor were cereal remains present. The weed seeds recorded would appear to represent a degree of disturbance of the habitat rather than the cultivation of crops in the area.

The large number of buttercup (*Ranunculus acris/bulbosus/repens*) seeds recovered from these sediments and the presence of taxa such as ragged robin (*Lychnis flos-cuculi* L.) and meadow rue (*Thalictrum flavum* L.) indicate the presence of areas of damp grassland. Although in Baker's (1937) comparison of meadows and pastures the latter two species are said to be absent from grazed pastures, Robinson (1979, 112) suggests that tussocky pastures may contain meadow species, and that indicators of pasture may be more reliable in distinguishing between grazed and ungrazed grasslands. Great plantain (*Plantago major* L.) and silverweed (*Potentilla anserina* L.) are typical of grazed and trampled grassland, and seeds of these species were recovered from both deposits.

It is probable that this disturbance was due to a certain amount of clearance of the alder carr vegetation to provide grazing on the damp, alluvial soils of the Kennet floodplain. Trampled areas with increased nitrogen and phosphorous levels due to the presence of animal dung would have been suitable for the growth of weeds of disturbed/cultivated soils.

Phase 1b: Trench XA

Samples from four features of this phase were examined, including two post-hole fills, 704 and 736, a dry ditch fill, 703, and a burnt flint concentration, 836. Although in total 31 litres of soil was subjected to flotation only one carbonised barley (*Hordeum* sp.) grain, an indeterminate cereal and a leguminous seed were recovered. The general sparsity of carbonised cereal remains from the Bronze Age features and channel silts suggests that crop processing activities were not taking place in the area. Of course, some caution should be applied when using negative evidence, since absence of material could be due the position of the samples or lack of preservation. An absence of domestic or crop processing waste seems to be typical of charcoal-rich samples from burnt mounds (Barfield and Hodder, 1987).

Phase 1c: Trenches XA and XB

The six samples taken from channel silts (contexts 640, 702, 710, 758, 788, 820) varied greatly in the quantities of plant remains preserved within them, but all contained a similar range of taxa. As mentioned above, river sediments may contain a mixture of material from a variety of sources, including redeposited remains and seeds carried in from upstream. It is also difficult to date such sediments and for these reasons they are of limited use in the interpretation of the site. However, some general observations and comparisons can be made.

The range of taxa and the percentages of the habitat groups obtained from the XA and XB silts were very similar to the earlier channel deposits from Trench XJ. Again, alder fruits and catkins dominated the assemblages and a few other woodland taxa were present, but not such a wide range as in the pre-Phase 1 samples. Although a large proportion of the alder remains may have been carried in from woodlands upstream of the site, it would appear that some alder carr still existed in the local area in the late Bronze Age. A lower percentage of woodland species was present in the Trench XA samples than XB which agrees with the apparent pattern of occupation of the area, though as only three samples are involved in this comparison its significance should not be stressed.

Amongst the other habitat groups the taxa showed few differences to those in Trench XJ. No carbonised cereal remains or other evidence of arable cultivation, such as waterlogged arable weed seeds, were recovered from samples of this phase. The evidence for human disturbance in the area of the Bronze Age waterfront was surprisingly slight. Although some weeds of disturbed/cultivated land were represented, such as thistles (*Cirsium* sp./*Carduus* sp.) and docks (*Rumex* sp.), these remains were not frequent.

Phase 1d: Trench XA, ditch 874

The primary silt of this ditch, 822, contained more remains of woodland taxa than samples from the two ditches of later phases, although they only amounted to 7% of the assemblage in total. Sedges, flote-grass (*Glyceria* sp.), gipsy-wort (*Lycopus europaeus* L.) and mint (*Mentha* sp.) were indicative of the stagnant or slow-flowing water present in the ditch. Of the weeds of disturbed/cultivated land represented, most were characteristic of soils containing high nutrient levels, such as Chenopodiaceae and stinging nettles. This may indicate enrichment of the soil by animal dung. The grassland species recovered included great plantain and silverweed indicating trampling. Thus, although dominated by seeds from the local ditch flora, this assemblage indicates a primarily open grassland vegetation which may have provided grazing for livestock.

Phase 1e: Trench XA, ditch 875

The slightly later ditch cutting ditch 874 contained no remains of woodland taxa in its primary silt, 814.

Other differences between this ditch and ditch 874 include the presence of ragged robin, spike-rush (*Eleocharis* subg. *Palustres*), purging flax (*Linum catharticum* L.), meadow-sweet (*Filipendula ulmaria* (L.) Maxim.), and greater quantities of meadow rue and bur-reed (*Sparganium* sp.). Taken together, the recovery of seeds of these taxa is an indication of hay production, since the plants will all be readily grazed. It is also possible that alternating regimes of grazing and hay production would enable some meadow plants to survive and set seed.

Although most of the taxa are typical of damp and marshy grasslands, the presence of purging flax, which prefers drier soils, could be due to the importation of hay to feed livestock from outside the immediate floodplain area. Great plantain and silverweed indicate the presence of trampled areas.

Phase 1f: Trench XJ, ditch 908

The complete absence of plant macrofossils from woodland/scrub taxa in the lowest fill of the ditch, 912, can be compared with the record of 50% from the river sediments into which it was cut. The problem of comparing sediments of different derivation has been discussed above, but from the pollen evidence it is clear that the alder carr vegetation had been reduced in the immediate locality by the late Bronze Age. Further evidence of clearance is that the insect remains recovered from this deposit included no wood or tree-dependent taxa (Robinson, this volume). However, some alder is likely to have survived along the valley a short distance away, since alder was the main source of timbers used structurally and some of the posts were from mature trees.

In addition, alder and other tree pollen remained quite high up to the formation of the secondary ditch silts. Since few alder remains were recovered from any of the ditches, when compared with the river sediments, there must have been very little flow of water from the river into the ditches and the alder trees must have been growing some distance away from the ditches.

The aquatic taxa recovered reflect the slow-flowing or stagnant nature of the ditch. Water-starwort (*Callitriche* sp.), flote-grass and speedwell (*Veronica* sp.) were almost exclusively confined to the lower fills of the ditch, 912 and 909, and these taxa are typical of drainage ditches where there is little water movement and which may dry out for short periods in summer (Haslam, 1978).

Several weeds of disturbed/cultivated land were recovered from the lower silts but none were strictly diagnostic of arable cultivation. However, a single carbonised barley (*Hordeum* sp.) caryopsis (context 909) and cereal-type pollen (Thompson and Allen, this volume, context 912) were recorded, so that it is probable that cereal cultivation was taking place in the vicinity, although perhaps not on the damp floodplain itself. Barley would be more suited to growing on the better drained calcareous soils of the river terraces.

The grassland taxa present indicated damp pasture with areas of trampling and this is corroborated by both pollen and insect remains. In the pollen analysis Thompson recovered evidence of hay meadow taxa in the lowest sample from 912 but these were not all present in the seed record. Rush (*Juncus* sp.) seeds, however, were numerous in the lower silts and some of these were identified to the *J. articulatus* group which are often present in wet hay meadows, since they can survive periodic cutting for hay.

Thus, the local vegetation would appear to have been grazed pastures with ruderal weeds growing in disturbed areas of site, such as along the bank where humans and stock gained access to the water. Hay production may have alternated with grazing in some areas of the site and cereals were probably cultivated on adjacent terraces.

Phase 3: Trench XB, the channel silts

The earliest Phase 3 deposits sampled were two channel silts in Trench XB; context 625 (Phase 3a) and 1612 (Phase 3c or later). These both produced fairly large quantities of alder catkins and fruits as was typical of the channel silts, indicating the continued existence or regeneration of areas of alder carr along the river, or possibly the reworking of earlier deposits. Small numbers of elder and hawthorn seeds and a hazelnut shell fragment also indicated woodland or scrub.

Other taxa represented provide little indication of a change in the nature of the vegetation, since most of the species were the same as those in the Bronze Age waterlogged samples. One interesting addition was the presence of a few cultivated flax (*Linum usitatissimum* L.) capsule fragments in both of the channel samples. Flax is commonly recovered from Saxon waterlogged deposits, particularly where flowing water may have been used in the retting process.

Phase 3f: The old land surface, 869

The presence of ploughmarks beneath this deposit provided the only clear evidence that cultivation had taken place in the area. Large amounts of soil were processed for carbonised plant remains from metre-squares 404, 470, 517. A few cereal remains were recovered including cf. spelt (*Triticum* cf. *spelta*) glume bases (identification based on measurements only as these remains were poorly preserved), emmer/spelt caryopses and glume bases, a barley caryopsis (*Hordeum* sp.) and indeterminate cereals.

The presence of cf. spelt suggests an Iron Age or Romano-British date for this layer, although spelt wheat is now increasingly being recovered from late Bronze Age sites in southern England. The artefactual evidence shows that although there is some Bronze Age residuality the majority of the pottery is from the Roman period. It is likely that the ploughing occurred during this period of agricultural expansion. The widespread cultivation of spelt in the Roman period may also be of relevance, as spelt wheat would have been better suited than barley to the heavy soils of the area.

In Trench XJ sediments overlying ditch 908 (contexts 904 and 903) produced very little evidence of woodland, but additional taxa characteristic of marshy areas such as pennywort (*Hydrocotyle vulgaris* L.), marsh marigold (*Caltha palustris* L. and cf. water dropwort (cf. *Oenanthe* sp.) were present. Sedges (*Carex* sp.) and rushes were numerous and fragments of moss were frequent in the uppermost of the two silts.

This, and the evidence of high counts of reedmace (*Typha* sp.) and Cyperaceae pollen, indicates the development of a reed-swamp vegetation following the silting up of the ditch. Plant macro- and microfossil evidence suggested some use of areas for grazing, as silverweed was present.

Phase 3g: Trench XA, pit 1070/1176

Two pits (contexts 1020, 1021) which appeared to cut through the old land surface produced only a spikelet fork and glume base of emmer/spelt wheat, even though 60 litres of soil were processed. It is possible that this material was residual, as emmer is primarily recorded from Bronze Age or earlier deposits and spelt is largely replaced by free-threshing wheats during the Saxon period.

Phase 5a: Trench XB, ditch 611

There may have been some regrowth of alder in the area when ditch 611 was in operation in the early medieval period, as some alder fruits and catkins were present (context 612). Aquatic and waterside taxa typical of still to slow-flowing water were frequent, including water-plantain (*Alisma* sp.), fool's watercress (*Apium nodiflorum* (L.) Lag.), mint and rushes.

Numerically the most dominant habitat group was the weeds of disturbed/cultivated land, in particular stinging nettles, demonstrating that human or animal disturbance had increased in the area by the medieval period. Buttercups and some other grassland taxa were present, including great plantain indicating trampled pasture.

Taxa recovered from this feature which were not in earlier samples include stinking mayweed (*Anthemis cotula* L.), a weed of heavy, disturbed or cultivated soils, whose occurrence is rare until the Iron Age, and hemlock (*Conium maculatum* L.), a weed of damp, disturbed soils not common prior to the Roman period.

Phase 6

The recovery of spruce pollen (Thompson and Allen, this volume) from the watermeadow deposit in Trench XJ (context 902) indicates that it originated in the post-medieval period. The plant macrofossil assemblages recovered from two samples from this deposit were dominated by weeds of disturbed/cultivated land, in particular stinging nettle seeds. There appears to have been some regeneration of alder judging from the small number of fruits and high percentages of alder pollen recorded. The pollen also provided evidence of hay meadows,

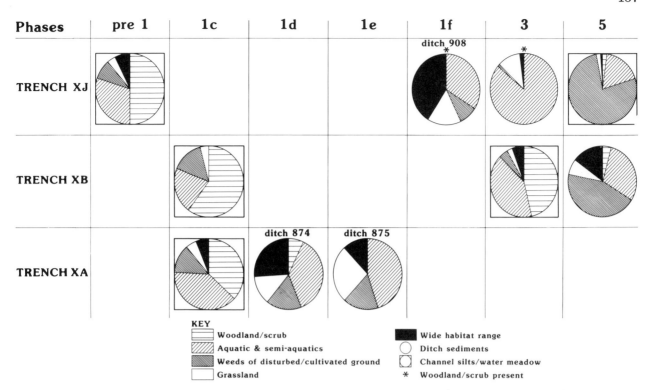

Figure 55   Anslow's Cottages: pie charts illustrating percentages of waterlogged plant macrofossil assemblages by phase

pasture and marsh, but the seeds were too few in number to demonstrate this.

Some marsh taxa were represented but a single achene of lesser spearwort was the only aquatic to indicate flooding in the operation of the watermeadow system. It is likely that periodic drying out of the meadow between the episodes of flooding had lead to some decay of plant macrofossils. A single carbonised *Galium* sp. seed was recovered.

Summary and discussion

Early channel deposits provided evidence of a predominately alder woodland vegetation with some signs of clearance. A few remains from weeds of disturbed/cultivated land were recovered, as well as grassland taxa indicative of trampled pasture and possible hay meadows.

Bronze Age silts from the river channel produced a similar range of plant material but with a smaller number of woodland taxa and an increased proportion of weeds of disturbed/cultivated land. The three late Bronze Age ditches examined produced very few remains from woodland taxa and much greater percentages of grassland species. Although the ditch sediments cannot be directly compared to the channel silts it appears that much of the alder woodland had been cleared from the immediate area to provide pasture and in some cases hay meadows for the rearing of livestock. Single grains of carbonised barley were recovered from a ditch sample and the burnt flint concentration. However, the late Bronze Age features generally produced very few carbonised

plant remains or fragments of charcoal. This suggests that activities associated with cereal processing, consumption and other domestic activities were not taking place in the area sampled. The use of land was probably confined to rearing stock on the lush pastures of the floodplain. Cereal cultivation was more likely to have taken place on the better drained gravel terraces a short distance from the site.

The only direct evidence for the cultivation of crops on the site was found in ploughmarks beneath the Phase 3f old land surface. The few carbonised cereals recovered from this buried soil provided evidence for cf. spelt wheat, spelt/emmer and barley.

A few fragments of a cultivated flax capsule in two Saxon sediments in Trench XB indicated possible use of the channel for flax retting. The Saxon samples were not otherwise notably different to the earlier waterlogged silts. The possible Phase 3f surface overlying the Phase 1f ditch in Trench XJ provided evidence of the development of reed-swamp vegetation following the silting up of the ditch.

Samples from the medieval ditch and post-medieval watermeadow system showed some signs of alder regeneration, but were dominated by weeds of disturbed/cultivated land, in particular stinging nettles, demonstrating an increased level of disturbance. Evidence of grazed pastures was present in these deposits, as in all of the previous samples examined.

The range of macroscopic plant remains recovered from Anslow's Cottages contrasts markedly with that from the middle Neolithic and

Table 30 Anslow's Cottages: summary of charcoal identifications

Phase	Trench	Context	Description	Ac	Al	Co	Fr	Qu	Po	Pr	Sa
1b	XA	703	fill of ditch 714	-	-	-	x	-	-	-	-
1b	XA	809	burnt flint concentration	x	X	-	x	x	x	x	X
1b	XA	836	burnt flint concentration	x	x	x	x	x	-	x	x
1b	XA	824	fill of ditch 848	x	x	x	-	x	-	x	-
?1c	AC	1178	layer in shallow hollow at edge of river channel	-	X	-	x	x	-	x	X
1d	Xa	800	scondary fill of ditch 874	-	x	-	-	x	-	x	-
1d	XA	822	primary fill of ditch 874	-	x	x	-	x	-	x	-
3g	XA	1020	fill of pit 1070/1176	x	-	-	x	x	x	x	x
3g	XA	1021	fill of pit 1070/1176	-	-	-	x	x	x	x	-

x = species present   X = dominant species.
Ac = *Acer*, Al = *Alnus*, Fr = *Fraxinus*, Qu = *Quercus*, Po = Pomoideae, Pr = *Prunus*, Sa = Salicaceae

late Bronze Age site at Runnymede (Greig 1991). Being a settlement site, Runnymede produced far more evidence of edible plants, in particular large amounts of well preserved cereal remains. However, like Anslow's Cottages, it also appeared to have alder carr growing along the riverbank in the vicinity.

Early Iron Age organic river bed sediments at Bidford upon Avon, Warwickshire, bore much closer resemblance to samples from Anslow's Cottages, producing a primarily open grazed grassland flora with only a little evidence of woodland and no indications of cereal cultivation (Greig, pers.comm.).

The late Bronze Age settlement sites of Aldermaston Wharf and Knight's Farm (Bradley *et al.* 1980) are situated in similar locations adjacent to the Kennet floodplain. Aldermaston Wharf produced no waterlogged plant material but far more carbonised cereal remains per litre of soil sieved than Anslow's Cottages. However, no evidence of crop processing debris was present leading to the conclusion that it was likely that the cereals were not grown in the immediate area. Knight's Farm produced less evidence for the cultivation of cereals. Waterlogged plant macrofossils from pond sediments on the site suggested that the local area was used primarily for grazing.

Late Bronze Age waterlogged deposits at Wallingford, Oxfordshire, on the banks of the Thames also produced evidence of primarily grassland environments (Thomas *et al.* 1986). The Iron Age site at Farmoor (Lambrick and Robinson, 1979), also on the Thames floodplain in Oxfordshire, appears to have been situated amongst grazed pasture, with no evidence having been recovered to suggest that cereals were grown on the floodplain itself. In contrast with all of these river valley sites, samples from middle Bronze Age deposits in the Wilsford Shaft (Robinson 1989), which is situated on the well drained chalk of the

Wiltshire Downs, produced more positive evidence of arable cultivation as well as that of chalk pasture.

Thus, the evidence from sites sampled to date indicates that the Kennet Valley floodplain provided lush pasture for grazing stock in the Bronze Age, and that cereals were grown on the better drained river terraces. The ploughmarks at Anslow's Cottages, however, demonstrate that alluvial soils were cultivated to some extent, possibly after the development of iron ploughshares which could cope with heavier soils as suggested by Jones (1981). The introduction of spelt wheat in the late Bronze Age or early Iron Age, which can grow on heavier soils, may also have been a contributing factor.

Charcoal, by R. Gale

Samples of charcoal from nine contexts were received for species identification using comparative anatomical methods. The individual fragments of charcoal were pressure-fractured to reveal clean, flat surfaces in the transverse, tangential longitudinal and radial longitudinal planes. These were supported in washed, fine sand and examined using an epi-illuminating microscope at magnifications of up to x400.

The samples from each context contained material from several different species. The structure of each fragment within these samples was compared and matched to authenticated reference material and the species present are listed in Table 30.

Habitat

The relatively high water table of the low-lying ground following the course of the river would have offered the damp habitat favoured by species such as *Alnus* (alder) and *Salix*/*Populus* (willow/poplar). On boggy ground alder and willow often form an alder carr. *Fraxinus* (ash) and *Quercus* (oak) also thrive on damp but not waterlogged soil. *Corylus* (hazel) and members of the Pomoideae group such as *Crataegus* (hawthorn) are generally shrubby but can form small trees when growing as understorey with *Fraxinus* and *Quercus*.

Acer (maple) and *Prunus* (blackthorn and wild cherry) prefer a drier environment; blackthorn often occurring as scrub on woodland margins or in more open areas.

Species selection

Any attempt to establish a pattern of selection or occurrence within a context was undermined by the wide range of species present.

The two contexts, 809 and 836, associated with the burnt flint concentration in Phase 1b varied in content, in that the former was dominated by *Alnus* and *Salix/Populus*, none of which make good fuel as wood. The other species present and mostly common to both contexts (*Quercus, Fraxinus, Prunus, Acer, Corylus* and the Pomoideae group) generally initiate higher temperatures when burnt. The fill of ditch 848 (context 824) of this phase contained a similarly wide range of species (*Quercus, Alnus, Prunus, Acer* and *Corylus*), whereas only minimal charred material was retrieved from the fill (context 703) of ditch 714 (*Fraxinus*).

A rather similar group of species was evident in Phase 1d. The primary fill of ditch 874 (context 822) included *Quercus, Alnus, Prunus, Acer* and *Corylus* (one fragment showed an area that may have been worked), and the secondary fill (context 800) had similar species but with *Alnus* in place of *Corylus*. The *Alnus* from the upper fill was in poor condition, probably due to charring at extremely high temperatures.

Phase 3g features (pit 1070/1176, contexts 1020 and 1021) which may have had a more industrial function, indicated a preference for *Quercus*, although many of the other woody species available in the area were also present. Context 1020 contained several large fragments some of which originated from fast growing trees, and some from heartwood suggesting that the material was from mature timber.

Pollen, by Belinda Thompson and Michael J. Allen

Pollen analysis was conducted by B. Thompson as an undergraduate dissertation at Reading University (1986). The work was supervised by M. Keith-Lucas who also checked and corroborated the identifications and interpretation. The dissertation was restructured, and is discussed in this report, by Michael J. Allen.

Fossil pollen and spore analyses were undertaken to reconstruct the vegetation history and determine the human impact upon, and use of, the site at Anslow's Cottages. There are relatively few palynological analyses within Berkshire and the Kennet Valley as a whole and a paucity of evidence from archaeological contexts. Major sequences in the Kennet include the Mesolithic sequences at Thatcham (Churchill 1962; Scaife forthcoming) and the biogeographical research of Holyoak (1980). Analyses from Cothill Fen (Clapham and Clapham 1939) provide another Mesolithic sequence and a Neolithic sequence was obtained from the excavations at Aldermaston (Clarke 1980). Bronze Age spectra are published from the barrows at Ascot in east Berkshire (Bradley and Keith-Lucas 1975) and Row Down, on the Berkshire Downs (Dimbleby 1962).

The area of the excavation investigated was confined to Trench XJ (Fig. 28). Two sequences were sampled for pollen. A short sequence of three samples was taken from the base of the sequence, from deposits pre-dating the Phase 1f ditch; a series of fifteen samples was taken through the fill of the Phase 1f ditch, 908, and the overlying sediments (Fig. 40, S.193).

Standard techniques were used to extract sub-fossil pollen and spores from the sediments (Moore and Webb 1978) using laboratory procedures outlined by Barber (1976). Samples of *c.* 1 cm^3 of sediment were prepared using sodium hydroxide to disperse the organic matter and sieving (180μ) to remove coarse sand and plant material. Hydrofluoric acid treatment was used to remove siliceous material and Erdtman's acetolysis to remove cellulose. The concentrated pollen was stained with safranin and mounted on slides with glycerine jelly. Approximately 200–300 grains were counted from each sample.

Identifications were made under x1000 magnification with the aid of the pollen reference collection in the Department of Botany, University of Reading, and the standard texts of Moore and Webb (1978), Faegri and Iversen (1975) and Erdtman *et al.* (1961; 1963). Algal spores were identified with reference to Van Geel *et al.* (1978) and plant macrofossils were identified by Carruthers (this volume); other microfossil evidence is presented in Table 32.

The results of pollen analysis are presented in archive and in diagram form (the percentages of total pollen are represented by points on a continuous curve) (Fig. 56), and summarised in Table 31. Pollen sums include tree, shrub and terrestrial herb pollen and excludes aquatic herb pollen and spores as they were invariably local species. Total pollen was used due to the difficulty of separating local and regional pollen spectra in such marginal deposits.

Pollen and spores were quite sparse and preservation was relatively poor. Although the clay silts were organic, the spectra had been affected by erosion and deposition of the sediments. The pollen assemblages can only be divided into two major zones representing the pre-Phase 1f deposits, which filled an old river channel, and the Phase 1f ditch and subsequent deposits. The later sequence could not strictly be divided into zones, since there was no marked change in the pollen, and is considered as

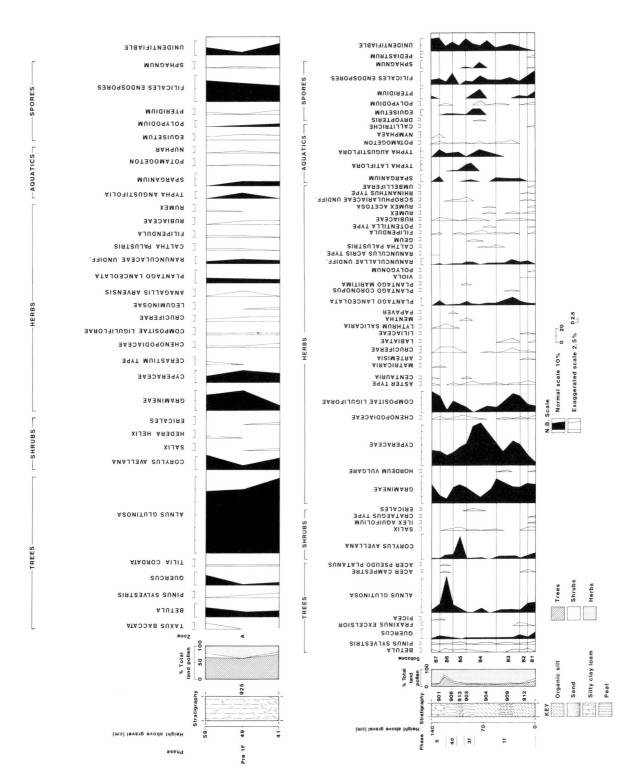

Figure 56 Anslow's Cottages: pollen diagrams

Table 31 Anslow's Cottages: summary of pollen analysis

Pollen zone	Context No.	Phase	Height above gravel	Local environment	Regional environment
B7	901	6	1.27–1.40 m	Land used as watermeadow. Flooded in winter, grazed in spring, and used to produce a hay crop in summer	Oak woodland with birch, spruce and pine
B6	901 902 906	5–6	1.09–1.27 m	Alder carr in marshy areas. Land used for pasture and hay production	Oak woodland with sycamore/maple, spruce
B5	913	?4d	0.93–1.09 m	Hay meadows and planting of hazel banks or colonisation of banks by hazel due to abandonment of grazing. Reedswamp	Oak woodland
B4	903	3f	0.55–0.93 m	Damp pastoral land. Reedswamp vegetation above ditch	Oak woodland. Peaty areas supporting *Sphagnum* and *Pteridium*
B3	904 909	3f 1f	0.25–0.55 m	Land was grazed. Erosion and infilling of ditch, probably caused by visiting animals. Arable land	Oak wood with some pine
B2	912	1f	0.15–0.25 m	Main landuse was for pasture	Oak woods with birch, pine and some ash. *Pteridium* in acid areas
B1	912 (ditch 908)	1f	0–0.15 m	Land used for grazing, hay and agriculture. Man-made ditch, probably visited by animals. Hawthorn growing locally	Oak woodland with sycamore/maple, ash and holly. *Pteridium* in acid areas
B		pre-1f		Grassland used for grazing animals. Cultivation of crops such as barley, and production of hay	Mixed oak woodland
A	925	pre-1f		Pastoral and cultivated land surrounded by alder carr. Waterside habitat near river channel	Oak and lime woodland with yew

one zone (B), but is divided into a series of sub-zones.

Pollen zone A: pre-Phase 1

The basal humic silty clay layer 925 was sealed by clay horizon 905, which was cut by ditch 908. The pollen spectra are characterised by high *Tilia* frequencies (to 6.5%) which is often under-represented in pollen spectra as it is not a prolific pollen producer and is insect-pollinated (entomophilous). This indicates a post-elm decline woodland prior to the anthropogenic selective clearance of lime typical of the 4th millennium BC, ie. late Neolithic. The predominantly lime woodlands were selectively felled between the later Neolithic and earlier Bronze Age (eg. Scaife 1987; Greig 1982).

Four main habitats can be recognised from the pollen spectra; oak woodland, alder carr (Alnetum), pasture and disturbed/cultivated land. The counts of *Quercus* suggest that there was oak woodland, probably on the higher ground. *Betula, Pinus, Taxus* and *Corylus* were also recovered and probably represent major constituents of a deciduous lime and oak woodland. Although today *Taxus* is restricted to the chalk in the south-east and limestone in the north-west of the country (Tittensor 1980), in prehistory it had a much wider distribution. During the Neolithic it certainly formed extensive woodland over the East Anglian Fens (Godwin 1975) and probably did so here too.

The high pollen counts of *Alnus* and the abundance of *Alnus* seeds and catkins suggests that alder grew locally, probably with Filicales and *Polypodium* which together represent an alder carr

(Alnetum) community. The *Polypodium* may have had an epiphytic existence on the *Alnus*, living on the alder trees. The alder carr was adjacent to open, slowly- moving water, as indicated by the spores of *Pediastrum* and presumably represents a river which contained aquatic species such as *Nuphar* (water lily), *Typha* and *Sparganium*.

Some of the land within the vicinity of the river channel may have been used as pasture for grazing since pollen of *Plantago lanceolata* and *Ranunculus acris* which are favoured by trampling were found. Gramineae pollen counts were, however, fairly low, possibly as a result of grazing. Indicators of disturbance were also recorded and include both pollen and seeds of Chenopodiaceae, and seeds of *Urtica dioica* (nettles) and *Sambucus nigra*. Today *U. dioica* occurs especially in disturbed and derelict areas and, like the small shrub *Sambucus nigra*, is characteristic of disturbed, base-rich and nitrogen-rich soils. The occurrence of *Anagallis arvensis* is of particular interest as it is possibly indicative of cultivated land and today is prevalent as an arable weed, like some members of the Chenopodiaceae family. This evidence may be taken to suggest that cultivation occurred in the vicinity prior to the late Bronze Age activity, and probably during the late Neolithic.

Pollen zone B: Phases 1f–6
The main sequence of fifteen samples was taken through the silts of ditch 908 and the later organic silty clays which sealed both the ditch (Fig. 40, S.193). This has been divided into seventeen sub-zones based on their vegetational characteristics, working from the gravel upwards.

Sub-zone B1 (0–0.15 m): Phase 1f
This sub-zone corresponds to the lower silty clay fill of ditch 908. The pollen spectrum is characterised by high Filicales endospore counts of c. 15% A total of five separate vegetational habitats can be recognised from the pollen spectra; woodland, arable, pasture, hay meadow and waterside.

The mixed deciduous woodland which probably grew on the higher ground was dominated by *Quercus* with *Fraxinus, Acer, Betula*, and localised stands of *Pinus. Corylus* and *Crataegus* are also recorded and probably contributed to the woodland composition. The *Crataegus* pollen count was, however, less than 1%, but as it is an insect-pollinated species it may be under-represented, and also of local origin.

The lower, wetter ground was dominated by *Alnus* and *Salix* with Filicales (ferns) growing in abundance beneath them. *Polypodium* probably grew in this habitat too, and *Pteridium* in very localised more acid and drier areas.

Pollen and seeds of Chenopodiaceae and *Rumex* can be taken to indicate the presence of anthropogenic activity in the area. The family Chenopodiaceae and genus *Rumex* contain many ruderals and weeds which grow on cultivated or disturbed land. The presence of *Artemisia* is also indicative of local disturbance. Cereal pollen,

predominantly *Hordeum vulgare*, was identified and was probably cultivated in the immediate proximity which would account for the presence of arable weed species.

Pasture is indicated by the presence of *Plantago lanceolata* and *Potentilla anserina* which both favour trampled environments; *Potentilla* is common, particularly in damp pastures. Both pollen and seeds of Ranunculaceae are present and include *R. acris* which is strongly resistant to grazing, *R. repens* and *R. bulbosus*, which are both common in pastures. Compositae–Liguliflorae is also considered an indicator of pasture. Other evidence suggesting that the land was used for grazing comes from the abundance of nematode eggs found in this sub-zone (Table 31). The sheer quantity of eggs suggest that the nematode was an animal parasite rather than a free-living species here.

Although the land was evidently grazed, it may also have been used as a hay meadow. Evidence for this may be provided by pollen of *Rhinanthus* (hay nettle) which is characteristic of hay meadow habitats, as a hemiparasite upon the roots of grasses. However, no remains of *Rhinanthus* were recovered from the plant macrofossils which did include a large number of *Veronica* (of *Rhinanthus* type) which is a weed of many environments. *Ranunculus repens, R. bulbosus* and some Umbelliferae, are common in both meadows and grazed pasture.

Freshwater is indicated by *Pediastrum* and algal spores, presumably occurring in the ditch itself. *Callitriche* would have occurred in the ditch, either completely submerged, or with floating leaves. *Sparganium* occurs in fresh water as well. Together with these fresh water species were a number of others typical of watersides which in- cluded the dominant *Filipendula ulmaria* and *Geum rivale*. Seeds of *Eleocharis*, which is recorded as a plant of open water margins, were also identified.

Sub-zone B2 (0.15–0.25 m): Phase 1f
This sub-zone also corresponds to the lower fills of the ditch and is characterised by high levels of Compositae–Liguliflorae which is typical of many damp pastures in the Kennet valley at the present day. Three distinct habitats could be recognised from the pollen spectra; woodland, pasture and waterside. The composition of the woodland can be seen to change with a decline in *Betula, Pinus, Acer* and *Corylus* in this sub-zone and this corresponds to a slight increase in *Quercus* and *Fraxinus*. The most dramatic changes in the tree species is the reduction of *Alnus, Salix* and Filicales. This evidence suggests that some forest clearance was taking place.

The land in the immediate vicinity of the ditch appears to have remained primarily as pasture and there is an increase in both *Plantago lanceolata* and Compositae–Liguliflorae. A decrease in Gramineae and the presence of nematode eggs confirms this. However, the increase of Cyperaceae from less than 15% to above 32% suggests that the pasture was

Table 32 Anslow's Cottages: Microfossil evidence identified during pollen analysis

Context No.	Depth above gravel	Microfossil	Implication
912	0–0.10 m	Abundant nematode eggs	These eggs are possibly from an animal parasite, suggesting grazing
		Algal spores	Suggests open water, which could result from flooding
912	0.12–0.20 m	Derived tertiary grain of Magnoliaceae and also possible grain of Bombaceae	Suggests that breakdown of Eocene formations occurred and some redeposition
		A few nematode eggs	Implication as above
		Algal spores including *Spyrogyra* types	Implication as above, although *Spirogyra* types indicate open, relatively eutrophic water. Optimal growth conditions for *Spirogyra* are over 20°C (Hoshaw 1968)
		Bryophyte spores	Local growth, damp places
912	0.20–0.30 m	*Spirogyra* type spores	Implication as above
		Zygnema type and other algal spores	*Zygnema* type indicate mesotrophic to eutrophic open water. Optimum temperature is 14–20°C (Hoshaw 1968)
909	0.30–0.40 m	As for 0.20–0.30 m, but a possible nematode egg was also found	As above. Animals or settlement nearby
909	0.40–0.50 m	As for 0.20–0.30 m, but also spores of *Mougeotia* were identified	Optimum temperature for growth of *Mougeotia* is 10–15°C. Could be caused by direct radiation on shallow water
904	0.50–0.80 m	As for 0.40–0.50 m	Implication as above
903	0.80–0.90 m	Algal spores as previously. Tertiary tree-compositae type grain	Implication as above
903	0.90–0.96 m	Algal spores as above	Implication as above
913	0.96–1.05 m	Algal spores of open water species	Implication as above
906	1.05–1.14 m	Algal spores of various species	Implication as above
902	1.14–1.21 m	Algal spores of various species	Implication as above
901	1.21–1 30 m	Algal spores of various species	Implication as above
901	1.30–1.40 m	Algal spores of various species	Implication as above

damp. A decrease and disappearance of many of the meadow species, such as *Rhinanthus* suggests that the land was no longer used to produce hay. Nor was there evidence of cultivation since there is a marked decline in the number of weed species found previously in sub-zone B1. Freshwater is indicated by the occurrence of *Sparganium* which requires a depth of water of between 1–5 cm (Haslam *et al.* 1976).

Sub-zone B3 (0.25–0.55 m): Phases 1f and 3f
The silts from the lower ditch fill and the more organic sitly clay of the upper ditch fill produced pollen spectra characterised by a continued increase in *Plantago lanceolata*. Three habitats could be recognised within this sub-zone; pasture, arable and waterside. The tree and shrub pollen remain low and more or less constant throughout this sub-zone.

The abundant *Plantago lanceolata* is accompanied by *Plantago coronopus* which is often considered a maritime plant, but also occurs inland on sandy and gravelly soils, particularly where heavy trampling is occurring, for example in farm gateways (Clapham *et al.* 1962). Other abundant pasture herb species include Compositae, particularly Liguliflorae.

The return of cultivation is indicated by the occurrence of pollen of *Hordeum vulgare*, and a rise in the level of Cruciferae. It is possible that the latter included *Brassica* species, such as *B. rapa* which could be cultivated as a crop. This could, however, represent waterside crucifers which grew around the edges of the ditch. A number of weed species associated with arable land includes Chenopodiaceae and *Rumex*.

The waterside habitat was represented by species such as *Sparganium* and *Filipendula ulmaria* which would have grown with Cyperaceae on the banks of the ditch in local marshy areas.

Sub-zone B4 (0.55–0.93 m): Phase 3f

The upper humic clay fill of the ditch and the peat above indicate that the environs were becoming damper and the two main habitat types represented were damp pasture and reed swamp. Pollen of *Typha*-type is high. According to Druce (1897) *Typha latifolia* has been found growing along the banks of the Kennet in modern times, but no *T. angustifolia* has been recorded in this location.

Herb pollen is dominant in this sub-zone; Gramineae comprised up to 39% whilst other herbs characteristic of pasture included *Plantago lanceolata*, Compositae-Liguliflorae, Ranunculaceae and *Potentilla*. Pasture is also suggested by the lower counts of *Sparganiun* which cannot withstand grazing. There is some evidence of local disturbance indicated by the presence of Chenopodiaceae, *Rumex* and *R. acetosa*.

Cyperaceae reaches a maximum of 59% suggesting the locality was very damp. Seeds of both *Juncus* and *Carex* sp. support this and may indicate a change from open water to reed swamp, following the infilling of the ditch. *Sparganium*, *Typha* and *Filipendula* could have grown within a reed swamp community. Water habitats, however, are indicated by the presence of *Potamogeton* and *Caltha*. *Sphagnum* is also present, along with *Pteridium* spores, indicating peaty areas nearby.

Sub-zone B5 (0.93–1.09 m): Phase 4d

The peat and humic silty clays in this sub-zone are characterised by high *Corylus* counts, which peak at 37% This is probably a very local effect as a result of the planting of hazel hedges or the abandonment of grazing and colonisation of the riverbanks. The increase of Gramineae may be taken to suggest a change of local landuse from pasture to meadow. This is supported by a decline in pasture herb species such as *Plantago lanceolata* and an increase in the herb species characteristic of hay meadows. Limited disturbance or cultivation is indicated in the vicinity by the presence of Chenopodiaceae and *Papaver*. The local vegetation, however, still appears to be reed swamp as indicated by the abundance of Cyperaceae, *Typha*, *Equisetum*, *Sparganium* and *Lythrum*. The reed swamp was probably surrounded by *Salix* and *Alnus*. The pollen count of *Salix* is relatively high (almost 5%), and, as it is a poor pollen producer, indicates that it must have been fairly abundant locally.

Sub-zone B6 (1.09–1.27 m): Phase 5–6

The upper alluvial sequence of clays is characterised by an increase in *Alnus* which reaches 53%. This colonisation of the marshy areas by *Alnus* may have been the result of reduced grazing. *Corylus* pollen declines, possibly as a result of the reduction of this species locally, or as a result of it

growing under the shade of canopies, thus reducing its pollen productivity. The latter is more likely because of the fairly high values of Filicales which would live under such a canopy.

Both *Acer campestre* and *Acer pseudoplatanus* are present, the latter of which was not introduced into the British Isles until the 16th century. Similarly *Picea* is recorded in this sub-zone and was introduced at about the same time. These species probably occurred in mixed woodland in the region which increased at this time, as is reflected by an increase in *Quercus* pollen. Herbs that are common in, but not exclusive to, meadows included Scrophulariaceae and members of the Ranunculaceae. Ranunculaceae are not, however, confined to meadows and do occur in pastures. Indeed *Plantago lanceolata* rises to over 10%, whilst Gramineae and Compositae–Liguliflorae fall dramatically which is also suggestive of pasture rather than haymeadow. The presence of flowering wet grassland species does indicate that some land was retained for hay production.

Marshy conditions remain, indicated by the high levels of Cyperaceae and *Typha*. Both *Lythrum* and *Equisetum* are also present. The occurrence of *Nymphaea* and *Potamogeton* indicates open water, possibly associated with the River Kennet, and deposited with the alluvium.

Sub-zone B7 (1.27–1.40 m): Phase 6

The upper alluvium contained an increase in *Pteridium* spores which had probably blown in from more acid areas. The grassland herb, and other, species suggest that the land was used as watermeadow and probably dates to the 18th century on the basis of the composition of the pollen spectra. Grazing of the land is indicated by *Plantago lanceolata* and *Ranunculus acris* and Compositae–Liguliflorae, while hay production is likely in view of the high Gramineae. The flowering of other herbs such as *Centaurea* supports the hypothesis of meadows. The local habitat remained quite damp as indicated by the levels of *Sparganium*, *Lythrum* and *Typha angustifolia*.

Summary, by Michael J. Allen

Although no associated archaeological or radiocarbon dating is available for the pre-Phase 1f palaeo-channel, the pollen spectra provide a fairly good chronological, as well as environmental, indicator. The lack of elm indicates a post-elm decline vegetation (*c.* 4900 BP (Scaife 1988)), whilst the relatively high percentage of lime, a poor pollen producer (Andersen 1970; 1973), is indicative of vegetation prior to the anthropogenically promoted *Tilia* decline (cf. Turner 1962). The fills of the palaeo-channel can, therefore, be attributed to the late 4th–early 3rd millennia BC.

It is evident that the palaeo-channel contained slow flowing, or static water, and the main vegetation cover which developed was one of alder carr (Alnetum) on the floodplain and mixed oak and lime (linden) woodland on the slightly higher land to the south. There is, however, evidence of anthropogenic activity in the form of both grazing and cultivation in the vicinity, possibly indicating limited clearance of the woodland on the floodplain margins.

There is an hiatus in the vegetation history until the sedimentation within the Phase 1f ditch began (late Bronze Age or later), by which time there is evidence of more widespread and formal anthropogenic use of the area. The ditch itself was waterlogged, containing water to a reasonable depth and having rank vegetation on its edges. Alder carr, comprised primarily of alder and willow, still existed in places on the floodplain.

Off the floodplain, the vegetation appears to have been mixed oak and scrubby woodland from which lime had been almost completely, and selectively, felled (cf. Turner 1962). More locally, a number of specific activities are indicated by the pollen and include cultivation, particularly of barley, pasture for grazing animals, and possibly hay meadows presumably for fodder production for livestock.

Later, within the period of the final use of the ditch and subsequently, the vegetation changed quite radically, with clearance of much of the woodland and woody species in the alder carr on the floodplain. Large areas were used predominantly for grazing livestock rather than for the production of hay and arable crops.

As the ditch continued to silt up, although it may still have contained water, the vegetation within the ditch increased raising the level of organic material in the silts. The area remained primarily one of damp pasture. The intensity of local grazing can be seen to have been quite severe, possibly as a result of livestock visiting the edge of the ditch to drink. Within the area as a whole the return of some arable activity locally is indicated by both the presence of barley and various arable weeds.

The ditch and bank were sealed by humic silty clay deposits which appear to have accumulated in the late Saxon period. Wetter conditions on the floodplain are reflected in localised changes in the vegetation. Reedswamp occurred and included the growth of *Typha* and *Juncus*, which were probably confined to the floodplain.

Elsewhere, grazing within the damp grassland remained in evidence. Over time the willow was allowed to grow back on the floodplain, but the reedswamp conditions remained, and damp grassland continued to be grazed, but limited hay meadow occurred.

Conditions on the floodplain continued to be neglected and by the 16th century alder carr became re-established in places. Pasture and hay meadows still existed and, further afield, the introduced spruce probably became a component of the oak woodlands. Later, as wet conditions prevailed, the area was used as watermeadow, but with little change in the vegetation.

6 Discussion

Although an overall sequence of events can be outlined for part of the site at Anslow's Cottages, interpretation of the whole area during the various stages of its development is not straightforward. The division between wet and dry areas most clearly shows the difficulties. Whereas the dry land sequence is (for the most part) clear, and features can be assigned to a particular phase or at least accommodated into the sequence with reasonable certainty, the same cannot be so easily managed for the river channel area. The complex intercutting watercourses could not be comprehensively investigated in the limited time and area available and the sequence there, as indicated earlier, has been suggested by the radiocarbon dates for individual timbers rather than by straightforward interpretation of the site records alone.

It is certain that the full extent of archaeological features at the site was not established, and it may be that areas not examined would have provided answers to questions that were not then and certainly cannot now be satisfactorily answered. It should also, perhaps, be considered that examination of a larger area might, in view of the difficulties encountered in a relatively small one, have led to more problems. This notwithstanding, the available evidence indicates a number of probably short-lived episodes of river-related activities of varying intensity, ranging from the late Bronze Age through Roman, middle, and late Saxon times.

Riverine activity in the earliest period was accompanied by land-based occupation. Such occupation may have occurred in later periods, although no evidence of it was found. Environmental evidence indicates that less intensive agricultural use has been practised in the area from the late Neolithic or early Bronze Age period into modern times.

The pre-Bronze Age landscape

Although no anthropogenic activity pre-dating the Bronze Age was identified, it is clear that humans had begun to have an impact on the environment in the vicinity of the site before then, possibly in the late Neolithic or early Bronze Age, indicated by the presence of *Tilia* in the pollen record. The pollen suggests a background of oak woodland with alder carr on the floodplain, although some clearance for arable is suggested by the pollen and the plant macrofossils, presumably on the higher ground to the south; there was also some open grassland which the insect evidence indicates was grazed.

Bronze Age

By the late Bronze Age the dry land on the southern bank of the river channel was being occupied, although the nature of this activity is not entirely clear. Some difficulty lies in determining whether certain of the features were contemporary, and also whether they were related to timber structure 873 at the southern riverbank. It may be reasonable to suppose that a structure in the river channel would have been acccompanied by some sort of activity nearby, however temporary or short-lived such activity might have been. The radiocarbon date for the timber structure indicates a date in the 7th or 8th centuries Cal. BC.

Of all the features south of the river, the shallow irregularly curving trackway, 1091, apears to be the earliest; the nature of the feature and the paucity of finds from the (admittedly few) excavated sections do not suggest any other more likely use than that suggested. Some of the post-holes may have been associated with this feature, although there was no evidence that this was the case. The trackway may have provided access to the river or to a crossing point from an unknown area of activity or settlement further to the south. The degree of compaction and mineralisation recorded in the fill of the feature suggests that it was well used.

Many of the other features south of the river may have been contemporary. If the stakes against the southern bank of the river, 873, are regarded as a small landing-stage, or revetment to prevent erosion at a well-used access point, there may be reason to suppose that access to the riverbank was restricted or controlled in the surrounding area. It is possible that the post-hole alignment and the interrupted ditches parallel to the river could have been left by a barrier constructed to achieve that purpose. The proximity of the post-holes to the river and the absence of others leading back from them suggest that they could have formed a single structure to protect the riverbank rather than part of a larger and more complex structure, such as a building.

The eastern end of the post-hole alignment and the interrupted ditch coincide so well that it seems likely that they were related features. The loss of the western end of the post-hole alignment, cut by later ditches 874 and 875, does not necessarily invalidate this suggestion. Within the river channel, organic deposits, similar to those recorded around the surviving timbers, extended to both to the east and to the west, suggesting that the timber structure in the water may have been more extensive.

The outer ends of the ditches were about 12.5 m (west) and 15 m (east) of the surviving outer stakes of the timber structure, giving a reasonably symmetrical arrangement overall. The widest gap in the post-hole alignment corresponded quite closely with the stakes in the river channel; if, as may have been the case, some stakes had originally existed in the area west of those surviving, the break in the post-holes could have been suitably placed to allow controlled access to the river across the landing-stage/revetment (there is no reason, of course, to assume that the whole arrangement had to be exactly symmetrical).

The function of the interrupted ditches is obscure; the gap between the two ditch sections does not correspond with a break in the post-hole alignment, nor does the interruption in the line of post-holes correspond with a break in the western ditch (the unexcavated area could have obscured a gap, however). The ditches may have been dug to provide soil to give further support to the posts themselves or to reinforce the fence line indicated by the post-holes; if the latter, perhaps a small bridge crossed the ditch at the appropriate place. Two post-holes (113, 180) lay between the alignment and the ditch, both of them near the gap in the alignment, opposite the timbers, and might perhaps have been part of such a bridge.

The timber structure would appear to have been intended for light use only judging by the selection of the wood type and the size of the stakes; with the exception of one oak stake all the others were of ash, alder or *prunus* sp., all of which would have been readily available on the river bank, and were an average 0.058 m in diameter. This contrasts with the alignment of posts, where a much more substantial structure is suggested by the closer spacing and large size of the post-holes (average 0.30 m diameter).

The other post-holes and pits lay to the south and east of the 'controlled' river access and could be (part of) an area of associated occupation on the slightly higher and therefore drier land to the south. Probably not all of the post-holes were contemporary and certainly some survived only as very shallow features; these may have been truncated by later activity related to the formation and cultivation of the buried land surface which sealed the site. Other features may not have been recognised because of the similarity between that layer and the fills of the features.

The excavated post-holes do not show any obvious or convincing structural groups, but the area available for excavation was so limited that any such patterns may have been lost in the destruction of the surrounding area. One group, the semi-circular arrangement cutting 1091 at the eastern end of 848, must be part of a single structure; these were some of the shallowest surviving features and may have been (part of) a later structure cut from a higher level.

Pits were few and scattered and usually contained little in the way of finds by which their function might have been determined. However, these observations might reflect the temporary nature of activity on the site; rubbish could most easily be disposed of in the river nearby. The upright jar was apparently deliberately placed in pit 1174, which lay outside the main concentration of excavated features, but the reason for its deposition there was not clear.

The position in the overall picture and the cause of the dense charcoal and burnt flint deposit, 809, (in the north-east corner of XA) are both uncertain. Another similar deposit occurred about 25 m east along the riverbank. It would be convenient to see them as contemporary with timber structure 873 and with the occupation features. Lying immediately beside the river, to the east of the timber structure and pits identified (downwind to minimise disturbance?), the burnt material was sealed by clean silts filling the upper level of and extending beyond the channel in this low-lying area. It may have been cut by the river but the proximity of the trench edge made it impossible to be sure; it was, however, cut by ditches 874 and 875.

There was no evidence to indicate an industrial purpose for the material. It is possible that this feature may have been associated with some sort of sauna or steam bath, although it lacks the characteristic pits or any other associated structural evidence (Barfield and Hodder 1987); however, evidence for a post-built structure may have been eroded by river action and/or truncated by later features. The quantity of burnt flint would seem too great simply for domestic hearth debris, although the interpretation as cooking places cannot be ruled out (O'Drisceoil 1988); this cannot be supported by the evidence of the faunal remains from the site, although gnawed bones were frequent and dogs may have played a part in keeping the site 'clean'. Again, however, this interpretation is flawed by the lack of an associated trough or pit, as is found in the Irish examples, although many excavated examples elsewhere in Britain are similarly lacking in associated structural features (Buckley 1990).

Domestic debris, which is common on other settlement sites of this period in the area (Bradley *et al.* 1980), is lacking at Anslow's Cottages and would tend to suggest that the features recorded do not represent habitation, although it is possible that the activities carried out at the site were on the periphery of a settlement, the nucleus of which was beyond the area investigated but not too far distant from the river. The insect and plant remains indicate some disturbance at the river edge but this is unlikely to be due to human habitation.

The plant remains also indicate that some alder carr still existed in the local area at this time. The river was a fast- flowing stream, but at some time during this period there was a noticeable change in the water supply. The volume of water must have decreased considerably, allowing finer silts to accumulate around the timber structure, eventually sealing it and filling the channel completely, forcing the edge of the water course to move northwards. The reason for this change remains unclear, but it may have led to the abandonment of the site. The area of the silted up channel reverted to wet, marshy grassland with some regeneration of woodland and scrub.

Following the abandonment of the site, but probably still within the late Bronze Age, two consecutive ditches (Phases 1d and 1e) were dug along the edge of the silted up channel. Ditch 875 was later than ditch 874. The course of 874 was irregular and it is possible that 362, an otherwise isolated short length of ditch in the south-west corner of XA, was a continuation of this feature; such a suggestion does present one difficulty, namely that the ditch did not cut the post-holes of the alignment which, had the ditch been continuous, it should have done (the recorded breaks within the post-hole alignment were generally not caused by the intrusion of later features, although some post-holes were lost to ditch 875 at the western end). If this indicates a break in the ditch then it may represent a gateway.

The later ditch, 875, was continuous and much straighter, diverging from the course of ditch 874 and the edge of the river channel at the eastern end of the trench. The function of the ditches is not known; all were quite shallow and may have simply marked boundaries, perhaps emphasising the division between the drier and wetter areas. The plant remains suggest that the two ditches contained stagnant or slow-flowing water and that animals continued to graze in the predominantly open grassland of the surrounding area.

The molluscan evidence from the silts sealing the river channel indicates unvegetated mudflat, which, it is suggested, may have resulted from animal trampling and over grazing. The plant taxa from the later ditch indicate a reduction in the woodland and suggest that hay making may have alternated with grazing. On the floodplain, ditch 908 (Trench XJ) appears to have been of similar nature to the two ditches to the south. The vegetation in the ditch fill again indicates slow-flowing or stagnant water and it is clear that by this time the alder carr vegetation on the floodplain had been largely reduced. The pollen suggests that some oak woodland was still present in the area, as well as some alder, probably along the banks of the river courses, although lime had been almost completely removed.

Seeds and pollen from the ditch fill also indicate arable cultivation in the vicinity, possibly on the drier ground to the south. This would suggest that the ditch may be later in date than the other two, possibly dating to the Romano-British period when there is some direct evidence for cultivation to the south of the river channel (*see below*). On the floodplain the insect remains, pollen and plant macrofossils indicate that the local vegetation was damp grassland which was grazed, perhaps alternating with some hay production. In the later use of the ditch, the pollen record indicates less hay production, perhaps eventually leading to the area being overgrazed, and clearance of much of the woodland.

Romano-British

All the features on the dry land to the south of the river channel were sealed by a humic soil, which became more peaty where it extended over the silted-up river channel. This horizon has been interpreted as an old land surface, representing a drier and more stable period which appears to have continued for a long time. The layer was very distinctive and markedly different from the underlying deposits. On the drier land quantities of Romano-British pottery, as well as residual Bronze Age material, were recovered which indicate a *terminus post quem* for the onset of this phase, although it clearly continued into the Saxon period (*see below*).

The Romano-British artefacts do not appear to relate to any features, nor do they conform to any pattern, and it is suggested that they are a result of spreading manure on the land in order to fertilise the soil. Arable cultivation is indicated by the ploughmarks which were preserved in the silty clay beneath the old land surface and which are thought to belong to this phase. A few cereal grains, including spelt, barley and some indeterminate cereals were recovered from the layer. Although it is possible that some of these may be residual there was very little evidence for arable farming in the preceding phases.

Some exploitation of the wetter floodplain in this period is indicated by the obviously fragmentary Roman 'structure' identified in the base of the river channel in Trench XB. This appeared to be a depression in the base of the channel which contained several angled stakes. The angle at which the stakes were lying when found suggests that, although their relationship to each other may have been preserved, they were probably not in their original positions. There was no indication of the full extent of the structure and its function is unclear. Nor is it clear whether there was an active stream at this period; if ditch 908 does belong to this phase then it clearly was not connected without constraint to an active stream, as it contained stagnant or slow-flowing water. The mollusc evidence initially indicates unstable, unvegetated mudflat, giving way to damp grassland or meadow with overbank flooding.

The Saxon period

By the mid Saxon period there was certainly at least one active stream running through the river channel area, although on a slightly different alignment to the Bronze Age channel, and this situation continued until the end of the Saxon period. The timber structures and features in the channel are difficult to interpret because of the extreme complexity of the shallow river-borne deposits in which they were found. Many different small streams crossed and recrossed the area and, although some sequences could be followed within the individual small trenches which made up XB/AB and in AAii, it was impossible to follow any single stream course across the whole excavation area. The groups of timbers have been described above and radiocarbon dating has enabled a broad sequence to be suggested, indicating activity in the 7th and 8th centuries AD, and again in the 10th and 11th centuries AD.

The environmental evidence from the earliest channel deposits, dating to the mid Saxon period, indicates some regeneration of alder (perhaps along the river), hazel and woodland or scrub, although damp open grassland generally persisted. The number of unstratified timbers within the channel deposits perhaps signify the collapse of earlier or contemporary structures, or that the those that were identified were more complex than the surviving timbers suggested.

The earliest feature was a shallow depression in the stream bed which contained angled timbers around one edge, seen only in section (Phase 3b), which may have functioned as a trap. The larger group of stakes, 1644, 1645, 1647 and 1648, may also have formed part of a trap, although there was no obvious indication of that, nor of a pattern suggestive of any other particular purpose. It is possible that they may not all have been contemporary. Three stakes further to the west, 1602, could have been associated with this group, but this was not determined. The stakes in AAii probably formed a discrete structure, perhaps a wild-fowl trap. They may have been placed in a pool or cut-off remnant of channel, since they were set in a shallow silty hollow and not surrounded by the coarse sands and gravels associated with many of the other *in situ* timbers.

In the later Saxon period the nature of the river activity appears to have changed slightly. Although trapping continued to be practised, as indicated by the wicker basket found in what may have been a backwater at the edge of the stream channel, the other timber structures suggest deliberate water control, possibly a type of watermeadow system. A narrow channel appears to have been confined by several posts along a possible bank on its northern edge and perhaps by a few stakes to the south. The three undated posts of 1602 could equally well relate to this phase as to the earlier one.

At the eastern end of this channel a cluster of timbers, 1594 and 1648, may have served as a barrage or similar shuttered device to control the flow of water. It is suggested that the horizontal beam may have supported a vertical sluice gate of which only the remains of the upright stakes survived, still pegged into the holes in the horizontal beam. The nature of the construction of this gate cannot be suggested, but presumably the stakes provided the framework for wattle or wickerwork which could then be lifted or dropped as required. Some erosion below this barrage was suggested, as the area immediately downstream appeared to open out into a broader channel or pool.

Environmental evidence for the Saxon phases is slight, probably because of erosion caused by subsequent rapid stream flow. The recovery of a few cultivated flax capsule fragments is interesting, perhaps suggesting that flax retting was taking place in the rapidly flowing water.

The coarse gravelly deposits which accumulated around and above the timber structures appear to indicate that the channel filled up rapidly. Wet conditions clearly prevailed over a broader area subsequently as the vegetation developed into reedswamp, resulting in the development of peat over the area of the river channels and onto the floodplain to the north. The conditions and causes of this dramatic change are not clear, although it is possible that the deliberate water management of the later Saxon period may have affected the hydrology of the area. Alternatively it has been suggested that increased grazing on the floodplain may have influenced the hydrology (Evans, this volume). The molluscan evidence suggests that there was a trend from grassland to mudflat and flooding prior to the development of reedswamp, suggesting a change from meadow to pasture. Clearly the final deposition and filling of the channel was very rapid and may signify a sudden collapse upstream. Management of the area appears to have gone into decline after this phase. Some damp grassland was available for grazing and limited hay meadow use occurred, but generally the area appears to have been neglected allowing willow to grow back on the floodplain.

On the drier land to the south a few features were observed which cut through the old land surface. These included ditches, 1019/1108, which probably marked a field boundary and possibly pit 1070/1176. Both ditch sections contained late Bronze Age pottery, which must be residual since their stratigraphic position indicates a Saxon, Roman or later date. The pit also contained late Bronze Age pottery, but its stratigraphic position is unclear. It has been suggested above that it could be a Phase 1 feature which survived as a visible landmark in the old land surface because of the remains of a superstructure. The pit was very irregular in shape and could be the result of small scale quarrying in the silty clay above gravel, although toward what purpose is unclear. Charcoal from the pit indicated that some mature oak woodland was still present in the area.

Medieval and post-medieval

It is not clear how long the reedswamp conditions prevailed on the floodplain but a change in the local environment is suggested by the abrupt horizon between the peat deposit and the overlying silts. A ditch was dug in the 14th century through the peat and across the top of the silted-up river channel. This was probably a field boundary and wet conditions clearly still prevailed, since the plant remains from the fill indicated slow-flowing water; increased grazing as well as cultivation in the vicinity is also suggested by the plant remains. However, the activity in this period must have been restricted or short-lived, as the pollen record indicates that alder carr had become re-established in places by the 16th century and conditions were fairly swampy. The introduction of the water-meadow system on the floodplain and adjacent fields appears to have corresponded to the clearance of the regenerated woodland and fields were opened up for grazing and some hay-making. The vegetation and landuse of the area appears to have continued unchanged on the floodplain into this century, although the drier ground has been cultivated periodically for arable crops in more recent times.

5 Theale Industrial Site, Archaeological Assessment

1 Introduction

In May 1986 an archaeological assessment was carried out on 19.2 hectares of land at Theale which were the subject of a planning application for redevelopment. Slight undulations in the surface and variations of soil type were observed in the two fields concerned, probably indicating the courses of former river channels. Ten trenches (Fig. 57) were excavated by machine, four of them down to the top of the gravel.

2 Results

In general, the excavations showed clay and silt deposits (beneath topsoil) ranging in depth from 0.25 m to at least 2.50 m, with some layers of peat and occasional lenses of fine redeposited tufa interleaved. Trench L and the southern end of Trench D contained very mixed silts, sands and gravels, often with organic debris, including occasional large pieces of timber. Occasionally but not consistently, layers of very dark clay up to 0.13 m thick occurred between 0.80 m and 0.90 m below the present ground surface. These layers may represent former ground surfaces which developed during periods of relative dryness and stability.

Peat occurred in Trenches A, B, D, G, J and M, varying in thickness from 0.04 m to 0.50 m and in depth from 0.80 m to 1.30 m below the present ground surface. In Trenches A, G and M and probably D, the peat lay between silt or clay deposits; in Trench J, although sealed by clay, the peat lay immediately above the gravel. In Trench A the peat and underlying clay were cut by a shallow de-

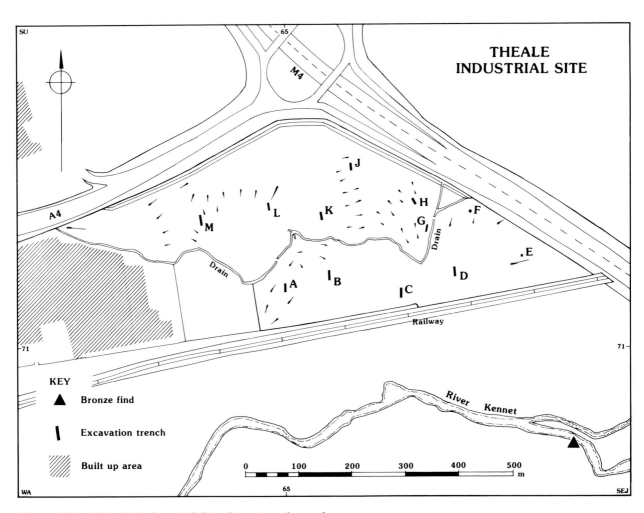

Figure 57   Theale Industrial Site: location of trenches

pression (not more than 0.60 m deep) at the northern end of the trench. This was filled with silty clay containing occasional sand lenses and some traces of organic material and may represent a pond or abandoned river channel which had silted up slowly.

The mixed organic silt, sand and gravel deposits in Trenches L and D indicated the positions of former river channels, both probably running west to east. The channel in Trench D was up to 7.50 m wide and cut through earlier clay and peat layers. The channel in Trench L would have been considerably larger, the sides not being apparent within the 14 m length of the trench. The bottom of neither channel was reached; in Trench L about 1.30 m and in Trench D about 0.85 m depths of deposits were excavated.

A wooden stake was recovered from the channel fill at the northern end of Trench L; a second stake was noted nearby but could not be excavated because of the angle at which it entered the section. Both stakes were apparently *in situ*, almost vertical, penetrating the channel fill to a depth of about 1.20 m below the ground surface, and probably formed part of a more extensive structure of undetermined function. There were no associated artefacts or occupation layers.

3 The Timber Stake

This stake was made on unprepared roundwood, approximately 0.08 m in diameter, with a faceted point, surviving to a height of 0.78 m. A sample of the timber was submitted for radiocarbon assay and produced a date of 1160±60 BP (HAR–8560) which calibrates to AD785–960 (1 sigma) and AD960–1000 (2 sigma) (Stuiver and Pearson 1986).

4 Summary

The trenches examined showed a substantial but uneven spread of alluvial soils across the whole site, truncated by the courses of former river channels. The channel identified within trench L was fairly substantial, the coarseness of its fills suggesting that they had been deposited by rapidly flowing water. The timber indicated that this channel was active in the mid-late Saxon period, and that at least 0.50 m of alluvial deposits accumulated after it silted up. The area has clearly been active floodplain until fairly recent times, with the areas of higher dry ground being too dispersed and small to be suitable for occupation. The timbers identified in the channel probably represent the remains of a temporary structure associated with fishing or similar riverine activity.

6 Development of the Landscape

by S.J. Lobb

1 Introduction

Prior to the Bronze Age the Burghfield Area appears to have been sporadically occupied in the Mesolithic and early Neolithic periods. A large number of Mesolithic tranchet axes have been recovered along the river corridor between Burghfield and the Kennet Mouth, and a few on the higher Plateau Gravel Terrace at Sulhamstead; in addition several early Neolithic flint and stone axes have been recovered in the area in similar locations. These perhaps reflect initial colonisation in the area, and the flimsy traces of occupation at Field Farm in these periods may be seen against this background. The activities may have been episodic as there is little evidence for major occupations.

2 Late Neolithic and early Bronze Age

It was not until the late Neolithic that the area began to be settled and the landscape opened up. The hearth, the Mortlake Ware bowl and associated features at Field Farm were located in a small grassy clearing in the oak and hazel woodland, by the side of a small stream. Some arable cultivation was suggested by the plant macrofossils. This is supported by the evidence from Anslow's Cottages where, although there was no direct evidence for habitation, alluvial soils had probably begun to accumulate in this period, possibly resulting from soil run-off caused by clearance in the area; the plants, pollen and insects indicate that the alder carr on the floodplain was partly cleared to provide areas for grazing, while the higher ground on the terrace appears to have supported some arable cultivation in clearings in the oak woodland. Artefactual material of late Neolithic date recovered during excavations, probably in residual contexts, from other ring-ditches in the area, is a further indication of occupation in this period (Healy forthcoming; Lobb 1985). In the early Bronze Age, dated by radiocarbon to 3650±80 BP (HAR–9139), the ring-ditch and probable associated mound at Field Farm were constructed in a grassy clearing, the mound apparently having sealed a soil containing sherds of Beaker and Collared Urn, indicating pre-existing occupation at the site.

The mound may well have served a mortuary function, even if the burial was only of a token nature, and appears to be one of several monuments of this type in the area. Many ring-ditches are indicated on the aerial photographs (Gates 1975, maps 7–11; Fig. 58) and excavation has shown that at least some were constructed in this period (Anon 1964, 99; Healy forthcoming; Lobb 1985). The isolated ring-ditch recorded during gravel extraction at Aldermaston, 8 km to the west, was of a comparable large diameter (approximately 55 m; Anon 1964). Similarly, the barrow cemeteries located on the Plateau Gravels to the south of the river at Mortimer (SU 6435 6500) and at Baughurst (SU 5770 6262) (Fig. 58) may be outliers of the great Wessex cemeteries and, although this is not confirmed by excavation, may date to this period.

These monuments all bear witness to a more stable population which was clearly farming the land fairly intensively (the charcoal from the silts of ring-ditch 417 at Field Farm indicated that further clearance of the primary oak woodland was taking place during the life of the monument) and burying some of their dead. The nature and location of their settlements, however, remain elusive.

The adjacent site at Knight's Farm provides further hints of occupation in the area; one of the ovens excavated, which was not associated with any artefacts, provided a radiocarbon date of 3630±50 BP (BM–1593) (Bradley et al. 1980, 260), which compares well with the dates for the construction of ring-ditch 417 at Field Farm. Furthermore, recent survey work in the Kennet Valley suggests that the gravel terraces at least were more fully occupied than was previously thought; the fieldwalking results from the Burghfield area, however, were inconclusive, although the distribution of surface finds may have been masked by the intensive occupation in the later Bronze Age and subsequent periods (Lobb and Rose forthcoming).

3 Later Bronze Age

Some continuity and intensification of landuse in the middle and late Bronze Age is indicated by the large number of finds and sites recorded in the area (Fig. 58). This has been discussed in some detail recently (Barrett and Bradley 1980; Bradley et al. 1980; Bradley 1986) and the evidence from Field Farm, Sulhamstead and Anslow's Cottages emphasises the intensity of occupation. Field Farm is immediately adjacent to the site at Knight's Farm and should be seen as part of the same extensive settlement.

There may have been occupation at this site in the early Bronze Age (see above), but the settlement appears to have become more established in the middle Bronze Age period as indicated by pits and post-holes and Deverel-Rimbury pottery, with an associated radiocarbon date of 3195±95 BP (BM–1594). The cremation cemeteries at Field Farm and Sulhamstead belong to this phase of occupation. It

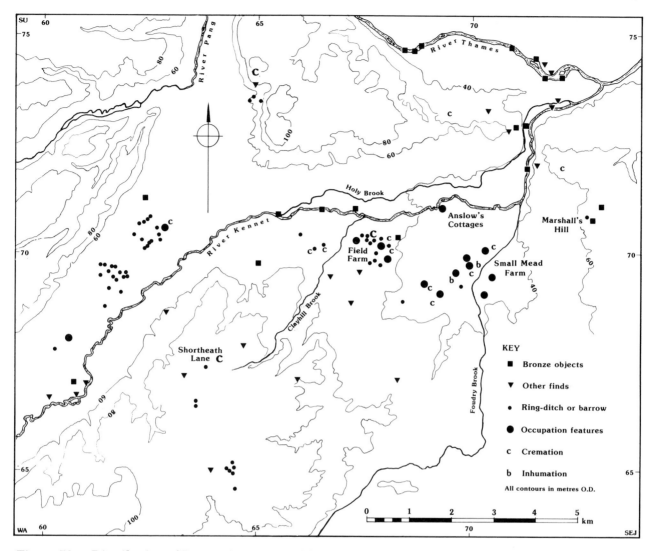

Figure 58   Distribution of Bronze Age sites and finds in the Burghfield Area

is clear that the landscape in the vicinity of the Field Farm site at this time was more open, although some primary oak woodland still survived. The plant remains indicate both grazing and arable as well as some scrub regeneration. Clearance of both the primary woodland and of secondary scrub growth continued; a burnt horizon in the silts of ring-ditch 417 contained charcoal of mature oak woodland while the ring-ditches at Sheffield Bottom and Heron's House both contained clearance horizons in their ditch fills containing charcoal of scrub species (Bradley and Richards 1980).

At Field Farm, cremations within both Collared Urns and Deverel-Rimbury Urns were inserted, alongside each other, into the edge of the mound of the earlier barrow. In addition, cremations exclusively within Deverel-Rimbury Urns were associated with the small ring-ditches; several unaccompanied cremations were also found between the monuments. The contemporaneity of the use of both types of urns is indicated by the overlap between the early date for the Deverel-Rimbury Urn from one of the smaller ring-

ditches (3690±120, HAR–9140) and the late date for a Collared Urn inserted into the edge of the mound of ring-ditch 417 (2890±60 BP, HAR–9143). Collared Urn sherds were also found beneath the barrow mound defined by ring-ditch 417, the construction of which is dated by radiocarbon to 3650±80 BP (HAR–9139), which also overlaps, rather enigmatically, with the early date for the Deverel-Rimbury Urn. Both the Collared Urn cremations contained other finds, which the Deverel-Rimbury Urns did not, and it is possible that they represent individuals of higher status, as has been suggested for the upper Thames region (Bradley 1986, 41). Perhaps the unaccompanied cremations represent a third tier in the status hierarchy.

The ring-ditches excavated prior to the construction of the motorway (Lobb 1985), to the south of Field Farm and Knight's Farm, may be part of the same cemetery, perhaps forming a boundary on the edge of the settlement area. The ring-ditches at Sheffield Bottom and Heron's House (Bradley and Richards 1980) to the south-west of the others, may also be part of this cemetery although, at approximately 1 km distance, they must be seen as outliers to the main group of ring-ditches. The radiocarbon dates from the Sheffield Bottom ring-ditch (3060±100 BP, HAR–2754, and 3040±90 BP, HAR–2749) suggest that these are later than those recorded at Field Farm.

The cemetery at Shortheath Lane, Sulhamstead, also falls within the middle Bronze Age period, the radiocarbon date of 3340±60 BP (HAR–9141) indicating contemporaneity with the cemetery at Field Farm. Two other urn cemeteries of this date are known in the vicinity, in similar locations to this site, on the opposite side of the river (Fig. 58): at Sulham (SU 6486 7416) seventeen cremations were recorded, fifteen with urns, clustered together in a group (Shrubsole 1907; Barrett 1973); and fragments of several urns were found at Tilehurst Road, Reading (ibid.).

Similarly, the barrow cemeteries in the area are also located on the Plateau gravel terrace well above the valley floor. In all cases there is no record of settlement in the near vicinity, although this may be because the evidence has been destroyed without recognition or simply because it has not yet been found. However, in the lower Kennet Valley in general, settlements of this period appear to be located on the valley floor, probably because the higher gravel terrace with poorer soils represented more marginal agricultural land.

It seems clear then that different burial practices were being carried out in the different topographical zones in this period. On the river gravel terrace cremations were being buried in and around ring-ditches around the edge of the settlement area. Clusters of ring-ditches visible on aerial photographs further west along the valley (Gates 1975, maps 7 and 8) indicate the existence of further such cemeteries. At the same time the dead were also being buried in flat urn cemeteries or barrow groups well away from settlement sites, perhaps on more marginal land. This would seem to suggest either different status for these high level cemeteries or different burial practices. These cemeteries probably represent family groups or communities (cf. Ellison 1980; Bradley 1981, 97), although only a selected few may have been buried, and the choice of location may have been influenced by pressures on agriculturally productive land, placing the cemeteries in more marginal areas.

By the late Bronze Age, population expansion led to the establishment of settlements over a much more extensive area on the river gravel terrace with two main foci, at Knight's Farm (Bradley et al. 1980) and at Small Mead Farm (Lambrick 1990) (Figs 2 and 58). Several individual settlements have been identified at Small Mead Farm and particularly around the southern margins of the gravel terrace, away from the river, at Pingewood (Johnston 1983–5), Moores Farm (SU 688 690; Oxford Archaeological Unit 1989) and Hartley Court Farm (SU 703 692; Moore pers. comm.).

The site at Anslow's Cottages indicates controlled access to, and presumably use of, the river at this time, and appears to stand out in relative isolation away from the main areas of settlement (Fig. 58), although this is not necessarily a true reflection of the settlement pattern as large parts of the gravel terrace have been extracted without archaeological observation (Fig. 2). The importance of the river, perhaps for the transport of goods, is indicated by the jetty at Anslow's Cottages, although the size of the structure and the depth of the stream channel could only have accommodated small craft, and certainly not those in any quantity. This period of settlement was long-lived with radiocarbon dates from Anslow's Cottages (2579±70 BP, HAR–9186) and Knight's Farm (2515±250 BP, BM–1597, and 2550±80 BP, HAR–1012) providing a terminus ante quem for the main phase of occupation.

The gravel terrace in this area is fairly low-lying and prone to periodic flooding and the environmental evidence from all the sites indicates that the landscape was predominantly open grassland in which a pastoral economy was exclusively practised. Faunal remains do not survive well on these sites, partly because of previously acid ground conditions, and information relating to the types of stock kept is consequently very slight. The few bones from Anslow's Cottages (Coy, this volume) and Pingewood (Cram 1985) indicate that cattle, sheep and pigs were all reared as well as horses, and there was also some suggestion that wild deer may have supplemented the diet. The floodplain adjacent to Anslow's Cottages appears to have been used for grazing and hay-making although some alder carr was still in existence.

Cereals were evidently consumed as small amounts of carbonised grains were found on many of the sites, but it is likely that these were not grown in the immediate neighbourhood, and were possibly imported from further upstream where the soils were better drained and more suited to cereal growing. It is significant that the contemporary site at Aldermaston Wharf, 8 km to the west, produced comparatively large quantities of carbonised cereal grains (Bradley et al. 1980).

The apparent burial practice in this period is markedly different to that of the preceeding middle Bronze Age. Cremations, often unaccompanied, as well as one or two inhumations were found among the settlement features at Knight's Farm (Bradley et al. 1980, 262), Pingewood (Johnston 1983–5, 26), Small Mead Farm (Lambrick 1990) and Moore's Farm (Oxford Archaeological Unit 1989). These burials represent very few individuals and, if the assumption is made that only high ranking people were afforded burial in this manner, then the apparent lack of ritual contrasts with the earlier period, perhaps suggesting less of a preoccupation with the ritual of the dead and less concern with the location of the burials.

Despite the increased population and inevitable pressure on land in this late period there is little evidence in the landscape for boundaries which might signify the need for territorial definition. Nor is there much evidence for any social hierarchy among the settlements. The contrast between these apparently low status sites engaging in intensive agricultural production and the concentration of high status metalwork around the confluence of the Kennet and the Thames, 7 km to the north-east, has already been pointed out (Bradley *et al.* 1980) and discussed (Barrett and Bradley 1980). It has been suggested that the site at Marshall's Hill on the Plateau Gravel to the east of the Burghfield settlements, overlooking both the Thames and the Kennet, may have been a high status structure of the Mucking Rings type, which could have exerted some power and influence over the settlements and production in the Kennet Valley while also controlling trade along the Thames (Bradley 1986). This site is now completely built over.

After the end of the Bronze Age much of the area appears to have been abandoned, perhaps due to the over-exploitation of natural resources and soil exhaustion, although some occupation lingered on. The river channel at Anslow's Cottages silted up, possibly because of intensification of arable agriculture further upstream, although several ditches were in use suggesting continued use of the land. Similarly, the stream running through the Small Mead settlements may have silted up in this period (Dawson and Lobb 1986). At Anslow's Cottages, the site continued to be used for grazing and hay making, although some regeneration of scrub growth is recorded. At Field Farm a radiocarbon date of 2240±120 BP (BM–1595) from charcoal in a pit is perhaps further indication of continued settlement, albeit at a low level.

4 Romano-British

Prior to the Romano-British period, evidence for occupation is provided by two cremation burials of middle or late Iron Age date at Pingewood (Johnston 1983–5) and a late Iron Age cremation on the bank of the river Kennet west of Anslow's Cottages at SU 6879 7086 (*Berkshire Archaeol. J.* 1958, 46–53). It was not until the 1st/2nd century AD that settlement was re-established in the area on any scale.

Aerial photographs indicate extensive settlement based on enclosures, fields and trackways along the margins of the gravel terrace (Gates 1975, map 11). This has been confmed by excavation at Pingewood, which appears to have been a poor farming settlement based on livestock (Johnston 1983–5). Traces of settlement were also recorded further east at Pingewood (Lobb and Mills forthcoming), and at Small Mead Farm (Dawson and Lobb 1986; Moore pers. comm.). Some occupation along the riverbank is also indicated by the salvage recording of occupation levels stratified within river silts at SU 6860 7081 (Boon and Wymer 1958).

At Anslow's Cottages, there was direct evidence for arable agriculture in the form of ploughmarks and an associated ploughsoil. The quantity of pottery which appears to have been spread on the land in this area, presumably with manure, suggests that a settlement was not far away and it is likely that the area to the south, which was

destroyed by gravel extraction without archaeological observation, may have supported settlement sites at this time.

The wooden trap in the stream, dated by radiocarbon to 1670±60 BP (HAR–9179), suggests exploitation of the river's resources. By this time the alder carr on the floodplain had been totally cleared and the area was used for grazing and hay-making.

5 Anglo-Saxon

It is not known how long the Romano-British settlements at Burghfield continued to be occupied, but there is very litle evidence for late Roman occupation. It is possible, however, that there was a Roman port at Reading serving Silchester (Astill 1978, 77). A logboat coffin containing the skeleton of a female adult found during gravel quarrying at Smallmead to the east of Anslow's Cottages provided radiocarbon dates of 1500±60 BP (BM–2096) and 1750±50 BP (BM–2096A) (Chadwick 1982, 104) indicating some human presence in the area in the sub-Roman period.

A Saxon settlement was probably established at Reading by the middle of the 5th century, perhaps reinforcing the defence along the Thames (Chadwick Hawkes 1986, 75). Early–mid Saxon metalwork and pottery was found during excavation in pre-Abbey levels (Slade 1973). The mixed cemetery at Earley to the east of the town, near the mouth of the Kennet, dates to the 5th and 6th centuries but does contain at least one early burial (Astill 1978, 77), and an urned cremation was found at Southcote, about 2 km south-west of Reading.

The cemetery at Field Farm provides an imperfect and enigmatic witness to an as yet undiscovered 7th century settlement in the Burghfield area to the west of Reading. An apparently isolated inhumation with a spearhead and shield-boss to the north of the river 1 km west of Reading may also date to this period, although the two sites are not connected. While the single burial is more likely to be associated with the occupation in Reading, the cemetery at Field Farm appears in some isolation, although occupation in the neighbourhood is likely as burials would generally be expected to be be quite close to the occupation site. The cemetery appears to represent a mixed group of people and was neither long-lived nor, probably, extensive in area. None of the surviving graves was overwhelmingly rich in the range and quality of its grave-goods, but this should not be taken as a clear reflection of the wealth, or lack of wealth, of the community to which the occupants belonged.

The floodplain and river resources were clearly being exploited in this period, as indicated by the stakes found at the edges of streams at Anslow's Cottages, and Coley Park Farm to the north of the river. At Anslow's Cottages three radiocarbon dates from *in situ* timbers within a backwater (1370±60 BP, HAR–9182; 1390±60 BP, HAR–9183; and 1300±60 BP) confirm a 7th or 8th century date for

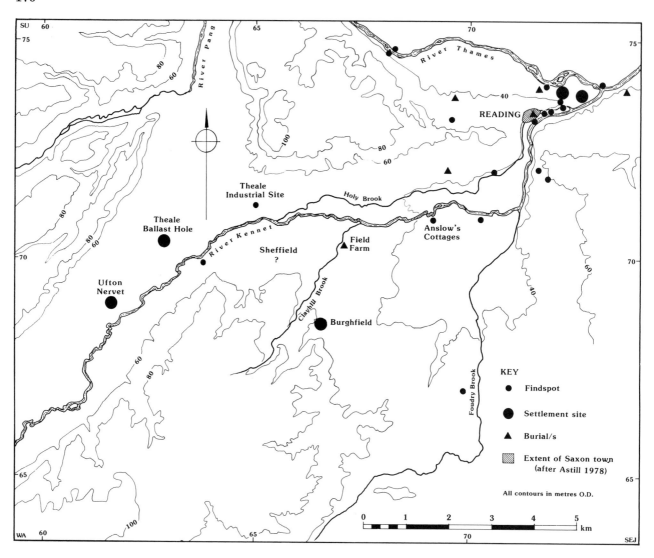

Figure 59   Distribution of Saxon sites and finds in the Burghfield area

this activity, which seems likely to represent fishing or trapping, although the number of unstratified timbers in the river channel possibly indicate more complex structures in the vicinity. These dates compare well with that from a stake at Coley Park Farm which appeared to be part of a revetment at the edge of the river channel (Hawkes and Fasham forthcoming).

The environmental evidence from Anslow's Cottages associated with the timbers indicates some regeneration of woodland or scrub although damp grassland was still predominant. Some woodland regeneration is perhaps also indicated by the charcoal from some of the graves at Field Farm where mature oak trees are predominantly indicated. However, at the latter site this need not indicate large numbers of trees.

In the mid–late Saxon period concern with the river margins grew and more rigid water control appears to have intensified. At Anslow's Cottages an arrangement of timbers, dated by radiocarbon (930±60 BP, HAR–9180; 1030±60, HAR–9181; 1030±70, HAR–9186) to this period, has been interpreted as an effort to control water flow. Similarly, one of possibly several stakes within a river channel at Theale Industrial Site was dated to this period (1160±60 BP, HAR–8560), and may suggest deliberate demarcation. The reasons for this water management may have been complex and cannot be deduced from the excavated record. The basket trap at Anslow's Cottages indicates that fishing continued, although this find is not necessarily related to the timber structure. The environmental evidence indicates that grazing intensified on damp grassland and it seems plausible to suggest that the late Saxon peoples were operating some form of watermeadow system along the Kennet floodplain.

The streams at both Anslow's Cottages and Theale Industrial Site appear to have been filled in fairly abruptly judging by the coarse nature of the sediments sealing the timbers at both places. The reasons for this are not clear, but a vastly increased water flow is indicated. This may have resulted partly from silting caused by a watermeadow system and partly because of climatic factors such as increased rainfall in this period; rapid silting also appears to have been a problem at this time in Reading itself, where several possible causes are suggested (Hawkes and Fasham forthcoming).

In the ensuing period wet conditions prevailed. At Theale Industrial Site, the peat and alluvial deposits sealing the river channel and covering the whole site indicate an active floodplain. At Anslow's Cottages, a layer of peat sealed the former river channel and extended onto the floodplain where reedswamp developed and there is some indication of willow regeneration. The remaining damp grassland continued to be grazed and limited hay-making was carried out, although the general impression is largely one of neglect until the late medieval or post-medieval period, when the regenerated alder carr was cleared for grazing and hay-making.

Burghfield is one of a band of parishes in this area which contain the element *feld* in their place names (Bradfield and Englefield to the north, Wokefield, Stratfield and Swallowfield to the south and Shinfield and Arborfield to the east). Gelling suggests that these names are connected with areas of common pasture in contrast to the forest areas to the east (1976, 836), and may represent open land between the kingdoms of Wessex and Mercia.

A settlement clearly existed at Burghfield (*Borgefelle*) by the 11th century (Fig. 59) as it is mentioned in *Domesday Book*, although the name also appears in a document of the 10th century (Gelling 1973, 204). A second settlement in this area (*Sewelle*) is mentioned in *Domesday Book* and it is suggested that the name of Sheffield, to the west, is a development of the Saxon name, although this village did not survive and its exact location is not known (Fig. 59); a low-lying situation on the gravel terrace is suggested.

Whether these villages grew out of earlier settlements is not known, and the location of the habitation sites of the earlier Saxon people represented in the cemetery at Field Farm also remains unknown. However, the location of earlier Saxon settlements at Ufton Nervet and possibly in the vicinity of Theale Ballast Hole (Fig. 59) further west, does suggest a preference for the low-lying areas of the gravel terraces and the floodplain. If Sheffield was similarly located on the lower ground, it is tempting to suggest that this may have been the main settlement focus in the middle Saxon period. Sadly the proof of this suggestion is unlikely to be made possible as the area has been almost entirely destroyed by gravel extraction.

Bibliography

Adovasio, J.M., 1977, *Basketry technology: a guide to identification and analysis*, Aldine manuals on Archaeology, Chicago, 15–52.

Alexander, J. and Ozanne, P.C. and A., 1960, 'Report on the investigation of a round barrow on Arreton Down, Isle of Wight', *Proc. Prehist. Soc.* 26, 236–302.

Andersen, S.T., 1970, 'The relative pollen productivity and pollen representation of North European trees, and correction factors for tree pollen spectra', *Danmarks geologiske Undersogelse* 2.96, 1–99.

——, 1973, 'The differential pollen productivity of trees and its significance for the interpretation of a pollen diagram from a forested region', in H.J.B. Birks and R.G. West (eds.), *Quaternary Plant Ecology*, Oxford, 109–15.

Annable, F.K. and Simpson, D.D.A., 1964, *Guide Catalogue of the Neolithic and Bronze Age Collections in Devizes Museum*, Wiltshire Archaeol. Natur. Hist. Soc.

Anon. 1964, 'Archaeological notes from Reading Museum', *Berkshire Archaeol. J.* 61, 96–109.

Arnold, C., 1980, 'Wealth and social structure: a matter of life and death', in P. Rahtz, T. Dickinson and L. Watts (eds.), *Anglo-Saxon Cemeteries 1979*, Brit. Archaeol. Rep. 82, 81–142.

Astill, G.G., 1978, *Historic Towns in Berkshire*, Berkshire Archaeol. Comm. Publ. 2.

Baker, H., 1937, 'Alluvial meadows: a comparative study of grazed and mown meadows', *J. Ecol.* 25, 408–20.

Balkwill, C., 1978, 'The ring-ditches and their neighbourhood', in Porrington, M., *The excavation of an Iron Age settlement, Bronze Age ring-ditches and Roman features at Ashville Trading Estate, Abingdon, Oxfordshire, 1974–76*, Counc. Brit. Archaeol. Res. Rep. 28, 28–30.

Barber, K.E., 1976, 'History of vegetation', in F.B. Chapman (ed.), *Methods in Plant Ecology*, Oxford, Blackwell, 5–83.

Barfield, L. and Hodder, M., 1987, 'Burnt mounds as saunas, and the prehistory of bathing', *Antiquity* 61, 370–9.

Barrett, J.C. 1973, 'Four Bronze Age cremation cemeteries from Middlesex', *Trans. London Middx. Archaeol. Soc.* 24, 111–34.

——, 1976, 'Deverel-Rimbury: problems of chronology and interpretation', in C. Burgess and R. Miket (eds.), *Settlement and Economy in the Third and Second Millennia BC*, Oxford, Brit. Archaeol. Rep. 33, 289–307.

——, 1980, 'The pottery of the Later Bronze Age in lowland England', *Proc. Prehist. Soc.* 46, 297–319.

—— and Bradley, R., 1980, 'The later Bronze Age in the Thames Valley', in Barrett, J.C. and Bradley, R. (eds.), *Settlement and Society in the British Later Bronze Age*, Oxford, Brit. Archaeol. Rep. 83, 247–71.

Bass, W.H., 1985, *Human Osteology*, Missouri, Missouri Archaeol. Soc.

Bird, J. and Bird, D.G. (eds.), 1987, *The Archaeology of Surrey*, Guildford, Surrey Archaeol. Soc.

Böhner, K., 1958, *Die fränkischen Altertümer des Trierer Landes*, Germanische Denkmäle Völkerwanderungs- zeit, Berlin.

Boon, G.C. and Wymer, J.J., 1958, 'A Belgic cremation-burial from Burghfield (Cunning Man Site), 1956', *Berkshire Archaeol. J.* 56, 46–53

Bordes, F., 1961, *Typologie du Paléolithique Ancien et Moyen*, Bordeaux.

Bradley, R., 1981, 'Urn cemeteries and settlements' in R. Chapman, I. Kinnes and K. Randsborg (eds.), *The archaeology of death*, London, Academic Press, 93–104.

——, 1984, *The Social Foundations of Prehistoric Britain*, Harlow, Longman

——, 1986, 'The Bronze Age in the Oxford area — its local and regional significance', in G. Briggs, J. Cook, and T. Rowley (eds.), *The Archaeology of the Oxford Region*, Oxford, Oxford Univ. Dept External Stud., 38–48.

——, 1983–5, 'The prehistoric pottery', in Johnston, J., 'Excavations at Pingewood', *Berks. Archaeol. J.* 72 [1987], 17–52.

—— and Keith-Lucas, M. 1975, 'Excavation and pollen analysis of a bell barrow at Ascot, Berkshire', *J. Archaeol. Sci.* 2, 95–108.

—— and Richards, J.C., 1979–80, 'The excavation of two ring ditches at Heron's House, Burghfield', *Berkshire Archaeol. J.* 70, 1–7.

——, Lobb, S., Richards, J. and Robinson, M., 1980, 'Two Late Bronze Age settlements on the Kennet gravels: excavations at Aldermaston Wharf and Knight's Farm, Burghfield, Berkshire', *Proc. Prehist. Soc.* 46, 217–95.

Brinkhuizen, D.C., 1986, 'Some notes on recent and pre- and protohistoric fishing gear from Northwestern Europe', *Palaeohistoria* 25, 7–53.

Brothwell, D.R., 1981, *Digging Up Bones*, 3rd edn., London, British Museum.

Buckley, V. ed., 1990, *Burnt Offering, International contributions to burnt mound archaeology*, Dublin, Wordwell Ltd.

Burgess, C., 1986, 'Urnes of no small variety; collared urns reviewed', *Proc. Prehist. Soc.* 52, 339–51.

Chadwick, P., 1981–2, 'Berkshire archaeological notes', *Berkshire Archaeol. J.* 71, 104.

Charles, D., 1979, *Aspects of the chronology and distribution of Silchester Ware Roman pottery*, unpubl. undergraduate dissertation, Univ. Reading.

Churchill, D.M. 1962, 'The stratigraphy of the Mesolithic sites III and V at Thatcham, Berkshire, England', *Proc. Prehist. Soc.* 28, 362–70.

Clapham, A.R. and Clapham, B.N., 1962, 'The valley fen at Cothill, Berkshire. Data for the studies of post-glacial history II', *New Phytologist* 38, 167–74.

——, Tutin, T.G. and Warburg, E.F., 1962, *Flora of the British Isles*, Oxford.

Clarke, A., 1980, 'Knight's Farm, pollen and spores', in Bradley *et al.* 1980, 279–80.

Clarke, A.J., Tarling, D.H. and Noel, M., 1988, 'Developments in archaeomagnetic dating in Britain', *J. Archaeol. Sci.* 15, 645–67.

Cleal, R.M.J. 1985, *The Later Neolithic in Eastern England*, unpubl. Ph.D. thesis, Univ. Reading.

Coles, J.M. and Orme, B.J. 1979, 'Multiple trackways from Tinney's Ground', *Somerset Levels Pap.* 4.

—— and ——, 1985, 'Prehistoric woodworking from the Somerset Levels: 3. Roundwood', *Somerset Levels Pap.* 11, 25–50.

Cook, A.M. and Dacre, M., 1985, *Excavations at Portway, Andover 1973–1975*, Oxford, Oxford Univ. Comm. Archaeol. Monog. 4.

Cram, L., 1983–5, 'The animal bone', in Johnston, J., 'Excavations at Pingewood', *Berkshire Archaeol. J.* 72, 47–9.

Crone, A. and Barber, J., 1981, 'Analytical techniques for the investigation of non-artefactual wood from prehistoric and medieval sites', *Proc. Soc. Antiq. Scot.* 111, 510–15

Crowfoot, E., 1985a, 'Textiles', in Hedges, J.D. and Buckley, D.G., 'Anglo-Saxon burials and later features at Orsett, Essex, 1975,' *Medieval Archaeol.* 29, 15–16.

——, 1985b, 'The textiles', in Hirst, S.M., *An Anglo-Saxon inhumation cemetery at Sewerby, East Yorkshire*, York, York Univ. Archaeol. Publ. 4, 48–54.

——, 1985c, 'Textiles', in Davies, S.M. 'The excavation of an Anglo-Saxon cemetery at Charlton Plantation, near Downton', *Wiltshire Archeaol. Natur. Hist. Mag.* 79, 140–3.

Crowfoot, G.M., 1953, 'The textile remains', in Leeds, E.T. and Shortt, H. de S., *An Anglo-Saxon Cemetery at Petersfinger, near Salisbury, Wiltshire*, Salisbury, South Wiltshire and Blackmore Museum, 61.

Cunliffe, B., 1978, *Iron Age Communities in Britain*, London, Routledge and Keegan Paul, 2nd edn.

——, 1984, *Danebury: an Iron Age hillfort in Hampshire. Vol. 2 The excavations 1969–1978: the finds*, London, Counc. Brit. Archaeol. Res. Rep. 52.

—— and Phillipson, D.W., 1968, 'Excavations at Eldon's Seat, Encombe, Dorset', *Proc. Prehist. Soc.* 34, 191–237.

Dacre, M.W., and Ellison, A.B., 1981, 'A Bronze Age urn cemetery at Kimpton, Hampshire', *Proc. Prehist. Soc.* 47, 147–203.

Davies, S.M., 1985, 'The Excavation of an Anglo-Saxon Cemetery at Charlton Plantation, near Downton', *Wiltshire Archaeol. and Natur. Hist. Mag.* 79, 109–54.

Dawson, R. and Lobb, S.J., 1986, *Reading Business Park: Axiom 4. Archaeological evaluation*, Salisbury, Trust for Wessex Archaeology.

Dickinson, T.M., 1973, 'Excavations at Standlake Down in 1954: The Anglo-Saxon graves', *Oxoniensia* 38, 239–57.

Dimbleby, G.W., 1962, *The development of British heathlands and their soils*, Oxford Forestry Memoirs 23.

Druce, G.C., 1897, *Flora of Berkshire*, Oxford, Clarendon Press.

Earwood, C., 1988, 'Wooden containers and other wooden artifacts from the Glastonbury Lake Village', *Somerset Levels Pap.* 14, 83–90.

Ellison, A.B., 1975, *Pottery and Settlements of the later Bronze Age in southern England*, Unpubl. dissertation, Univ. Cambridge.

——, 1980, 'Deverel-Rimbury urn cemeteries: the evidence for social organisation', in Barrett, J. and Bradley, R. (eds), *Settlement and Society in the British Later Bronze Age*, Oxford, Brit. Archaeol. Rep. 83.

Erdtman, G., Berland, B., and Praglowski, J., 1961, *An introduction to a Scandinavian flora*, Stockholm, Almqvist and Wiksell.

——, Praglowski, J., and Nilsson, S., 1963, *An introduction to a Scandinavian pollen flora*, II, Stockholm, Almqvist and Wiksell.

Evison, V.I., 1963, 'Sugar-loaf shield bosses', *Antiq. J.* 43, 38–96.

——, 1987, *Dover: The Buckland Anglo-Saxon Cemetery*, London, English Heritage Archaeol. Rep. 3.

——, 1988, *An Anglo-Saxon Cemetery at Alton, Hampshire*, Hampshire Fld. Club Archaeol. Soc. Monog. 4.

Faegri, K., and Iversen, J., 1975, *Textbook of pollen analysis*, 3rd edn, Copenhagen, Munksgard.

Ford, S., Bradley, R., Hawkes, J., and Fisher, P., 1984, 'Flint-working in the metal age', *Oxford J Archaeol.* 3.2, 157–73.

180

Froom, F.R., 1976. *Wawcott III. A Stratified Mesolithic Succession*, Oxford, Brit. Archaeol. Rep. 27.

Gates, T., 1975, *The middle Thames Valley, an Archaeological survey of the river gravels*, Oxford, Berkshire Archaeol. Comm.

Geel, G. van, and Van der Hammen, T., 1978. 'Zygnemataceae in quaternary Colombian sediments', *Rev. Palaeobotany Palynology*, 1.25, 377–95.

Gelling, M., 1973, *The Place Names of Berkshire: Part I*, Cambridge.

——, 1976, *The Place Names of Berkshire: Part III*, Cambridge.

Gejvall, N., 1969, ' Cremations', in Brothwell, D.R., and Higgs, E. (eds), *Science in Archaeology*, Cambridge, Univ. Press, 468–79.

Gibson, A.M., 1982, *Beaker Domestic Sites*, Oxford, Brit. Archaeol. Rep. 107.

Godwin, H., 1975, *History of the British flora*, 2nd edn, Cambridge, Univ. Press.

Gray, H., 1977, *Anatomy*, New York, Bounty.

Green, H.S., 1980, *The Flint Arrowheads of the British Isles*, Oxford, Brit. Archaeol. Rep. 75.

Greene, K., 1978, 'Imported fine wares in Britain to AD 250: a guide to identification', in Arthur, P. and Marsh, G. (eds), *Early Fine Wares in Britain and Beyond*, Oxford, Brit. Archaeol. Rep. 57, 15–30.

Greig, J., 1991, 'The botanical remains', in Needham, S., 1991, 234–61.

Grigson, C., 1965, 'Faunal remains: measurements of bones, horncores, antlers and teeth', in Smith, I.F., *Windmill Hill and Avebury*, Oxford, Clarendon Press, 145–67.

——, 1974, 'The craniology and relationships of four species of *Bos*: part 1', *J. Archaeol. Sci.* 1, 353–79.

——, 1978, 'The craniology and relationships of four species of *Bos*: part 4', *J. Archaeol. Sci.* 5, 123–52.

Harcourt, R.A., 1971, 'The animal bone', in Wainwright, G.J. and Longworth, I.H., *Durrington Walls: excavations 1966–68*, Res. Comm. Soc. Antiq. London Rep. 29, 338–50.

——, 1974, 'The dog in prehistoric and early prehistoric Britain', *J. Archaeol. Sci.* 1, 151–75.

Harding, P.A.H., 1990, 'The comparative analysis of four stratified flint assemblages and a knapping cluster', in Richards, J.C., *The Stonehenge Environs Project*, London, English Heritage Archaeol. Monog. 16

——, 1991, 'The worked stone', in Woodward, P.J. *The South Dorset Ridgeway: Survey and Excavations 1977–84*, Dorset Natur. Hist. Archaeol. Soc. Monog. 8.

——, 1992 'The flint', in Gingell, C.J., *The Marlborough Downs: a later Bronze Age landscape and its origin*, Wiltshire Archaeol. Soc. Monog. 1, 123–33.

——, forthcoming, 'The flint ', in Lobb, S.J. and Morris, E.L, *The investigation of Bronze Age and Iron Age features at Riseley Farm*, Berkshire Archaeol. J.

Härke, H., 1989, 'Remarks and observations on the weapons', in West, 1988, 11–14.

Haslam, S.M., 1978 *River Plants*, Cambridge.

——, Sinker, C.A., and Wolseley, P.A., 1975, 'British Water Plants', *Fld Stud.* 4, 242–351.

Hawkes, J.W. and Fasham, P.J., forthcoming, *Excavations on Reading Waterfront Sites 1979–1988*, Berkshire Archaeol. J. Monog.

Hawkes, S.C., 1973, 'The dating and social significance of the burials in the Polhill cemetery', in Philp, B. (ed.), *Excavations in West Kent 1960–1970*, Dover, Kent Archaeol. Rescue Unit, 186–201.

——, 1986, 'The Early Saxon period', in Briggs, G., Cook, J. and Rowley, T. (eds), *The Archaeology of the Oxford Region*, Oxford, Univ. Dept External Stud, 64–94.

H.B.M.C.E., no date, *Recommended variables for anthropological observations on human skeletal remains*.

Healy, F., forthcoming, 'The excavation of a ring ditch at Englefield, Berkshire by John Wymer and Paul Ashbee, 1963', *Berks. Archaeol. J.*

Healey, E. and Robertson-Mackay, R. 1983, 'The lithic industries from Staines causewayed enclosure and their relationship to the other earlier Neolithic industries in southern Britain', *Lithics* 4, 1–27.

Hillman, G., 1982, 'Appendix 6: Charred remains of plants', in Birdnell, W., 'The excavation of two round barrows at Trelystan, Powys', *Proc. Prehist. Soc.* 48, 198–200.

Hirst, S.M., 1985, *An anglo-Saxon inhumation cemetery at Sewerby, East Yorkshire*, York, York Univ. Archaeol. Publ. 4.

Holyoak, D.T., 1980, *Late Pleistocene Sediments and Biostratigraphy of the Kennet Valley, England*, Unpubl. Ph.D. thesis, Univ. Reading.

Hoshaw, R.W., 1968, 'Biology of the filamentous conjugating algae', in Jackson, D.F. (ed.), *Algae, man and the environment*, New York, Syracuse Univ. Press.

Jackson, J.W., 1943, 'The animal bone', in Wheeler, R.E.M., *Maiden Castle, Dorset*, Res. Comm. Soc. Antiq. London Rep. 12, 360–71.

Janaway, R., 1983, 'Textile fibre characteristics preserved by metal corrosion: the potential of SEM studies', *Conservator* 7, 48–52.

Jarvis, K.S., 1983, *Excavations in Christchurch 1969–80*, Dorset Natur. Hist. Archaeol. Soc Monog. 5

Jarvis, M.G., Hazelden, J., and Mackney, D., 1979, *Soils of Berkshire*. Soils Survey Bull. 8, Harpenden.

Jenkins, J.G., 1974, *Nets and Coracles*, ??, David and Charles, 44–66, 263–87.

Jewell, P.A., 1962, 'Changes in size and type of cattle from prehistoric to mediaeval times in Britain', *Zeitschrift für Tierzuchtung und Zuchtungbiologie* 77, 159–67.

Johnston, J., 1983–5, 'Excavations at Pingewood', *Berkshire Archaeol. J.* 72, 17–52.

Jones, M., 1978, 'The plant remains', in Parrington, M. *The excavation of an Iron Age settlement, Bronze Age ring- ditches and Roman features at Ashville Trading Estate, Abingdon (Oxfordshire) 1974–76*, London, Counc. Brit. Archaeol. Res. Rep. 28, 93–110.

——, 1981, 'The development of crop husbandry', in Jones, M. and Dimbleby, G. (eds), *The Environment of Man: the Iron Age to the Anglo-Saxon Period*, Oxford, Brit. Archaeol. Rep. 87.

Katz, D. and Sutchey, J.M., 1986, 'Age determination of the male *os pubis*', *Amer. J. Physical Anthrop.* 69, 427–36.

Lambrick, G., 1990, 'Farmers and shepherds in the Bronze and Iron Age', *Current Archaeol.* 121, 14–18.

—— and Robinson, M., 1979, *Iron Age and Roman riverside settlements at Farmoor, Oxfordshire*, London, Counc. Brit. Archaeol. Res. Rep. 32.

Lobb, S.J., 1980, 'Notes from the Wessex Archaeology Committee', *Berkshire Archaeol. J.* 70, 9–20.

——1985, 'Excavation of two ring ditches at Burghfield by R.A. Rutland', *Berkshire Archaeol. J.* 70, 9–20.

—— and Mills, J., forthcoming, *Observations and excavations in the Pingewood area*, Berkshire Archaeol. J.

——, and Morris, E.L., forthcoming, 'Investigations of Bronze Age and Iron Age features at Riseley Farm, Swallowfield', Berkshire Archaeol. J.

—— and Rose, P.G., forthcoming, *An Archaeological Survey of the Lower Kennet Valley, Berkshire*, Wessex Archaeol. Rep.

Longley, D., 1980, *Runneymede Bridge 1976: Excavation on the site of a Late Bronze Age settlement*, Guildford, Surrey Archaeol. Soc. Res. Report 6.

Longworth, I., 1984, *Collared Urns of the Bronze Age in Great Britain and Ireland*, Cambridge, Univ. Press.

——, Ellison, A.B. and Rigby, V, 1988, *Excavations at Grimes Graves, Norfolk, 1972 1976. Fascicule 2. The Neolithic, Bronze Age and later pottery*, London, British Museum.

Louwe Kooijmans, L.P., 1985, *Sporen in Hetland: de Nederlandse Delta in de Prehistorie*, Amsterdam, Meulenhoff Informatief.

Luniak, B., 1953, *The identification of textile fibres*.

Lynn, C. J., 1978, 'A rath in Seacash Townland, County Antrim', *Ulster J. Archaeol.* 41, 55–74.

McKinley, J.I., 1989, 'Cremations: expectations, methodologies and realities', in Roberts, C.A. *et al.* (eds), *Burial archaeology; current research, methods and developments*, Oxford, Brit. Archaeol. Rep. 211.

——, forthcoming, *The Anglo-Saxon cemetery at Spong Hill, North Elmham. Part VIII. The cremations*, E. Anglian Archaeol.

McMinn, R.M.H., and Hutchings, R.T., 1985, *A colour atlas of human anatomy*, London, Wolfe.

Meaney, A.L., and Hawkes, S.C., 1970, *Two Anglo-Saxon cemeteries at Winnall, Winchester, Hampshire*, Soc. Medieval Archaeol. Monog. 4.

Montague, R., forthcoming 'The metalwork', in Market Lavington, check ref with PW

Morris, E.L., 1992 *The Analysis of Pottery*, Salisbury, Wessex Archaeology Guideline No. 4, 3rd edn.

Moore, P.D., and Webb, J.A., 1978, *An Illustrated Guide to Pollen Analysis*, London, Hodder and Stoughton.

Moffett, L. Robinson, M.A. and Straker, V., 1989, 'Cereals, fruit and nuts: charred plant remains from Neolithic sites in England and Wales and the Neolithic economy', in Milles, A., Williams, D. and Gardener, N. (eds), *The Beginnings of Agriculture* , Oxford, Brit. Archaeol. Rep. S496, 243–61.

Needham, S.P., 1987, 'The Bronze Age' in Bird, and Bird, 1987, 97–137.

Needham, S.P. and Longley, D., 1980, 'Runnymede Bridge, Egham. A Late Bronze Age riverside settlement' in Barrett, J., and Bradley, R., (eds), *Settlement and Society in the British Later Bronze Age*, Oxford, Brit. Archaeol. Rep. 83, 397–436.

O'Connell, M., 1986, *Petters Sports Field, Egham: excavation of a late Bronze Age/Early Iron Age site*, Guildford, Surrey Archaeol. Soc. Res. 10.

O Drisceoil, D., 1988, 'Burnt mounds: cooking or bathing?', *Antiquity* 62, 671–80.

Ohnuma, K., and Bergman, C., 1982, 'Experimental studies in the determination of flaking mode', *Bull. Inst. Archaeol. London* 19, 161–70.

Orme, B.J. and Coles, J.M., 1983, 'Prehistoric woodworking from the Somerset Levels: 1. Timber', *Somerset Levels Pap.* 9, 19–43.

Ortnar, D. and Putschar, G.J., 1985, *Identification of Pathological Conditions in Human Skeletal Remains*, New York, Smithsonian Inst.

Owen-Crocker, G.R., 1986, *Dress in Anglo-Saxon England*.

Oxford Archaeological Unit, 1989, *Archaeological Assessment, Burghfield: Moores Farm, Pingewood*, Oxford, Archaeol. Unit.

Pader, E., 1980, 'Material symbolism and social relations in mortuary studies', in Rahtz, P., Dickinson, T., and Watts, L. (eds), *Anglo-Saxon Cemeteries 1979*, Oxford, Brit. Archaeol. Rep. 82, 143–69.

Pearson, G.W., and Stuiver, M., 1986, 'High precision calibration of the radiocarbon timescale, 500–2500 B.C.', *Radiocarbon* 28.2B, 839–62.

Pitts, M.W., 1978, 'On the shape of waste flakes and an index of technological change in lithic industries', *J. Archaeol. Sci.* 5, 17–37.

Pryor, F.M.M., French, C.A.I. and Taylor, M., 1985, 'An interim report on excavations at Etton, Maxey, Cambridgeshire, 1982–84', *Antiq. J.* 65, 275–311.

——, —— and ——, 1986, 'Flag Fen, Peterborough I: discovery, reconaissance and initial excavation (1982–85)', *Proc. Prehist. Soc.* 52, 1–24.

Rahtz, P., 1978, 'Grave orientation', *Archaeol. J.* 135, 1–14.

Richards, J.C., 1985, 'Scouring the surface: aproaches to the ploughzone in the Stonehenge environs', *Archaeol. Rev.* 4, 27–42.

Riley, D.N., 1947, 'Late bronze age and iron age site on Standlake Downs, Oxon.', *Oxoniensia* 11/12, 27–43.

Robinson, M., 1979, 'The biological evidence', in Lambrick, G. and Robinson M., *Iron Age and Roman riverside settlements at Farmoor, Oxfordshire*, London, Counc. Brit. Archaeol. Res. Rep. 32.

——, 1981, 'The Iron Age to Early Saxon Environment of the Upper Thames Terraces', in Jones, M. and Dimbleby, G. (eds), *The Environment of Man: the Iron Age to the Anglo-Saxon Period*, Oxford, Brit. Archaeol. Rep. 87, 251–77.

——, 1988, 'Molluscan evidence for pasture and meadowland on the floodplain of the upper Thames basin', in Murphy, P. and French, C. (eds), *The Exploitation of Wetlands*, Oxford, Brit. Archaeol. Rep. 186, 101–12.

——, 1988, 'The significance of tubers of *Arrhenatherum elatius* (L.) Beauv. from site 4, cremation 15/11', in Lambrick, G. *The Rollright Stones*, English Heritage Archaeol. Monog. 6, 102.

——, 1989, 'Macroscopic plant remains from the Wilsford Shaft, Wiltshire', in Ashbee, P., Bell, M. and Proudfoot, E. (eds), *Wilsford Shaft Excavations, 1960–2*, English Heritage Archaeol. Monog. 11.

——, 1991, 'Neolithic and Bronze Age insect assemblages, in Needham, S., *Excavation and Salvage at Runnymede Bridge 1978*, London, Brit. Mus. Press

Royal County of Berkshire, 1989, *Replacement Structure Plan for Berkshire*, Reading, Co. Counc.

Saville, A., 1981, *Grimes Graves, Norfolk. Excavations 1971–72. Vol.II. The flint Assemblage*, London, H.M.S.O.

Scaife, R.G., 1988, 'The *Ulnus* decline in the pollen record of South east England and its relation to early agriculture', in Jones, M. (ed.), *Archaeology and the flora of the British Isles*, Oxford, Univ. Comm. Archaeol. Monog. 14, 21–33.

——, forthcoming, 'The pollen', in Healy, F., Heaton, M. and Lobb, S., 'Excavation of a Mesolithic site at Thatcham, Berkshire', *Proc. Prehist. Soc.*

Shrubsole, O.A., 1907, 'On a tumulus containing urns of the Bronze Age, mear Sunningdale, Berkshire, and on a burial place of the Bronze Age at Sulham, Berkshire', *Proc. Soc. Antiq.* 21, 303–14.

Slade, C.F., 1973, 'Excavation at Reading Abbey', *Berkshire Archaeol. J.*, 66, 65–116.

Smith, I.F., 1965, *Windmill Hill and Avebury: excavations by A. Keiller 1925–39*, Oxford, Clarendon Press.

——, 1974, 'The Neolithic', in Renfrew, C. (ed.), *British Prehistory: a New Outline*, London, Duckworth, 100–36.

Sparks, B.W. and West, R.G., 1959, 'The palaeoecology of the interglacial deposits at Histon Road, Cambridge', *Eiszeitalter und Gegenwart* 10, 123–43.

Speake, G., 1989, *A Saxon Bed Burial on Swallowcliffe Down; Excavations by F. de M. Vatcher*, English Heritage Archaeol. Monog. 10, 27–30.

Steinbock, R.T., 1976, *Palaeopathological Diagnosis and Interpretation*, Springfield, Thomas.

Stone, J.F.S., 1941, 'The Deverel-Rimbury settlement on Thorny Down, Winterbourne Gunner, South Wiltshire, *Proc. Prehist. Soc.* 7, 114–33.

Stuiver, M. and Pearson, G.W., 1986, 'High precision calibration of the radiocarbon timescale, A.D.1950–500 B.C.', *Radiocarbon* 28 (2B), 805–38.

Suchey, J.M., 1979, 'Problems in the ageing of females using the *os pubis*, *Amer. J. Physical Anthrop.* 51, 467–70.

Stewart, T.D., 1979, *Essentials of Forensic Anthropology*, Illinois, Charles C. Thomas.

Swanton, M.J., 1973, *The Spearheads of the Anglo-Saxon Settlements*, London, Roy. Archaeol. Inst.

——, 1974, *A corpus of pagan Anglo-Saxon spear types*, Oxford, Brit. Archaeol. Rep. 7.

Thomas, R., Robinson, M., Barrett, J. and Wilson, B., 1986, 'A Late Bronze Age riverside settlement at Wallingford, Oxfordshire', *Archaeol. J.* 143, 174–200.

Tittensor, R.M., 1980, 'The ecological history of Yew (*Taxus baccata* L.) in southern England', *Biol. Conserv.* 17, 243–65.

Tixier, J., Inizau, M.L. and Roche, H., 1980. *Préhistoire de la pierre taillée: terminologie et technologie*, Cercle de Recherches at d'Études Préhistoriques, Antibes.

Trotter, M. and Gleser, G.C., 1952, 'Estimation of stature based on measurements of stature taken during life and long bones after death', *Amer. J. Physical Anthop.* 10, 463–514.

—— and ——, 1958, 'A re-evaluation of stature based on measurements of stature taken during life and long bones after death', *Amer. J. Physical Anthrop.* 16, 79–123.

Turner, G.M. and Thompson, R., 1982, 'Detransformation of the British geomagnetic secular variation record for Holocene times', *Geophysical J. Roy. Astronomical Soc.* 70, 789–92.

Turner, J, 1962, 'The *Tilia* decline: an anthropogenic interpretation', *New Phytol.* 61, 328–41.

Van Beek, G.C., 1983, *Dental Morphology*, Bristol, P.S.G. Wright.

Veen, van der, M., 1985, 'Evidence for crop plants from north-east England: an interim overview with discussion of new results', in Fuller, N.J., Gilbertson, D.D. and Ralph, N.G.A. (eds), *Palaeobiological investigations: research design, methods and data analysis*, Oxford, Brit. Archaeol. Rep. S266, 197–219.

——, 1987, 'The plant remains', in Olivier, A.C.H., 'Excavation of a Bronze Age funerary cairn at Manor Farm, near Borwick, North Lancashire', *Proc. Prehist. Soc.* 53, microfiche 3.

Wainwright, G.J., and Longworth, I.H., 1971, *Durrington Walls: excavations 1966–1968*, London, Res. Comm. Soc. Antiq. London Rep. 29.

Warrick, R. and Williams, P.L. (eds), 1980, *Grey's Anatomy*, 36th. edn, London and New York, Longman.

West, S.E., 1988, *The Anglo-Saxon Cemetery at Westgarth Gardens, Bury St Edmunds, Suffolk: Catalogue*, Ipswich, E. Anglian Archaeol. 38.

White, R.H., 1988, *Roman and Celtic Objects from Anglo-Saxon Graves*, Oxford, Brit. Archaeol. Rep. 191.

Workshop of European Anthropologists, 1980, 'Recommendations for age and sex diagnosis', J. Human Evol. 9, 517–49.

Young, C.J., 1977, *The Roman Pottery Industry of the Oxford Region*, Oxford, Brit. Archaeol. Rep. 43.

Index, *by Lesley and Roy Adkins*

The following abbreviations have been used: BA (Bronze Age), EBA (Early Bronze Age), IA (Iron Age), LBA (Late Bronze Age), MBA (Middle Bronze Age), Meso (Mesolithic), Neo (Neolithic), RB (Romano-British). Numbers in **bold** indicate the main entries. Environmental remains have not been indexed according to species.